FEDERICO FELLINI

Centenary Essays

Federico Fellini

Centenary Essays

EDITED BY MARCO MALVESTIO, JESSICA WHITEHEAD, AND ALBERTO ZAMBENEDETTI

UNIVERSITY OF TORONTO PRESS
Toronto Buffalo London

© University of Toronto Press 2025
Toronto Buffalo London
utorontopress.com
Printed in the USA

ISBN 978-1-4875-4398-3 (cloth)   ISBN 978-1-4875-4399-0 (EPUB)
                                 ISBN 978-1-4875-4400-3 (PDF)

Toronto Italian Studies

___

Library and Archives Canada Cataloguing in Publication

Title: Federico Fellini : centenary essays / edited by Marco Malvestio, Jessica
   Whitehead, and Alberto Zambenedetti.
Names: Malvestio, Marco, editor | Whitehead, Jessica (Lecturer in communication
   and languages), editor | Zambenedetti, Alberto, editor
Series: Toronto Italian studies.
Description: Series statement: Toronto Italian studies | Includes bibliographical
   references and index.
Identifiers: Canadiana (print) 20240458478 | Canadiana (ebook) 20240458524 |
   ISBN 9781487543983 (cloth) | ISBN 9781487544003 (PDF) |
   ISBN 9781487543990 (EPUB)
Subjects: LCSH: Fellini, Federico – Criticism and interpretation. | LCGFT: Essays.
Classification: LCC PN1998.3.F45 F43 2025 | DDC 791.4302/33092 – dc23

___

Cover design: Val Cooke
Cover image: Federico Fellini, Anita Ekberg, and Marcello Mastroianni on the set of
Intervista, 1987. (Photo credit: Emilio Lari. German poster, item no. 1065, courtesy of
Fellini Forever Inc.)

We wish to acknowledge the land on which the University of Toronto Press
operates. This land is the traditional territory of the Wendat, the Anishnaabeg, the
Haudenosaunee, the Métis, and the Mississaugas of the Credit First Nation.

This volume was published with support from the Emilio Goggio Chair in Italian
Studies at the University of Toronto and under the patronage and with the financial
assistance of the Istituto Italiano di Cultura of Toronto.

University of Toronto Press acknowledges the financial support of the Government of
Canada, the Canada Council for the Arts, and the Ontario Arts Council, an agency of
the Government of Ontario, for its publishing activities.

In memory of Marguerite Waller and Ottavio Cirio Zanetti

Contents

List of Illustrations xi

Acknowledgments xiii

Introduction: Fellini at 100 – The Lingering Celebration 3
MARCO MALVESTIO, JESSICA WHITEHEAD, AND ALBERTO ZAMBENEDETTI

Film-Makers on Fellini

Reflections on *8 ½ Screens* 17
ATOM EGOYAN

Q&A on *The Rabbit Hunters* (2020) 21
GUY MADDIN

The Unexpected Moment 24
DEEPA MEHTA

In Memoriam

Introduction: Ottavio Cirio Zanetti – In Memoriam 29
ANDREW A. MONTI

Federico Fellini's Urban Planning 32
OTTAVIO CIRIO ZANETTI

Fellini's Graphic World 37
OTTAVIO CIRIO ZANETTI

Deleuzional Ponderings: The Fellinian Symbolic
(in Memory of Marguerite Waller)   45
FRANK BURKE

Centenary Essays

What Is in the Modern Look? Federico Fellini and the
Photography of William Klein   71
GIULIANA MINGHELLI

Fellini, Theorist of Culture, 1950–1972   100
VERONICA PRAVADELLI

Oenothea's Gaze: Donyale Luna in *Fellini Satyricon*   114
SHELLEEN GREENE

Consumer Capitalism, National Identity, and Heterotopia in
Fellini's *Le tentazioni del dottor Antonio*   130
ELEONORA SARTONI

Fellini, Dante, *Il viaggio di G. Mastorna*, and Dreams   144
MIRKO TAVONI

Il viaggio di G. Mastorna's Constellation at the Crossroads of
Arts and Media   162
MARINA VARGAU

The Genesis of Steiner: *La dolce vita* as Authorial Melting Pot   177
FEDERICO PACCHIONI

Amarcord: Fascism, Nightmares, and the Spectator's
Autobiography   190
EMILIANO MORREALE

Spectres of Venice: Gothic Apparitions in *Il Casanova di
Federico Fellini*   201
MARCO MALVESTIO AND ALBERTO ZAMBENEDETTI

Sense of Place and "Placelessness": Fellini's Rome   216
ANDREA MINUZ

Framing Women in Fellini's Films and Drawings   231
DISHANI SAMARASINGHE

Originals in the Dark, Imitations in the Light: Fellini's
Ginger e Fred 240
GIOVANNA CATERINA LISENA

"The Tyrant Spectator": Intermediality, Spectatorship, and
Subjectivation in Fellini's Work 255
GIACOMO TAGLIANI

Imaginary Worlds and Startling Creatures: Fellini and
Popular Culture 271
MANUELA GIERI

The Megaphone Ran Out of Battery: The Invitation of
Fellini's Voices 287
GAIA MALNATI

Watch Out! Flashback! Fellini's Memory Films 302
RUSSELL J.A. KILBOURN

Fellini's Notes on Camp to John Waters 322
ELEONORA LIMA

The Mastrangelo Collection and Fellini's Distribution in Canada 343
JESSICA WHITEHEAD AND CHRISTINA STEWART

"Women with Big Breasts and Wide Hips": Fellini's Cinema
in Chinese Media Essays 358
GAOHENG ZHANG

Contributors 371

Index 379

Illustrations

1. Image from Federico Fellini's *Book of Dreams*   18
2. Images of the projector in front of the cinema from *8 ½ Screens*   19
3. Image of Luisa leaving the cinema as seen projected in *8 ½ Screens*   20
4. Ottavio Cirio Zanetti   30
5. Ottavio Cirio Zanetti   31
6. "Selwyn, 42nd Street, 1955" and "Wings of the Hawk, 1955" in *Life Is Good and Good for You in New York*   78
7. The mambo dance from *Le notti di Cabiria*   79
8. Escaping a police raid in *Le notti di Cabiria*   81
9. In front of the Piccadilly club, from *Le notti di Cabiria*   82
10. "Cadillac show-room, 1955" in *Life Is Good and Good for You in New York*   83
11. Lazzari + neon, from *Le notti di Cabiria*   83
12. The Lux cinema theatre, from *Le notti di Cabiria*   84
13. Cabiria in front of a bar, from *Le notti di Cabiria*   85
14. The mysterious light on Lake Bracciano, from *Le notti di Cabiria*   86
15. "Atom Bomb Sky, 1955" in *Life Is Good and Good for You in New York*   87
16. Fight at the Passeggiata Archeologica, from *Le notti di Cabiria*   89
17. "Girls laughing, Puerto Rican neighbourhood, 1955" in *Life Is Good and Good for You in New York*   89
18. Close-up of Marisa, from *Le notti di Cabiria*   90
19. Close-up of Oscar, from *Le notti di Cabiria*   90
20. Cabiria's final shot, from *Le notti di Cabiria*   91

21 "Stucco sculptures that have performed in 'War and Peace,' Cinecittà, ca. 1957" in *Rome: The City and Its People* 95
22 Children on scaffolding, from *Le notti di Cabiria* 95
23 Cabiria perched between the old and the new, from *Le notti di Cabiria* 96
24 Anita's billboard, from *Le tentazioni del dottor Antonio* 133
25 Close-up of Anita, from *Le tentazioni del dottor Antonio* 136
26 Illustration from Milo Manara's *Due viaggi con Federico Fellini* depicting an imagined scene from *Il viaggio di G. Mastorna* 149
27 Image from Fellini's *Il libro dei sogni* 153
28 Page from a fourteenth-century manuscript of Dante's *Divine Comedy* 156
29 Plate from the exhibition *Il Viaggio di Mastorna: Il sogno di un film messo in scena* 169
30 Drawing from *Fellini en Roma* by Tyto Alba 171
31 Photograph of a scene from the stage play *Le voyage de G. Mastorna* 172
32 Saraghina (Eddra Gale) in *8 ½* (1963) 324
33 Edie (Edith Massey) in *Pink Flamingos* (1972) 324
34 The tobacconist (Maria Antonietta Beluzzi) in *Amarcord* (1973) 325
35 Aunt Ida (Edith Massey) in *Female Trouble* (1974) 325
36 Suzy (Sandra Milo) in *Giulietta degli spiriti* (1965) 333
37 Lady Divine (Divine) in *Multiple Maniacs* (1970) 333
38 The Marquis Du Bois (Daniel Emilfork Berenstein) in *Il Casanova di Federico Fellini* (1976) 334
39 Aunt Ida (Edith Massey) in *Female Trouble* (1974) 334
40 Partygoer (Franca Pasut) in *La dolce vita* (1960) 335
41 Raymond and Connie Marble (David Lochary and Mink Stole) in *Pink Flamingos* (1972) 335
42 Carla (Sandra Milo) in *8 ½* (1963) 336
43 Divine/Babs Johnson (Divine) in *Pink Flamingos* (1972) 336
44 Frame from *Fellini Satyricon* (1969) 337
45 Dawn Davenport (Divine) in *Female Trouble* (1974) 337

Acknowledgments

The editors wish to thank the Department of Italian Studies at the University of Toronto and its current and former Emilio Goggio Chair, Luca Somigli and Nicholas Terpstra, for their generous support of this project from its inception. We are also greatly indebted to the faculty and staff of the Cinema Studies Institute at the University of Toronto. We owe a special debt of gratitude to Giovanna Lisena, Daniele Iannucci, and Katherine Birrette for their impeccable editorial assistance throughout this volume's long journey to press. The graduate students in our two iterations of the "100 Years of Federico Fellini" helped us sharpen our thinking and deepen our scholarship on the Maestro, and for this we are deeply grateful to them. We are also sincerely thankful for the logistical support we received from Elizabete Lourenco and Lucinda Li when the COVID-19 pandemic thwarted our plans for an in-person conference in Toronto. Alessio Aletta came to our rescue when platforms like WordPress, Zoom, and YouTube became the only option for scholarly gatherings, and we truly appreciate his knowledge and patience. The Istituto Italiano di Cultura of Toronto has been a staunch supporter of our activities around Fellini's centenary, from the conferences in 2020 and 2021 to this very publication; we are forever indebted to its current and former directors, Veronica Manson and Alessandro Ruggera. Finally, we would like to acknowledge the precious help of Mark Thompson, who acquired this volume for the University of Toronto Press and oversaw its publication, and of Beth McAuley, who masterfully copyedited its many different essays.

FEDERICO FELLINI

Centenary Essays

Introduction:
Fellini at 100 – The Lingering Celebration

MARCO MALVESTIO, JESSICA WHITEHEAD, AND
ALBERTO ZAMBENEDETTI

In January 2020 the first cases of the 2019 coronavirus disease were reported in North America. Shortly thereafter, the world braced for the devastating impact of the COVID-19 pandemic. Many countries, including Canada, attempted to contain the spread of this deadly virus by issuing stay-at-home orders and closing their borders. Most forms of socialization, including academic gatherings and film screenings, were discouraged, if not outright prohibited. As the pandemic claimed the lives of many, exposed entrenched systemic inequalities, and restructured our entire way of relating to one another, we learned how to adapt to this new world and, when possible, pressed on with our activities, albeit with a heavy heart, mindful of the many relatives, colleagues, and friends we might never see again.

In the world of Italian cinema, the year 2020 also corresponded with the one-hundredth anniversary of Federico Fellini's birth. Scholars and cinephiles, including the editors of this volume, were preparing to celebrate this macro-event when concerns over the pandemic rightfully overshadowed all else, including Fellini's friend and collaborator Alberto Sordi's identical milestone, which by comparison went relatively unnoticed. Instead, Fellini's centenary turned into a moment of reflection, an opportunity for debate and confrontation that coexisted, at times in emotionally and intellectually surprising ways, with one of the most trying challenges of the twenty-first century, one that would have set the Maestro's imagination ablaze. In many ways, the taking stock of his enormous cultural legacy ended up corresponding with the rethinking of the entire academic edifice. At least in some venues, it felt as if any discussion of the centenary was a discussion about the ways in which we talk about cinema itself.

Like many of our colleagues, we had lofty ambitions for the centenary. We participated in the planning of two international conferences that were to take place in Rome and Toronto in the summer and fall of 2020, respectively; we intended to publish the proceedings of these events right after they took place; we team-taught two monographic graduate seminars at the University of Toronto; we coordinated the involvement of our doctoral students in the Toronto International Film Festival's (TIFF) public programming of a comprehensive Fellini retrospective; similarly, we offered our help to the Istituto Italiano di Cultura in Toronto (IIC), which was to sponsor a large exhibition of Fellini paraphernalia; finally, we applied for a Social Sciences and Humanities Research Council (SSHRC) Connection grant to support many of the aforementioned activities. Of course, the TIFF retrospective was cancelled, as was the exhibition; the Toronto conference was held fully online and the Rome one was postponed to 2021. We threw out our original plans and regrouped, our efforts stretching into the years following the centenary. One thing remained certain: as documentaries, books, and rereleases of his classic films planned before the pandemic poured into the marketplace, we maintained the belief that Fellini remains one of the most celebrated directors and profitable brands in all of cinema's history.[1] We wanted to contribute to this conversation, but we needed to adapt to the new working conditions. Given the unusual circumstances under which the conferences took place, we scrapped the idea of publishing proceedings. Instead, we decided that an edited collection that situates Fellini in the present would be a better way to consider this strange moment. In this work, we welcomed a wide array of scholarly approaches that eschewed purely celebratory tones, and embraced a multitude of perspectives that, we hope, will bring complexity and nuance to a cultural force that continues to reverberate through the history of cinema.

An acclaimed and sometimes controversial author whose career spanned the second half of the twentieth century, Fellini is still a central part of the Italian cultural imagery, and the object of ongoing debates and critical scrutiny at home and abroad. Our collection contains contributions from renowned Fellini authorities (Burke, Gieri, Minghelli, Minuz, Morreale, Pacchioni, Pravadelli, Tavoni, Vargau, Zanetti), scholars occasionally engaged with his cinema (Greene, Kilbourn, Lima, Malvestio, Sartoni, Stewart, Tagliani, Whitehead, Zambenedetti, Zhang), as well as emerging academics of extraordinary promise (Lisena, Malnati, Samarasinghe). We also elicited short essays from a group of distinguished Canadian film-makers (Egoyan, Maddin, Mehta) who reflect on the ways in which Fellini's work reverberates through theirs. Thanks to the variety of approaches employed, the contributors collectively assess the film-maker's legacy in twenty-first century global culture. From literary influences to pictorial references, from artistic collaborations to politics, from exhibition history to revivals, the chapters in this volume cover the pivotal aspects of Fellini's poetics through contemporary methodological tools.[2]

A testament to Federico Fellini's legacy is the continuing attention paid to his life and work by the international scholarly community since his passing in 1993. Beginning with his early days as a radio dramatist, the legendary Italian director left behind a complex and multifarious oeuvre, from screenplays to comic strips, from the notebooks in which he collected his dreams to the fragments of his incomplete or aborted projects to his mature films. Time and attention have also been devoted to the work of Fellini's collaborators, from his wife Giulietta Masina (Angelucci 2014, 2021; Sani 2021), who starred in many of his films, to Nino Rota (Dyer 2010; Giaquinto 2021; Sorino 2020, 2022), the legendary composer whose scores accompanied so many of Fellini's iconic images, to the writers and intellectuals who worked with Fellini and inspired his work – from Pier Paolo Pasolini to Tullio Pinelli, from Bernardino Zapponi to Andrea Zanzotto and Milo Manara (Pacchioni 2014). Similarly, scholars have examined the contaminations between Fellini's work and the history of painting, from Velazquez and Hogarth to Picasso and Francis Bacon (Aldouby 2013). The persistence of his influence on today's film-makers, and we would argue on the culture at large, is evidence of the fact that Fellini's imagery has become a shared patrimony, a common currency that is exchanged with daily frequency in our media-saturated lives. Gelsomina's tears, Marcello's sunglasses, and Anita's fountain bath have become global signifiers not only for Fellini and Italian cinema but also for Italy itself: they are as firmly lodged in the world's collective unconscious as the Colosseum's arches and Venice's gondolas.

Fellini's work has touched the most different aspects of Italian culture and politics: from ancient Rome to eighteenth-century Venice, from machismo to Catholicism, from Fascism to Berlusconi. Even when he retreated to the sound stages of Cinecittà and seemed to disengage with the outside world, Fellini in fact always paid close attention to Italian history, politics, and cultural heritage. Most importantly, with an allegorical and yet realistic gaze, skilfully but not didactically, Fellini portrayed the economic and social changes taking place in postwar Italy. Sceptical of "high art" and flaunted erudition, Fellini was instead fascinated with popular art forms such as comics and radio-dramas, as well as with the occultural tendencies of modern Italy (exemplified in his attention to the supernatural and the subconscious). The multiplicity and diversity of these sources of inspiration contributed to Fellini's shaping of an imagery that continuously merged low and high culture, the trivial and the historic, the solemn and the grotesque. Especially in his later work, Fellini did not eschew controversy, often taking polemical stances against ideologies (as in his critique of feminism) and "new" media (such as his ambivalent relationship with television).

In recent years, several publications have returned to Fellini's cinema and assessed it from a variety of novel vantage points, testing its resilience against the latest contributions in critical theory and making a compelling case for the need of the sort of re-evaluation we perform with our edited collection. For instance, in his *Political Fellini: Journey to the End of Italy* (2015), Andrea Minuz argued that, contrary to popular belief, the film auteur was not an aloof dreamer but an artist who was profoundly immersed in his cultural milieu, pondering the questions of his time, and responding with an honesty that was uncommon, often disarming, and certainly problematic. If Minuz focused on secular institutions, Alessandro Carrera turned to religion in his *Fellini's Eternal Rome: Paganism and Christianity in the Films of Federico Fellini* (2018), exploring the uneasy mélange of beliefs, fate, and spirituality in the works of the director, underscoring how life-affirming Franciscanism and repressive Counter-Reformation dogmatism co-exist and clash throughout Fellini's catalogue. The late Ottavio Ciro Zanetti, to whose memory this collection is dedicated, published his *Tre passi nel genio: Fellini tra fumetto, circo e varietà* in 2018; in his book, the scholar explored Fellini's interest in cinema's sister visual and performing popular arts, of which the director was a both an early practitioner and a lifelong admirer. Marina Vargau has focused on Rome as the urban catalyst of Fellini's attractions, pursuits, and simulacra in her *Romarcord: Flânerie, spectacle et mémoire dans la Rome de Federico Fellini* (2021), and Minuz zoomed in on the Maestro's meditation on Italy's capital in his *Fellini, Roma* (2020), whereas Marco Bertozzi widened the scope of his investigation to the entire peninsula in his *L'Italia di Fellini. Immagini, paesaggi, forme di vita* (2021).

Books devoted to Fellini's films appear in print with regular cadence, from Roberto Chiesi's monograph *8 ½ di Federico Fellini* (2018) to Rosita Copioli and Gérard Morin's edited collection *Il Casanova di Fellini: ieri e oggi 1976–2016* (2017), from *Fellini 23½* by Aldo Tassone (2020) to Richard Dyer's exploration of *La Dolce Vita* (2020). In the occasion of the centenary, 2020 also saw the publication of compendia such as Oscar Iarussi's "alphabet" *Amarcord Fellini. L'alfabeto di Federico* and *A Companion to Federico Fellini*, edited by Frank Burke, the late Marguerite Waller (also a dedicatee of this collection), and Marita Gubareva.

Additionally, Burke reprinted an expanded edition of his landmark volume *Federico Fellini's Film and Commercials: From Postwar to Postmodern* ([1996] 2020). Our collection builds and elaborates on this sea of contributions, adding a primarily Canadian voice to the conversation on the legacy of this celebrated cinematic juggernaut. In fact, out of the twenty-seven people involved in this enterprise in one role or another (editor, contributor, translator), at least fourteen are Canadian citizens and/or are (or were, if postdoc or emeritus) affiliated with Canadian institutions of higher learning, as well as active members of prominent Canadian professional associations such as the Film and Media Studies Association of Canada (FMSAC) and the Canadian Association for Italian Studies (CAIS). We do not wish to purport that the book's content is exclusively Canadian, of course, nor do we argue that its focus is confined to Fellini studies in Canada. As stated, our goal was to include essays that reflected the multitude of diverse scholars engaged in academic work on Fellini; we believe that this is, in fact, the strength of this entry in the vast Fellini catalogue.

The first section of this collection, "Film-Makers on Fellini," is dedicated not to scholarly work but rather to the reflections on Fellini of three contemporary Canadian directors: Atom Egoyan, Guy Maddin, and Deepa Mehta. Atom Egoyan, who directed the acclaimed *Exotica* (1994), *The Sweet Hereafter* (1997), and *Chloe* (2009), reflects on his experience creating *8 ½ Screens*, a Fellini-inspired installation for the inauguration of the TIFF Bell Lightbox in downtown Toronto in 2010. For Egoyan, this project meant finding in Fellini the intersection between the oneiric and the cinematic experience; by reconfiguring and interpolating the screen tests sequence of *8 ½*, Egoyan creates a rich metatextual net, in which viewers can watch the director and his aids interact with the filmed auditions of characters from the protagonist's life, who employs cinema as a way to reimagine, and stage, his own past, present, and future. The critically acclaimed director and screenwriter Guy Maddin – famous for his films *Dracula, Pages from a Virgin's Diary* (2002), *The Saddest Music in the World* (2003), and *My Winnipeg* (2007) – discusses his latest short film, *The Rabbit Hunters* (2020), which stars Isabella Rossellini as a Fellini-inspired character. In his Q&A with Jessica Whitehead, Maddin reflects on Fellini's influence on him as a film-maker and how *The Rabbit Hunters* was conceived to visualize a Fellini dreamscape. Indo-Canadian director Deepa Mehta, best known for her *Elements Trilogy* (*Fire*, 1996; *Earth*, 1998; and *Water*, 2005), shares her thoughts on *La strada* and *Le notti di Cabiria*, and on the experience of watching Fellini while growing up in India. In 2011, TIFF organized a series titled *Fellini/Felliniesque: "Dream" Double Bills*, for which Mehta paired *La notti di Cabiria* with Satyajit Ray's *Devi* (1960), highlighting the Italian Maestro's global influence.

The second section of this volume is, sadly, an in memoriam one. In early 2020, two superb Fellini scholars died: Ottavio Cirio Zanetti and Marguerite Waller. Zanetti, born in 1983, was both a film-maker and an essayist; he directed several shorts and published countless online reviews, as well as the aforementioned volume *Tre passi nel genio: Fellini tra fumetto, circo e varietà*. We are proud and moved to include two previously unpublished essays by Zanetti in this volume. "Federico Fellini's Urban Planning" (which Zanetti was scheduled to present in person at the Toronto conference) deals with the representation and reinvention of urban spaces in Fellini's cinema, as well as with the influence of comic strips in his depiction of cities. "Fellini's Graphic World" investigates the relationship between Fellini's imagination and the comic strip authors of his youth, from Attalo to Lee Falk, as well as the way in which his own experience as an author of comics in the 1940s contributed to shaping his later work. Andrew A. Monti of York University, a media studies scholar and a long-time friend of Zanetti, generously translated (with Camilla Bozzoli) and edited his two essays.

Marguerite Waller was Professor of Comparative Literature and Chair of the Department of Gender and Sexuality Studies at the University of California, Riverside. She published on a vast array of topics, from Dante and Petrarch to Shakespeare and feminist theory. As a Fellini scholar, she co-edited *Federico Fellini: Contemporary Perspectives* (2002). Here, Frank Burke, one of the great authorities of Fellini of his generation, pays homage to her with an essay titled "Deleuzional Ponderings: The Fellinian Symbolic." Drawing on Waller's research and reflection on Fellini's work, Burke uses Jung and Deleuze to interpret some crucial passages of Fellini's cinema and his *Book of Dreams*. Like Fellini, Burke argues, Waller "saw a thousand things at once in a way that exploded simple reference, allegory, or arid conceptualization. She created fissures in seeming textual homogeneities while refusing any complacent relationship to Fellinian signification."

The "Centenary Essays" section collects the main bulk of the chapters of this volume. The section opens with Giuliana Minghelli's essay "What Is in the Modern Look? Federico Fellini and the Photography of William Klein," in which Minghelli recounts Fellini's crucial encounter with American photographer William Klein. Famous for his 1956 photobook *Life Is Good and Good for You in New York: Trance Witness Revels*, Klein unofficially collaborated in Fellini's *Le notti di Cabiria*, and his innovative way of representing life in a modern metropolis influenced Fellini's work of the late 1950s and 1960s, especially his use of light.

While Rome is no New York, Klein's gaze helped Fellini highlight new and unexpected aspects of Italy on the cusp of the economic boom. Charting a series of thematic and iconographic occurrences in both artists, Minghelli investigates the reciprocal influence Fellini and Klein had on each other. Similarly, Veronica Pravadelli explores the way in which Fellini exploited and engulfed other forms of art in his work, and the theoretical premises and consequences of this assimilation. Her essay "Fellini, Theorist of Culture, 1950–1972" touches on an essential point in Fellini's scholarship: the role of popular culture (and especially its visual aspects, from *varietà* to *fotoromanzo*) in shaping Fellini's gaze as a film-maker and his understanding of Italian society. Pravadelli shows how Fellini's interest in spectacle and the spectacular mirrored and expanded contemporary debates on high and low culture, overcoming the more conservative positions of Croce's idealism and of Frankfurt School theory.

Shelleen Greene's "Oenothea's Gaze: Donyale Luna in *Fellini Satyricon*" offers an insightful account of the role of African-American model and actress Donyale Luna in Fellini's adaptation of Petronius's *Satyricon*, in which she played the goddess Oenothea. While *Fellini Satyricon* is often regarded as the director's most experimental film and a reflection on contemporary counterculture, Greene reads Luna's performance through the framework of the Civil Rights movement and decolonization processes. Still a non-professional actress at the time, but already a cultural icon, Luna's stardom challenged traditional representations of Black bodies in Italian cinema, as well as the country's reticence to address its colonial and racist past.

Eleonora Sartoni's essay "Consumer Capitalism, National Identity, and Heterotopia in Fellini's *Le tentazioni del dottor Antonio*" discusses Fellini's contribution to the omnibus film *Boccaccio '70* in relation to social changes in post-economic boom Italy. In the picture, Rome's EUR (Esposizione Universale di Roma) business district becomes simultaneously a Foucauldian heterotopia of compensation and the heterotopia of illusion. According to Sartoni, *Le tentazioni del dottor Antonio* is a critique of the capitalist illusion of being able to overcome social class disparities thanks to economic growth. A distinctive example of Fascist architecture and urban planning, in Fellini's film the EUR allowed the re-emersion of this past in the context of a more modern country – one characterized by mass consumerism and advertising – for which the director and his protagonist felt simultaneously repulsion and attraction.

Mirko Tavoni explores the relationship between Fellini and one of Italian culture's unavoidable models, Dante Alighieri. Several scholars have argued, not always convincingly, for a direct link between the contents of Dante's work and Fellini's imagination. In his "Fellini, Dante, *Il viaggio di G. Mastorna*, and Dreams," Tavoni argues that one of the works where this influence is more tangible is *Il viaggio di G. Mastorna*, Fellini's long prepared and never realized project about the afterlife. Together with Dante, Tavoni also explores the role of Jungian psychoanalysis in helping Fellini express his oneiric and visionary poetics. "The most famous film *never* made in the history of cinema" is again the topic of Marina Vargau's essay "*Il viaggio di G. Mastorna*'s Constellation at the Crossroads of Arts and Media." Rather than with the influences that defined this project, Vargau is interested in the many ways in which Mastorna has cast its shadow across arts and media, from the 1992 comic book by Fellini and Milo Manara to Fellini's later production, to a variety of works by other artists and film-makers, such as McMullan's documentary *Deragliamenti/Derailments* (2011); Mion, Corvi, and Izzo's experimental film *Il viaggio di G. Mastorna, esperimento di ricostruzione* (2013); the exhibition *Il Viaggio di Mastorna. Il sogno di un film messo in scena* (2017); Tyto Alba's comic book *Fellini en Roma* (2017); and the theatrical performance *Le voyage de G. Mastorna* (2019), staged by Marie Rémond.

In "The Genesis of Steiner: *La dolce vita* as Authorial Melting Pot," Federico Pacchioni explores one of the most disturbing and mysterious figures in Fellini's cinema: Steiner, Marcello's intellectual friend who killed himself and his children. Pacchioni digs into the cultural and literary origins of the character, pointing out to the intellectual influences (Christian dramaturgy, existentialism, musicology) and the real-life figures (Roberto Longhi, Cesare Pavese) behind Steiner. Pacchioni also investigates the role of Fellini's collaborators, most notably Tullio Pinelli and Brunello Rondi, in shaping Steiner as we see him on screen, while also highlighting their different understandings of the character.

Translated by Giovanna Caterina Lisena, Emiliano Morreale's essay "*Amarcord*: Fascism, Nightmares, and the Spectator's Autobiography" underlines the generational value of *Amarcord* as a depiction of Fascism in Italy. By means of his oneiric imagination, Fellini created a portrait of Fascist-era Italy that resonated with the experience of other writers and intellectuals of the time. The film's autobiographical dimension is put into question, separating it from its literal sense to give it the broader meaning of a generational autobiography. Memory, history, and imagination blend into a recreation of a crucial period in modern Italy, and in the lives of the director and spectators alike.

In "Spectres of Venice: Gothic Apparitions in *Il Casanova di Federico Fellini*," Marco Malvestio and Alberto Zambenedetti discuss the influence of Gothic imagery in *Il Casanova di Federico Fellini*. This influence is explored with reference to the Gothic *filone* of the 1960s, as well as to Fellini's interest in the occult and in Zapponi's knowledge of horror and the Gothic. The relationship between Fellini and the Gothic is not simply an iconographic one, as the director exploited the inherently Gothic (and, at the same time, profoundly postmodern) theme of the double (in the forms of automata and mannequins) to question his protagonist's agency.

Andrea Minuz, in "Sense of Place and 'Placelessness': Fellini's Rome," reads the director's renditions of the Italian capital (especially in the eponymous film) in tandem with the so-called *mondo* movies of those same years. In this essay, translated by Giovanna Caterina Lisena, Minuz interprets *Roma* as a safari into the unknown dimensions of a city that, for Italians, is simultaneously the epitome of Italianness and an indecipherable mystery. In Minuz's argument, the *mondo* genre of Italian cinema, which centres on the exhibition/exploitation of exotic locations as a thinly veiled excuse to show nudity and violence, has influenced Fellini's work by bringing him to direct this exoticizing gaze on the most famous symbol of the nation: Rome, the eternal city. The documentary, yet imaginative and rhapsodic approach that Fellini adopted in this film was influenced, according to Minuz, by a genre of Italian cinema mostly employed to look outside Italy and to represent "otherness"; *Roma* thus casts an estranging and uncanny light on something that Italians believe to know well.

Dishani Samarasinghe explores Fellini's cinema alongside his own drawings, a crucial, yet understudied, area of his artistic production. In her "Framing Women in Fellini's Films and Drawings," Samarasinghe adopts the concept of interartiality to discuss the relationship between Fellini's *Book of Dreams* (and thus the role of Jungian analysis) and two of his best-known films, *8 ½* and *La città delle donne*, and the representation of women, a subject that famously obsessed Fellini in a variety of forms. Samarasinghe investigates to what extent psychoanalysis, artistic influences (mainly by Picasso), and oneiric imagery helped Fellini develop his distinct (and problematic) approach to femininity, and how his cinematic work and his drawings interacted and enhanced each other.

"Originals in the Dark, Imitations in the Light: Fellini's *Ginger e Fred*" by Giovanna Caterina Lisena addresses Fellini's relationship with television. A crucial topic in Fellini's later years, he criticized television (and especially commercial television) as a superficial and consumerist medium that allowed spectators to view more than a program at once, and constantly interrupted films with commercials. At the same time, Lisena argues, *Ginger e Fred* was imbued with nostalgia for the times of the *avanspettacolo*, which in the film was replicated on the set of a TV variety show, thus casting a light of unreality and lack of authenticity of the celebrated reunion. Lisena evokes Baudrillard's concept of the simulacrum to address the conflicting issues in *Ginger e Fred*, thereby reflecting on the postmodern dimension of his work. A similar topic is discussed by Giacomo Tagliani in "'The Tyrant Spectator': Intermediality, Spectatorship, and Subjectivation in Fellini's Work." The author deals with the intermedial critique in Fellini's works – which is to say, how Fellini employed a medium (specifically cinema) to criticize others, and especially television. By doing so, Fellini commented on the changes in the way spectators experience films, connecting them to broader social and cultural changes in post-economic boom Italy.

Manuela Gieri's "Imaginary Worlds and Startling Creatures: Fellini and Popular Culture" centres once again on the importance of popular culture in shaping Fellini's imagination. His unique vision, Gieri argues, was influenced not by highbrow cinema but rather by a vast array of popular art forms ranging from comic strips to the *varietà*, from circus to television. Early in his career, Fellini himself authored such products, as his collaboration with *Marc'Aurelio* shows. Comic strips were for Fellini a preparatory stage towards the world of moving images, while the insertion of advertising in his movies widened the narrative space in a metaphorical direction.

The role of Fellini's voice, which starting from a minor appearance in *I vitelloni* would become central in later movies such as *Fellini: A Director's Notebook* (1969), *I clowns* (1970), *Roma* (1972), and *Intervista* (1987), is the focus of Gaia Malnati's essay "The Megaphone Ran Out of Battery: The Invitation of Fellini's Voices." Fellini's use of his own voice in his films was a key element of his self-representation as an auteur. By diminishing the distance between director and spectator, Fellini's voice deceived the audience into believing that they were at the centre of the diegetic space. Fellini's world, at the same time, constantly hinged on the spectacular and the inauthentic, and his use of his voice was not dissimilar, as he employed it as a tool to enhance the autobiographical dimension of his movies while simultaneously negating it in the mise-en-scène.

Russell J.A. Kilbourn focuses on another distinctive characteristic of Fellini's cinema and authorship: the non-normative use of flashbacks. In "Watch Out! Flashback! Fellini's Memory Films," Kilbourn merges flashback studies and memory theory to provide an overview of this often overlooked aspect of Fellini's poetics and technique. The role of memory in Fellini's later works should be, according to Kilbourn, balanced with the consistent refusal of autobiographical readings of such films.

In her "Fellini's Notes on Camp to John Waters," Eleonora Lima investigates Fellini under the critical lens of camp studies. By reconstructing

Fellini's influence on cult American director and camp pioneer John Waters, Lima explores Fellini's "aesthetics of bad taste" and his love of the unnatural, the exaggerated, the artificial. Framing Fellini within a camp aesthetic means understanding his work and cultural influence in dialogue with postmodernity. At the same time, by detailing the influence Fellini had on Waters, Lima traces underinvestigated genealogy of "bad taste" in contemporary cinema, expanding the areas where Fellini's legacy can be observed.

Jessica Whitehead and Christina Stewart examine Fellini's impact on international film distribution in Canada. Unlike the United States, art-house Italian cinema did not traditionally receive wide-spread distribution in Canada. The authors argue, through an analysis of exhibition data, that because of Fellini's unique relationship with the North American press, he was able to evolve from traditional grass-roots exhibition practices to more mainstream distribution by becoming a widely recognized director in Canada. The chapter is also an example of a new way to study Fellini with a focus on exhibition and audiences. This novel approach helps us understand how Fellini was able to permeate global film cultures through his distinctive press-persona and gives us a deeper understanding of how international audiences received Fellini and his work.

The essay that closes the volume, Gaoheng Zhang's "'Women with Big Breasts and Wide Hips': Fellini's Cinema in Chinese Media Essays," focuses on the complex reception of Fellini's work in China. In 2020, the year marking the fiftieth anniversary of the establishment of diplomatic relations between Italy and China, several Fellini retrospectives took place. Zhang explores the Fellini-related publications produced in this occasion, showing the many ways in which Fellini's distinctive style is mediated for a Chinese audience, and the role that Western film criticism plays in this mediation.

NOTES

1 At the time of writing, the Italian national television platform RaiPlay (www.raiplay.it) lists no fewer than nine documentaries devoted to the Maestro.
2 We should note that, given the diversity of our contributors, the sources they employ in their essays are often written in multiple languages. We provide in-text English translations of the quotes, whereas the original language can be found in the endnotes. If a published translation of a source existed, we omitted the original language and relied on the work of the translators to minimize word count in our own volume. Unless otherwise noted, all translations are by the essays' authors.

REFERENCES

Angelucci, Gianfranco. 2014. *Giulietta Masina. Attrice e sposa di Federico Fellini.* Rome: Edizioni Sabinae.
– 2021. *Giulietta Masina.* Rome: Edizioni Sabinae.
Bertozzi, Marco. 2021. *L'Italia di Fellini. Immagini, paesaggi, forme di vita.* Venice: Marsilio Editori.
Burke, Frank. (1996) 2020. *Federico Fellini's Film and Commercials: From Postwar to Postmodern.* Bristol, UK: Intellect.
Burke, Frank, and Marguerite R. Waller. 2002. *Federico Fellini: Contemporary Perspectives.* Toronto: University of Toronto Press.
Burke, Frank, Marguerite R. Waller, and Marita Gubareva, eds. 2020. *A Companion to Federico Fellini.* Hoboken, NJ: Wiley Blackwell.
Carerra, Alessandro. 2018. *Fellini's Eternal Rome: Paganism and Christianity in the Films of Federico Fellini.* London: Bloomsbury Academic.
Chiesi, Roberto. 2018. *8 ½ di Federico Fellini.* Rome: Gremese.
Copioli, Rosita, and Gérard Morin, eds. 2017. *Il Casanova di Fellini: ieri e oggi 1976–2016.* Rome: Gangemi editore.
Dyer, Richard. 2010. *Nino Rota: Music, Film, and Feeling.* New York: BFI/Palgrave Macmillan.
– 2020. *La Dolce Vita.* 2nd ed. London: BFI/Palgrave Macmillan.
Giaquinto, Pasquale. 2021. *La biblioteca ermetica di Nino Rota.* Manfredonia: Andrea Pacilli Editore.
Iarussi, Oscar. 2020. *Amarcord Fellini. L'alfabeto di Federico.* Bologna: Il Mulino.
Klein, William. 1956. *Life Is Good and Good for You in New York: Trance Witness Revels.* London: Photography Magazine.
Minuz, Andrea. 2015. *Political Fellini: Journey to the End of Italy.* New York: Berghahn Books.
– 2020. *Fellini, Roma.* Rome: Rubbettino Editore.
Sani, Marco. 2021. *… e adesso parlo io. Giulietta Masina si racconta.* Taranto: Antonio Dellisanti Editore.
Sorino, Tino. 2020. *In Seicento o a spasso con Nino Rota. Ricordi e documenti dagli archivi dei suoi amici.* Rome: NeP edizioni.
– 2022. *Nell'intimità di Nino Rota. Curiosando ancora tra le carte di Prudenzina Giannelli.* Rome: NeP edizioni.
Tassone, Aldo. 2020. *Fellini 23½. Tutti i film.* Bologna: Edizioni Cineteca di Bologna.
Vargau, Marina. 2021. *Romarcord: Flânerie, spectacle et mémoire dans la Rome de Federico Fellini.* Montreal: Guernica World Editions.
Zanetti, Ottavio Cirio. 2018. *Tre passi nel genio: Fellini tra fumetto, circo e varietà.* Venice: Marsilio Editori.

FILM-MAKERS ON FELLINI

Reflections on 8 ½ Screens

ATOM EGOYAN

Even though I thought I felt close to the art of Fellini, it was not until I came across the pages of his magnificent *Book of Dreams* that I fully appreciated the depth and complexity of this great creative genius.

It was at a large retrospective at the Jeu de Paume in Paris in November of 2009. The exhibition was full of various objects, photos, and props from his films, as well as projected clips and interviews. In the final room of the show, the viewer got to see Fellini's *Book of Dreams*, which he had transcribed from his subconscious mind (see image 1). It was like viewing storyboards from every film he had ever made and many that were only imagined. I was in awe.

I had already been asked by the Toronto International Film Festival to make an installation for the inauguration of the TIFF Bell Lightbox the following year, and I had chosen a very special site. Cinema 4 of the new building would house the Cinematheque and I wanted to create a piece that would honour the spirit of cinephilia.

The original idea of this installation/consecration of Cinema 4 was to compile a selection of classic images of characters watching films, from such diverse sources as *Taxi Driver* (watching porn), *A Clockwork Orange* (watching horror), *Cinema Paradiso* (watching classic movies), *Sunset Boulevard* (watching oneself) ... In short, the list was long and full of options.

But the moment I experienced Fellini's *Book of Dreams* I changed my mind and decided to find a way of mirroring the experience I had in Paris, that of vertiginously falling into the physical crucible of a great film-maker's inspiration. I wanted to find a way of sculpturally placing the viewer into one of Fellini's dreams.

Of course, it can be argued that cinema itself does this quite effortlessly. *8 ½* is full of these immersions with unforgettable dream sequences and passages into the great artist's subconscious.[1] The challenge here was to take one sequence from the film – a sequence that was *not* a dream

18   Atom Egoyan

Image 1. Image from Federico Fellini's *Book of Dreams*. Copyright Comune di Rimini/Francesca Fabbri Fellini, Archivio del Fellini Museum di Rimini.

Image 2. Images of the projector in front of the cinema from *8 ½ Screens*. Image courtesy of Atom Egoyan.

sequence – and transform it into a physical experience that evoked the fractured logic of a dream state.

All films try to create a sense of internal reality by harnessing the energy of the performers with a series of actions that move a plot forward. Unless the film comes to a stop, which happens in Fellini's *8 ½*. The production comes to a stop.

I love how *8 ½* captures this sense of suspended time whilst moving forward in its *own* space – that is to say the time that Fellini's *actual* film takes to unfurl on a screen – with such vigour and force. Fellini has made a film about an artist's block and by cinematically displaying this block, he is able at the same time to miraculously unleash all of the creative potential that has been locked in the artist's imagination, unable to find expression.

In this way, it is a completely unique work. It gives the viewer full access to both an internal and external dynamic in an utterly original way, inviting us to concomitantly experience a sense of stasis and tremendous movement. It is full of great beauty, charm, and erotic tension. How could I honour the power and possibility of this work and celebrate its unique construction?

I immediately thought of placing a film projector *in front of* the screen thus displacing the conventional format of projection (see image 2). This projector would then show a single scene from *8 ½* that occurs near the end, fracturing this scene into its component shots. It would

20 Atom Egoyan

Image 3. Image of Luisa leaving the cinema as seen projected in *8 ½ Screens*. Image courtesy of Atom Egoyan.

simultaneously break down the scene and allow the viewer to reconstruct it, depending on their physical placement and movement through the cinema itself.

The scene itself takes place in a screening room, where we encounter one of the densest scenes of collective film-watching ever captured. The complexity of the relationships between the viewers in this scene (a film director, his frustrated producer, his luminescent muse, his alienated wife, her bemused friend) and the screen auditions they are viewing (for the part of an alienated wife, a frustrated mistress, and idealized prostitute) is quite overwhelming. By the end of this scene as the director's wife, Luisa, leaves the theatre, the marriage is effectively over. Mastroianni's Guido is metaphorically hung out to dry (see image 3).

Curious viewers experience the installation through reconfiguring and reformatting the pieces of this scene – *8 ½* shots projected on *8 ½* screens made from torn bedsheets and suspended in the theatre with strings and wooden clothes pegs – into their own unique way of imagining this moment. I invite them to move around the cinema to explore possibilities.

This very personal project is a fantasy fuelled by one of the greatest imaginations of Italian cinema. I offer the work with deep respect, more than little nostalgia, and tremendous excitement.

NOTE

1 On this diegetic fluidity, see Russell J.A. Kilbourn's chapter in this volume.

Q&A on *The Rabbit Hunters* (2020)

GUY MADDIN

Questions written by Jessica Whitehead

JW: It is clear that you have a close relationship with Italian cinema. For example, Isabella Rossellini's presence in many of your films and the forward you wrote for Angela Dalle Vacche's book *Diva: Defiance and Passion in Early Italian Cinema*. How was Italian cinema formative for your film-making practice and how has this relationship evolved through the years?

GM: I came to Italian cinema relatively late, well after I acquired my ardent passion for certain tendencies in 1930s American cinema. Yes, I knew and loved the major De Sica and Fellini works early, and I loved Max Ophüls's *La signora di tutti* (1934), but I was well over forty when I discovered the narcotic enchantments of the diva films and of *Cabiria* (1914) with Maciste. One of the oddest Italian films I have seen is Felix Feist's disaster film *Deluge* (1933), which was an entirely American production shot in the United States with all the Hollywood trimmings. It was sent out into the world where it was dubbed into the languages of various markets and then, like so many early movies it was lost, or even intentionally tossed out by its distributors. A copy turned up around 2008 in Italy, dubbed into Italian. No other copies exist, so to market the picture in English DVD markets, the film was subtitled back into English. This is the only form in which it exists, this American film shot in English, dubbed into Italian, then subtitled back into its original language. Watching *Deluge* is an uncanny experience. All the American actors seem so Italian. I can imagine their off-screen lives as Italian thespians. Their hair seems darker, more Mediterranean, their hand gestures more expressive than their Hollywood counterparts of the era, and the plot seems downright operatic compared to American films of the period, all because of this strange dub-and-subtitle process the film underwent. In short, I feel more at home with this USA product after its Italianization than I would've with the original had it been available to me. I must be on some Italian wavelength. And though I am Icelandic by ethnicity, I adored the disinhibition of the operatic cultures. I feel like my creative spirit is a hybrid similar to Isabella Rossellini's, half Scandinavian, half Mediterranean. That's probably why she and I hit it off so quickly, so naturally.

JW: How was *The Rabbit Hunters* project first developed?

GM: It was a commission from the Pacific Film Archive at Berkeley. They planned a series of screenings and fundraisers to celebrate the Fellini centennial in 2020. We completed *The Rabbit Hunters* (2020) on time, but the events were cancelled at the last second in the first days of the COVID-19 shutdowns. It was nice to have the film on our résumés, but it never really got a proper premiere anywhere. Too bad. The film is minor, maybe, but we took on the project with a lot of love for it and for the Maestro himself.

JW: Russell J.A. Kilbourn in his chapter in *A Companion to Federico Fellini* (2020), "Il ritorno in patria: From Rimini to Winnipeg by Way of the Alps," explores how *I vitelloni* (1953) influenced your film *My Winnipeg* (2007). How did Fellini's exploration of his hometown of Rimini shape your own ongoing cinematic relationship with Winnipeg?

GM: *I vitelloni* knocked me out so much when I first saw it that decades later, when I received the commission to make a documentary about my hometown, I decided to structure *My Winnipeg* (2007) after this Fellini film about the useless twenty- and thirtysomethings of Rimini. The Rimini of that film is defined by the immaturity of its main characters, just as the Winnipeg I knew best was populated mostly by similarly overaged young men, my city's pieces of veal.

JW: Fellini's dreams play a pivotal role in the plot of *The Rabbit Hunters*. Why do Fellini's dreams resonate so much with you as a film-maker?

GM: I talk about my dreams with a lot of people. I guess it's the surrealist in me. I love the topic. I am often surprised by how different from mine other people's dreams are. But Fellini, who kept and even published an illustrated dream diary, dreamt as I dream. I feel I would have gotten along with him, if only on the subject of dreams. When we received *The Rabbit Hunters* commission, we knew the only way to approach the film was by shooting some of the dreams recounted by Fellini. But we had so little time to complete the project and certainly no money to pay for a lawyer or rights clearances to excerpt the great director's diary, so we used our dreams instead of Fellini's for our script. Maybe this way was far more honest anyway. Our dreams – my film-making partner Evan also keeps a dream diary – were already similar to Fellini's but we were the film-makers now, so we felt fine with sliding our own sleeping experiences into the script. We didn't have to pay for the rights to our own dreams either.

JW: Why did you cast Isabella Rossellini in the role of Fellini in the film? Did her family's long-standing relationship with Fellini and Masina come into play?

GM: Federico has a million anxiety dreams about his wife Giulietta, probably because he cheated on her so much, hurt her so often. But it sure seemed like a lifelong love bound the two great talents together no matter what, they even died a short time apart, as if one could not survive without the other. So, it occurred to us that having Isabella play both the husband and the wife crammed into one body, a dream duality, was a nice idea from which to start building up the events of the story. And, yes, it helped that Isabella knew both Federico and Giulietta through her father. If work on our film was rushed, there was at least going to be some genuine spiritual connections between us and the film's subject matter!

JW: How did the relationship between Fellini and his wife Giulietta Masina influence the development of Isabella's character?

GM: I can't for the life of me think in complicated terms about performance, so we just put Isabella in a man's suit and let her femininity blast through it all. And of course, Isabella is a comic genius, so I think she identified far more with Giulietta. The result is some kind of strange hybrid, but we barely had any control over what that hybrid produced on screen.

JW: How do you see Fellini's influence continuing to impact your films?

GM: Now that I have made twelve features and reached my sixty-sixth year, I see better how Fellini's films were put together, and why he made them. I feel a far closer affinity to the director now than I ever did as a young man. There must be something in his temperament that allows me clear access to his heart. I feel like I know him. I feel that way about Buñuel as well. So even without attempting to imitate Fellini, I feel I can keep improving as a film-maker by being more like him. And since I am more like him with each passing year, I feel I can make my own Fellini films for the rest of my life. No one will see Fellini in these pictures because they may represent roads down which Fellini never travelled, but he will be there at my side nonetheless.

The Unexpected Moment

DEEPA MEHTA

When I think about Federico Fellini and his work, it takes me back to the first time I watched one of his films. It was back when I was studying at Delhi University, and the film was *La strada*. It was an eye-opening experience, one filled with wonderment, which I carry with me, even today.

I had grown up in the northern city of Amritsar on a steady diet of commercial Indian cinema (now known as Bollywood). We considered ourselves lucky if the monotony of our cinematic experience was upended by the viewing of a Western film; by the likes of an Elvis Presley or Cliff Richard dirge on a Sunday morning show at our local movie hall, Ashok Cinema. Non-English language films, or "foreign movies" as they were called, were an anomaly and my first exposure to them was only when we moved to Delhi from Amritsar. Dragged by a friend whom I considered sophisticated by the virtue of her knowing Italian, I sat on a steel-backed chair in the screening room of some cultural centre on Curzon Road, utterly mesmerized by what was unfolding before me on the screen. It was Fellini's *La strada*. I clearly remember walking out after the movie and sitting on the curb of the road quite gobsmacked. How does one react to, say, the taste of something completely unique and completely other worldly and yet, shockingly, completely accessible? With awe, I would guess. It felt like I had just witnessed not just a piece of art but also something tangible. Something human.

Until then, the only film-maker whose work, for me, reflected a similar kind of humanness was Satyajit Ray, whom I have always considered one of the greatest humanitarian film-makers. A few years ago, the Toronto International Film Festival asked me to pair a Fellini film with a feature film that reflected similarities, in theme or style, for their program called "Fellini/Felliniesque: Dream Double Bills." I paired

Fellini's film from 1957, *Le notti di Cabiria*, with Ray's film from 1960, *Devi*, because of the strong connection I felt between the two.

Le notti di Cabiria is about a prostitute, Maria "Cabiria" Ceccarelli, who wants to start her life afresh and find true love. I was so moved by her ability to rise above where life and her circumstances had left her, to find human dignity. Which is what reminded me of the protagonist in *Devi*, Doyamoyee, a woman whose father-in-law makes her believe that she is the reincarnation of the Hindu goddess Kali. And though the stories of the two women are far from alike, I felt they were tied together by the protagonist, a woman whose ultimately tragic outcome had been framed by the expectations and pressures put on her by society and her own beliefs – about herself and the world around her. And both film-makers, Fellini and Ray, had executed the story of such a woman with finesse while carefully walking the fine line between reality and fantasy.

When I was in my third year of university, I remember watching *Subarnarekha*, a Bengali film made by Ritwik Ghatak. It was both tragic and sublime. There was a scene, close to the end of the film, in which the protagonist goes to a fancy Western restaurant in Calcutta and gets drunk. In the background of that scene, there was a Western tune that was so haunting in its effervescence that it remained with me for years. The juxtaposition of Ghatak's scene of a man hitting rock bottom while a completely alien piece of music played in the background was startling in what it said about the collision of emotions coinciding with the coming together, so harmoniously, of diverse cultures. A few years later, when I watched Fellini's *La dolce vita* at Max Mueller Bhavan (or it might have been Alliance Française in New Delhi), I felt a sense of familiarity but couldn't pinpoint what it was for a while. And then it hit me: in the background of the orgy scene at the end of the film was the same piece of music I had first heard in Ghatak's film, *Subarnarekha*. When I did some research, I found out that the tune was called *Patricia* and because Ghatak was so taken in by what Fellini revealed with that track in *La dolce vita*, he used it to make a statement in *Subarnarekha* five years later. Ironically, I had seen the films backwards – *Subarnarekha* first, at a film festival, and *La dolce vita* later. The films were very dissimilar and so were the scenes, and yet I found them to be so similar in emotional content. That is the beauty of film, isn't it? How two disparate worlds, so different and far apart, can have a common inspiration and how that translates into an emotion both in the mind of the film-maker and in the heart of the audience.

As I watched more of Fellini's work, I could see the thread of social consciousness that went hand-in-hand with his neorealistic approach and bound together the narratives he created based on the daily lives of ordinary average Italian people. He portrayed their struggle in a humanistic way, as if from the point of view of one of their own and not someone looking into their world from the outside. I don't think one would need to be a film critic, part of the film industry, or a cinema buff to connect with Fellini's films for this very reason. You'd just need to be human to be able to relate.

I think I feel connected to Fellini as a film-maker as well because the stories I am curious about are based on the lives of the average South Asian, the marginalized "other," and women. His choice of casting non-actors opened up new paths within the world of cinema and is a tool that I used in my film *Anatomy of Violence* (2016), which is a dramatized improvisation of a gang-rape case that took place in Delhi and had a non-professional actress stepping into the shoes of the victim.

There's a lot that one can say about Federico Fellini. But if I had to put it in a nutshell, which is hard to do given the person and film-maker that he was, I would say that he was somebody who was magical and whose cinema carries that same magic even today. He had the power to create pieces that made worlds come together in a most unexpected way. His command over cinema was so strong that he had the gift of being able to take up the most ordinary subject and make it something totally extraordinary and push it beyond our imagination. Like the opening sequence of *La dolce vita*, where the statue of Jesus is moved in the most brilliantly unbelievable way – by helicopter over the city as people look at the spectacle from below. In fact, Fellini came to mind a few weeks ago when I watched Paolo Sorrentino's film *È stata la mano di Dio* (2021). It made me think of Fellini's semi-autobiographical film *Amarcord*. And I think that could be one of the biggest reasons why I loved *È stata la mano di Dio* so much. During an intimate salon conversation that I attended over Zoom, Sorrentino spoke about how Fellini had influenced him and continues to do so.

What's not to love about Federico Fellini? He created unexpected moments not for the sake of being unexpected. He took something simple and mundane to the average person and championed it. He made the ordinary special and understood its value and meaning. He created cinema that was, above everything else, still human no matter how fantastical his approach was. I am extremely humbled and honoured to be a part of the celebration of one of the most tantalizing film-makers the world has seen, and probably will ever see.

IN MEMORIAM

Introduction:
Ottavio Cirio Zanetti – In Memoriam

ANDREW A. MONTI

Ottavio Cirio Zanetti was born in Genova on 15 September 1983. I will never forget his birthday because he was my best friend and the best best-friend I could ever ask for. He was generous, caring, and trustworthy. If it wasn't for his rare congenital disease – neurofibromatosis type 2 – that later developed into a malignant tumour, he would still be with us, researching and writing on his favourite topic: film and the art of cinematography (image 4).

Ottavio's first foray into film started at a young age as he supplemented his final secondary school exams with term papers centred on cinema and its relationship with literature, art, history, and mathematics. Upon graduation, he started working in film, with significant experiences alongside directors Michele Soavi, Marco Ponti, and Lina Wertmüller.

He was just nineteen years old when he produced and directed his first documentary, on Emanuele Luzzati, the great theatre and opera set designer. A few years later, Luzzati designed the closing credits of Ottavio's short film *The Honey of Luxembourg*. This short, autobiographical, Proustian thriller is set in three time periods: contemporary Paris, Paris in the early 1990s, and the Paris of the Three Musketeers. The short includes a cameo appearance by Umberto Eco and was selected at the Annecy Film Festival where Ottavio was the youngest director.

In 2007, Ottavio wrote and directed *Sipario*, a medium-length film in which four stories of actors' ordinary quarrels are intertwined as they take place on the backstages and frontstages of four theatres. *Sipario* starred Valentina Cortese, Adriana Asti, Francesca Benedetti, and Luca Ronconi, and the score was composed by Nicola Piovani. In 2009, the Bergamo International Art Film Festival awarded *Sipario* the Acting Prize for Valentina Cortese's performance and the Director Prize. In the same year, he curated a column on art and cinema in Kataweb's

Image 4. Ottavio Cirio Zanetti.

Katalibri magazine and directed documentaries for RAI, the Italian public broadcaster; in 2015, he joined the photography team of the Hermitage Museum in St. Petersburg, Russia (image 5).

For more than seven years starting in 2013, Ottavio held a column of film criticism on the online newspaper *InPiù*. A collection of Ottavio's best film reviews appears in his posthumous *300 dichiarazioni d'amore al cinema* (300 declarations of love for cinema) published by Erga in 2021. At the University of Roma Tre, where until his passing he worked as "Cultore della Materia" (subject matter expert), he received two degrees: his first with a thesis on Alfred Hitchcock, titled "Il regista che sapeva troppo" (The director who knew too much), which explored the relationship between cinema and art; his second with a research paper titled "Tre passi nel genio" (Three steps into the genius) that examined Federico Fellini's cinema and focused on the influence that comic art, circus entertainment, magazines, and variety theatre exerted on his cinematic style. "Tre passi nel genio" won the Filippo Sacchi Prize with a special mention for its originality and was published in book form by Marsilio Editori in 2018. *Tre passi nel genio* features original extended interviews with Fellini's main collaborators: Nicola Piovani, Milo Manara, Lina Wertmüller, Paolo Villaggio, Claudia Cardinale, and Dante Ferretti among others. Ottavio filmed these interviews and was planning on including them in a documentary project he was working

Image 5. Ottavio Cirio Zanetti.

on while undergoing chemotherapy. His personal computer abounds with research material for what would have been his second book on Federico Fellini, *L'urbanistica di Fellini* (Fellini's urban planning), an outline of which he was slated to present at the University of Toronto conference on Fellini in 2020.

In July of 2019, I visited Ottavio in Genova for what would be our last summer hang. At the time, the malignant tumour on his brachial plexus had paralyzed his right arm and hand, and so he taught himself how to type and write with his left. Though he was on strong pain meds, his wits were still remarkably sharp, and he carried on researching and writing. In December 2019, his condition worsened rapidly, and despite the best efforts of the medical team at the Rovigo Hospital, he passed away on 24 January 2020, with his mum and me by his side. Although he is no longer with us, Ottavio's contributions to the scholarship on cinema are permanent, and so is the mark he left on the people he loved and who loved him back.

Federico Fellini's Urban Planning

OTTAVIO CIRIO ZANETTI

Translation by Andrew A. Monti and Camilla Bozzoli

Federico Fellini used cities not only as sets for his films but in some cases as protagonists – this is the case of *Roma* (1972) and Rimini in *Amarcord* (1973) – or co-stars of his stories – for example, Venice in *Il Casanova di Federico Fellini* (1976) – by building a sort of personal urban planning justified not only by aesthetic values, but also by analyses of social behaviour, urban functions, and definitions of the territory.

The work analyzes how Federico Fellini "depicted" the cities in his films, how he photographed them, how he chose them in his shots and presented them in editing. Or, how he reinvented them. Fellini was impressed by *Barry Lyndon* (1975), shot by Kubrick at the same time as *Casanova*. Kubrick expanded the eighteenth century into very large frames, while Fellini did the opposite: he compressed it into small spaces. Fellini's eighteenth-century Venice was completely rebuilt (Davis 1975, 89) in Cinecitta's Studio 5 with the help of a surprisingly large number of set designers, assistant designers, and architects: Danilo Donati, Antonello Geleng, Rinaldo Geleng, Giovanni Giannesi, Giantito Burchiellaro, Giorgio Giovannini, and Fellini himself as the author of the "scenographic creation."[1]

To emphasize the deliberate fakeness of Venice, even the lagoon is visibly artificial, represented by a plastic sheet. Venice would have been the protagonist of another film by Fellini, meant for television but never made due to production setbacks (Iacoli 2014, 174). Fellini was fascinated by the concealed Venice, the one hidden from the eyes of Venetians and tourists: a forest of stilts supporting the city's foundations. "I saw the underwater photos of the foundations of Venice, impressive, poles as dense as the trees of the Amazon rainforest"[2] (Cirio 1994, 11). Venice, as was Rimini, was never actually shot by Fellini and was completely rebuilt in Cinecittà. "I totally invented my childhood"[3] (Maltese 2006, 36), he said, so as to make it more authentic by relying upon false memories. His childhood memories thus took shape in the same old Studio 5 in Cinecittà: the legendary Grand Hotel, the boats in the Adriatic saluting the Rex, the squares, the corso, the church, partially similar, partially reinvented with the help of the great Danilo Donati.

I vitelloni (1953), a sort of virtual prequel to *Amarcord*, is instead the result of an urban collage. Not a single frame of the film was shot in Rimini. In this case not so much to trick the memory, but rather to chase Alberto Sordi who was at the time engaged in a theatrical tour between Rome, Florence, and Viterbo. The train station in Rimini whence Moraldo leaves for Rome (and ideally for the film *Roma*) is actually the train station in Ostia. The Rome described in *Roma* (1972) seems based on a sort of schizophrenic urban planning, which combines degradation with monumental excellence. A chaotic urban planning in space: open-air trattorias, children in the streets, a cheap boarding house, traffic jams in Rome's ring road, an *avanspettacolo* theatre, the construction of a subway tunnel, Trastevere and the "Festa de Noantri,"[4] the hippies in Piazza di Spagna, an old brothel, motorcycles roaring in the night. It is also a chaotic urban planning in time, juxtaposing the times of young Fellini's arrival in Fascist Rome with events that happened in the year of the film, 1972: the director shoots in crowded touristic locations, defends himself from students claiming that he didn't care about politics, stages an ecclesiastical fashion show, and Anna Magnani's last screen appearance.

The representation of the nostalgic urban planning of Rome experienced by Fellini upon his arrival in 1939 affectionately imitates Attalo's cartoons. The illustrator of the satirical magazine *Marc'Aurelio* authored characters such as "Il Gagà che aveva detto agli amici" (The Gagà who had told his friends) and "Genoveffa la racchia" (Ugly Genoveffa). Fellini was a great admirer of Attalo and met him in the *Marc'Aurelio* editorial office, where the future director, then eighteen, contributed short stories and cartoons. "When I made the film *Roma* I really wanted to evoke Attalo's cartoons, first of all out of authentic inspiration, and then also in order to pay homage to this kind, gentle and violent illustrator"[5] (Antonelli and Paolini 1995, 10; see also Chiesa 1988, 13). Attalo's Rome is lower-middle class, deformed and heavy, as genuine as it is far from the arrogant stereotypes imposed by Fascist rhetoric *Agenzia matrimoniale* (1953), one of the six episodes of the film *L'amore in città* (1953) created by Cesare Zavattini. Before the degraded capital of *Roma*, Fellini had featured the myth of the city's ancient origins in *Fellini Satyricon* (1969), based on the text by Petronius Arbiter. Instead of Attalo, the reference point had been the contribution of Danilo Donati, a refined creative mind and author of the scenography together with

Luigi Scaccianoce. For Fellini, the film was supposed to be a science fiction of the past. The construction of a decadent capital city, a welcoming place for collective memory, imposes itself with a flamboyant figurative invention. The capital of decadence is arcane, delusional, mysterious, dreamlike. It is Jungian (Carotenuto 1977, 137).

If *Fellini Satyricon* (1969) explores a possible archaic myth, *Roma* (1972) helped to re-establish a contemporary and international myth of Rome, with an unprecedented staging of its locations, even the most touristic ones. Anita Ekberg bathing in the Trevi Fountain gives the monument a new identity, destined to remain intact over time, as legendary as Marilyn Monroe's blowing skirt in *The Seven Year Itch* (1955). Via Veneto in *La dolce vita* (1960) becomes the perfect place to bury neorealism, thanks to a dry and fatuous celebration of a capital city that has adopted cosmopolitan attitudes nourished by weeklies and promoted by the economic boom. It implied a spiteful satirical touch represented as a parody in *Totò, Peppino e ... la dolce vita* filmed in 1961 by Sergio Corbucci, recycling the expensive scenography of Fellini's film. Anita Ekberg in *Le tentazioni del dottor Antonio*, an episode of *Boccaccio '70* (1962), helps glorify the EUR (Esposizione Universale Roma) district, made majestic by Fellini who thus fulfilled his dream of filming Baudelaire's *La Géant*. Peppino De Filippo stands at the feet of the young, gigantic woman like a cat that is barely sensual, yet tormented by disturbances as sesquipedalian as his partner.

An older Anita Ekberg reappeared in 1987 in *Intervista*, an autobiographical film set in what Fellini really considers his personal territory, the city that really belongs to him and that he also uses as a psychoanalyst's couch: Cinecittà. He is interviewed by a team of Japanese television journalists about *America*, a film project based on Kafka's novel, and takes the opportunity to ramble on. He reminisces about his first encounter with Cinecittà in 1940, where he was interviewing a famous diva. Fellini once again presents the schizophrenic urban planning already covered in *Roma* (1972). Like a combination of buildings from different times in a city, his memories approach and contrapose contemporary events: old generals in uniform together with Marcello Mastroianni in Mandrake's tailcoat. As Fellini would have liked to make a film on the comic wizard created by Lee Falk (Zanetti 2018, 20), Mastroianni swirls Mandrake's magic wand and makes the images of *La dolce vita* (1960) reappear, together with his own dance with Anita Ekberg. In the finale, Cinecittà is in danger: a group of feathered Native Americans (sic) on horseback surrounds the film studios and fight using television antennas as spears. After *Ginger e Fred* (1986), Fellini once again mentions his dislike and distrust of television in an attempt to exorcise it, to prevent Cinecittà from becoming an archaeological find, like Rome in *Satyricon*.

As for Venice, Fellini wanted to make a film about the city that would compare reality to fiction, propose a stylistic reality, and reveal an unknown image of the lagoon, the forest of stilts down below (Citati 2016, para. 3; see also Angelucci 2016, para. 4). Beyond Venice immersed in the lagoon, Fellini was attracted by the bird's-eye view of the city, as seen from a plane, "an indecipherable alphabet of hieroglyphs and signs"[6] (Citati 2016, para. 3). Indeed, the film about Venice would show his dislike of television, to the point of imagining Venice being acquired by a Berlusconi-like character. Fellini wrote: "The film would have been a series of pieces that separated, disintegrated the story in a molecular decomposition, constantly threatened by an inner fragmentation, yet one that still reveals as a whole the mirage of unity or vision"[7] (Citati 2016, para. 5). Fellini had imagined doubling himself for the occasion into an elderly American director visiting the degraded city, invaded and occupied by hordes of threatening tourists. Aboard a bathyscaphe, Fellini visits Venice underwater. And once the vision emerges, the film would entertain a love story between the director and a Venetian lady, meeting again after years of separation. All Venetian women have her face, which reflects past and possibly future reality: Fellini imagines the city underwater, permanently swamped by molten glaciers. Compared to other cities, such as Rimini and Rome, this Fellinian Venice was intended to represent another urban experience, a completely reinvented Venice at the border of fact and fiction, suspended between sky and lagoon, between reality and invention, an ancient and unprecedented Venice.

NOTES

1 "Ideazione scenografica," in Credits, *Il Casanova di Federico Fellini*.
2 "Ho visto le foto subacquee delle fondamenta di Venezia, impressionanti, pali fitti come alberi della foresta amazzonica"
3 "Mi sono del tutto inventato la mia infanzia"
4 Neighbourhood festival typical of Trastevere.
5 "Quando ho fatto nel 1972 il film *Roma*, ho voluto proprio ricordare [le vignette di Attalo], intanto come ispirazione, e poi anche per fare un omaggio a questo gentile, delicato e violento disegnatore"
6 "un indecifrabile alfabeto di segni e di geroglifici"
7 "il film avrebbe dovuto essere una serie di tasselli che si separavano, disintegravano il racconto, in una scomposizione molecolare continuamente minacciata da un'ulteriore frammentazione, e che pure svela nel suo insieme il miraggio di un'unità o di una visione"

REFERENCES

Angelucci, Gianfranco. 2016. "Venezia e i fantasmi di Fellini." *Articolo21*, 27 December. www.articolo21.org/2016/12/venezia-e-i-fantasmi-di-fellini-racconto-di-natale/.
Antonelli, Lamberto, and Gabriele Paolini. 1995. *Attalo e Fellini al Marc'Aurelio: Scritti e Disegni*. Rome: Napoleon.
Carotenuto, Aldo. 1977. *Jung e la Cultura Italiana*. Rome: Astrolabio.
Chiesa, Alfredo. 1988. *Il meglio del Marc'Aurelio*. Rome: Napoleone.
Cirio, Rita. 1994. *Il mestiere del regista. Intervista con Federico Fellini*. Milan: Garzanti.
Citati, Pietro. 2016. "Fellini, la Venezia mai vista." *Corriere della Sera*. Last modified 23 December. www.corriere.it/cultura/16_dicembre_22/fellini-venezia-mai-vista-c3196068-c872-11e6-b72f-beb391d55ecd.shtml.
Davis, Melton. 1975. "Federico Fellini's Far-Out Casanova." *The New York Times*, 31 August, 89.
Iacoli, Giulio. 2014. "'Quell'esile filo che ti lega a Venezia vorrei che diventasse un canapo': Su un film mai girato, tra Fellini e della Corte." In *Una raffinata ragnatela: Carlo della Corte tra letteratura e giornalismo nel secondo Novecento Italiano. Quaderni Veneti Studi e Ricerche* 1, edited by Veronica Gubbato and Silvia Uroda, 171–88. Venice: Edizioni Ca' Foscari. https://edizionicafoscari.unive.it/media/pdf/books/978-88-97735-70-0/978-88-97735-70-0.pdf.
Maltese, Curzio. 2006. "A Spasso con Scorsese nella Rimini di Fellini." *La Repubblica*, 8 January, 36. https://ricerca.repubblica.it/repubblica/archivio/repubblica/2006/01/08/spasso-con-scorsese-nella-rimini-di.html.
Zanetti, Ottavio Cirio. 2018. *Tre passi nel genio. Fellini tra fumetto, circo e varietà*. Venice: Marsilio.

Fellini's Graphic World

OTTAVIO CIRIO ZANETTI

Translation by Andrew A. Monti and Camilla Bozzoli

"Felliniano": The Dream of Being an Adjective

Federico Fellini was one of those rare film directors whose name became an adjective, "Felliniano," thus fulfilling his childhood dream. "Felliniano ... I always dreamed of being an adjective when I grew up"[1] (Castellacci 1993, 33). Yet Fellini himself admitted that he did not know what "Felliniano" meant, and it was first invented by critics, but then also widely used in common language as a synonym for grotesque, surreal, dreamlike. Fellini's films transcended neorealism, but also broke entirely away from realism in order to manipulate the products of the new mass culture industry – such as comics, caricatures, magazine theatre, *avanspettacolo* theatre, as well as the circus – instead of the products of elite culture favoured by critics (Zanetti 2018, 11). Thus, the "Felliniano" Fellini was a forerunner of pop art, whether he was aware of it or not, convinced by it or not, but certainly for 1950s critics, he was juxtaposed to the aristocratic art of a director like Visconti, who instead handled elite cultural products, such as paintings, literature, theatre, and melodrama.

Heterodox, elusive to definitions and classifications, unrealistic, and dreamlike, Fellini was "Felliniano" not only in relation to realism and neorealism and political militancy (Canova 2014), but also towards the more pragmatic Hollywood rules on how to make a film. Fellini did not follow the three-act rule: presentation of facts, identification of conflicts, positive or negative resolution of conflicts. Rather than following Greek tragedy rules or Hollywood-style structures, he seemed to model his films after comic strips, the framed compositions of the revue theatre and *avanspettacolo* theatre, and the surprising attractions of the circus. Starting from *Le notti di Cabiria* (1957), an open sequence structure prevails in his films. Fellini said:

"A film doesn't need a real story. Put six or seven sequences together and the film is done"[2] (Zapponi 1995, 29).

Fellini's Graphic World

Before shooting his films, Fellini drew them up with felt-tip pens and preferred to reconstruct his sets in Cinecittà's Studio 5, to give a graphic imprint to his creativity. The preliminary illustration work for his films, characters, locations, and atmospheres is a sort of preview of the screenplay, a storyboard, a graphic testing before auditions and shootings (Zanetti 2018, 13). Illustrating was for Fellini a kind of indispensable language, a primary form of checking reality as well as dreams, the most immediate way to give artistic value to emotional and sensorial perceptions.

Fellini was born in 1920. His upbringing took place during the Fascist era. As a boy he was a passionate cinema viewer and an avid reader of comic books, which in the 1930s were also a seductive antidote to the propaganda that Mussolini aimed at youth, and which was in direct competition with Catholic youth organizations in Italy. Fascism was particularly interested in shaping the awareness and knowledge of the Italian youth, by providing a framework for their future training. In *Amarcord* (1973), Fellini tells the story of his scholastic experience during the Fascist years, and even the uncle of the young protagonist "Lallo detto il Patacca" (Lallo known as the arrogant boaster) (Gaudenzi 2002, 159), played by Nando Orfei, is made up to resemble the caricature of "il Gagà che aveva detto agli amici" (Gagà who had told his friends), invented by Attalo, the great illustrator of *Marc'Aurelio*, a successful satirical magazine that had among its contributors many Italian screenwriters and directors. Among these was Fellini himself, who always greatly admired Attalo, a Roman illustrator who inspired many of Fellini's characters and situations. These showed a world of cynical, lower-middle class people living in Rome, idle and physiologically resistant to any sort of fascist rhetoric. "When I made the film *Roma* in 1972, I really wanted to remember Attalo's [comic strips] and also pay homage to this kind, gentle and violent illustrator"[3] (Antonelli and Paolini 1995, 10).

Among the non-comic heroes on the pages of *L'avventuroso*, Fellini preferred Mandrake. He always wanted to make a film about the character created by Lee Falk (Zanetti 2018, 20). He succeeded in part in *Intervista* (1987), a film about film-making in which Fellini himself is shooting an adaptation of Kafka's *America*. He is interviewed by a Japanese television crew in Rome. While he is at the table with his team, Marcello Mastroianni appears all dressed up as Mandrake for a commercial. This provides a great opportunity to recall the past, *La dolce vita* (1960), and particularly, Anita Ekberg. Fellini and Mastroianni pay Ekberg a visit in her Castelli Romani home, where Mandrake Mastroianni can thus perform one of his tricks. A movie screen magically appears in her living room, and Anita and Marcello, dressed in Mandrake's tailcoat, dance once again to the tunes of Nino Rota (reworked by Nicola Piovani). This was a magic moment that Lee Falk would have appreciated as well. Fellini also had the opportunity to meet the creator and stunt double for Mandrake while he visited Italy. Upon meeting his comic book hero, this time without a tailcoat and top hat, Fellini could not resist playing a fun trick. As he was shooting at the Colosseum, Fellini had already placed the spotlights to light up his set. He had arranged with the electricians to suddenly turn the lights on and told Falk: "I too can do magic. Lend me your cane."[4] He then tapped it on the ground and the electricians blasted all the lights much to Falk's surprise (Zapponi11 1995, 691).

Fellini also wanted to make a film about Disneyland and Walt Disney, whom he met when he won the Academy Award for *La strada* (1954). "It seems strange to me that no one has ever made a film about Disneyland. It would have been a unique way to describe America, as a documentary"[5] (Cirio 1994, 99–100). Fellini himself acknowledged his connection to American comic strips when he shared the fact that Italian publishers secretly continued printing American cartoons entrusting the work to Italian illustrators and screenwriters despite Fascist regime censorship. For example, it is widely assumed that an adventure of the legendary Flash Gordon was completed by the illustrator Giove Toppi based on a script written by Fellini, who had left Rimini and joined *L'avventuroso* in Florence as a contributor (Bellano 2020, 63). But Fellini's recollection is doubtful, as he himself admitted that "sometimes I say things that I invent and end up really believing them"[6] (Placido 1992, 29).

In Florence, Fellini worked for *420* magazine, published by Nerbini, who was also the publisher of *L'avventuroso*. Fellini, who went by the signature of "Fellas," published seventy-six illustrations and fifty-one short stories, thus fulfilling his childhood dream of working for the satirical magazines he used to read in Rimini. The visual style was partly inspired by the surrealism of the great humorist Saul Steinberg, who at the time worked in Italy. Fellas's crowded illustrations in some ways foreshadowed his future autobiographical films, *I clowns* (1970), *Roma* (1972), and *Intervista* (1987), often entrusted to his favourite leading character, Marcello Mastroianni. After his experience in Florence with *420*, Fellini's next professional step in the world of satire took place in Rome working for the most coveted of magazines, *Marc'Aurelio*. This transition was showcased in the 1972 film *Roma*, and more recently in 2013 by director Ettore Scola in his film *Che strano chiamarsi Federico*. The film recalls the editorial meetings of young Fellini, who then went by the signature of "Federico," with future directors and screenwriters of the calibre of Steno, Metz and Marchesi, Age and Scarpelli, Maccari, Zavattini, Zapponi, and the very young Scola himself, as well as the legendary Attalo.

Marc'Aurelio was a great success. It sold 350,000 copies in 1935 (Zanetti 2018, 24; Chiesa 1988, 12), and introduced jokes and characters that would become household names, such as "il Gagà che aveva detto agli amici" (Gagà who had told his friends) and "Genoveffa la racchia" (Ugly Genoveffa), both created by Attalo. To avoid trouble with fascist censors, the magazine's editors and illustrators had decided to issue two versions of the weekly: one meant for insiders that lampooned old generals, imperial eagles, and huge crowds; and another meant for newsstands that wisely avoided politics and limited itself to social commentary satire (Antonelli and Paolini 1995, 11). Despite his admiration for Attalo, Fellini's humour was "a little more surreal, not very suitable to Attalo"[7] for *Marc'Aurelio* (Zanetti 2018, 25; Casetti and Caruso 1999, 79; Antonelli 1986, 8). Fellini held a regular column in the magazine titled "Ma tu mi stai a sentire?" (Are you listening to me?) in which he addressed characters from everyday life. In the difficult post-war years, *Marc'Aurelio* had suspended publications. To survive, Fellini continued to draw caricatures for allied soldiers. With other illustrators he had opened a store that exhibited the sign "Funny Face Shop" (Borini 2009, 16).

Two Comic Book Films: *Viaggio a Tulum* and *Il viaggio di G. Mastorna detto Fernet*

Fellini's love for comics also compelled him to take a break from filming and create, using ink and paper, two films that had long remained scripts: *Viaggio a Tulum* and *Il viaggio di G. Mastorna detto Fernet*, both illustrated by Milo Manara under the guidance of Fellini.[8] Scripted by Fellini, together with Tullio Pinelli, the text was published in *Corriere della Sera* (18–23 May 1986) and then in colour and comic form in the magazine *Corto Maltese* (1990). Fellini told his readers that the story had really happened.[9] The journey's destination was Mexico, in search of Carlos Castañeda, "an enigma wrapped in a mystery wrapped in a tortilla," as *Time* magazine put it in the March 1973 cover article (Burton 1973, 37). By his own admission, Fellini had been troubled by Castañeda's books and had decided to make a film about magic and sorcery

(Zanetti 2018, 27). After reading the film script, Milo Manara, who illustrated the posters for *Intervista* and *La voce della luna*, asked Fellini to turn it into a comic book. Fellini accepted but asked Manara to replace the leading character with Mastroianni (Manara, Mollica, and Fellini 2001, 102). Fellini wrote the story and in collaboration with Manara directed the making of the comic book, contributing to the selection of frames, streaks of light, and characters' expressions.

In the case of Mastorna, "the most famous film in the history of cinema that was never made"[10] (Mollica 2008, 7), Fellini was so keen on the project that he singlehandedly drew a very detailed storyboard of the first episode, which was later created by Manara with aquatint to emphasize the dreamlike atmospheres of the story. The first challenge was giving the leading character a face. Paolo Villaggio was chosen and summoned to Cinecittà to be photographed dressed as a clown. The photos then served as a model for Manara's illustrations. The first episode of the Mastorna comic strip was published in *Il Grifo* magazine (Fellini and Manara 1992, 8). Two more episodes were planned, but due to a typo, the final word of the last cartoon was "End" instead of "the story continues in the next episode." Fellini saw it as an omen[11] and decided not to follow up with the story though he had already drafted the second episode. It was an obsession of his. Fellini dreamt Mastorna as well (Fellini, Kezich, and Boarini 2007, 569).

The Book of Dreams

Fellini experienced his dream fantasies vividly, so much so that he would write them down and draw them in his *Book of Dreams* upon awakening. The book consists of two bound albums. The first spans from November 1960 to August 1968, and the second from February 1973 to the end of 1982. The two volumes were published after his death and collect the drawings and comments of Fellini's dreams; an endless storyboard of films that were only imagined, "a divine comedy of dreams" (D'Orrico 2007).[12] The monumental *Libro dei sogni* (Book of dreams) is a sort of *liber monstrorum* of the real and imaginary characters that populated Fellini's dreams and nightmares. Brightly coloured, gaudy, funny, and distressing, Fellini's drawings feature large and available women (Gaillard 2010, 43), threatening landscapes, looming architecture, absurd animals. The graphic style is both sophisticated and common, halfway between James Ensor and *Il Corriere dei Piccoli*,[13] in a playful attempt to reconcile dream and reality, life and death (Zanetti 2018, 38).

NOTES

1 "Felliniano … Avevo sempre sognato, da grande, di fare l'aggettivo"
2 "Un film non ha bisogno d'una vera storia. Metti insieme sei o sette sequenze e il film è fatto"
3 "Quando ho fatto nel 1972 il film *Roma*," Fellini said, "ho voluto proprio ricordare [le vignette di Attalo], intanto come ispirazione autentica, e poi anche per fare un omaggio a questo gentile, delicato e violento disegnatore"
4 "non solo tu fai i prodigi: anch'io. Prestami il bastone"
5 "Mi sembra strano – ha raccontato Fellini – che nessuno abbia mai girato un film su Disneyland. Sarebbe stato un modo di raccontare l'America unico, come un documentario"
6 "a volte racconto delle cose, inventandole, e finisco davvero per crederle"
7 "un pochino più surreale, non molto adatto ad Attalo"
8 About Fellini's *Il viaggio di G. Mastorna*, see the chapters by Marina Vargau, Mirko Tavoni, Frank Burke, and Manuela Gieri in this volume.
9 See Tripodi and Dalla Gassa (2010).
10 "il film mai realizzato più famoso della storia del cinema"
11 The story goes that Mago Rol, a famous magician and psychic from Turin whom Fellini consulted his whole life, predicted to him that if he made the film about Mastorna he would die soon after. "A Fellini, che era solito consultarlo, sconsigliò – mentre le carte della sceneggiatura veleggiavano per l'aria – di ultimare 'Il viaggio di G. Mastorna'" (Fellini was used to consulting Rol, and he advised Fellini against completing "The journey of G. Mastorna" – while the pages of the screenplay floated in the air) (Mondo 1994, 1). Though this version of events was denied by Rol (Quaranta 1993, 12), Fellini never shot the film and instead turned it into a comic book with the help of Milo Manara.
12 "una divina commedia onirica" (book jacket blurb).
13 Literally, "The Courier of the Little Ones," a weekly magazine for children published between 1908 and 1995.

REFERENCES

Antonelli, Lamberto, ed. 1986. *Attalo*. Rome: Napoleone.
Antonelli, Lamberto, and Gabriele Paolini. 1995. *Attalo e Fellini al Marc'Aurelio: Scritti e disegni*. Rome: Napoleone.
Bellano, Marco. 2020. "Fellini's Graphic Heritage: Drawings, Comics, Animation and Beyond." In *A Companion to Federico Fellini*, edited by Frank Burke, Marguerite Waller, and Marita Gubareva, 59–78. Hoboken, NJ: Wiley Blackwell.

Borini, Andrea. 2009. *Federico Fellini*. Rome: Mediane.
Burton, Sandra. 1973. "Don Juan and the Sorcerer's Apprentice." *Time*, 5 March, 36–45. https://time.com/vault/issue/1973-03-05/page/1/.
Canova, Gianni. 2014. "Fellini politico: a sua insaputa?" In *MicroMega N.9: Fellini il Cinema e le Donne*. Rome: MicroMega.
Casetti, Giuseppe, and Rossella Caruso. 1999. "Comunicazione: Disegni inediti dall'archivio De Bellis." In *Federico Fellini autore di testi. Dal "Marc'Aurelio" a Luci del Varieta' (1939–1950)*, edited by Massimiliano Filippini and Vittorio Ferorelli, 76–9. Bologna: Quaderni IBC. www.yumpu.com/it/document/read/16120624/federico-fellini-autore-di-testi-pdf-2142-kb-istituto-per-i-beni-.
Castellacci, Claudio. 1993. "L'America voleva colorare la Dolce vita." *Corriere della Sera*, 30 March, 33.
Chiesa, Adolfo. 1988. *Il Meglio del Marc'Aurelio*. Rome: Napoleone.
Cirio, Rita. 1994. *Il mestiere di regista. Intervista con Federico Fellini*. Milan: Garzanti.
D'Orrico, Antonio. 2007. "Nota in Risvolto di Copertina." In *Federico Fellini. Il libro dei sogni*. Milan: Rizzoli.
Fellini, Federico, and Milo Manara. 1992. "Il Viaggio di G. Mastorna detto Fernet." *Il Grifo*, no. 15: 8–30.
Fellini, Federico, Tullio Kezich, and Vittorio Boarini. 2007. *Il libro dei Sogni*. Milan: Rizzoli.
Gaillard, Christian. 2010. "Taking Wing and the Ordeal of Immersion: Reflections on Federico Fellini's *Il Libro dei sogni*, Rizzoli, 2007." *Jung Journal: Culture & Psyche* 4, no. 2: 31–61. https://doi.org/10.1525/jung.2010.4.2.31.
Gaudenzi, Cosetta. 2002. "Memory, Dialect, Politics: Linguistic Strategies in Fellini's *Amarcord*." In *Federico Fellini: Contemporary Perspectives*, edited by Frank Burke and Marguerite R. Waller, 155–68. Toronto: University of Toronto Press.
Manara, Milo, Vincenzo Mollica, and Federico Fellini. 2001. *Due viaggi con Federico Fellini. Viaggio a Tulum – Il viaggio di G. Mastorna detto Fernet*. Milan: Mondadori.
Mollica, Vincenzo. 2008. "Prefazione: Sulla vicenda cinematografica." In *Federico Fellini: Il viaggio di G. Mastorna*, edited by Ermanno Cavazzoni, 7–14. Milan: Quodlibet Compagnia Extra.
Mondo, Lorenzo. 1994. "È Morto Rol il 'mago' di Fellini." *La Stampa*, 22 September, 1. www.archiviolastampa.it/component/option,com_lastampa/task,search/mod,libera/action,viewer/Itemid,3/page,1/articleid,0755_01_1994_0260_0001_10729398/.
Placido, Beniamino. 1992. "Fellini e Mollica, due uomini due fumetti." *La Repubblica*, 28 January, 29. https://ricerca.repubblica.it/repubblica

/archivio/repubblica/1992/01/28/fellini-mollica-due-uomini-due-fumetti .html.

Quaranta, Bruno. 1993. "Intervista. L'Amico Occulto." *La Stampa*, 3 November. www .archiviolastampa.it/component/option,com_lastampa/task,search/mod,libera /action,viewer/Itemid,3/page,12/articleid,0809_01_1993_0300_0012_11352975/.

Tripodi, Antonio, and Marco Dalla Gassa. 2010. *Approdo a Tulum: le Neverland a fumetti di Fellini e Manara*. Venice: LT2.

Zanetti, Ottavio Cirio. 2018. *Tre passi nel genio. Fellini tra fumetto, circo e varietà*. Venice: Marsilio.

Zapponi, Bernardino. 1995. *Il mio Fellini*. Venice: Marsilio.

Deleuzional Ponderings: The Fellinian Symbolic (in Memory of Marguerite Waller)

FRANK BURKE

Introduction

Federico Fellini's *Il libro dei sogni* (2007) is an ever-present horizon, looming but also beckoning, to my thoughts about the director – and one that I am approaching cautiously because of its magnitude. One of the things that has occurred to me in contemplating *Il libro dei sogni* is that the oneiric, for which Fellini is so well known even aside from his dream diaries, is part of a larger category of the symbolic and imaginal. This larger category is rich, and I have chosen, as a research strategy, to explore it in Fellini's film work before addressing its presence in the dream book. Accordingly, most of what follows will be related to Fellini's cinema, though I will conclude by discussing a well-known dream from *Il libro dei sogni*. In keeping with both the conference from which this chapter derives and the dedication of the volume in which it will appear, I will take this opportunity to pay tribute to the work of Marguerite Waller, who died unexpectedly in March 2020 and whose loss has been deeply felt within numerous academic communities, including Italian film and literary studies, and non-academic communities as well. Margie's readings of Fellini, which have garnered responses such as "magisterial" and "brilliant" from distinguished readers and reviewers, are extraordinarily useful tools for illustrating the Fellini symbolic.

Symbolic Interpellation

The symbolic in its most limited form in Fellini's work comprises meaningful images, icons, representations, and so on that evoke or command feelings of familiarity, admiration, consent, even belonging. They can be religious (the Vatican, various statues and representations of Christ, the Madonna), political (the Altar of the Fatherland, fascist spectacle in various forms, the *Rex* ocean liner), cultural (the Lupa del Campidoglio, the Grand Hotel, Casanova, Edmea Tetua, Fellini himself in *Intervista* [1987]), and pop-cultural (the White Sheik, Sylvia Rank, Ginger and Fred, Mandrake the Magician, and all symbols, even the most revered such as Dante, that get decontextualized and mass reproduced in Fellini's despised televisual/advertising industry). Limited as well are many of the more personal symbols that characters construct out of culturally prefabricated materials to express anxieties, project desires, and fulfill fantasies. To name just a few: Wanda's White Sheik, Giudizio's gilded angel (*I vitelloni*, 1953), Gelsomina's (and Il matto's) existential pebble (*La strada*, 1954), the innumerable "big scores" of *Il bidone* (1955), Dr. Antonio's monumental "Anitaaa" (*Le tentazioni del dottor Antonio*, 1962), Guido's woman-in-white (*8 ½*, 1963), Giulietta's countless spirits (*Giulietta degli spiriti*, 1965), Toby's she-devil (*Toby Dammit*, 1968), Fellini-the narrator/character's Rome-as-Woman (*Roma*, 1972), Titta's Gradisca (*Amarcord*, 1973), Casanova's "uccellino" and automaton lover (*Il Casanova di Fellini*, 1976), Snàporaz's hot-air Madonna/Soubrette/Ideal Woman (*La città delle donne*, 1980) the townsfolks' Miss Farina (*La voce della luna*, 1990). There are many more, but this seems a reasonable sampling.

In their broadly cultural manifestations, the symbols are instruments of interpellation, suturing people, via habitual responses, into ideological conformity. In their more personal forms, they are instruments of self-delusion that prevent characters from maturing and developing a healthy relationship to their world. Ultimately disempowering, they contribute to the characters' surrender to existing relations of power. (In this respect, they too are ultimately interpellating.) However, there is a yet another mode of the symbolic fundamental to Fellini's work and dreams and at times present even among his characters – those most capable of engaging creatively with their worlds and recognizing the numinous possibilities of a world encountered with openness and imagination.

Creative Symbolization

Fellini's interaction with his world was largely symbolic in this last sense – the product of a sensibility that sought to identify in every moment its meaningfulness in a profound and suprarational way and at the same time to imbue the moment with momentousness, transforming it into a creative event. In part, this hearkens back to Fellini's memories of childhood experience.

For an adult Fellini, there was always the risk of losing this fresh, unfiltered, and unconsciously inflected sense of the world, but there was also the accumulation of conscious experience that, if wedded to a vibrant unconscious, offered the promise of even more meaningful experience. The vibrancy of the unconscious was to him made manifest and available in dreaming, which fuelled artistic activity, and which was profoundly symbolic. Dreams were a means of enriching conscious life, avoiding the "adult-eration" of experience and promoting the "ever-increasing becoming-conscious" of which Gilles Deleuze speaks below.

It is this open, creative, and imaginative aspect of the symbolic that I would like to address in this chapter, incorporating Jungian notions, to which Fellini was indebted for certain of his formulations; then moving onto Deleuze, whose expansive sense of the symbolic is invaluable in dealing with the Fellinian symbolic; and incorporating Marguerite Waller's extraordinary readings of Fellini's work. Largely because of my focus on the creative and imaginative, I bypass the semiotic poststructuralist theoretical stream that posits language as the bedrock of consciousness and expression – even visual – and thus denigrates the image.[1] Not that this stream does not have its uses. Symbolic interpellation could be read fruitfully in conjunction with the theorizations of Jacques Lacan, and scholars such as Van Watson (2002) have had great fun with Casanova's phallic lack as evidenced in, among other things, his mechanical bird and sex partner.

The symbolic as I approach it derives largely from the Romantic tradition, which influenced Jung and crucial twentieth-century aestheticians such as Gaston Bachelard, and has become a staple in literary and art criticism. In the case of Deleuze, it derives more broadly from post-Kantian romantic thinkers opposed to Enlightenment rationality (Ramey 2012, 5) and Neoplatonism from Plotinus to the Renaissance (6). Indebtedness to Neoplatonism and Renaissance humanism (as well as the Romantics) also characterizes the work of post-Jungian James Hillman, for whom Fellini had great respect (Hillman 1975, 193–226; Bentivoglio 2003). The stream to which Fellini's notions of the symbolic belong also includes the work of Ernst Cassirer, who designated "man" a "symbolic animal," and Susanne Langer, who followed, with great originality, in Cassirer's footsteps. Deleuze and Langer, in turn, were heavily influenced by Alfred North Whitehead, and his contributions to symbolic discourse. This is not to suggest that Fellini immersed himself in the work of these thinkers; only that Fellini's sense of the symbolic was very much in the air among major thinkers in the twentieth century.

For Fellini, as for many "symbol-minded" artists and thinkers, symbol and image are largely inseparable; the latter is inevitably symbolic.

This is especially the case in dreams: "Dreams are a language made up of images. There is nothing more true than a dream, because dreams resist obvious interpretation – dreams use symbols instead of concepts" (Chandler 1995, 204).[2] But it is also the case in conscious life. In expressing his resistance to meditation, Fellini said: "Perhaps I was afraid if I ever turned off my images, my waking dreams, they might be startled away and never come back, and I would be left alone without them" (Chandler 1995, 152). And, of course, Fellini attributed his love for filmmaking to his fondness for images.

Implicit in Fellini's sense of images is the assumption that they are not just literal or representational, but psychic – charged with energy and meaning. In this regard, he is firmly in tune with Jung, who maintains, "Everything of which we are conscious is an image, and that image *is* psyche" (Jung 1967, 50; emphasis Jung's), and, "'Experience' is, in its most simple form, an exceedingly complicated structure of mental images" (Jung 1969, 327). Following upon Jung, James Hillman (1975) asserts, "All consciousness depends on ... images. Everything else – ideas of the mind, sensations of the body, perceptions of the world around us, beliefs, feelings, hungers – must present themselves as images in order to become experienced" (23).

Gilles Deleuze, while not sharing Jung's and Hillman's totalizing views of the imaginal, offers a view of the symbolic that helps shed light on Fellini's. He employs a discussion of D.H. Lawrence to identify "characteristic features":

> The symbol is a concrete cosmic force ... It is a dynamic process that enlarges, deepens, and expands sensible consciousness; it is an ever-increasing becoming-conscious, as opposed to the closing of the moral consciousness upon a fixed allegorical idea. It is a method of the Affect, intensive, a cumulative intensity, which merely marks the threshold of a sensation, the awakening of a state of consciousness: the symbol means nothing, and has neither to be explained nor interpreted, as opposed to the intellectual consciousness of allegory. It is a rotative thought, in which a group of images turn ever more quickly around a mysterious point, as opposed to the linear allegorical chain. (1997, 48)

Here, as in so much of his writing, Deleuze rescues thought from the realm of concept, rational reflection, and abstraction to which it is so often consigned – and that was anathema to Fellini – making it a vital, experimental, open-ended activity.[3]

For Fellini, Jung, Hillman, and Deleuze, the ability of the symbol to embrace multiple impulses, emotions, intensities, and nonconceptual meanings makes it simultaneously unitive (the root meaning of "symbol" is "to throw together") and centrifugal. The energy produced by the work of synthesis propels the symbol outwards, forwards, and beyond. In that respect, and Deleuze is particularly insistent on this point, the symbolic is ultimately an activity: both a call to action and a response – and perhaps most of all a becoming.

The Fellinian Symbolic and Marguerite Waller

Marguerite Waller had the perfect sensibility for articulating the Fellinian symbolic, particularly as refracted through a Deleuzian lens. She, like Fellini, saw a thousand things at once in a way that exploded simple reference, allegory, or arid conceptualization. She created fissures in seeming textual homogeneities while refusing any complacent relationship to Fellinian signification. Let's take for example her reading of a crucial sequence in *La dolce vita* (1960):

> In the elegant living room of Steiner ... a young woman of colour wearing a sari sits cross-legged on the floor singing and accompanying herself on the guitar. An old colonial [world traveler] holds forth on the "Oriental" woman as the essence of true femininity, hinting that his [experience] has included intimate investigation in this area ... Some moments later, Steiner's two young children, a boy and a girl, appear. Steiner interacts very directly with his son but very little with his daughter, whom he refers to in the third person. Steiner's differential response ... silences his daughter's ... voice. He would dismiss the question she once posed to him – "Chi è la madre del sole?" ("Who is the mother of the sun?") – by aestheticizing it as "poetic" (and nonsensical), failing to hear in it, as we may, a challenge to his Olympian stance toward a messy world ... Meanwhile ... [as the woman of colour] sings ..., it becomes obvious that she is not Asian at all but rather African American, not "Eastern" but rather a particularly loaded signifier of "Western" culture ...
>
> ... Not present in any literal way, but not absent either, are the hypertextual links that one might begin to pursue between and among Orientalism, colonialism, Western constructions of gender and race, Oedipal family dynamics, the roots of U.S. economic and military dominance in the slave trade, the binarism of the Cold War (Steiner refers to threat of nuclear war as the reason for his alienation), bourgeois aesthetics. (2002a, 5–6)

Here, Waller reveals Fellini's symbolic sensibility to be richly meaningful without being abstract: infinitely complex in and because of its striking concreteness, provocative of multiple interpretations because of its density but also because it refuses to preach or resort to coercive "messages." Waller's analysis reflects Deleuze's description of "a group of images [that] turn ever more quickly around a mysterious point, as opposed to [a] linear allegorical chain" (Deleuze 1997, 48).

The open-endedness of the Fellinian symbolic, implied in Waller's above discussion, is beautifully illustrated in her reading of what she terms "separation sequences" in *La dolce vita* in which characters, while present to each other in one way or another, are not consistently shot in the same frame or related to each other via shot-reverse shot (Waller 2002b, 109–13). She singles out Marcello's phone conversations with his mistress Emma, the famous "chamber of serious discourse" scene between Marcello and Maddalena, and the even more famous concluding scenes of Paola and Marcello on the beach. In terms of the last, she notes how the "classic" separation strategy – Paola and Marcello isolated in disparate shots – is itself "separated" by shots that place the two together but in such a way (e.g., via a telephoto lens) as to emphasize their distance from each other. "Separation to the second power," as Waller calls it. Then she also notes the separation between moments of deafening noise of wind and sea and moments of sufficient quiet to allow Marcello's dialogue (monologue, really) to be heard. She concludes that "unresolved sequences, in which the characters are never shown in the same frame, are paradigmatic of the film's refusal to resolve either visually or narratively the sexual and political conflicts it unfolds" (110). She further notes that these separation shots loosen any identification on our part with Marcello. "Once we recognize that we do not have to identify with Marcello but are freed by the cinematic text to make our own connections, many further potent rearrangements of the elements of this and other scenes suggest themselves. Determinations of centre and periphery, foreground and background, actions and setting, may shift dramatically" (112). One of the things that Waller's readings suggest is that the Fellinian symbolic is disruptively specific and non-isomorphic in its practices.

Waller contrasts the liberating irresolution and de-dentification of *La dolce vita* with Marcello's attempts to turn Paola, in an earlier scene, into an "Umbrian angel" (arguably guaranteeing his inability to recognize her at the beach): "By lending to Raphael's angels the status of a disembodied ideal and by then assimilating Paola into that ideal, Marcello is doing just the opposite of what Fellini's film does: he is flattening her into a static, two-dimensional image (quite literally when he has her pose for him in profile) and detaching that image from the context ... [of] the young woman in front of him" (2002b, 112). Waller thus identifies one of Deleuze's major bugbears: the (anti)symbolic "closing of ... consciousness upon a fixed allegorical idea."

Waller's 1993 essay "Neither an 'I' Nor an 'Eye': The Gaze in *Giulietta degli spiriti*" performs a profoundly Deleuzian-Fellinian function in unhinging the gender-essentialist and disproportionately influential (in part because it is so Hollywood-centric) 1975 Laura Mulvey essay "Visual Pleasure and Narrative Cinema."[4] Employing her usual priceless talent for close reading, born in part of her first-hand knowledge of film language (she studied film-making at NYU and Harvard), Waller details how Fellini de-essentializes the gaze in the opening moments of the film:

> In an elaborate mirror shot, the maid, Teresina, appears to have her back to the camera as Giulietta, seated before her dressing table mirror, debates what wig to wear, but the picture changes radically the moment Teresina leaves the frame, screen right, and simultaneously re-enters it screen left ... Fellini's camera was not, in fact, lined up with Teresina's and Giulietta's gazes toward the image in the dressing table mirror, but must actually have been facing almost 180 degrees away from Giulietta and about 90 degrees away from Teresina. It must have been positioned between the two women rather than outside the space of their relationship, its gaze directed toward a different mirror than the one Giulietta looks in, to create the illusion that all three gazes were pointed in the same direction.
>
> ... The revelation that the camera has been recording a mirror image that, for a moment, made several disparate gazes – ours, the camera's, Teresina's, and Giulietta's – appear to converge, deliteralizes or denaturalizes the shot and completely restructures the film's mode of address to the spectator. It is as if there were two cameras here, one making the conventionally objective shot and a second, shooting the same scene from a 180-degree reverse angle which includes the first camera in it ... The physical, visual field upon which we would ground our perception having been disrupted, our own position also becomes an issue. We don't know where we are; we know only that we are positioned – no less than the camera – and that our position is a determining factor in both what, and how, we perceive. (1995, 217–18)

The gaze operates like the Deleuzian symbolic – "between" as Waller stated it, or, as Deleuze put it above, "always in the middle ... between things." As Waller goes on to argue, "the looks of the camera, the characters, and the spectators do not coincide but potentially and open-endedly interact with one another" (1995, 219) and, as a consequence, "[the film] never fixes us, never allows us to remain in one place for very long. It denies us the sensation of cognitive mastery that we might ... think we want, positioning us instead to ... change our perceptions" (221).

These last two quotations point to a major aspect of both Waller's and Deleuze's work: relationality. The former's emphasis on intertextuality in *La dolce vita* and on the gaze's various and irreducible "immanences" in *Giulietta degli spiriti* is, above all else, a privileging of the relational over the ontologically stable. Relationality is an ongoing process, not a relationship in a traditional sense. It is a never-ending putting-into-relationship, rather than a linking of, say, subject to object, individual consciousness to world, one distinct person to another.

Waller performs relationality in several of her final writings on Fellini. In her "*Il Maestro* Dismantles the Master's House" from the *Companion to Federico Fellini*, she puts *Le tentazioni del dottor Antonio* in relation not only with the Japanese monster movies to which the towering Anita Ekberg obviously refers, but with the "radioactive rain" from hydrogen bomb testing that poisoned milk, thus providing an insidious inflection to the film's advertising jingle: "bevete più latte" [drink more milk] (2020, 321). She also puts Fellini's Casanova in relation with a centuries-old history of colonial masculinities and fear of women, in light of which she sees Fellini demolishing the myth of Casanova created by the Venetian poseur and generations of gender-impaired *casanovisti* (314–17). But perhaps most stunningly, she puts Fellini in creative relationship with feminism in a film so often despised by feminists, *La città delle donne*:

> The film is dense with references to ... the explosion of feminist theory, performance art, and activism of the 1970s. The laughter on the soundtrack that prefaces the opening credits evokes the work of Hélène Cixous, one of French feminism's founders, whose widely translated essay, "The Laugh of the Medusa," was published in the mid 1970s. The theorizing of another French feminist, Luce Irigaray (1980), author of "When Our Lips Speak Together," echoes in the commentary accompanying a slide show on female genitalia at the feminist convention Snàporaz finds himself in the midst of. (The commentator urges, "Let's explore her with her lips perpetually kissing.") The convention also invokes Mary Shelley's Frankenstein ... and indirectly her mother Mary Wollstonecraft's "A Vindication of the Rights of Woman" in a crude but very funny and beautifully choreographed feminist skit portraying the typical housewife as the victim of a Frankensteinian monster husband. Later in the film, Snàporaz's extended exploration of Katzone's heavily defended but soon to be demolished

"master's house" pays homage to ... African-Caribbean-American poet and essayist Audre Lorde (1984). Lorde's presentation, "The Master's Tools Will Never Dismantle the Master's House," at a 1979 feminist conference in New York City (alluded to by several attendees in the film's convention) charged the predominantly white, middle class, heterosexist feminist movement with excluding differences of race, class, sexuality, and age – the very differences from which its strength needed to come if it were not to reproduce colonial patriarchy. (323)

It is well known that Fellini researched feminism extensively and communicated with several noted feminists in his preparation of the movie, and Waller's contextualization helps correct the false impression that *La città delle donne* was merely a mean-spirited assault on feminism. It was, instead, a thoughtful engagement with something Fellini took seriously, even though at times he parodied ideological excess and, far more important, critiqued the aporias of masculinity that led his protagonist – much more than Fellini himself – to react blindly and defensively to changing times and mores.

Waller's writings on Fellini unequivocally demonstrate a symbolic imagination ceaselessly putting multiple meanings, emotions, intensities into play. She provides indisputable proof that a Fellini text can never be merely what it might seem to be; it is always in motion towards somewhere else.

The Creative Symbolic in Fellini's Cinematic Oeuvre

As I have argued in *Fellini's Films and Commercials*, the first part of Fellini's career seems to embody a consistent movement towards creative symbolization on the part of Fellini's characters. However, symbolization proves to be a complex issue. Cabiria is the first Fellini figure to display truly imaginative power, envisioning an ideal self, named "Maria," and an ideal other/lover in Oscar. Not by accident, this occurs when she is able to connect oneirically with her unconscious, under hypnosis. On the one hand, this activates the penultimate stage in her journey towards self-realization;[5] on the other hand, the symbolization itself must be surpassed. It is allegorical – directed towards the fixed constructions of Self and Other – not open-ended and "rhizomatic." Oscar implodes as a fraud, and Cabiria must refashion an identity on-the-move, entering a path at film's end that is enchanted but without clear destination. Her journey does not conclude, it begins anew.

Fellini's two films of Jungian individuation, *8 ½* and *Giulietta degli spiriti*, perform something similar. Guido's allegorical structures –

principally his film and his woman-in-white – fail to provide the resolution he seeks, and the concluding scenes trigger vacillation between euphoria and confusion before setting him, like Cabiria, on the move: promenading around the circus arena with Luisa and his other fellow travellers and then mobilizing his allegorical boy-in-white, who ultimately breaks the film's final frame. Giulietta must renounce her allegorical spirits – most notably her mother and grandfather and binary figures such as Iris and Olaf – and put herself in motion, always centred, but always taking the centre with her, in an ending that, like Cabiria's, is a beginning.

Toby Dammit offers perhaps the most graphic renunciation of fixed and fixing symbolism or "allegory," particularly in what we might still consider Fellini's Jungian phase. Toby himself is the symbol. He is an actor or persona and thus "represents" everything that others want him to represent. He must speak others' lines, be it Hamlet or Christ, depending on the wishes of theatre directors or movie producers. Consequently, "To be" he must "Damn It" – annihilate himself in a "suicide" in which he leaves behind his talking head: the symbol everyone else in the film has sought to possess (Foreman 1977; Burke 2020, 135–41). He also must leave behind his principal oppositional symbol, the girl-in-white she-devil.

The renunciation of self as persona becomes a significant factor in three of Fellini's succeeding movies: *Fellini: A Director's Notebook*, in which Marcello Mastroianni has become too much of a "Latin lover" to serve Fellini's needs for "Il viaggio di G. Mastorna," and *I clowns* and *Roma*, in which Fellini himself as director and "star" must disappear for the films to reach satisfactory conclusions.

While *Toby Dammit* may be the most graphic example of the rejection of allegory, *Roma* may be the most definitive. The film is loosely organized around two strongly Jungian symbols: the quest for a centre, or in psychoanalytical terms, a self, and the Great Mother – with Rome playing the role of the Mediterranean archetype. In terms of the first, Walter C. Foreman has argued: "The particular form that the movement of the eye takes in Roma is related to a basic mythic process: the foundation of a city, of a city which is a 'Center,' a center of society, of culture, of religion, but also a psychic center, a center of human wholeness" (1980, 151). There are several centres with which Fellini seeks to connect. As Foreman suggests, the all-encompassing one is Rome, as Fellini undertakes a "documentary" – or as he puts in in the original English-language version of the film, a "portrait" – of the city, seeking to illuminate its ontology and meaning. This mega centre embraces multiple more specific ones, as Rome functions as a centre of

Western civilization, both historical (the references to Roman history) and religious (the ecclesiastical fashion show); a fantasized centre of male desire; a centre of community, both in the 1930s and the 1970s; and even, with the appearance of Anna Magnani, as a centre of Italian cinema.

Fellini's film offers numerous incarnations of the Great Mother: the She-wolf of the Capitoline, the gigantic and imperiously maternal pensione proprietress, the dark-haired trattoria matron who takes special care of the young Fellini during the outdoor eating sequence, the large prostitute in the fields outside Rome shortly thereafter, and so on.

The film fails to arrive at a centre. Two salient examples: the trip on the Grande Raccordo Anulare ends up blocked, unable to reach the Colosseum, and the metropolitana "journey to the centre of the earth" ends up with the evaporation of the ancient Roman frescoes. This latter sequence has obvious psychoanalytical overtones: a descent into the underworld of the unconscious and imaginal – that is, a potential means of achieving centred selfhood in Jungian terms – dominated by rational/technological/phallic/"day-world" instruments that destroy the possibility of meaningful access.[6] Ultimately the movie must let go of its quest for both a centre and the Great Mother. In the penultimate sequence, Fellini encounters Anna Magnani whom he tries to turn into a totalizing ("centring") figure – "a living symbol" of Rome. He also seeks to describe her as the mythically mothering She-wolf of Rome, no doubt having in mind that Magnani had acquired the identity of "Mamma Roma" in Pasolini's eponymous film.[7] She rejects his attempts, closing her door in his face and saying, "I don't trust you."

The centre and the Great Mother are not only allegorical, they are also interpellating: culturally produced ways of organizing experience and psychic life. Instead, the concluding motorcycle ballet of *Roma* is the epitome of the Fellinian/Deleuzian symbolic. It comes from nowhere and ends on the move, with no determinate destination. It seems liberated from a single point of view – Fellini the director, appears to have left the scene once he has been renounced by Magnani – and the sensation I, for one, have watching it is very much that of immanent participation, not distanced observation. The camera eye and I, as audience, seem swept up in the motion and the headlight revelations of the motorcyclists, everywhere yet nowhere. To the extent that we might posit the reappearance of Fellini as camera eye, he is manifest only in what is seen, not as seeing subject. The sequence is centripetal and centrifugal, linear and circular, darkness and light, as the riders encircle and abandon, illuminate and obscure. In its ceaseless penetration of new spaces – and hypothetically new horizons at film's end – it is rhizomatic and omni-relational. The sequence is profoundly and intensely sensual in its vibrant flood of sound and image, eliciting (with a good sound system) powerful vibrations within the body of the viewer/auditor. It has the quality of dream, of an eruption from the creative unconscious. (The subway sequence redeemed.) Though consciously conceived and choreographed, it is clearly shaped, as well, by strongly intuitive, non-rational powers. Finally, partly because of its oneiric nature, it is meaningful beyond understanding, open-ended and undecidable, utopic and dystopic at the same time.[8]

Following *Roma*, Fellini is no longer tempted by the kind of symbolism (Jungian for the most part) that seems to promise a kind of liberation or enlightenment for his characters – or for himself as protagonist – but that is, ultimately, allegorical in a Deleuzian sense. His films are always symbolically rich and multiform in ways suggested above by Waller, but not directed towards a particular epistemological or psycho-spiritual end. *Amarcord* is a good example of a film in which symbolic energy is diffused throughout a landscape of memories, unattached to a single "I" despite the title of the film ("amarcord" = "I remember"). Even a film such as *La città delle donne* – dream from the beginning virtually to the end – does not arrive at any kind of culminating point. The symbols within the dream – for instance Snàporaz's "Ideal Women" – are largely created in order to be superseded or destroyed, and the "message" of the film is to "stay with the dream" for the sheer pleasure and excitation of oneiric activity, not for purposes of individuation or enhanced lucidity. In Fellini's later work, symbolic diffusion is accompanied by narrative diffusion, another way in which the director seeks to no longer confine his visions within fixed structures.

Il viaggio di G. Mastorna

I would like to conclude my discussion with what I feel to be two intriguing examples of the Fellinian/Deleuzian open-ended symbolic that occur outside his cinematic production: *Il viaggio di G. Mastorna*[9] and an oft-discussed (especially by Fellini himself) dream recounted in *Il libro dei sogni* and in Fellini interviews and writings.

Vincenzo Mollica calls *Il viaggio di G. Mastorna* "the most famous unmade film in the history of cinema"[10] (Mollica 2008, 7). The story emerged in the shadow of the unexpected death of Ernst Bernhard, the Jungian psychoanalyst so important to Fellini in the early 1960s, and it was profoundly marked by a near-death experience of Fellini in 1967: anaphylactic shock plus fear of an incurable disease prior to proper diagnosis and treatment. *Mastorna* detailed the protagonist's death in a plane crash and his gradual recognition that he is living in the afterlife. Whereas he was able to carry off the less personal and Edgar Allan Poe–derived *Toby Dammit* – his other death-themed story of the moment – Fellini could not bring *Mastorna* to fruition. On the other hand, the film provided raw material for virtually every other film Fellini made until his death. *Mastorna* is the fulfilment of the symbolic experience as predicated by Deleuze and, implicitly, Fellini. The dynamism, energy, open-endedness, and rhizomatic nature of the symbolic makes it, ultimately, an ongoing and interminable activity rather than the mere production of discrete forms. In fact, one could argue that imaginative work that eventuates in symbolic form(s) runs some risk of becoming allegorical, at least to the extent that it arrives at some degree of closure. A formidable paradox for any artist.

With this in mind, what we might call the "Mastorna complex" that lasted for years, continued to metamorphose, and refused to offer itself up for finalization, constituting symbolic activity in its purest form. The greatest evidence of this are the countless "other stories and dreams" that the *Mastorna* matrix nurtured. As Marcus Perryman notes, Fellini "repeatedly plundered the script for his new films" (2013, 10). Perryman provides numerous examples as does Alessandro Carrera (2020) in his discussion of the diffusion of *Mastorna* throughout Fellini's oeuvre. Anyone who reads the script carefully will find even more Fellinian moments indebted to the evergreen but never completed project. One can hypothesize that, born amidst a moment of great crisis and his own confrontation with death, *Mastorna* was too "symbolic" in a Deleuzian sense, too numinous, too intense for Fellini to fossilize in final form.

Il libro dei sogni: The Airport Dream

Il viaggio di G. Mastorna is linked to another "activity" in Fellini's life that seems to me to fulfil the requisites of the Fellinian/Deleuzian symbolic in such a way as to defy encompassment. In this case, we are not talking about an incomplete project but rather a dream that keeps haunting Fellini because it is emotionally and morally irresolvable and – in its irresolution – endlessly meaningful and provocative. Immediately following the above-cited discussion of "Mastorna," Fellini says, "A dream I had a long time ago may be related to this chimeric film, or better yet to my attitude toward it, one consisting of fascination and suspicion, making me feel excited and skeptical, attracting and repelling me" (Fellini et al. 2015, 104). This is the famed (within *felliniana* circles) airport dream in which Fellini feels he must make an immigration decision about a foreign traveller. I will discuss what I feel to be the symbolic play of both it and a dream that follows on the same night and that, to my knowledge, has never been interpretively linked to the first. I will then suggest how the composite dream experience seems to function (as Fellini himself suggests) much in the same way as did "Mastorna," particularly in terms of its insistence and dispersiveness.

The two dreams, with some elision, are as follows:[11]

> In flight, inside a small airplane ... We [passengers] ... are comfortable together, happy and upbeat. The airplane lands in a north European city (Denmark? West Germany?) ...
> ... A youngish, elegantly dressed lady ... tells me she is the mother of a girl who worked in one of my films [and] she shows me ... a well-wishing message ... I had sent the girl, two typewritten lines: the meaning was to suggest some kind of advice on how to face life.
> Now I'm seated behind a desk, I'm an important manager at the airport, responsible for running the place. Facing me, with a dignified air, is a mysterious-looking traveler of unknown race, who provokes subservience, fear, and revulsion in me all at once.
> Who is he? Where does he come from? What does he want from me? This person with Mongolian features could be an immigrant, he undoubtedly wants a resident's permit, a visa, from me.
> His attitude was that of someone who has no doubts about his own rights and is waiting faithfully. The dignity and strength that emanate from this person, miserable and filthy to look at, gave me a sense of ... [page is cut]
> I told him that it wasn't possible for me to let him in. I wasn't really responsible for this, but I felt equally guilty all the same, I was [despicable, of little worth] ... "I'm not the real boss of the airport," I said, turning red. "I don't have the authority to let you in ..." But I knew that I wasn't being completely sincere, and I was ashamed by my cowardice. The [Oriental] waited, immobile, his face closed, inscrutable. Loyal and threatening. This unknown man emanated a great force that intimidated me, frightened me like the final call of something. The dream ends with a close-up of this mysterious face.

That same night 27 December 1960:

> Immense Villa Borghese, all covered with rain, what a [gloomy] night!
> All around in the darkness whores and prostitutes peek out from amid the bushes, tree trunks, and marble busts.
> I wander around, tense, agitated, I have a date with Delia Scala ..., and now I am waiting for her so that we can make love.

Two night guardians on bicycles stop me. They scrutinize me ... Pimps and whores who have emerged from the tenebrous humidity surround me, everyone snickers, the guardians and prostitutes are disgusted with me, taking me for a bizarre sleepwalker, a foreigner to their world.

I move away from those scornful gazes ... and I realize I am naked, white, thin.

"Filthy faggot!!" they yell after me, snickering, "Homo!"

And to me it seems like they're right. (Fellini 2019, 484)

The initial dream presents us with two Fellini figures. The first is the happy, "upbeat" cosmopolitan European-on-the-move: travelling and adventuresome, comfortable in the presence of an elegant woman, and capable of providing paternal advice to a young admiring actress. The second is a Eurocentric authority figure, no longer travelling but deskbound at an airport. He is no longer offering advice and is, in fact, refusing to offer assistance. He is not only motionless himself, he is also impeding motion – and perhaps more important, boundary crossing. He is intimidated by and closed to the cultural difference presented by the foreigner.

Fellini's dream ego (and/or Fellini recounting) seems to adopt a couple of strategies to negotiate difference. He first says the stranger is of "unknown" race. Then, he talks of "Mongolian" traits, and finally he describes him as "Oriental." (The use of this problematic term is contextualized later in this chapter.) It is as though he is trying to make the stranger more specific, definable, and perhaps more familiar as the dream (or recounting of the dream) progresses. In fact, by the time he is recounting the dream in the 1980s, the figure has become "Chinese." At the same time, the dream ego/recounting enacts a subtle shift from dream to film saying that the dream ends with a large "close-up" ("un grande primo piano") of the mysterious face. Gianfranco Angelucci (2019) has noted the curious fact that, in one of his sketches, Fellini identifies his dream persona as "Director," an English word that can also mean "regista" or film director,[12] and one could argue that having lost his authority as airport director in the face of radical difference, the dream ego seeks to reclaim it as cinematic authority, controlling the "final shot" (256). However, the effect of the "grande primo piano" is to suggest the subjection of the dream ego to the mysterious figure, not vice versa. The "director" is overcome by his "subject" – and by his guilty subjectivity.

There are a number of elements of the first dream – particularly the encounter with the "Oriental" – that prepare for the dream that follows: Fellini's crisis of authority, his sense of self-abasement, his descriptions of himself in the dream in terms that are not entirely divergent from his perceptions of the stranger. The latter is "miserable" and "filthy to look at" while Fellini sees himself as "despicable" and "of little worth" – qualities that to a large extent characterize the Fellini of the second dream. A small but intriguing detail is that Fellini changes skin colour, turning red, towards the end of the first dream. It seems like an innocent and plausible detail in the dream context, but "pellerossa" is a term used by Italians, in imitation of Americans, to describe Native Americans. (The term appears insistently in the screenplay to *Intervista*.) With this "gesture," it is as though the Fellini dream ego becomes a "man of colour," taking on the marginality that would link both the Native American and the stranger. All this leads oneirically, in my reading, to the second dream, in which the Fellini/dream ego is not protected by the cultural complacency of the first figure and the (albeit paralyzing) institutional authority of the second. It seems that his dream ego's demoralization at not being able to embrace the stranger punishes him by making him experience the full brunt of the difference he could not accept earlier. Also, his claim "I don't have the authority" (which really meant the moral fibre and openness), becomes a crushing lack of agency in the second dream.

Things start off as a sexual adventure, with Delia Scala a transmutation of the earlier "elegantly dressed" woman, signalling perhaps an oneiric escape from the moral accountability of the preceding dream. The rain and gloom somewhat offset this, while the "respectable" romanticism of the anticipated escapade is strongly qualified by the whores and prostitutes peeking out everywhere. Then, suddenly, the dream ego is subjected to authority figures who exert the kind of scrutiny that he was empowered to employ with the stranger – though, in fact, his xenophobia foreclosed the kind of close attention that scrutiny entails. He is then subjected to the misrecognition, disgust, contempt, and rejection (as well as condescension) at the root of the second Fellini's inability to accept the "Oriental." In having to occupy the role of the stranger, the dream ego becomes, in a sense, sexually demeaned which is consistent with classic Orientalizing attitudes.[13] And in a poetically just ironic reversal, the Fellini figure becomes painfully aware of his naked and thin whiteness. His mockers are indeed "right," as the dream ego suggests, if they are identifying whiteness as a principal villain in this dream narrative.

When Fellini recounted the airport dream to Bernhard, the latter commented, "The day you understand this figure here before you will be an extraordinary one"[14] (Fellini 2007, 559). It seems to me that Fellini's unconscious understood the dream perfectly well, on the very night it occurred. The fact that he appears to title this dream "The Tao Symbol" in his *Book of Dreams* sketch, with a representation of the symbol, seems to suggest that, whenever he arrived at this title and "logo," he recognized the two faces, the Self and Other, as it were, of the dream.

The dream can be read in autobiographical terms, given Fellini's aversion to travel or even to shoot on location – a phenomenon that begins with *La dolce vita*, hence at the same general moment as the dream. His unwillingness to venture far beyond Theatre 5 at Cinecittà suggests a strongly conflicted relation to adventure, much less difference. However, my emphasis here is on the broader symbolic function of the dream. The stranger himself is powerful in this respect: impenetrable (a classic "attribute" of the East in Western eyes), mysterious, contradictory. Loyal and threatening at the same time, he tempts one to ask: loyal to whom, and, if loyal, why threatening? But most important, he is numinous: arousing strong feelings, unsettling certitudes, and setting in motion questions without answers. Most important, he – and the dream – won't go away. Fellini repeatedly returned to it. First of all, he sketched and annotated it on 27 December 1960. Then he seems to have insistently resketched it. Angelucci has several other images that feature an oversized woman (Lea Giacomini in Angelucci's opinion) on the desk next to him – one of which has the identifying plaque "Director" in front of the Fellini figure. Fellini seems to have become quite possessed by it in the late 1970s and early 1980s. On 28 September 1977, he sends yet new sketches and a new recounting of the dream[15] to the American journal *Dreamworks* for its debut issue that will appear in the spring of 1980 (Fellini 1980a). Then, in 1980, he provides a lengthy description of the dream in his *Fare un film* (Fellini 1980b, 67–8). In the early 1980s, he recounts it to Charlotte Chandler for an interview that appears in *The Ultimate Seduction* (Fellini 1984, 132).[16] Interestingly, he tells Chandler he has never told anyone the dream when, in fact, he had sent it to *Dreamworks* several years before and drafted a recounting for *Fare un film*.[17] It seems that "confessing" the dream, even long after its occurrence, causes Fellini some of the same discomfort and shame he experienced with the dream itself. Intriguingly, the very process embodied by the airport dream becoming the Villa Borghese dream – a cosmopolitan and comfortable male dream ego undergoing horrifying experiences that destroy all complacency – resurfaces in Fellini's final film work, in the first and third of his 1992 Banca di Roma commercials.

Most important, as a haunting and "floating" signifier, the dream, like "Mastorna," finds echoes throughout Fellini's work, putting into relationship all its many issues: insularity, openness, difference, xenophobia, whiteness, arbitrary authority, marginalization, shame, and so on. There is a good deal of pre-dream sensitivity to these issues as early as *Lo sceicco bianco*, which critiques popular-culture colonization of the East – even to the extent of making the absurd sheik "white."[18] Though Oriental(ist) encounters do not abound in the early films, Fellini's awareness of the problem is rooted in his provincial experience, upon which he drew for *Lo sceicco bianco* and which finds fullest expression in *Amarcord*. Turkish scholar Cihan Gündoğdu, writing from the perspective of the East and addressing the film's harem sequence, cites Fellini's observations that "adolescent Italians of a certain period ... are filled with absurd dreams concerning the Orient" and of "sensuously exotic Oriental women" (Fellini 1975, quoted in Gündoğdu 2020, 437). Gündoğdu argues that the harem scene "is critical of the average provincial Italian male" (437). Conclusive support for Gündoğdu's opinion is found in a deleted scene from the film, in which "Patacca," whose nickname ("phony," "fraud") indicates his untrustworthiness and who turns out to be a fascist collaborator, assails a Chinese character in a bar with a series of profoundly racist assumptions based on total ignorance.[19] Patacca's assault and Fellini's critique are so crude, they exceed the bounds of satire or parody, hence, no doubt, Fellini's decision to cut it, but their excessiveness seems charged with Fellini's regret for his fearful and cowardly response to the airport stranger, ultimately identified by Fellini as Chinese. The critique of Patacca helps place in perspective the encounter of the young Fellini figure in *Roma* with a Chinese pensione boarder who, on the one hand, seems clichéd in his hyperactivity and desire to please, but who, on the other hand, is being seen from the point of view of both a provincial youth newly arrived in Rome and Fellini, as film-maker, recalling his own provincial proclivity for circumscribing ethnic others in cliché.

The "Oriental" resurfaces in a number of ways in other of Fellini's films and dream diaries. It can be associated with the same fear, anxiety, negative reaction, and shame of the airport dream, as in his dream of being prisoner to a group of Chinese prostitutes "as treacherous as wild beasts" (Fellini 2019, 495)[20] whom he then treats violently to his regret. He dreams of being in the charge of a Chinese taxi driver who seems to put him at some risk (560).[21] In a dream of 22/5/1967 (515), there is an association between a Chinese figure and Fellini's brother Riccardo – a recurrent source of angst in the dream diaries, arising from their estrangement.

There are also quite positive associations with the East, one of which occurs only a week after the airport dream, perhaps confirming my sense that Fellini had, in fact, come to terms with the meaning of that dream by the end of his night's sleep. In his notation of a dream from 3/1/1961 (Fellini 2019, 485), Fellini describes Giulietta sitting in a pose reminiscent of "Oriental monks," while her throat and neck contain an engraved or stitched sentence that conveys to him "a sense of liberation" and "a sense of joyous stupor." He reports that the phrase "clarified all my doubts and left me reassured and happy." Here in a sense, Giulietta "becomes" the mysterious stranger as the vehicle of ineffable revelation. This dream might be seen negatively as an act of de-othering familiarization, but more affirmatively as a sign that Fellini is struggling to embrace rather than reject the figure of the "Oriental."

The most positive role for Chinese figures in the Fellinian imaginary occurs in *Il viaggio di G. Mastorna*, bringing us back to the seemingly inevitable pairing of that never-completed work and Fellini's airport dream and allowing me to once again invoke the work of Marguerite Waller. Having undergone a series of bizarre adventures that only gradually push Mastorna to the recognition that he is in the afterlife, he comes upon a little plane made of sticks and twine (sibling, as it were, to the grandfather's plane in *Giulietta degli spiriti*). He boards, and Waller describes and interprets:

> Reaching the cockpit ... he discovers that there are no controls; the pilot, an elderly Chinese man is asleep; and the plane is somehow being flown by a laughing Chinese girl of four or five. The "bimbetta cinese" takes the plane through several cartwheels, thoroughly bashing the terrified Mastorna, particularly his head. The moment he gives up any attempt to master the situation, the little girl announces that they have arrived ... Fellini's association of Mastorna with European high culture [he is a symphony cellist], coupled with Mastorna's initial, almost willed, obliviousness to the dramatic change he has undergone, seems to express a certain mindset rooted in homogeneity, stasis, impermeability, hierarchy, and the illusions of clarity and mastery. An unruly Chinese bimbetta, in this sense, is the precise obverse of Mastorna's subject position. Recognizing the dependence of his persona on the condensed figure of all that he has been defined against seems to be a crucial step in Mastorna's radical psychological transformation en route to a fully relational universe. (Waller and Burke 2020, 8–9)

Although one might dispute just how relational things become by the end of Fellini's story and while one might note that Fellini has to put the "mysterious stranger" to sleep and replaced him with a less threatening little girl, it is clear that in reconfiguring the airport dream in *Il viaggio di G. Mastorna*, Fellini has, as he did in the dream of Giulietta, found a way to make some peace with the once-threatening "other."

The vitality and "morphability" of the Chinese traveller match the vitality and transmutability of the ever-travelling Mastorna as both protagonist and text. They confirm the Fellinian symbolic as something that at its best never settles in one place, never lapses into facile allegory hence inevitable disuse, but insistently migrates, pondering imponderables and sleuthing out mysteries that remain unresolved but provocative in a never-ending journey. One can also hypothesize – though the proof lies beyond the confines of this chapter – that the greatest example of the Fellinian symbolic lies not in his films or unfinished works or specific dreams but in his marvellously sprawling, centrifugal, uncontainable *Book of Dreams* – which, like *Il viaggio di G. Mastorna*, was an invaluable source of inspiration and imagery throughout the Fellini oeuvre.

NOTES

1 See Martin Jay (1993) for an excellent overview of French image-phobic, language-dominant theory that, paradoxically, held a tight grip on film studies for several decades, contributing to a striking neglect of Fellini's work.
2 Aside from a foreword and afterword, Chandler's *I, Fellini* consists entirely of Fellini's words, so I will avoid the tedium of writing "quoted in" every time I cite the text.
3 "At its apex, thought, for Deleuze, manifests an intensity that expands and alters the limits of human subjectivity, bringing mental life closer to the life of animals and rocks, but also to imperceptible forces, and to the imbricated rhythms of affective dynamisms, the deep pulsations and vibrations of the cosmos itself" (Ramey 2012, 27).
4 I seek to do something of the same in my discussion of *La città delle donne* in *Fellini's Films and Commercials: From Postwar to Postmodern* (2020, 337–41).
5 For more, see my discussion in *Fellini's Films and Commercials* (2020, 187–8.)
6 I thank Antonella Sisto for noting the psychoanalytical implications during a roundtable discussion at the American Association of Italian Studies Virtual Conference, 5 June 2021.
7 There is irony in the designation of Magnani as "Mamma Roma" in Pasolini's film; her character has a painfully difficult time throughout. So, built into Fellini's choice of Magnani as a Great Mother is a kind of inevitable disavowal of the archetype.
8 For a longer discussion, see my *Fellini's Films and Commercials* (2020).
9 For more about *Il viaggio di G. Mastorna*, see the chapters by Marina Vargau, Mirko Tavoni, Ottavio Cirio Zanetti, and Manuela Gieri in this volume.

10 "il più famoso film mai fatto nella storia del cinema"
11 I am using the English translation from the Rizzoli 2019 edition of *The Book of Dreams*, but with close attention to the Italian original to make sure that *traduzione* is not *tradimento*. In certain instances, in brackets, I substitute translations that are more accurate than those of Rizzoli.
12 This is not visible in the sketches that appear in *The Book of Dreams*, but it appears clearly in a sketch Fellini made of the dream that included one of his powerful women, advising him to "cast away" the mysterious stranger. For a specific discussion, see Angelucci (2019, 256).
13 In using a slur against the LGBTQ+ community, the Fellini figure is arguably "othered," which Orientalism does repeatedly to the East. Though this implies problematic stereotypes on Fellini's part regarding homosexuality, the point here is that a stanchly heterosexual identity – clear from the dream ego's anticipated dalliance with Delia Scala – is being placed under erasure.
14 "Il giorno in cui lei realizzerà questa figura che le sta dinnanzi sarà un giorno straordinario."
15 The new account seems to add some details just to make the dream more understandable in the new context – details that were not important to the initial recounting of the dream and that were probably not part of the dream experience. The same is true with the accounts of the 1980s.
16 The dream reappears in Chandler's 1994 *I, Fellini* (208–9), but this is merely the republication of the same account.
17 It is unclear exactly when in the early 1980s Chandler interviewed Fellini. It is conceivable that his comments to her and his drafting for *Fare un film* were more or less simultaneous.
18 For an excellent discussion of race, whiteness, and colonization in Fellini's work, see Shelleen Greene's chapter in this volume.
19 For more, see Maurizio Mein's film, *Diario segreto di Amarcord* (1974).
20 Dream dated 1/3/1967 in *The Book of Dreams*.
21 Dream dated June 1970 in *The Book of Dreams*.

REFERENCES

Angelucci, Gianfranco. 2019. *Glossario Felliniano. 50 voci per raccontare Federico Fellini il genio italiano del cinema*. Rome: Avagliano editore.
Bentivoglio, Leonetta. 2003. "A 10 anni dalla scomparsa del regista/intervista a James Hillman." *La Repubblica*, 1 November. https://ricerca.repubblica.it/repubblica/archivio/repubblica/2003/11/01/10-anni-dalla-scomparsa-del-regista.html?ref=search.

Burke, Frank. 2020. *Fellini's Films and Commercials: From Postwar to Postmodern*. Bristol, UK: Intellect.

Carrera, Alessandro. 2020. "Il viaggio di G. Mastorna": Fellini *Entre Deux morts.*" In *A Companion to Federico Fellini*, edited by Frank Burke, Marguerite Waller, and Marita Gubareva, 129–39. Hoboken, NJ: Wiley Blackwell.

Chandler, Charlotte. 1995. *I, Fellini*. New York: Random House.

Cixous, Hèléne. 1976. "The Laugh of the Medusa." *Signs* 1, no. 4: 875–93. www.jstor.org/stable/3173239. https://doi.org/10.1086/493306.

Deleuze, Gilles. 1997. "Nietzsche and Saint Paul, Lawrence and John of Patmos." In *Essays Critical and Clinical*, translated by Daniel W. Smith and Michael A. Greco, 36–52. Minneapolis: University of Minnesota Press.

Fellini, Federico. 1975. "*Amarcord*: The Fascism within Us – An Interview with Valerio Riva." In *Federico Fellini: Essays in Criticism*, edited by Peter Bondanella, 220–6. Oxford: Oxford University Press.

– 1980a. "Dream Report." *Dreamworks* 1, no. 1: 4–6.

– 1980b. *Fare un film*. Turin: Einaudi.

– 1984. "Interview with Federico Fellini." In *The Ultimate Seduction*, edited by Charlotte Chandler, 111–52. New York: Doubleday.

– 2007. *Il libro dei sogni*. Edited by Tullio Kezich and Vittorio Boarini with a contribution by Vincenzo Mollica. Milan: Rizzoli.

– 2019. *The Book of Dreams*. Edited by Sergio Toffetti. Translated by Aaron Maines and David Stanton. New York: Rizzoli.

Fellini, Federico, Italo Calvino, Liliana Betti, and Chistopher Burton White. 2015. *Making a Film.* Translated by Christopher Burton White. New York: Contra Mundum Press.

Foreman, Walter C., Jr. 1977. "The Poor Player Struts Again: Fellini's *Toby Dammit* and the End of the Actor." In The 1977 *Film Studies Annual: Part 1, Explorations in National Cinemas*, edited by Ben Lawton, 111–23. Pleasantville, NY: Redgrave.

– 1980. "Fellini's Cinematic City: *Roma* and Myths of Foundation." Reprinted in *Perspectives on Federico Fellini*, edited by Peter Bondanella and Cristina Degli-Esposti, 151–6. New York: G.K. Hall & Co.

Gündoğdu, Cihan. 2020. "Fellini and Turkey: Influence and Image." In *A Companion to Federico Fellini*, edited by Frank Burke, Marguerite Waller, and Marita Gubareva, 435–38. Hoboken, NJ: Wiley Blackwell.

Hillman, James. 1975. *Re-visioning Psychology*. New York: Harper & Row.

Irigaray, Luce. 1980. "When Our Lips Speak Together." *Signs* 6, no. 1. Part 2: 69–79. www.jstor.org/stable/3173966. https://doi.org/10.1086/493777.

Jay, Martin. 1993. *Downcast Eyes: The Denigration of Vision in Twentieth-Century French Thought*. Berkeley: University of California Press.

Jung, C.G. 1967. "Commentary on 'The Secret of the Golden Flower.'" In *Collected Works of C.G. Jung*. Vol. 13, *Alchemical Studies*, translated and

edited by Gerhard Adler and R.F.C. Hull, 1–56. Princeton, NJ: Princeton University Press.
– 1969. "Spirit and Life." In *Collected Works of C.G. Jung*. Vol. 8, *The Structure and Dynamics of the Psyche*, 2nd ed., translated and edited by Gerhard Adler and R.F.C. Hull, 319–37. Princeton, NJ: Princeton University Press.
Lorde, Audre. 1984. "The Master's Tools Will Never Dismantle the Master's House." In *Sister/Outsider: Essays and Speeches by Audre Lorde*, 110–13. Freedom, CA: The Crossing Press.
Mein, Maurizio, dir. 1974. *Diario segreto di Amarcord*. Rome: RAI: Radiotelevisione Italia. Film.
Mollica, Vincenzo. 2008. "Sulla faccenda cinematografica." In *Federico Fellini. Il viaggio di G. Mastorna*. Edited by Ermanno Cavazzoni, 7–14. Macerata: Quodlibet.
Mulvey, Laura. 1975. "Visual Pleasure and Narrative Cinema." *Screen* 16, no. 3: 6–18. http://doi.org/10.1093/screen/16.3.6.
Perryman, Marcus. 2013. "Introduction." In *The Journey of G. Mastorna: The Film Fellini Didn't Make*, by Federico Fellini. Translated and with a commentary by Marcus Perryman, 1–14. New York: Berghahn Books.
Ramey, Joshua. 2012. *The Hermetic Deleuze: Philosophy and Spiritual Ordeal*. Durham: Duke University Press.
Shelley, Mary Wollstonecraft. (1818) 1994. *Frankenstein; or, The Modern Prometheus*. Peterborough, ON: Broadview Literary Texts.
Van Watson, William. 2002. "Fellini and Lacan: The Hollow Phallus, the Male Womb, and the Retying of the Phallus." In *Federico Fellini: Contemporary Perspectives*, edited by Frank Burke and Marguerite R. Waller, 65–91. Toronto: University of Toronto Press.
Waller, Marguerite. 1993. "Neither an 'I' Nor an 'Eye': The Gaze in *Giulietta degli spiriti*." In *Perspectives on Federico Fellini*, edited by Peter Bondanella and Cristina Degli-Esposti, 214–24. New York: G.K. Hall & Co.
– 2002a. "Introduction." In *Federico Fellini: Contemporary Perspectives*, edited by Frank Burke and Marguerite R. Waller, 3–25. Toronto: University of Toronto Press.
– 2002b. "Whose *Dolce Vita* Is This Anyway? The Language of Fellini's Cinema." Reprinted in *Federico Fellini: Contemporary Perspectives*, edited by Frank Burke and Marguerite R. Waller, 107–20. Toronto: University of Toronto Press.
– 2020. "*Il Maestro* Dismantles the Master's House: Fellini's Undoing of Gender and Sexuality." In *A Companion to Federico Fellini*, edited by Frank Burke, Marguerite Waller, and Marita Gubareva, 311–28. Hoboken, NJ: Wiley Blackwell.
Waller, Marguerite, and Frank Burke. 2020. "Introduction." In *A Companion to Federico Fellini*, edited by Frank Burke, Marguerite Waller, and Marita Gubareva, 3–12. Hoboken, NJ: Wiley Blackwell.
Wollstonecraft, Mary. (1792) 1988. *A Vindication of the Rights of Woman*. New York: Norton.

CENTENARY ESSAYS

What Is in the Modern Look? Federico Fellini and the Photography of William Klein

GIULIANA MINGHELLI

There is a turning point in the cinematic world of Federico Fellini, a poetic visual shift that coincides with the seismic global changes of the late 1950s, a time when the postwar world seemingly emerged from an ice age to embark once again – yet as if for the first time – into mass modernization. In Italy, these earth-shaking times are dispatched with a clipped moniker: *miracolo economico* (economic miracle). *Le notti di Cabiria*, Fellini's 1957 film, powerfully, if cryptically, inhabits this watershed. It is here that Fellini's image acquires that modern look that a few years later will become iconic of transnational cinema via *La dolce vita* (1960).[1] The encounter with American photographer William Klein and his defining photobook, *Life Is Good and Good for You in New York: Trance Witness Revels* (published in France and Italy in 1956), was a key inspiration for this visual change. Klein's (uncredited) collaboration on the 1957 film was instrumental to the evolution of Fellini's aesthetics in the late 1950s.

Through a comparative reading of Klein's photobook and *Le notti di Cabiria*, this chapter will explore the formal influence of Klein's photography on Fellini and highlight the richness of cultural exchanges across countries and media in the postwar moment. What does it mean to look at Rome as if it were New York? The answer to this question lies in the film's shimmering nights and dramatic choreography of light – sites where modernity flares up as an effect of the photographic surface. A study of the new energy of Fellini's cinematic image will highlight the impact of Klein's photography as well as the commonality of vision of two artists bound to a love for the human figure and a reality veined with the expressionistic and surreal. Like Rome, the lovely Cabiria, protagonist of the film, is an unlikely icon of modernity. Her direct gaze, however, still engages contemporary spectators, interrogating their own relation to what is modern. Cabiria's position on the precipice of a new era sheds light on our present ongoing "transition" towards an even less decipherable future.

Fellini's *livre de chevet*

> I was a Fellini groupie and when he came to Paris in 1956 to present *I vitelloni*, I wanted to meet him. In that time, heroes were accessible. I phoned his hotel, "Mr. Fellini s'il vous plait," and they put me through. I said, "I just did a book on New York. I'd like to show it to you." He replied, "Come tomorrow at four," and I went.
>
> He said: "You know, there's an Italian edition, I have a copy next to my bed. I like it a lot." And we talked. In a few minutes he said: "Why don't you come to Rome and work on my new film, be my assistant?" I'd never seen a film being shot and had no idea what an assistant did and told him. He said, "No problem, if I'm sick you shoot." (Klein 2009, 6)[2]

So William Klein remembers his first encounter with Fellini in 1956. Fellini was thirty-six, already a world-renowned film-maker about to start shooting *Le notti di Cabiria*. Klein was twenty-eight, a fairly obscure photographer who earlier that year had published his first photographic book with the French publishing house Petite Planète under the auspices of Chris Marker. The book, *Life Is Good and Good for You in New York*, is a milestone in the history of photography. With it, Klein inaugurated a new, irreverent and revolutionary visual aesthetic that, shot by shot, interrogated New York and its myth of modernity, bringing to the surface the visual and social unconscious of the city. This is what Fellini brought back to Italy, along with the photographer himself.

After the Paris rendezvous followed the usual antics in Fellini's travelling circus. Upon arriving in Rome two weeks later, Klein discovered he was one among a sprawling retinue of assistants. The shooting of the film was constantly delayed – Giulietta Masina broke her leg, Fellini's father died, the funds ran out. To kill time, Klein did in Rome what he had done a few years before in New York: he wandered through the city taking photographs, chaperoned by some of Italy's leading artists and intellectuals – Moravia, Pasolini, and Feltrinelli. The resulting body of photographs made up *Rome*, his second photobook, published in 1959, the year Fellini was filming *La dolce vita*.

Eventually, Klein's "collaboration" with Fellini took off. His task, Klein remembers, was to follow Fellini "to find whores who wanted to be in the film ... My job was to photograph likely prospects, someone else took their names and phone numbers" (2009, 6). Working as an anonymous stage photographer may have spectacularly fulfilled the dream of the Fellini groupie, but it was certainly a let-down for the aspiring "assistant." Klein was not the only person whom Fellini had taken for a ride. Pier Paolo Pasolini (the only assistant to be credited in the film titles) recounts his collaboration with Fellini as endless gallivanting through Rome's suburbs in search of a mythical prostitute called "la Bomba." Recalling the spell Fellini had on him, Pasolini describes the film-maker as "a huge snail as big as a city into whose innards one could enter like a Rabelaisian hero … But then, slowly realizing that the snail-labyrinth digests and assimilates everything in its horrendous and radiant innards: it will digest you as well, if you don't watch out" (1999, 700). Seemingly playful and casual, the collaborations with the charming and benevolent *lumacone* (big snail) disguised a treacherous act of cannibalism. On the surface, Klein, the American expatriate from Paris, simply lent an exotic touch to Fellini's entourage, a cosmopolitan glamour that would later become the very stuff of that rambling epic of jetsetters that is *La dolce vita*. But his involvement was more profound, entailing, as Pasolini suggested, an act of cannibalistic assimilation. What exactly was Fellini feasting upon?

Klein's Ongoing Moment

In 1956, Klein could not publish his photographs in the US. The raw, straight look into the face of an American society not yet wary of the camera and thus nakedly exposed to its revelatory power unveiled, together with the irrepressible vitality of the city, the arrogance of money, the pervasiveness of poverty, and the incongruous coexistence of rituals old and new (sports, religion, advertising). "What is this shit?" Klein remembers, was the standard comment of the prospective publishers to the book. The New York they saw was not a New York that they knew or wanted to know. "The whites," Klein wrote in one of the book's captions, "never go to Harlem, never even think of it, for Harlem lies off-limits somewhere in the bad conscience of the city."[3] Because of this challenging commentary, a raw aesthetic indifferent to technical and stylistic norms, and its playful unconventional layout, Klein's photobook irrupted into an ordered photographic world dominated by Henri Cartier-Bresson's carefully calibrated image. Published in 1952, Cartier-Bresson's seminal *Images à la Sauvette*, translated into English as *The Decisive Moment*, had by the mid-1950s become a photographic bible of sorts. Ironically, Klein's first camera previously belonged to Cartier-Bresson. Harshly framed, often grainy, even out of focus because of the extreme closeness of the subject, Klein's photographs convey an alternative topsy-turvy universe, the furthest thing from Cartier-Bresson's silent and stubborn pursuit of the perfect moment.

Photography for Klein is an up-close, personal, and impulsive sensual engagement with the world. Poised in an unfolding moment, overflowing with life and possibility, the photographs of *Life Is Good* are like an ongoing conversation that gestures to a before and after, to a beyond the frame, that "blind field" that Roland Barthes associated with the surplus of life in cinema's moving image (1980, 57). Klein, who started his career as a painter before moving to photography and eventually cinema, is an artist whose vision unfolds in an intermedial space. One could say that he wields the photographic camera with a sense of movement suggestive of a desire to shoot a film, but it is also his photographer's eye for composition that guides his work as a cinematographer. Hence, as it has been observed, his photographs look like film stills, while, conversely, any frame of his films looks like a photo.[4]

An ethical and political stance towards the world informs Klein's aesthetic. Born in New York to a Jewish family ruined in the 1929 market crash, Klein early on embraced art as a way to escape the hardships and squalor of his environment. In his photographs, the myths and iconography of New York as the majestic point of entry to a modern world of freedom and opportunity are rubbed against his experience of growing up in Manhattan's West Side and the street-level reality of poverty, struggle, and indifference. Far from "incomprehensible" (as an Italian journalist observed), the title of the book, *Life Is Good and Good for You in New York*,[5] ironically borrowing the language of advertising, announces a trenchant critique of the American Dream and its accompanying myths of the unqualified goodness of capitalism, modernity, and progress.

At first sight, the *Life Is Good* photobook is aligned with the tradition of documentary photography. However, the intensity of Klein's realist vision – blurred, deformed, and out of focus – gives rise to an aesthetic of excess verging on the surreal that constantly threatens to breach the boundaries of social photography and the objectivity of the witness. If the ironic title was not enough, the subtitle, *Trance Witness Revels*, unmistakably reframes expectations. For Klein, the encounter with reality is a mixed experience that stretches the boundaries of documentary photography: witnessing can fade into trance and explode into revel. This complex aesthetic points to the deeply democratizing nature of Klein's photographic practice, which, unlike that of Cartier-Bresson and many other photographers, places photographer and photographed subject on the same plane. "You feel," David Campany noted, "this very collaborative theatre in the pictures" (quoted in Bright 2012, 24:24), a collaboration that has the expansive effect of pulling us, the belated spectator, into the spectacle.

Undoubtedly, Fellini and Klein had much to talk about during their first encounter in Paris. The countless affinities that immediately emerge between the two artists – the love for the human face and the mysterious alchemy of crowds; the camera as the site of a happening and the photographer/cinematographer as an enabler of a travelling spectacle; the mixed status of the image as document and dream, reality veering towards the deformed and expressionistic – make the impact of Klein on Fellini's cinema at once profound and lasting. "Trance, witness, revels" could just as well summarize Fellini's own ethos and aesthetic vade mecum as he transitioned away from neorealism.

The 1956 Watershed

When did Fellini become modern? Critics seem to agree that the ferrying from the "primitive" shores of neorealism to avant-garde auteur cinema was completed with *La dolce vita*, which set a global standard for modernism in the medium.[6] The understanding of what counts as cinematic modernism remains tentative, however. In the case of Fellini, the main points of reference have been the visual avant-garde of the early and mid-twentieth century – Fellini himself first likened his method to Cubism and Picasso (Kezich 2006, 196) – and, later on, the abstract expressionism of Pollock, Rothko, and Tobey, which evoked notions of "action filming" (Brunetta 2001, 514–15).[7] But how exactly can a cinematic image be likened to a cubist painting or Pollock canvas? Rather than invoking the high church of painterly or literary modernism, what is moulding Fellini's aesthetic evolution lies close at hand in the contemporary medium of photography. While present since *Lo sceicco bianco*'s (1952) world of *fotoromanzi*, photography had a central impact on both the form and content of *La dolce vita*. But it was in *Le notti di Cabiria* that Fellini aesthetically confronted and absorbed the most avant-garde lessons of the medium. Klein played a crucial role in this moment of aesthetic transition to cinematic modernism, one that would, through his rough tabloid-like take on the streets, his expressionistic use of the camera, and his persona of the photographer as a daring explorer of urban modernity, become the core of *La dolce vita*.

Before 1956, Fellini's cinema lived in the provinces, either among a sleepy middle class or the world of marginal travelling performers. *Il bidone* (1955) marks a moment of crisis in this universe. In that film, the petite bourgeois and the down-at-the-heels artist merge into a crowd of petty criminals, swindlers, and forgers. Augusto and his friends – decayed *vitelloni* without the youth, fantasy, or verve to redeem the emptiness of their lives – inhabit an uncertain geography precariously balanced between the primeval landscapes of the countryside and the phony and theatrical scenarios of the city. For this humanity, time is suspended, with no horizon to seek, no childhood to mourn – an empty temporality representative of the film's uncertain historicity.

One element that does anchor *Il bidone* to its time is the recently introduced television. Ubiquitous in both peasant houses and nouveau riche apartments, the TV sets project a belittled and vaguely demoralizing modernity, epitomized in the image of the party revellers huddled around the small screen awaiting the announcement of the New Year. On the other hand, the iconic cinematic embodiment of the cutting edge, the trope of the nightclub, offers the most revealing example of the film's and Fellini's temporal/aesthetic blockage. With its tentative mix of Matisse- and Kandinsky-inspired decor and performances harkening back to a 1920s Paris jazz club or even earlier *café chantant*, the nightclub of *Il bidone* is, like its protagonists, out of step and strikingly anachronistic. It is from this muddled nowhere land at the margins of modernity that Fellini leaps with *Le notti di Cabiria* to the forefront of a new aesthetic.

Days and Nights of Cabiria

Nights, the time of parties when the everyday world recedes and the universe expands in a glow of lights that make everything seem possible, are the pulsating heart of Fellini's world. Foregrounded in the title, the nights occupy more than half the film's running time. The story of the lovely and resilient Cabiria, a prostitute proudly independent and cruelly cheated by her lovers, is told in a series of loosely connected episodes rotating around the nocturnal setting of the Passeggiata Archeologica – a gathering place of female and male prostitutes next to the Terme di Caracalla. Cabiria's adventures – the encounters with the actor Alberto Lazzari and the mysterious man of charity, the collective visit to the Madonna del Divino Amore, and the nightmarish adventure in the variety theatre – take off from and return to this nocturnal stretch of road. After first meeting Oscar, the daytime outings will occupy the greater narrative time, but each date with the sinister swindler will still be followed, as a sort of running commentary, with a return to the Passeggiata.

However, it is a sun-scorched ex-urban landscape that introduces us to *Le notti di Cabiria*. This bright day sets a strong counterpoint to the dark brilliance of the night scenes immediately to follow. At the same time, Cabiria's close brush with death and comedic rescue on the harshly lit banks of the Tiber foreshadow her final heartbreak in the waning light on Lake Bracciano. The opening day of *Le notti di Cabiria* documentaristically reveals the poor, seemingly abandoned periphery of Rome inhabited by a marginal humanity, living on expedients in makeshift buildings. Neither countryside nor city, this is a space seemingly outside of time, belonging to all times. However, an occasional advertisement and the omnipresent horizon of advancing cranes and new buildings announces the approach of the future. Nothing separates temporally or geographically this eternally diurnal landscape, ancient with exhaustion and desolation, from the night world of the Passeggiata Archeologica, Cabiria's workplace, an even more ancient scene of toil, squalor, and violence. Nonetheless, Fellini's night seems to inaugurate a different historical era.

Night, with its artificial lighting, entertainments, and around-the-clock activity, is the archetypal time of modernity. With its phantasmagoria of lights, the modern night overrides geographical and historical differences, drawing closer the widest corners of the globe. If by day, mid-1950s Italy is still a country barely on the threshold of modernization, by night, with its ancient landscapes blanketed in shadows, it too can bask in the first glimmers of this new world, so much so that even the squalor and ruins of the Passeggiata can become the backdrop of an alluring modernity. Because, after all, isn't being modern first a question of appearances – the stuff of image making, a play of surfaces, of photography, of writing with light?

From Broadway to the Passeggiata Archeologica

Perusing Klein's New York book, with a film about nightlife in the making, Fellini must have found the photographs of Broadway by night to be show-stopping: the bright neons and lacquered blacks expressing the cutting-edge look of the city that never sleeps, the electrifying promise of all that is modern (see, for example, image 6). What is the essence of this nocturnal modernity? How can it be evoked in the Roman landscape? Beyond the realist display of the obvious icons of modern life – cars, huge marquees, nightlife – these photographs foreground light as the very substance of modernity. But more important than the direct illumination of the bulbs and marquees are the reflecting surfaces. The reflections powerfully structure the images in a striking abstract arabesque of lights and shadows that distorts and enlivens the solidity of the world. Klein's vision transforms the night into an expanding and

Image 6. Two photographs from the page spread "Selwyn, 42nd Street, 1955" and "Wings of the Hawk, 1955" in *Life Is Good and Good for You in New York* (Klein 1956, 50, 51). © William Klein Estate.

endlessly duplicating world through such reflection.[8] In this exciting and disorienting topsy-turvy space, a night palpable and fluid like an aqueous environment, an anonymous humanity wanders like opaque shadows lost in a mysterious pool. Nothing could be further from the glow of Broadway than Rome's Passeggiata Archeologica, yet there Fellini undertook the construction of his nocturnal stage through Klein's lens. But how to recreate this shimmering modern look in a world of crumbling bricks, dusty roads, and dry underbrush?

The first thing that Fellini adopted – mediated by the vision of his cinematographer Aldo Tonti, who had developed the look of American *noir* in Luchino Visconti's *Ossessione* (1943) – was the basic quality of Klein's black-and-white photography: full of high contrasts; rich in deep and saturated blacks. Shedding the greyer tones of previous films, *Le notti di Cabiria* embraces Klein's extreme palette. But what allowed Fellini to make the Roman night pulsate with the electricity of modern life is precisely those reflecting surfaces and their dramatic choreography of lights. Water is a crucial medium of this visual amplification. Surprisingly for Rome, all the nights at the Passeggiata Archeologica are wet with dew, fog, and veritable downpours. A trickle of water on

Image 7. The mambo dance from *Le notti di Cabiria*.

the asphalt and the reflection of rain on a black umbrella discretely focus on and magnify the water element in the introductory shots to the night sequences. These are not decorative, casual elements. The trickle of water will become a crucial structuring element for lighting and set design during Cabiria's first irresistible mambo performance (image 7). Spreading on the asphalt into a complex web of rivulets that recalls the aerial view of a river delta, the water transforms the surface of the road into a maze of light and shadow. Through water and lighting, the drab asphalt becomes an arabesque dance floor, glittering with sparkle and a deep liquid darkness. The Roman arch in the background creates a monumental backdrop for this open sky nightclub, while in the foreground Marisa's new white FIAT Seicento, symbol of the impending *miracolo economico*, sparkles with its own reflected light.

As the dancing continues, a dark car drives by. The combined effects of the water on the ground, the contrasting brilliance of the black and white vehicles, and a solitary floodlight in the furthest distance charge the antique setting with the vibes of modernity. However, in the cinematic appropriation of the modern look of Klein's Broadway an inversion takes place: the human beings step to the foreground while the lights choreograph and spectacularize the action. But this does not imply that the lights play a secondary role. As much as character and setting, lighting contributes to the affective structure and symbolism of the film.

In *Le notti di Cabiria*, modernity is equally bound to the night and to its inhabitants: the brutal underworld of criminality and transgression and, to a lesser extent, the glamorous life of the privileged (which would become the exclusive focus of *La dolce vita*). This humanity is the raw matter that approximates the thrilling intensity of modern life. But it is through light, on the photographic surface, that this matter is transformed into the illusion of unbounded freedom, mystery, and adventure that makes up that intensity. Finally, and most importantly, it is through light that Fellini explores and tests the desire for the modern against both secular and metaphysical horizons of promise. In the second night sequence, while Cabiria and her friends discuss a visit to the sanctuary of the Divino Amore, a religious procession crosses the Viale delle Terme di Caracalla. The wet reflection on the street surface as well as the overall atmosphere are quite changed. The jazzy glimmer is now replaced by a concentrated and powerful glow. Since the light source remains invisible, the illumination seems otherworldly, creating a sense of suspension and mystery – a similar effect later repeated during the police raid (see image 8). In both instances, the visual focus of the scene is the glow, but a glow that the slightly tilted camera and an oppressive canopy of leaves seems to want to pin to the ground, giving the impression that the light emanates from the street. This light, that rather than illuminate makes the night seem darker, announces a chthonian dimension of modernity.

Light is the condition of material visibility yet also the materialization of an invisibility, a gesturing to "a hidden counterpart, of which [things] are, so to speak, merely the adumbration" (Bazin 2004, 88). Complementing Bazin, we could add that in Fellini, this hidden counterpart could be at the same time archaic and modern, sacred and profane. In the lights of *Le notti di Cabiria*, the tantalizing reflection of secular modernity coexists with the timeless manifestation of the numinous, a sacrality that outstrips the cheap commerce of institutionalized religion. The "cosmic nocturnal light" (Pasolini 1999, 705) of the Passeggiata Archeologica points to a hybrid metaphysics torn between the modern promise of secular happiness and the religious possibility of grace and redemption. In either case, as Klein's photographs of Broadway suggest, the glimpse of a beyond might turn out to be simply the effect of a reflection. After the dances and the procession are over, Fellini leaves

Image 8. Escaping a police raid in *Le notti di Cabiria*.

us with a light fallen to earth. This illumination will return and attain a truly cosmic dimension towards the end of the film, once again inspired and mediated by Klein's imagery.

Neons

Like photography, modernity is a writing with light, and neon signage is its most literal manifestation. William Klein's photographs insistently feature neon lighting whose omnipresent and compulsive messaging maps the real and dreamlike topography of the city (see, for example, image 10). Likewise, throughout the film, Fellini uses neon logos as signposts of the new intense life brightening up nocturnal Rome. On the other hand, neons are only newer iterations of previous forms of luminous writing like old fashioned bulbs and candles, which advertise the aura of sacred and profane spectacle. Ultimately, Fellini exposes all these lights as cheap and illusory trappings of metaphysical and earthly promises.

Image 9. In front of the Piccadilly club, from *Le notti di Cabiria*.

Neon illuminates Cabiria's night with the movie star Alberto Lazzari. From its first appearance announcing the Kit Kat Club, the neon spells out in words puzzling as a magic incantation a shorthand for all that is modern and exciting. Unlike the Passeggiata Archeologica, the nocturnal world of the privileged is, like the neons, milky and incandescent, from the whiteness of Lazzari's immaculate suit to his lover's fur and the huge convertible.[9] Like Olympians, celestial apparitions of the modern and glamorous, the actor and his lover loom large in the foreground while the dark figure of the doorman and the tiny Cabiria recede in the distance. Yet unexpectedly, upon climbing into Lazzari's car, Cabiria too steps into the world of glamour and light.

At the second night club, the Piccadilly, the neon and its reflection on Lazzari's car offers a minor key version of the Broadway-by-night photographs of Klein (image 9). But it is in two medium close-ups of Lazzari and Cabiria that Fellini more extensively elaborates a recurrent motif of Klein's urban landscape: the overlapping presence of people and neons (see images 10 and 11).

Here the signage advertising modernity is transformed into an electric halo hovering around the heads of Lazzari and Cabiria. In Fellini, modern

Image 10. "Cadillac show-room, 1955" in *Life Is Good and Good for You in New York* (Klein 1956, 41). © William Klein Estate.

Image 11. Lazzari + neon, from *Le notti di Cabiria*.

Image 12. The Lux cinema theatre, from *Le notti di Cabiria*.

glamour and its spectacle (cinema being a part of it) are closely intertwined with religious ritual, the church and the stage equally catering to (or praying on) the same human yearning for a beyond. Fellini's cinema inhabits these human spaces of promise and enchantment while debunking their heartless manipulations and wilful illusions. Lazzari's house, a symphony of smooth, shiny surfaces, transparent glass, and reflecting mirrors, is the arrival point of Cabiria's journey into the realm of light. This is what paradise on earth looks like: a posh, pretentious, and hollow set, where the star rehearses a drunk and hysterical melodrama every night.[10]

Paradoxically, yet fittingly, the closest approximation in the film to Klein's modern Broadway is the phantasmagoria of candles and bulbs illuminating the sanctuary of the Divino Amore. There, Cabiria, neé Maria Ceccarelli, contemplates in her candlelit name the promise, both tawdry and numinous, of redemption. But the miracle does not happen, and after the bitter, disillusioned party on the sanctuary grounds, Cabiria lands in front of the sinister neon light of the Lux cinema theatre. Immersed in a night dark as pitch, this ironic and lusterless "LUX" (Latin for "light") seems to mark the entrance of an infernal den gaping for its victim (image 12). With its illusionist tricks, the variety theatre appears a perfect secular counterpart to the church's histrionics, both

Image 13. Cabiria in front of a bar, from *Le notti di Cabiria*.

of them equally damaging to Cabiria. After the theatre, violated in her soul, Cabiria with Oscar, the devil conjured by the "magic" show, stops at a bar. The place is about to close. A lonely neon "R" hovers in the air (image 13). In this desolate *periferia*, the furthest outpost before modernity succumbs to ex-urban night, Cabiria reaches the end of the night. From now on, what is to come, her cruel love story with Oscar, will unfold under the flat, unforgiving light of day.

The Mysterious Light

Beyond the empty displays of modernity and organized religion, light in Fellini also conveys the appearance of the truly numinous. In its most obvious manifestations, with the charity man and the religious procession, powerful beaming lights, whose source remains hidden, create a metaphysical effect. While these arc lights remain connected to an understood and thus reassuring source of projection, there are other instances, like the glow on the road discussed earlier, when the source of light remains not just hidden but uncertain and untraceable, a sheer

Image 14. The mysterious light on Lake Bracciano, from *Le notti di Cabiria*.

manifestation. This uncanny light, pointing beyond the human story, is the closest the film comes to representing the sacred.

Arriving at the clifftop over Lake Bracciano where Oscar has lured her, Cabiria comments: "Che luce strana …" The light is truly uncanny, but what makes it so strange? The illumination seems to come from different sources: the light of the invisible setting sun descends on Cabiria and Oscar, creating sharp shadows, but the scene is enveloped in a glare of light emanating from the surface of the water enclosed by the dark line of woods (image 14). The sky is darker than the lake, the night has already reached the woods, and the characters are dark silhouettes suspended against a background of earth, water, and an empty sky. With an effect akin to the glowing asphalt in the Passeggiata, but now on a cosmic scale, the light seems to have fallen to earth. This is an upside-down light; more than reflected, it seems trapped under the water like molten lava rising from the deep volcanic hollow containing the lake. An ominous light – what Barthes (1977) would call obtuse – it has no use, does not illuminate, has no meaning, simply is. Cabiria kneels as a sacrificial victim in front of this treacherous glow, the manifestation

Image 15. "Atom Bomb Sky, 1955" in *Life Is Good and Good for You in New York* (Klein 1956, 188–9). © William Klein Estate.

of an indifferent deity who presides over a life barren of meaning and humanity.

This mysterious luminosity finds a precedent in the closing photograph of Klein's *Life Is Good* photobook. A bird's eye view of New York shows a dark sky dominated by a shapeless glow, an apocalyptic light enveloping the capital of modernity (image 15). Is this the luminescence of a sickened sun or the afterglow of a catastrophic explosion? The setting, scale, and positioning of the lights are different, but the same inversion is behind the strange quality of the two images. Is the light descending and spreading on earth or is it rising from the ground? Either way, the glowing dusty light transforms the towering modernity of New York, the site of the promise of a secular beyond, into a shadowy profile of uncertain ruins. Just like Cabiria on Lake Bracciano, the city stands at the world's post-human edge.

Modernity's lights come to an end, for both Klein and Fellini, in an ominous glow; the street-level pyrotechnics pale in front of the intimation of a cosmic showdown. These images of impending material dissolution feature at their centre a figure of extreme human vulnerability:

Cabiria and the city lie prostrate, crushed shadows under the cosmically indifferent light. This luminescence lays bare the betrayal and greed at the heart of alluring promises, be they the seductions of Oscar, the small time crook, or of a modernity blindly driven by capitalist expansion. In both cases, the effect is photographically the same: "All that is solid melts into air" (Marx 1977, 224) – or rather, light.

The Emancipated Actor/Spectator

The human presence ultimately endures: Cabiria survives the terrible light on Lake Bracciano; Klein's teeming humanity – laughing, shouting, performing before the camera – cannot be erased by the closing apocalyptic panorama. The photographing of people is where the dialogue between Fellini and Klein is at its most intense, where the visual grammar of photography endows Fellini's sensual cinematic vision with a heightened energy. Klein's signature close-ups, so near and candid as to blur the images, giving the impression that people are about to jump off the photographic surface, are a crucial influence (for example, image 17). In *Le notti di Cabiria*, this can be detected in the reduced distance between lens and subject that heightens the violent sense of movement (for example, image 16).

Most importantly, the adherence of Klein's camera to its subjects speaks of an innovative entanglement of photographer and world photographed that transforms the image into the site of a collective performance, eventually pulling the spectators into its theatre as well. This appeal to participation colours many cinematographic close-ups. Well before Cabiria's final look into the camera, the spectators are directly summoned by her to moments of thoughtful intimacy; they are challenged by the direct gaze into the camera of an enraged Marisa (image 18); and, most eerily, they are brought face to face with murder through an extreme close up of Oscar (image 19).

But it is in the final frame that the cinematic moves closest to the photographic, producing what Barthes calls "the look," the archaic frontal pose of a subject looking another subject in the eyes.[11] Cabiria's final gaze into the camera (image 20), "the boldest and most powerful shot in the whole of Fellini's work" (Bazin 2004, 91), while exceptional in cinema, is standard fare in photography. However, as noted, Klein pushed this photographic trope to new levels, openly foregrounding the engagement between posed subject and photographer. How does Fellini adapt this photographic trope? As in Klein, "the look" bypasses the impersonality of the camera (the nothing that you are looking through) to posit a direct interrogation. But radical differences also

Image 16. Fight at the Passeggiata Archeologica, from *Le notti di Cabiria*.

Image 17. "Girls laughing, Puerto Rican neighbourhood, 1955" in *Life Is Good and Good for You in New York* (Klein 1956, 108). © William Klein Estate.

Image 18. Close-up of Marisa, from *Le notti di Cabiria*.

Image 19. Close-up of Oscar, from *Le notti di Cabiria*.

Image 20. Cabiria's final shot, from *Le notti di Cabiria*.

separate this effect in Klein and Fellini, pointing to radical divergences in their aesthetics and ethics, their concepts of photography, and their stances towards reality.

Klein shares with Fellini a love for reality, but what that reality is and how the medium expresses this love differ profoundly. For Klein, reality is something that explodes in the photographer's eye. His love for reality (the city and its inhabitants) is a love at first sight, unfolding in a happening that is a shared act of invention and communication. The photographic encounter, at times blunt but always warm, is predicated on freedom, improvisation, and self-expression. If Cartier-Bresson photographed on the sly, Klein cherished the pose because the deliberate self-positioning of the subject in front of the camera becomes the occasion for a life story to unfold.[12] Klein's participatory photography puts into practice Jacques Rancière's "redistribution of the sensible" as a redistribution of power. Klein is an example of "photography as a new scene of equality" (Rancière 2011, 22). Unlike street photography, cinema unfolds in an environment where the artistic practice fosters an absolute control over all aspects of production and of the world represented.

Pasolini links Fellini's seductive autocratic power to an omnivorous vision that sees and appropriates all. Fellini's camera, Pasolini notes, is sensitive and all-embracing ("it photographs even the air"), but the "intensity of passion for the world" makes his eye "brutal and obsessive" (1999, 702). This quality, at once loving and violent, changes according to the object portrayed, giving rise to two distinct stylistic modes. When approaching the "'real' reality" of the peripheries, the landscapes and everyday life, the camera embraces a documentaristic openness; but with the human figure, the lens displays "an aprioristic lyricism in assaulting reality" (703). This affective and formal unevenness creates a metaphysical "unknowability between characters and environment" (705). The reality of Fellini is a mysterious world where any possibility of communicability and knowledge is called into question. Within the context of cinema and Fellini's personal artistic practice – where photography is a technique to master reality, and reality a depository of forms in the service of the film-maker's vision – there is no space for Klein's photographic emancipation of the human actor/spectator. Nonetheless, and perhaps under the prodding of Klein's stylistic lesson if not his ethos, Fellini manages to stage a powerful instance of emancipation in the final parting sequence.

When Cabiria, crushed with sorrow by Oscar's betrayal, emerges from the woods onto the road, she is surrounded by a group of young revellers twirling around her. This walking carousel, where everybody is both performer and spectator, achieves the "blurring of the boundary between those who act and those who look; between individuals and members of the collective body" (Rancière 2011, 19), thus lifting Cabiria into a free community. Further widening this circle, Cabiria gazes directly into the camera, summoning us to join in. As Bazin notes, her look "removes us quite finally from our role of spectators, inviting us to follow on the road" (2004, 92). In Cabiria's sparkling eyes Fellini's Rome meets Bazin's Paris, Klein's New York, and our late modern globe, marking the birth of a global spectator/actor entering a new shared historical and geopolitical moment.[13]

But in 1957, it was not this unique moment of cinematic intersubjectivity that defined Cabiria. Pasolini, and many others in his wake, read Cabiria as a figure of incommunicability, a creature lost in a mysterious world. The cipher of a diffuse metaphysical condition in Fellini is transformed in Pasolini into the allegory of "a moment of our history," mid-1950s Italy, a vague "interregnum," a mysterious "moment of transition" (1999, 706). This figural status erases Cabiria's subjectivity and tames the power of her gaze, thus relieving us from the task of confronting the historicity that binds together character, film-maker, and spectators. As a result, subjectivity and history descend into mystery and incommunicability. What is within Pasolini's "moment of transition"? With hindsight the answer seems direct: a modernization about to explode, the *miracolo economico* that, for Pasolini, will permanently disfigure Italian culture. However, far from being a historical moment limited to provincial, underdeveloped Italy, "transition," synonymous with "development" and "progress," is the very condition of a modernity perennially changing. The throes of its creative destruction, which will soon overtake the Roman peripheries, will, in those same years, on the other side of the globe, transform the downtowns of the great American cities into equally dismal peripheries.[14] Cabiria's eyes inaugurate a silent interrogation that is a mutual recognition: What is awaiting us down that road on which, after so many years, we keep walking? What beckoning to a shared future is contained in the shimmering eyes of Cabiria, the last powerful glimmer of light on which the film closes?

Conclusion: A Future at the Periphery

The youthful improvisation and serendipity of Klein's encounter with Fellini are the hallmark of Klein's evolution as an artist. Stationed in Europe at the end of his military service in 1948, Klein took advantage of the GI Bill[15] to study painting in Paris with Fernand Léger. It was in Italy, however, well before his meeting with Fellini, that Klein as photographer was born. In 1951, he had been invited by avant-garde theatre director, Giorgio Strehler, to exhibit his work in Milan. Spotted by architect Angelo Bangerotti, Klein got his first commission: to recreate one of his abstract paintings on a series of rotating room dividers in a Milanese apartment. It was in the process of documenting these panels in motion that Klein started experimenting with photography, specifically blurred abstract images. His abstract photographs appeared throughout the 1950s as cover illustrations of the prestigious architectural magazine *Domus*, founded by Gio Ponti. The cover of Klein's New York photobook – a cutting-edge embodiment of American modernity – is a reworking of a cover designed for the Italian magazine. This to and fro from the heart of modernity to its outskirts – war-scarred Europe and provincial Italy – maps a complex geography of postwar modernity that is multidirectional, multitemporal, postmodern. A reflection on the role of peripheries in Fellini and Klein highlights these tensions.

Both Klein's 1956 photobook of New York and Fellini's 1957 film dwell on a discrepancy between the look of modernity and its reality. There is a fluid agreement about what a modern look is, but what being modern means remains a matter of uncertainty. Beyond the surface reflections, Fellini's film gives expression to a global stance towards modernity as an ever-receding promise, something akin to what Italo Svevo called "an anxious hope." *Le notti di Cabiria* pitches the nocturnal dreams of modernity against the desolate landscapes of the Roman periphery, seeming proof of Italy's underdevelopment. Nonetheless, is it not exactly this dreary landscape punctuated with lonesome ads and derelict structures coexisting with new buildings that is the true look, the substance in eternal transition, of our current global modernity, both vanguard and refuse of its unstoppable march?

During a day of wandering on 30 September 1967 in the suburbs of Passaic, New Jersey, dotted with construction sites, conceptual artist Robert Smithson took photographic records of an allegorical landscape of modernity: pipes, cranes, and abandoned buildings as "the monuments of dislocated directions," or "ruins in reverse," new constructions that "rise into ruin before they are built" (1996, 72). This periphery in the throes of an ongoing process of dissolution is at one time archaeological and the front lines of modern times. Confronted with this heap of past and future, Smithson muses: "Has Passaic replaced Rome as The Eternal City?" (1996, 74).

The media of modernity are self-critically included in Smithson's critique. Photography and cinema, by constantly projecting new skins on the world, do not simply represent but actively contribute to this "map of infinite disintegration and forgetfulness" (1996, 74) and fall victim to its incessant movement. In Klein's *Rome*, a photograph of Cinecittà bridges Rome and Passaic (image 21). The caption reads: "Excavation of Cinecittà ca. 1958 A.D. Stucco sculptures that have performed in 'War and Peace,' roofless and dispossessed like so many Romans" (1959, 76). Even Cinecittà has been displaced by capitalist modernization. What is left in its wake are the dreams of yesterday, precariously – and yet how oddly caringly – huddled under a shack. Here, as in New Jersey, "the future is lost somewhere in the dumps of the non-historical past ... in the false mirrors of our rejected dreams" (74). Nonetheless, a touch of unlikely and gratuitous care saves the Roman periphery from the ghostly posthuman monumentality of Smithson's Passaic.

To sum up their outlooks on modernity, both Fellini and Smithson place at the heart of their peripheries "monuments" of play and childhood. Smithson's essay closes on a forgotten sandbox within which he imagines a bunch of children running around in circles eternally mixing the same sand. Across from Cabiria's home, a form of "ruin in reverse," Fellini places a scaffolding – whimsical, improbable, temporary, and playfully poetic – on which a group of children are perched like a bunch of modern cherubs (image 22). If the sandbox offers a dreary allegory of

Image 21. "Stucco sculptures that have performed in 'War and Peace,' Cinecittà, ca. 1957" in *Rome: The City and Its People* (Klein 1959, 106–7). © William Klein Estate.

Image 22. Children on scaffolding, from *Le notti di Cabiria*.

Image 23. Cabiria perched between the old and the new, from *Le notti di Cabiria*.

a capital-driven modernity bound to a circular, mindless, destructive, and unrelenting logic, Fellini's scaffolding evokes the appeal and tenuousness of modernity's emancipatory dream. For both artists, modernity is a shaky enterprise, but in Fellini, periphery's monstrous and heartless unfolding is seemingly kept in check by poetry's airy promise and a stubborn "belief in life" (Bazin 2004, 86).

For the children acrobats, as for Cabiria, the squalor of the periphery is inseparable from a promise of emancipation. Like the children on the aerial and improbable scaffolding, Cabiria is precariously and improbably perched between light and shadow, between the old and the new, a defeated figure of emancipation and the vulnerable and resilient face of a redeemed time (see image 23). In 1957, the economic "miracle" will hit backward Italy full blast, luring people forward indefinitely with its promise. In the unmonumental and forever dissolving periphery of modernity, Cabiria stands as a signpost, mysteriously marking the frontier between past and future. Her look, her unstable body, her stubborn belief in life give the lie to the greed, sham appearance, and mindless destructiveness that dominate modernity and its fast dreams. Her presence, like the presence of the vibrant humanity in Klein's images, raises the question of the future and what it should look like: modernity not as a fate but an aspiration.[16]

NOTES

1 Fellini's relation to modernity is usually explored in reference to the visual arts and literature. Photography remains notably absent from these discussions. Analyzing "the exhausted modernist aesthetic" of *La dolce vita*, for example, Alessia Ricciardi (2000, 201–19) references painting, music, and architecture.
2 For an autobiographical overview and critical appraisal of Klein's career, I refer the reader to the excellent two-hour interview with the artist curated by David Campany at the Museum of Arts and Design (MAD) in New York, held in the spring of 2013; see MAD (2013).
3 The commentary on Klein's photographs is separate from the images and collected in an accompanying booklet.
4 David Campany made the first statement in "The Many Lives of William Klein" (Bright 2012, 43:50–43:53); Chris Marker made the second observation (50:00–50:04).
5 See Smargiassi's (2010) review of Klein's first exhibit in Italy, "William Klein Rome Photos – 1956/1960," which ran from 13 April to 25 July 2010 in Rome's Trajan Market. With a similar tone, Smargiassi describes the *Rome* photobook, the focus of the exhibition, as "quell'indigeribile libro-antimonumento" (that indigestible anti-monument book).
6 In the rich literature on cinema's relation to modernity and aesthetic modernism, see De Vincenti (1993); on auteur cinema as modernist, see Jameson (1992); on Hollywood's vernacular modernism, see Hansen (2000); and for the emergence of the category of world cinema, see Andrew (2004). On Fellini's position between modernism and postmodernity, see Burke (1996) and Ricciardi (2000).
7 For a more sustained analysis, see Ricciardi (2000).
8 In 1958, Klein pursued this vision in the short documentary *Broadway by Light* (1958).
9 For a discussion of the 1956 DeSoto Firelite driven by Alberto Lazzari (played by Amedeo Nazzari), see Zambenedetti (2021).
10 See Schoonover (2014) for a discussion of Cabiria's trouble with surfaces.
11 There is wide agreement, following Bazin (2004), that Cabiria's closing gaze is a disruption of film aesthetics. See Brown (2012) for an extensive discussion of Cabiria's returned gaze for cinema.

12 In a comment in *Rome*, Klein writes: "Here the Theory of the Revealing Character of the Posed Photo is demonstrated. Unposed, caught unawares, we would see noses being picked, brows creased in vague internal contemplation, ambiguous, illegible, perhaps meaningless, expressions. Allow, however, the subject to reveal his attitude towards life, towards his neighbour, towards the photographer, and we have, rich in information, a self-portrait" (1959, 10).
13 This event is much more radical than the renegotiation of "the relationship of international spectator to realist spectacle" pointed out by Schoonover (2014, 98). See his analysis of Cabiria's bodily histrionics as a challenge to "the complacent and sequestered spectator."
14 See David Harvey's *The Condition of Postmodernity* on "creative destruction and destructive creation" (1989, 18–19) in capitalist modernity and its economic and aesthetic impact on the urban environment.
15 The United States' Servicemen's Readjustment Act of 1944, also known as the GI Bill, was a law that provided a range of benefits for some of the returning veterans of the Second World War (commonly referred to as GIs).
16 I would like to thank Pierre-Louis Denis, curator at the Studio William Klein, for his generous support.

REFERENCES

Andrew, Dudley. 2004. "An Atlas of World Cinema." *Framework: The Journal of Cinema and Media* 45, no. 2 (Fall): 9–23. www.jstor.org/stable/41552405.

Barthes, Roland. 1977. "The Third Meaning." In *Image, Music Text*, translated by Stephen Heath, 52–68. New York: Fontana Press.

– 1980. *Camera Lucida: Reflections of Photography*. Translated by Richard Howard. New York: Hill and Wang.

Bazin, André. 2004. "Cabiria: The Voyage to the End of Neorealism." In *What is Cinema?*, translated by Hugh Gray, 83–92. Vol. 2. Berkeley: University of California Press.

Bright, Richard, dir. 2012. *Imagine*. Season 20, episode 5, "The Many Lives of William Klein." Aired 12 November 2012, on BBC.

Brown, Tom. 2012. "*Le Notti di Cabiria* (1957)." In *Breaking the Fourth Wall: Direct Address in the Cinema*, 78–115. Edinburgh: Edinburgh University Press.

Brunetta, Gian Piero. 2001. *Storia del cinema italiano: Dal Neorealismo al miracolo economico 1945–1959*. Vol. 3. Rome: Editori Riuniti.

Burke, Frank. 1996. *Fellini's Films: From Postwar to Postmodern*. Woodbridge: Twayne Publishers.

De Vincenti, Giorgio. 1993. *Il concetto di modernità nel cinema*. Parma: Pratiche.

Hansen, Miriam. 2000. "The Mass Production of Senses: Classical Cinema as Vernacular Modernism." In *Reinventing Film Studies*, edited by Christine Gledhill and Linda Williams, 332–50. London: Bloomsbury Academic.

Harvey, David. 1989. *The Condition of Postmodernity: An Enquiry into the Origins of Cultural Change*. Oxford: Basil Blackwell.

Jameson, Fredric. 1992. *Singularities of the Visible*. New York: Routledge.

Kezich, Tullio. 2006. *Federico Fellini: His Life and Work*. Translated by Minna Proctor with Viviana Massa. New York: Faber and Faber.

Klein, William. 1956. *Life Is Good and Good for You in New York. Trance Witness Revels*. Paris: Petite Planète.

– dir. 1958. *Broadway by Light*. France: Argos Films.

– 1959. *Rome: The City and Its People*. New York: Viking Press.

– 2009. *Rome + Klein*. New York: Aperture.

Marx, Karl. 1977. "The Communist Manifesto." In *Karl Marx: Selected Writings*, translated by David McLellan, 221–47. New York: Oxford University Press.

Museum of Arts and Design (MAD). 2013. "In Conversation: William Klein." YouTube video, 1:51. 22 March 2013. www.youtube.com/watch?v=AMkZZkk9zqE.

Pasolini, Pier Paolo. 1999. "Nota su *Le notti*." In *Saggi sulla letteratura e sull'arte*, 699–707. Vol. 1. Milan: Mondadori.

Rancière, Jacques. 2011. *The Emancipated Spectator*. Translated by Gregory Elliott. London: Verso.

Ricciardi, Alessia. 2000. "The Spleen of Rome: Modernism in Fellini's *La dolce vita*." *Modernism/Modernity* 7, no. 2 (April): 201–19. http://doi.org/10.1353/mod.2000.0044.

Schoonover, Karl. 2014. "Histrionic Gestures and Historical Representation: Masina's Cabiria, Bazin's Chaplin and Fellini's Neorealism." *Cinema Journal* 53, no. 2 (Winter): 93–116. https://doi.org/10.1353/cj.2014.0002.

Smargiassi, Michele. 2010. "La dolce vita di William Klein." *La Repubblica*, 10 April 2010. https://roma.repubblica.it/cronaca/2010/04/11/news/la_dolce_vita_di_william_klein-3269234.

Smithson, Robert. 1996. "A Tour of the Monuments of Passaic, New Jersey." In *Robert Smithson: The Collected Writings*, edited by Jack Flam, 68–74. Berkeley: University of California Press.

Zambenedetti, Alberto. 2021. "Conclusion to Part One: Driving the Flâneuse: *Le notti di Cabiria*." In *Acting across Borders: Mobility and Identity in Italian Cinema*, 105–10. Edinburgh: Edinburgh Univeristy Press.

Fellini, Theorist of Culture, 1950–1972

VERONICA PRAVADELLI

Fellini's cinema is grounded in the idea that spectacle, visual entertainments, and popular culture at large are essential to the development of subjectivity. Spectatorship and cultural consumption are formative experiences in the shaping of modern and postmodern identities. For Fellini, each visual medium and cultural form – theatre, circus, advertising, the *fotoromanzo*, cinema, television – engages vision, pleasure, and knowledge in its specific ways. Fellini's discourse on spectacle and culture is developed in particular by interlocking two major scenarios: Italian modernity and contemporary debates on popular and mass culture. In terms of Italian modernization, Fellini's films stress the dichotomy between urban and small town/rural lifestyles. At the same time, his work so consistently addresses the "status" of popular and mass art that Fellini can be considered a protagonist in the contemporaneous debate on culture occurring in both Europe and North America.

The mise-en-scène of spectacle and popular culture goes through several modes from *Luci del varietà* (1950) to *La voce della luna* (1990). Fellini is torn between the desire to keep spectacle as an element of the diegesis, a fact to be represented – most of his films are about artists putting up a show – and the idea that spectacle is not a show separated from reality but a basic feature of reality itself. In other words, in Fellini's work there is a tension between spectacle as performance and reality turned into spectacle. *Roma* (1972) is the apotheosis of this tension: here we not only have spectacles and shows, but Rome itself – even more than in *La dolce vita* (1960) – has become a total spectacle to the extent that the spectacular seems to be the new condition of reality itself.

The duality between spectacle and the spectacular operates on a couple of levels. Fellini manifests a fondness for older popular arts, such as variety theatre and the circus, but he also develops a sophisticated discourse on contemporary mass culture, especially cinema, the *fotoromanzo*, television, and advertising. At the same time, the tension between spectacle and the spectacular involves a discourse on subjectivity and agency, including issues relating to consumption and gender. Overall, Fellini shows that both reality and the subject have no essential or a priori meaning or quality, but that meaning is created through mise-en-scène and performance. He reveals how different arts and cultural forms participate in these processes, elaborating in effect a theoretical project that contributes to contemporary debates on popular art, mass culture, and the renewed status of the image in the age of mass communications. Therefore, I view Fellini as a theorist of culture.[1]

Fellini, Theories of Popular Culture, and *Luci del varietà*

When Fellini started his career as a director, the cultural debate in Italy was still dominated by Benedetto Croce's idealism and aesthetic theory. Since the publication of his *Estetica* (1902), Croce's thought has continued to influence Italian intellectuals, artists, and literati. In particular, his notions of "art as intuition" and "intuition as form," cornerstones of Croce's definition of poetry, loom large in discussions of art and literature. Of course (true) art is the product of human beings with special skills and sentiments whose "intuitional knowledge" cannot be compared to everyday experience or other forms of knowledge (scientific, historical, etc.) (Croce 1990). Popular culture can hardly find a place among Croce's followers.

Though antithetical to Croce's aesthetics, in the late 1940s neorealism also nourished skepticism towards popular and mass culture by promoting "serious" realist art and literature. These tenets would be reinvigorated in the 1950s when Lukács's ideas – especially his notion of realism – would affect Italian Marxist thought as well as film criticism – look no further than the *querelle* on Visconti's *Senso* (1954) (Aitken 2001). Therefore, when Fellini starts his film career, Italy is a rather "inhospitable place" for popular and mass culture. While some of his films betray close relations to realism – *La strada* (1954) and *Il bidone* (1955) *in primis* – I would argue that, in contrast to the other major filmmakers of the time (Rossellini, Visconti, and Antonioni), Fellini's main interest is in telling stories of how cultural consumption affects people in a modernizing Italy. Fellini's interest in popular and mass culture can be seen in the context of an international debate that is emerging on both sides of the Atlantic.

Starting with Max Horkheimer and Theodor Adorno's essay "The Culture Industry: Enlightenment as Mass Deception" (1947), many intellectuals, in both Western Europe and North America, participated in heated debates on the status of popular and mass culture after the Second World War. Critical accounts could be hostile or sympathetic, but overall the most important contributions stressed the necessity to consider the phenomenon seriously. Daniel Horowitz notes that the nature of the debate has ranged "across national borders because writers were simultaneously raising similar questions in different places" (2012, 14). From Roland Barthes's *Mythologies* (1957) to Dwight Macdonald's *Masscult and Midcult* (1960), from Stuart Hall and Paddy Whannel's *The Popular Arts* (1964) to Umberto Eco's *Apocalittici e integrati* (1964) and Marshall McLuhan's *Understanding Media* (1964), thinkers investigated the nature of mass art in relation to other forms of artistic and cultural production. Other scholars engaged specifically with the status of the image and of spectacle: for example, Daniel J. Boorstin's *The Image: A Guide to Pseudo-Events in America* (1962) and Guy Debord's *The Society of the Spectacle* (1967).[2] And key thinker Edgar Morin addressed these and related matters in *The Cinema, or The Imaginary Man* (1956), *The Stars* (1957), and *L'esprit du temps* (1962). This voluminous output reflects issues that shape all of Fellini's cinema.

A recurring trope in Fellini's work is the crisis of popular art forms at the hands of progress, technological and otherwise. Fellini mourns, even more so, the decline of the circus and the variety show at the hands of cinema and television. His work is imbued with a strong Benjaminian dichotomy between live and reproduced art forms. Such a dichotomy is paradoxically enmeshed with the author's biography. The circus and popular theatre – along with cinema – were Fellini's favourite mediums of entertainment as a child. Therefore, their disappearance creates a sense of loss and nostalgia and sadly reminds him of his own aging. Yet, as a film-maker, he contributes to their crisis. As Helen Stoddart argues, "when Fellini mourns the disappearance of the clown ... he must of course acknowledge his own complicity in this, since it is the mass media of cinema and television that have superseded the circus in popularity and dominance" (2002, 59). The cultural relationships between the circus and the cinema can be extended to Fellini's treatment of the decline of *varietà*, which coincided with the rise of cinema (Forgacs and Gundle 2007, 50).

In his first film, *Luci del varietà*, co-directed with Alberto Lattuada, Fellini tackles the decline of the variety show and links this cultural turn to modernity and mass culture. Even though there is no specific reference to other forms of entertainment, one senses that the crisis of the *varietà* is related to the emergence of new forms in the context of a growing urban modernization. For this reason, the film converges with Hall and Whannel's arguments in *The Popular Arts*.

Richard Dyer has argued that the definition of popular culture proposed by Hall and Whannel has a dual nature. It is positioned in "a tradition of engagement with culture grounded in philosophical and literary writings" (2018, viii). The work of F.R. and Q.D. Leavis is crucial and explains Hall and Whannel's interest in proposing value judgements such as "authentic" vs. "meretricious" (x). But the book is also a New Left project, offering "a sense of social urgency about popular culture," the idea that popular culture matters to the underprivileged and that taking it seriously serves "deeply-felt needs" (xii).

Fellini's attitude towards popular culture is not too far from Hall and Whannel's and shares a similar dual nature. Most of his films are about shows and spectacles. One gathers that popular and mass culture are essential to people's lives; they shape people's imaginaries, their desires, fears, and identities. Implicitly or explicitly, Fellini's narratives also foster value judgements on culture, often juxtaposing different art forms. Yet, while Hall and Whannel contrast popular and mass culture in terms of the opposition between authentic and inauthentic and consider mass culture "a corrupt form of the popular" (Horowitz 2012, 264), Fellini doesn't settle the question once and for all. At first sight, he also seems to value popular culture over mass culture, but a closer look reveals that his perspective may vary from film to film: for Fellini, no form or medium has an ontological essence.

The convergence between Hall/Whannel and Fellini on the popular is crucial in relation to the function they assign to the music hall and the variety show, respectively. In Hall and Whannel's account, the music hall is a "transitional form … between earlier 'folk' and later 'popular' art" (1964, 56). The music hall dealt "with a whole range of familiar experiences" and "moral attitudes" shared by audience and artists. At the same time, it was not "the art of a community" but "an art of the performer," and this aspect positions the music hall within the realm of popular rather than folk culture.

The *varietà* is the Italian version of the British music hall. Stefano De Matteis (2008) explains the emergence of *varietà* in relation to modernity; that is, the migration of large sectors of the population to urban areas. As somebody who comes from a small town and moves to the big city, Fellini transforms his experience into a powerful discourse on the transformations of popular culture, media, and entertainment at large. He shows how the new cultural landscape and the growing impact of images in modern and postmodern society make it difficult for premodern forms of entertainment to survive. At the same time, he shows the different temporalities of small town and rural life vis-à-vis the modern metropolis (Simmel 1971).

Even though the class discourse of *Luci del varietà* is not too far from that of neorealism, the film's imagery is reminiscent of Hollywood: in particular, early sound cinema between the end of the 1920s and the early 1930s. Liliana, the young, beautiful, and relatively talented dancer who is able to use Checco and his shabby travelling troupe as stepping stones to joining a big-time revue, recalls Hollywood's focus on young, self-assertive, and sexy women coming to the big city in search of success on Broadway. The metropolis as the locus of women's emancipation is key to understanding both modernity and twentieth-century "new womanhood" (Pravadelli 2015). What changes in *Luci del varietà* is the representation of show business and the story's point of view. The title and opening credits evoke the glamour of the theatre, but the story only stresses the everyday problems and difficulties of the company and its members. The film never sentimentalizes show business, especially in its provincial manifestations. In contrast to Hollywood films about modern New Women, Fellini and Lattuada tell the story from Checco's perspective, not Liliana's. They choose the "losers" rather than the "winners," those left behind by modernity. At the end, in Termini station, Checco's company and Liliana cross paths as they are getting on their respective trains: the former is going to a small town and a poor theatre; Liliana is heading to urban and rich Milan.

While Liliana's story is not the film's main focus, a contemporary viewer cannot help but notice how "modern" she is. Apart from her skill and ambition, she has the physique of a Hollywood heroine: she is skinny, and her legs are thin and soft as opposed to the fleshier legs of the other performers. De Matteis (2008, 83) recalls that speaking of the girls' legs was common in publicity materials and newspapers, and that the opposition between the two physical types bespoke a larger opposition between urban and rural/provincial variety, rich and poor entertainment.

By adopting Checco's perspective, the film seems to maintain a certain distance from modernity and the female character. And yet, there is no real sympathy for the male protagonist nor nostalgia for the past. In other words, while the film does not fully embrace the promises of modernity, it does not mourn the decline of older cultural forms either. What is important is that Fellini will fill up the distance towards modern culture and femininity in his first solo work, *Lo sceicco bianco* (1952).

Lo sceicco bianco, the *fotoromanzo*, and Female Agency

Lo sceicco bianco focuses on the *fotoromanzo*, a fundamental product of Italian mass culture in its nascent phase. Here Fellini remaps the relations among modernity, popular culture, and femininity in a radical way. The film embraces the woman's point of view, that of the young and innocent newlywed Wanda, an avid reader of *fotoromanzi*, who comes to Rome with her husband Ivan for their honeymoon but sneaks off in search of her idol, the "White Sheik" of the eponymous *fotoromanzo*.

Lo sceicco bianco engages with debates on mass culture based on differing emphases on the relations among author, text, and reader or viewer. For detractors of mass culture, the problem was the top-down relation between producers – Horkheimer and Adorno's infamous culture industry – and consumers. While folk culture was "collectively" produced, as it was based on a "direct relationship between performer and audience" (Hall and Whannel 1964, 52–3), mass culture was divorced from consumers' values and lifestyles. The culture industry created "false" desires and expectations in its audience and produced standardization among individuals because culture was "infecting everything with sameness" (Horkheimer and Adorno [1947] 2002, 94). As Dwight MacDonald has stated, "the mass man is a solitary atom, uniform with the millions of other atoms that go to make up 'the lonely crowd,' as David Riesman correctly calls our society. A community, on the contrary, is a group of individuals linked to each other by concrete interests" ([1960] 2011, 8). However, at about the same time, Umberto Eco rejected the most determinist aspects of mass culture theorizations, specifically in relation to consumption. In "Lettura di 'Steve Canyon'" he states: "In what way, we should ask ourselves, does consumption change in relation to class, cultural background, age and sex? In other word, how do the categories of sex, age, class, cultural background endow consumers with a specific code different from others? ... It is clear that, if we frame the argument in this way, the fetish of the 'mass' and of the 'mass-man' – both methodologically useless – start to crumble"[3] (Eco 1964, 164–5).

Fellini's narrative of Wanda's passion for *fotoromanzi* takes the perspective of the female protagonist and constructs, consistent with Eco's position, an implied female viewer in a manner far more progressive than *fotoromanzi*. Visiting the editorial offices of *Incanto blu*, the magazine in which her favourite *fotoromanzo* appears, Wanda, as a consumer, is emphatically revealed. She declares that she reads *fotoromanzi* avidly because where she lives there is nothing else to do. She insists that reading and dreaming are her real life. The magazine is well aware of the importance of consumer agency, and the manager asks Wanda for advice on how to write some dialogue for the issue they are working on. Then, as the crew is leaving the city for a shoot at the beach, Wanda is given the opportunity to go along. This episode is the core of the film: Wanda meets the White Sheik, is seduced (somewhat) by him, and plays a character in the scene being shot. But her dream comes true only for a moment. At the end she will reunite with her husband, presumably to return to her native place and boring life.

Fellini's position vis-à-vis mass culture is striking, as the film's ideology relies on the opposition between religion and *fotoromanzi*. Ivan is a conservative, old-fashioned young man who wants to spend his time with his patriarchal family in Rome visiting monuments and meeting the pope. His exposure to culture is at the opera. He doesn't seem to know what a *fotoromanzo* is and is certainly unaware that his wife reads them. Like the film, the viewer cannot but sympathize with Wanda, who entertains herself with a recent cultural product – and one that disseminates discourses about female desire and agency.

While grounded in references to the world of *fotoromanzi*, the film is consistently more progressive than its "source." Lucia Cardone has argued that the implied female consumer of *Grand Hôtel*, at the time the most widely read *fotoromanzo* in the country, is somebody "to educate and warn with serene severity" (2004, 42–3). The magazine's "explicit ideology ... coincide[s] with the most conservative rules of the Catholic church and Communist morality." Motherhood is the "supreme ideal" and "the couple must be preserved at all costs." The implied reader is allowed a "controlled transgression," but is then happy to go back to conservative normalcy (45).

In contrast to the *fotoromanzi*, *Lo sceicco bianco* appears as a direct critique of bourgeois marriage and of small-town life. In the few moments we see Wanda and Ivan together, we see no sign of affection or eroticism. Their desires are incompatible, they seem strangers to each other, they spend the vast majority of the film separated, and they reunite only at the end and under false pretences, as Wanda unconvincingly pronounces Ivan her sheik. The opposition of religion vs. mass culture, pope vs. sheik, can easily be translated into a dichotomy between past and present, tradition and modernity: husband and wife are doomed to live in two different cultural temporalities.

Fellini's film is an important episode in women's long-term connection with mass culture, a connection that, starting with Nietzsche, has pervaded the discourse on culture and modernity in the West. In a highly influential study, Andreas Huyssen reveals that, during the nineteenth century, "mass culture is somehow associated with woman while real, authentic culture remains the prerogative of men" (1986, 47). The first figure to embody such a relation is Flaubert's Emma Bovary, who loved to read sentimental novels to escape the boredom of provincial life. Germaine Dulac's feminist film *La souriante Mme Beudet* (The smiling

Madame Beudet, 1923) is an iteration of the same link and an implicit precursor of Fellini's film. Like *Lo sceicco bianco*, *La souriante Mme Beudet* ends with the protagonist looking at the camera almost pleading for help while her husband hugs her. Both Madame Beudet and Wanda interlock the (female) spectator's gaze while their spouses are unaware of what is happening. While the diegesis ends with irresolvable contradictions – how can Wanda and Ivan's marriage last, considering how different their values and lifestyles are? – the look inscribes a complicity among women that furthers knowledge and awareness about female agency and desire.

Lo sceicco bianco and *Le notti di Cabiria*: Cinema, Popular Culture, and Illusion

Lo sceicco bianco and *Le notti di Cabiria* (1957) both focus on young women's attraction to popular culture and, more specifically, how female consumers can indulge in fantasies and daydreaming that compensate for everyday frustrations. While the role of cinema is central, Fellini shows that "illusion" is a pervasive feature of popular culture at large.

The illusory power of popular culture and of the image problematizes the "real" as well as the subject's relation to both. Fellini accentuates the problem through a mise-en-scène of looking, showing how human perception has been shaped by "technological reproducibility" to the extent that the dichotomy between reality and image has become tenuous. In both films there is a specific moment where the protagonist has difficulty believing what she sees: Wanda when the White Sheik "magically" appears on a swing hung unrealistically high among the trees, and Cabiria when the movie idol Alberto Lazzari (Amedeo Nazzari) unexpectedly appears on the street in front of her. Both scenes are centred on the protagonists' mesmerized look, and in both the meeting will develop into a short "relationship." If Wanda's illusions are the product of reading *fotoromanzi*, Cabiria constantly falls prey to fantasy and is easily deceived by images and men.

Fellini's narratives of illusion and fantasy are symptomatic of how far he is from neorealism. In different yet complementary ways, Marxist ideas around neorealism and orthodox film theory – especially apparatus theory and the ideological approach of Jean-Louis Baudry – have taught us to renounce cinema's illusory quality and pleasure in favour of "reality" and of conscious, deconstructive, viewing processes. Fellini's take on this issue constitutes an important part of his unconventional attitude towards popular culture.

On the issue of illusion, we can read Fellini in dialogue with Edgar Morin, especially his book *The Cinema, or The Imaginary Man* (1956). Morin has never really entered the pantheon of film theorists, precisely because his position on cinema and popular culture was antithetical to Althusserian Marxist thought, which inspired French and Anglo-American 1970s and 1980s film theory. As Morin recalls, in the early 1960s on more than one occasion he was attacked by French intellectuals for his ideas on popular culture because he did not consider it a "capitalist mystification" or "an instrument of alienation" (quoted in Mortimer 2001, 78). Seeing Hollywood and much auteurist European cinema as both, particularly in their supposed seduction of the viewer through various kinds of cinematic pleasure, a large number of film scholars preferred avant-garde and Brechtian films.

Morin argues that there is a structural link between cinema and illusion: cinema is a modern technology that "effects a kind of resurrection of the archaic vision" ([1956] 2005, 154). The aesthetic experience of the film spectator "is that of a divided consciousness, participating and sceptical at the same time" (155). While visual representations and images are presented as "nonreality," they invade the subject's psyche and become central to his or her process of knowledge-making. For Morin, cinema is an "imaginary spectacle" in which "the illusion of reality is inseparable from the awareness that it is really an illusion, without, however, this awareness killing the feeling of reality" (225). Morin's idea that in cinema there is not only a "distinction" but also a "confusion" and "complementarity" between "real and imaginary," and that illusion has a productive and positive effect on spectators is highly suggestive for a discussion of *Lo sceicco bianco* and *Le notti di Cabiria*.

Both films end with the main character's looking at the camera. As in the meeting with the star, Cabiria's final look is a repetition of Wanda's. Both characters seem to ask the viewer to participate to their quandaries, to give some advice on what to do. Cabiria's look is more empathic, longer, and shot with the camera closer to the protagonist. A citation of Chaplin, as Bazin first suggested, the shot "carries the film on a higher level, making the viewer identify with the heroine" ([1957] 1986, 333). I interpret Cabiria's bright look as a readiness to enter the realm of illusion once again. But her look is also an invitation to follow her, "tearing us apart from our position of spectator" (333). Bazin's conclusion might not be too far from Morin's: Cabiria's look to the camera asks us to participate and identify, but also to become aware of and self-conscious about her trajectory and about the power and danger of illusion. The idea of cinema's double consciousness implies a dichotomy between the character and the viewer's knowledge. The double or divided consciousness Morin speaks about might be weak in Fellini's heroines but is preserved and reinforced for (female) viewers of Fellini. Therefore, his films are based on the same "kind of duality ... at the very core of romances," that is, "the relation between an 'informed' reader and a necessarily innocent heroine" (Modleski 2008, 23).

Wanda and Cabiria become aware of illusion when it is too late. And yet, Fellini's choice to link escapism and popular culture to female consumers is somewhat a "feminist" move: reading and watching popular stories allows Wanda and Cabiria to nourish their imaginations and "to imagine" a transformation. One needs to imagine, to envision a change in order for it to happen. As Fellini shows, the main obstacle to their desires is less modernity and popular culture than the men closest to them. With the exception of Moraldo in *I vitelloni* (1953), male characters in Fellini's 1950s films are all "outside" of modernity: Ivan is an old-fashioned bigot, while Giorgio and Oscar (in *Le notti di Cabiria*), like their counterparts in *La strada* and *Il bidone*, are violent tricksters, members of what Marx and Engels defined Lumpenproletariat, a "parasitical group," "remains of older, obsolete stages of social development" that could have no part in modernity (Bussard 1987, 677). With Marcello Rubini, *La dolce vita* will offer a model of masculinity totally in tune with modernity (and postmodernity).

La dolce vita and *Roma*: The Spectacle of Modern and Postmodern Life

La dolce vita represents a transition from the representation of spectacle and popular culture to reality as mise-en-scène, as spectacle and image. *Roma* will take the spectacle of the real to an unexpected apex. As Fellini shifts his attention from consumers of popular culture to producers or authors (journalists, photographers, intellectuals, and so on), gender dynamics also shift.

La dolce vita may best be defined as what Franco Moretti (1996) has called a "world text," or a modern epic. Moretti takes Hegel's theory of the epic form as his starting point. For Hegel, (traditional) epic was concerned with the manifestation of a totality: in epic, action is "connected with the total world of a nation and epoch" and is "inseparable from individuality: a world that takes form thanks to a hero, and recognizes itself in him" (quoted in Moretti 1996, 11, 12). For Moretti, modern epic is truly different: the hero is passive; he does not act but rather becomes a spectator. His "presence seems always to leave things as they are, in a kind of gigantic spectacle" (1996, 16). Finally, in the modern epic, inertia offers the only opportunity for totality: "in this new scenario, the grand world of the epic no longer takes shape in transformative action, but in imagination, in dream, in magic" (16).

In *La dolce vita* we identify a convergence among the crisis of the hero, his passivity, and the mise-en-scène of Rome as a spectacle. While Marcello wanders in the city streets all day and night, the city of Rome is filmed in its startling beauty. If the Eternal City is a spectacle for Marcello's look, the image is a spectacle for the viewer. In *La dolce vita* everything is on display, and events matter only in so far as the media transform them into something that matters. This thesis is the core of Daniel Boorstin's *The Image*, which anticipated key aspects of the debate on postmodernism. Boorstin argues that newspapers fabricate news. Because our demand for novelties and illusions is almost insatiable, media must "make up for the world's deficiency" ([1962] 1992, 9). Reality is transformed into events, but events are fabricated and thus become pseudo-events. The value of an event "depends on its being photographed and reported in newspapers, magazines, newsreels, on radio, and over television. It is the report that gives the event its force in the minds of potential customers" (10). Starting from Hegelian and Marxist premises, a few years later Guy Debord similarly argued that reality had become "a pseudo-world apart" ([1967] 1983, 1) and that "in societies where modern conditions of production prevail, all of life presents itself as an immense accumulation of spectacles" (2). Moreover, spectacle "is not a supplement to the real world, an additional decoration. It is the heart of the unrealism of the real society" (6). For Debord, reality is a pure phantasmagoria in Marx's sense of the fetishism of commodities.

For Fellini, as for Boorstin and Debord, any aspect of life can become a spectacle, from the most obvious, such as female beauty, to the less evident, such as religion. When Marcello looks at Sylvia bathing in the fountain, the film employs one of the basic codes of classical cinema, the male look at the sexy female body. But the mise-en-scène of Anita Ekberg's beauty is so excessive that it might question the very code upon which it is based. In modern epic, as Moretti would say, the male loses control of space and diegesis. Therefore, even though the film preserves the "classical" paradigm theorized by Mulvey, it is Sylvia who possesses Marcello, and not vice-versa.

While female beauty is an essential component of *La dolce vita*'s discourse on spectacle, such a discourse encompasses every aspect of the social fabric, including religion (Bertetto 2010), as in the opening sequence and in the episode of the fake miracle. If the film has rightly been heralded as a paradigmatic example of modern cinema, its discourse focuses on a key aspect of postmodern culture and aesthetics: the supremacy of image over reality.

As a sort of follow-up to *La dolce vita*, *Roma* offers an intense radicalization of Fellini's postmodern aesthetics. The film is structured like an endless mise-en-abyme, so to speak, of spectacle itself. *Roma* is driven by dissemination and by the deferral of meaning. One might speculate that such a structure perfectly fits the film's argument: while not an orthodox essay film, *Roma* does indeed have a thesis. The Eternal City is offered to the viewer's eye in any space and time as an ongoing spectacle. Most episodes, if not all, are structured around the gaze and, more specifically, point-of-view shots of spectators looking at shows: the religious fashion show, the variety show, and the two visits at the brothel are all grounded on desire, voyeurism, and visual pleasure. Similarly, Fellini transforms into spectacles specific locations, such as the subway under construction and the Grande Raccordo Anulare, by using travelling shots. Of course, every episode can be interpreted, but the film's structure is driven by the principle of addition typical of experimental (for example, structural) cinema rather than cause and effect. The experience Fellini creates for the spectator is akin to his own. The director's presence in front of the camera adds a biographical level also centring on spectacle: Fellini has shaped his ideas of Rome by looking at shows and pictures about the Eternal City since he was a child in Rimini. For him, Rome is not a set of concepts but a catalogue of images.

The ending of *Roma* appears as a logical outcome. Fellini follows a group of bikers coursing noisily through the city's historical centre at night. The image defies meaning as it registers pure movement and pure noise. Fellini seems fascinated and shocked at the same time by such a spectacular nonsense. It is a provocative instance of what Jean-François Lyotard at the time defined as "acinema." In "Acinema," Lyotard ([1973] 1989) praises experimental (and postmodern) cinema for breaking the rules of representation in relation to movement, narrative, and film music. Representation implies a "selection" of bodies in motion, actions and sounds, and the "exclusion of others." By contrast, experimental cinema "accept[s] what is fortuitous, dirty, confused, unsteady, unclear." Any movement or image is "given to the eye-ear of the spectator for what it is: a simple *sterile difference* in an audiovisual field" (169–70). Cinema must be like fireworks, an art of pyrotechnics "leading nowhere," to "what the physicist calls the dissipation of energy" (171). With *Roma*, Fellini takes the discourse on the postmodern to a new level and reasserts, once again, his role as theorist of culture.

NOTES

1 About the connections between Fellini's films and popular culture, see the chapters by Ottavio Cirio Zanetti, Manuela Gieri, and Eleonora Lima in this volume.
2 In their respective chapters in this volume, Eleonora Sartoni and Giovanna Caterina Lisena also comment on the relationship between Fellini and the society of spectacle theorized by Debord.
3 "In che modo, chiediamoci ora, le varie fruizioni variano a seconda della classe, della categoria intellettuale, dell'età e del sesso del fruitore? In che modo cioè appartenenza a una classe, a una categoria intellettuale, a un tipo psicologico, a un'età e a un sesso forniscono al fruitore un codice di lettura che si distingue dagli altri? ... È chiaro che, una volta impostato il problema in questo senso, si frantuma il feticcio della 'massa' e dell'"uomo-massa,' che risultano entrambi metodologicamente paralizzanti."

REFERENCES

Aitken, Ian. 2001. *European Film Theory and Cinema: A Critical Introduction*. Bloomington: Indiana University Press.
Bazin, André. (1957) 1986. "*Le notti di Cabiria* o il viaggio al termine del neorealismo." In *Che cosa è il cinema?*, edited by Adriano Aprà, 325–33. Milan: Garzanti.
Bertetto, Paolo. 2010. "*La dolce vita*: Microfilosofia della spettacolarità." In *Le dieu caché? Lectura christiana des italienischen und französischen Nachkriegskinos*, edited by Uta Felten and Stephan Leopold, 143–50. Tübingen: Stauffenburg Verlag.
Boorstin, Daniel. (1962) 1992. *The Image: A Guide to Pseudo-Events in America*. New York: Vintage Books.
Bussard, Robert L. 1987. "The 'Dangerous Class' of Marx and Engels: The Rise of the Idea of the Lumpenproletariat." *History of European Ideas* 8, no. 6: 675–92. https://doi.org/10.1016/0191-6599(87)90164-1.
Cardone, Lucia. 2004. *Con lo schermo nel cuore: Grand Hôtel e il cinema (1946–1956)*. Pisa: Edizioni ETS.
Croce, Benedetto. (1902) 1990. *Essays on Literature and Literary Criticism*. Annotated and translated by M.E. Moss. Albany: State University of New York Press.
Debord, Guy. (1967) 1983. *The Society of the Spectacle*. Detroit: Black & Red.
De Matteis, Stefano. 2008. *Il teatro delle varietà. Lo spettacolo popolare in Italia dal café chantant a Totò*. Rome: La casa Usher.
Dyer, Richard. 2018. "Introduction to 2018 edition." In *The Popular Arts*, by Stuart Hall and Paddy Whannel, vii–xxvi. Durham, NC: Duke University Press.

Eco, Umberto. 1964. "Lettura di 'Steve Canyon.'" In *Apocalittici e integrati*, 131–83. Milan: Bompiani.
Forgacs, David, and Stephen Gundle. 2007. *Mass Culture and Italian Society from Fascism to the Cold War*. Bloomington: Indiana University Press.
Hall, Stuart, and Paddy Whannel. 1964. *The Popular Arts*. London: Hutchinson Educational.
Horkheimer, Max, and Theodore W. Adorno. (1947) 2002. "The Culture Industry: Enlightenment as Mass Deception." In *The Dialectic of Enlightenment*, 94–136. Edited by Gunzelin Schmid Noerr. Translated by Edmund Jephcott. Stanford: Stanford University Press.
Horowitz, Daniel. 2012. *Consuming Pleasures: Intellectuals and Popular Culture in the Postwar World*. Philadelphia: University of Pennsylvania Press.
Huyssen, Andreas. 1986. *After the Great Divide: Modernism, Mass Culture, Postmodernism*. Bloomington: Indiana University Press.
Lyotard, Jean-François. (1973) 1989. "Acinema." In *The Lyotard Reader*, edited by Andrew Benjamin, 169–80. Oxford: Basil Blackwell.
MacDonald, Dwight. (1960) 2011. "Masscult and Midcult." In *Masscult and Midcult: Essays against the American Grain*, edited by Joan Summers, 3–71. New York: New York Review of Books.
Modleski, Tania. 2008. *Loving with a Vengeance: Mass-Produced Fantasies for Women*. 2nd ed. New York: Routledge.
Moretti, Franco. 1996. *Modern Epic: The World System from Goethe to Garcia Marquez*. London: Verso.
Morin, Edgar. (1956) 2005. *The Cinema, or The Imaginary Man*. Minneapolis: University of Minnesota Press.
Mortimer, Lorraine. 2001. "We Are the Dance: Cinema, Death and the Imaginary in the Thought of Edgar Morin." *Thesis Eleven* 64, no. 1 (February): 77–95. http://doi.org/10.1177/0725513601064000006.
Pravadelli, Veronica. 2015. *Classic Hollywood: Lifestyles and Film Styles of American Cinema, 1930–1960*. Translated by Michael Theodore Meadows. Urbana: University of Illinois Press.
Simmel, Georg. 1971. "The Metropolis and Mental Life." In *Georg Simmel on Individuality and Social Forms*, edited by Donald Levine, 324-39. Chicago: University of Chicago Press.
Stoddart, Helen. 2002. "Subtle Wasted Traces: Fellini and the Circus." In *Federico Fellini: Contemporary Perspectives*, edited by Frank Burke and Marguerite R. Waller, 47–64. Toronto: University of Toronto Press.

Oenothea's Gaze:
Donyale Luna in *Fellini Satyricon*

SHELLEEN GREENE

In the Fellinian oeuvre, model and actor Donyale Luna (1945–79) may seem like a footnote, having appeared most famously in *Fellini Satyricon* (1969) as the earth goddess Oenothea. A raucous, visionary adaptation of Petronius's *Satyricon* (first century CE), *Fellini Satyricon* captures the spirit of the late 1960s youth generation and countercultural moment through the escapades of the student Encolpio (Martin Potter) and his friend Ascilto (Hiram Keller). Luna's Oenothea appears relatively late in the film. After a near-death encounter with a Minotaur, Encolpio loses his sexual potency, and he and Ascilto visit Oenothea in the hopes of regaining his virility. At first, Encolpio envisions the beautiful Oenothea, portrayed by Luna, who then transforms first into a decaying corpse, then into an aged, full-figured woman with whom he copulates (Greene 2020b, 339–40). While her part in the film is brief, Luna's striking appearance – appearing in a long, flowing black sheath gown accentuated with gold-plated jewellery designed by legendary art director Danilo Donati – has become one of the most iconic images of the film.

Fellini Satyricon has been hailed as "Fellini's most experimental film" (Sisto 2020, 252), a work influenced by the radical politics and counterculture of the 1960s, the space age, pop art, Fellini's encounters with Jungian psychoanalysis, and experimentation with psychedelics (Villa 2020, 485). Indeed, *Fellini Satyricon*'s emphasis on the incomplete and fragmentary status of Petronius's text creates a series of beguiling, oneiric passages through ancient Rome animated by the tumultuous political and cultural present. In order to capture the era's zeitgeist, Fellini often drew upon the artistic and celebrity circles in which he moved, casting performers among his friends, non-professional actors, and models, such as Luna. However, Luna's performance speaks to the wider presence of Black women within Italian print, film, and televisual culture during the 1960s and 1970s – a presence that not only registers its position within a rapidly transforming global media environment but also the country's colonial legacies (Caponetto 2012). Fellini's oeuvre is seldom read in relation to questions of racial discourse and postcoloniality,[1] and Luna's presence in *Fellini Satyricon* offers an opportunity to place Fellini within the period's broader political and cultural currents, including the civil rights movement and decolonization.

By expanding the analytic frameworks for Fellini's films, I am not suggesting a progressive political stance on the part of the auteur. Indeed, Fellini's films offer manifold instances of racial stereotypes in the form of blackface performance, orientalism, and the fetishization of non-white bodies (O'Healy 2009). In addition, while several of the non-white artists who appear in Fellini's films are credited for their work, including actor John Kitzmiller, singer Gloria Jones, choreographer Archie Jones, and model Hylette Adolphe, non-white actors were not always credited (Greene 2020b, 333). Luna falls within a liminal position, widely known as an international fashion model – the first Black supermodel – but also a "non-professional" actor who was often cast as herself and only had a few minor acting credits prior to her appearance in *Fellini Satyricon*.[2] Luna was often cast because of her physical appearance, her exceptional personality, and her status as a model. However, Luna was also exoticized in her print and film appearances, and this is evident in *Fellini Satyricon* and its paratexts.

In this chapter, I draw upon an alternate archive by which to interpret *Fellini Satyricon* following the career trajectory of Donyale Luna from the US civil rights era, to Swinging London, to Italian experimental film of the 1970s. By tracing the "minor" performer's journey through the various global centres of avant-garde art and culture during the 1960s and 1970s, this chapter attempts a retrieval of Luna's insurgent, radical presence, her art of being – one that in its transnational impulse and self-(re)invention proposes an emergent postmodernism that both reorientates and moves beyond the Fellinian imaginary.

I.

Prior to her appearance in *Fellini Satyricon*, Luna was already an icon of the period. Born Peggy Ann Freeman in Detroit, Michigan, in 1945, Freeman changed her name to Luna while a teenager, then involved with the city's traditional and experimental theatre scene, including the Concept East Theater, a Black theatre company (Powell 2008, 88). Throughout her career, Luna was an agent of her own myth-making, describing herself as alien, modifying her accent, and creating her own origin stories. In one 1967 feature, Luna – her full name printed as Peggy Donyale Zazea Dogonea Freeman Luna – stated: "Most people call me Luna. I'm from the southside of the moon. I've had two births, but I only recognized the second, which happened about four years ago, when I was 16, in Detroit" (quoted in Agel 1967, 64). Her striking appearance – she stood at five foot ten – led to various descriptions such as "Gauginesque to Egyptian," "faunlike" and "gamine" (*Time* 1966). Surrealist Salvador Dalí, for whom Luna became a muse, called her the "reincarnation of Nefertiti" (Bowman 2015, 302), and she was described by British *Vogue* editor Beatrix Miller as "all sort of angular and immensely tall and strange" (quoted in *Time* 1966).

At eighteen, she was discovered by photographer David McCabe and soon moved to New York City (Brown 2019, 242).[3] Luna's daughter, Dream Cazzaniga, notes that her mother's entrance into modelling occurred at a period of momentous political change in the United States, notably the passage of the Civil Rights Act of 1964 (Cazzaniga 2019). As fashion scholar Janice Cheddle argues, "within any analysis of the history of black models within the Anglo-American fashion industry and fashion image it is necessary to examine the intertextual relationship between *race, fashion and social protest*" (Cheedle 2002, 62). While Luna did not align herself with political activism or a racial politics (she identified as being of mixed heritage, including African American, South American, and European descent), in this context, Luna was a groundbreaking model, gracing the pages of *Harper's Bazaar* – first illustrated for the January 1965 cover, then in an April feature spread – through her collaboration with legendary fashion photographer Richard Avedon, garnering a dedicated *Time* magazine fashion feature called "The Luna Year." Luna also became the first Black model to appear on the cover of British *Vogue* in 1966, photographed by David Bailey, and she even had a mannequin designed in her likeness by Adel Rootstein (Brown 2019, 257). Luna's accomplishments in international fashion led the way for later Black supermodels such as Naomi Sims, Beverly Johnson, Grace Jones, Iman, and Naomi Campbell.

Luna's 1965 collaboration with Avedon was timely. Avedon was already advocating for greater diversity in the fashion industry, attempting to connect the insular community with the burgeoning civil rights movement through fundraising activity (Brown 2019, 243–4). Avedon's efforts eventually led to a collaboration with his friend and high school classmate, writer and activist James Baldwin, which resulted in *Nothing Personal* (1963), a photographic and literary examination of the complexities of humanity's struggle with race and racism in the United States and globally. The volume contains Avedon's searing photographs of human and civil rights activists Malcolm X and Julian Bond, as well as William Casby, at the time one of the last living Americans born in slavery (see Baldwin 2021). For his 1965 *Harper's Bazaar* spread, Avedon collaborated with then fashion director China Machado, another groundbreaking model of Chinese and Portuguese descent who was also photographed by Avedon and became the first non-white model to appear in *Harper's Bazaar* (Friedman 2016). It was Machado, McCabe, and *Bazaar* editor-in-chief Nancy White who introduced Avedon to Luna and laid the ground for what would eventually be Luna's breakthrough assignment. As Elspeth Brown states, "Avedon's work with Luna at *Harper's* emerged on the heels of Avedon's engagement with the civil rights movement and his increasing impatience with the fashion industry's racism" (2019, 243–4).

The *Bazaar* issue was controversial, with several Southern states boycotting the magazine due to the appearance of a Black model, resulting in a loss of advertising revenue for the company. After the issue, Avedon ended his relationship with the magazine, later stating that he left "for reasons of racial prejudice and the economics of the fashion business" (quoted in Gefter 2017).[4] Luna, meanwhile, due to the discrimination she faced in the US fashion world as a Black model, moved to London, entering the cultural arena known as the Swinging Sixties. As with many other African American artist-expatriates, moving to Europe allowed Luna new career possibilities and creative expression.

II.

While still in New York, Luna's bold, expansive character and unique physicality led her into the celebrity and avant-garde art circles of the time, including those of Sammy Davis Jr., Miles Davis, and Andy Warhol. Luna may have joined Warhol's circle due to her connection to McCabe, who between 1964 and 1965 became Warhol's exclusive photographer, documenting the artist's creative practice and life at the Factory.[5] Nevertheless, Luna soon became one of Warhol's "superstars," featured in Warhol's *Camp* (1965) and starring in a thirty-three-minute short segment from the twenty-five-hour-long *Four Stars* called *Donyale Luna* (1967), perhaps ironically also known as *Snow White*. Her *Snow White* performance conveys a personality and effervescence; she takes on a British accent and humorously, sometimes forcefully, confronts the white male models who serve as her "dwarfs."[6]

Luna also appeared in two of Warhol's *Screen Tests* from 1966. In one, Luna is filmed in close-up on a white studio backdrop. She is dressed in a striped shirt with her hair pulled into a crowing bun to place greater emphasis on her angular face and dramatic eyes. Unlike many of Warhol's *Screen Tests*, Luna does not hold still for the camera but rather addresses the camera as though looking in a mirror, frequently using her hands to frame her face and draw attention to her eyes. In one moment, she playfully winks or makes a funny face; in another, she looks at her manicured nails as though bored, only to catch herself again, as she turns her head, poses, and the film fades. In her other screen test, Luna emerges on screen in a long shot that reveals the length of her body occupying the studio with its white screen and single key light. Luna poses in a dress shirt and skirt, then sits in preparation for a close-up. Moving through a series of gestures, Luna directs her attention off screen, perhaps speaking to someone outside the frame, stands again and poses, performs short dance movements, then seats herself as the film runs its course.

Prior to Luna's appearance in *Fellini Satyricon*, another future Warhol superstar, Nico (Christa Päffgen), played herself (then a fashion model) in *La dolce vita* (1960), performing as one of the eclectic nomads Marcello encounters on the streets of Rome. While there is little scholarship on Fellini's engagement with Andy Warhol and his experimental cinema, there exists between the two an interest in celebrity and the moving image, and models such as Nico and Luna moved among and bridged the arenas of celebrity, fashion, the avant-garde, and auteur cinema.[7]

The *Screen Tests*, Warhol's series of over 500 black-and-white silent film portraits shot on a Bolex 16mm camera between 1964 and 1966, reference the Hollywood screen test in which an actor is gauged for their suitability for a role, both in terms of performance and their screen appeal or "magnetism." As Gary Needham argues, Warhol's *Screen Tests* and other filmic work convey "certain tendencies and obsessions … around portraiture, the technological agency of the recording apparatus, experiments in duration and temporality, and the fascination with 'superstars,' their performances, personalities and the abstract quality of possessing 'screen presence'" (2016, 128). Warhol's *Screen Tests* are not preparation for an eventual film but rather appropriate the form to interrogate the production of stardom. As Brigitte Weingart argues, "what is actually tested here – as a pre-condition for 'screen magnetism' – is not just the capacity to turn oneself into a living picture; rather, it is the capacity to bear the gaze of the camera, eye to eye, without any distraction, let alone an escape into a pre-scripted role" (2010, 50).

Luna, as fashion model, brings to the *Screen Tests* her familiarity with the camera's gaze from her work in still photography, and as Weingart further argues, "it is no wonder that both professional models, such as Holzer and Donyale Luna, and Factory 'superstars' such as Edie Sedgwick clearly quote the mimetic and gestural repertoire of Hollywood – or, are generally, 'old school' – glamour" (55). As mentioned, Fellini was known for casting not only non-professional performers for their unusual appearances, but also fashion models, including Anita Ekberg and Nico in *La dolce vita*, and Capucine (Germaine Hélène Irène Lefebvre) in *Fellini Satyricon*. These models-turned-actors aided in the promotion of Fellini's films, not only allowing him to merge the fashion and film industries but also to capitalize on the model's "star" personality and appeal. As fashion critic Gianluca Lo Vetro states,

> When he used real models in his films, he chose not the beautiful ones, but the particular ones, such as Capucine (as Trimalchio's wife), Donyale Luna (*Fellini – Satyricon*) and Nico (*La dolce vita*). Their physical distinctiveness, together with their peculiar personalities, immediately dispels the stereotypical idea of cover-model models virtually opposed to the system to which they belong. In this way, Fellini shows that he knows how to exploit the power of fashion, sensing the need for new standards capable of capsizing the conventional perceptions. (quoted in Burke, Waller, and Gubareva 2020, 157)

Lo Vetro's comment directs us to the potential of the non-conventional model-performer to intervene and challenge "conventional perceptions." I suggest that Luna's appearance (as well as other Black model-performers) offers such a provocation by both activating and contesting colonial visual regimes during a period of heightened global media production and distribution.

III.

If we read Luna's performance in *Fellini Satyricon* by way of her collaboration with Warhol, her sequence emerges as an interrogation of perception, its seductive and deceptive qualities, and its powers of revenge. Indeed, the narrative (which does not appear in Petronius's original text) concerns a sorcerer who falls in love with the young Oenothea. She does not return his favour; rather, she mocks his affections, and for this she is punished by being forced to issue fire from her genitals. In the opening frames of the episode, we see Oenothea in a long shot, walking across a field with attendants. The camera then moves to a close-up of Oenothea in which she glances at the sorcerer, laughs, turns away from the camera, then turns back to the camera in semi-profile. Luna's performance becomes a series of beguiling poses, smiles, and glances.

When Encolpio arrives at Oenothea's enclosure, the camera zooms in on Oenothea, who appears seated, smiling behind a raging fire. Encolpio at first sees the young Oenothea, but soon this vision is transformed into a decaying corpse. Upon closing and reopening his eyes, Encolpio once again sees the young Oenothea. As Ascilto is murdered, Encolpio has his final vision of the full-figured earth goddess.

Luna's performance requires a kind of stasis as she is posed, and for the most part silent, in her role as the goddess. As in her fashion photography, Luna hovers somewhere between agency and objectification, at once reified and insurgent. Fellini not only draws upon Luna's fashion modelling but also captures the self-reflexivity of the *Screen Tests*, in the sense that *Fellini Satyricon* is a revisionist adaptation that is also a "highly self-conscious examination of cinematic and narrative technique" (Burke 2020, 1). As Warhol produces screen tests for a film never to be made, Fellini engages linear narrative subversion and the fragment, or "the missing parts; that is, the blanks between one episode and the next" (Fellini, quoted in Burke 2020, 155). While I do not argue for a direct correspondence between Warhol's and Fellini's projects, I suggest a parallel in their postmodernist orientations to rupture grand narratives through self-reflexivity, intertextuality, and estrangement.

The world of fashion and its ties to beauty, celebrity, and a consumer culture that generates desire by way of illusion seem a fitting reference for *Fellini Satyricon* as Encolpio, after his drug-induced vision and encounter with the earth goddess, leaves Ascilto to die and gains little to no insight into his own journey. As Frank Burke argues, Encolpio's passage may be read as anti-heroic, in the sense that "the realm of imaginative or heightened experience, so affirmative in earlier Fellini films, leads not just to a cure but to a fatal disconnection" (2020, 157). *Fellini Satyricon* ends with the death of the "old world," signalled by the poet Eumolpus's cannibalization by his would-be heirs, replaced by a youth generation, led by Encolpio, which is bound for North Africa. While it is tempting to suggest further connections between Warhol and Fellini, particularly in terms of their engagement with the psychedelic experience through the creation of expansive audio-visual environments, such as Warhol's synaesthetic *Exploding Plastic Inevitable* (1966–7) and *Fellini Satyricon*'s "pan-sonorous and estranging ethnocacophony" (Sisto 2020, 252), I return to Luna's Oenothea, who directs us towards another node of the postmodern.

Beginning in the 1960s, Fellini's productions are often characterized by a nascent postmodernism. Through an analysis of Fellini's films, such as *Fellini Satyricon*, *Toby Dammit*, and the never realized *Il viaggio di G. Mastorna*, Burke argues that Fellini begins to register the postmodern "'death-of-the-subject' – the demise of the kind of self-determining individual or center of consciousness" prompted by political, social, cultural, and personal crises of the late 1960s (2020, 11). Further, Burke notes that "as the 1970s progressed, postmodernism became part of the cultural atmosphere in which Fellini lived and worked" (12). Along with challenging the modernist distinction between high and low cultures, universalist claims, and notions of progress, postmodernism also ushered in a new awareness of difference, notably in terms of ethnicity, race, gender, sexuality, and class. Along with the "disillusionment with individual autonomy," a particular form of difference is also registered in Fellini's work from the 1960s onward, influenced by the growth of consumer society, globalized media in the form of television, satellite, and cable, as well as new patterns of global migration (Burke 2020, 11). However, as theorists Stuart Hall, Gayatri Spivak, Paul Gilroy, Cornell West, and others note, theories of the postmodern ushered in a critique of the coherent subject and the so-called death of the author at the moment when marginalized groups begin to assert resistance and agency in the form of postcolonial and critical theories of race, gender, and sexuality. Furthermore, within the postmodern era, complex identity formation is often subsumed under a commodity multiculturalism, producing cultural difference for circulation within a global market.

As a Black fashion model working transnationally and bridging print and electronic media, Luna's performance in *Fellini Satyricon* signals this shifting global media environment of the late 1960s and 1970s. Luna, along with other African-descent artists, including Lola Falana, Beryl Cunningham, and Zeudi Araya, entered the Italian media landscape, indexing not only the decline of the Italian film industry in the early 1970s and the growing influence of television, but also an emergent Italian postcolonial condition (Greene 2020a, 168). As Áine O'Healy argues, "In the history of Italian colonialism ... the representation of the black female body did not adhere to an entirely stable or uniform pattern, but vacillated between images of exotic beauty and those evoking abjection or repulsion" (2009, 177). O'Healy further contends that "the occasional, fleeting appearances of black women in prominent Italian art films of the post-war and Cold War era have also left a decisive trace in the Italian imaginary" (178). In several Italian films of the period, this re-emergence of Italian colonial legacies becomes exemplified in the trope of the "Black Venus" (see Caponetto 2012; Harris 2019; Greene 2020a).

As Rosetta Giuliani Caponetto has argued, the figure of Eritrean-Italian actor Araya in Luigi Scattini's *filone esotico erotico* (exotic erotic subgenre) "exhumes" the colonial stereotype of the Black Venus, the "figure deeply rooted in the Italian imagery since the nineteenth century, whose exotic sexuality has been historically portrayed alongside a sense of danger" (2012, 191). And as Sandra Ponzanezi writes, the persistence of the Black Venus trope can be seen in its use in Italian advertising campaigns, thereby implicating the trope in the commoditization and global consumption of "difference" (2005, 181). Produced within this complex milieu, Fellini's films disclose an ambivalent and problematic relation to racial, ethnic, and gendered difference that speaks to the broader debates within postmodernism and postcolonialism.

In his chapter in this volume, Andrea Minuz discusses Luna's performance in *Fellini Satyricon*, suggesting as much in his reading of the controversies surrounding the poster design for Fellini's *Roma* (1972). The poster reimagines the sculpture *Lupa Capitolina* (Capitoline Wolf), the she-wolf who nurses Romulus and Remus, the founding brothers of Rome. In the design, the she-wolf is replaced by a non-white woman, posed on her hands and knees, with three breasts, an image inspired by Donyale Luna. The image was condemned for its exploitative nature, but Minuz argues that through the racial ambiguity surrounding this image, we can excavate other traces and meanings; to paraphrase, he argues that the *Roma* poster is in keeping with the film's contamination of styles, imaginaries, and ethnicities, with its special blend of Roman science fiction. Of course, the *Lupa Capitolina* was also closely associated with the Italian fascist regime, as Benito Mussolini copied and disseminated the sculpture to various countries, often with the purpose of solidifying nationalist sentiment among the Italian diaspora. The images of the *Lupa Capitolina* and Donyale Luna, travelling through time and space, conflate within the profane *Roma* poster image, gesturing towards an Italian (post)colonial libidinal economy, within and against which, I suggest, Luna operates through her experimental impulse.

IV.

Luna was subject to racial fetishization in both her modelling and film careers, and she is both within and without the history of Italian colonialism and its exploitation of Black femininity. After *Fellini Satyricon*, Luna starred in Carmelo Bene's *Salomè* (1972), a "psychedelic" adaptation of Oscar Wilde's 1891 play. Luna plays the titular role, the daughter of King Herod, who after failing to seduce John the Baptist performs a dance for her father in exchange for the prophet's head. While *Salomè* exhibits some of the exploitative elements found in the "soft pornography" period films produced in Italy at this time, such as Piero Vivarelli's *Black Decameron* (1972), Bene was also a major figure in the Italian avant-garde and brought his experimentation in theatre to the screen, making "baroque use of zooms, dollies, cranes, elaborate pans and exaggerated camera angles" (Pendleton 2012; see also Le Cain 2002). With a bald head, Luna appears otherworldly throughout the film, more alien than simply seductress.

Although Luna played a leading role in the film, *Salomè* is rarely mentioned as part of her screen performances, particularly as an example – through her collaboration with Fellini and Bene – of her continued engagement with experimental film and the avant-garde in the Italian context. As art historian Richard Powell suggests, Luna's enigma is partially due to her liminal relationship to the fashion industry and her avant-garde projects. He argues:

> Luna herself is implicated in the near disappearance of her facsimile, in part because of her unconventional relationship to modeling, her decision to perform in experimental theater and film projects, and finally, her reluctance to participate in the race-centered image discourses that emerged in the late 1960s. Yet it is precisely this obscure and inaccessible aspect of Donyale Luna – the opposition to conventional art forms, the embrace of an unorthodox black identity, her uncustomary rapport with image makers – that I find fascinating. (2008, 87)

It is also during this period that Luna begins to settle in Italy. In her Italian press coverage from the late 1960s to 1970s, Luna is mostly featured in her role as Oenothea in *Fellini Satyricon*, but also as a celebrity fashion model, photographed dancing at Roman nightclubs and on the streets of Trastevere. In a *La Stampa* article from 1969, Gigi Ghirotti writes of Luna:

> The languid stride, a gaze struck with a violet-blue light, a black queen advances along the street. Extremely tall, skin and bones enveloped in a faded military tunic and a pair of dirty velvet socks. From what planet has Donyale Luna descended, the sorceress Enotea from Fellini's *Satyricon*? "From the moon," she responds raising a very long, thin finger to the sky. (1969, 3)

While Luna made a strong impression on Italian society, she was also subject to some controversy. In 1973, she was nearly deported from the country under an archaic fascist statute that rendered her "undesirable" for unexplained reasons (Madeo 1973, 7). At the time, the 1931 statute was invoked to expel "foreigners" and those deemed politically "dangerous." While Luna's racial identity is not mentioned in the article, her expulsion order is referred to as "incomprehensible" and a "sensational and disturbing ... abuse of power" (Madeo 1973, 7). Luna was eventually allowed to stay and work in the country, and she later married and had a daughter with photographer Luigi Cazzaniga.

Luna's life came to an end in Rome, in May 1979, after she suffered an accidental overdose at the age of thirty-three. During my research, I visited the Biblioteca Luigi Chiarini to find additional information on Luna and her work on *Fellini Satyricon*. After some searching, I found a file devoted to her tucked away in a larger binder containing news clippings for the film. Luna's pathbreaking career as a model and actor, including her signature film role in *Fellini Satyricon*, seemed muted by the details of her untimely passing. Considering Luna's legacy, Powell writes: "Despite Luna's wide exposure in the late 1960s and early 1970s, projects like her Rootstein mannequin and fire-begetting role in *Fellini Satyricon* simultaneously weakened that eye-catching display to something delusory or inextricably bound by someone else's designs" (2008, 122). Drawing upon the work of visual theorist Michelle Wallace, Powell argues further that Luna becomes subject to a "visibility/invisibility trap" in which "black feminist creativity ... operates 'as the Incommensurable, or as Variations on Negation'" (122). In this sense, Powell argues that "Luna is reduced to a noted insignificancy, a metaphoric 'black hole' (to again, quote Wallace), which, despite an abundance of imagination, complexity, and critical reflexivity, is assumed to be without content" (122). Yet Donyale Luna – La Luna – is here with an insurgent, experimental impulse that confounds and alters the archive.

A *La Stampa* article from July 1994, titled "Una Luna tutta felliniana: Donyale, regina della sfilate di moda" (A full Fellinian moon: Donyale, queen of the runway), offers a glimpse of Luna's presence within Italian cultural memory. Indeed, the full article title reads: "In those days, between government crises and mysterious crimes, a full Fellinian moon"[8] (14). Beyond the title, the article only mentions Fellini once when quoting the 1969 Ghirotti article. Instead, departing from the 1969 Apollo moon landing, the article is a rumination on the last twenty-five years of Italian postwar history, then culminating in the collapse of the Christian Democratic Party. The article surveys a quarter century of political and cultural upheaval, from the 1969 Piazza Fontana bombing, to student uprisings in Milan, to sensational tabloid murders and the scaling of the Matterhorn, and in the centre, as a sort of fulcrum, stands Luna, modelling in the legendary fashion shows held on the Campidoglio: "But above all, the splendid figure of black American Donyale Luna, 24 years old, stood out among the dense ranks of the models ... Donyale died ten years later, in Rome. The moon had betrayed her"[9] (14). In the accompanying photograph, Luna poses in front of the ruins of ancient Rome, staring pensively into the distance. If 1969 signalled the culmination or a turning point of the era, the article suggests that Luna's mediatic presence in print, film, and television placed her as a nodal point for the political and cultural shifts that mark Italy's transition into late twentieth-century globalism.

In perhaps what can be read as a kind of coda to Luna's under-acknowledged experimental practice is photographer Nan Goldin's *Sirens* (2019), a film dedicated to Luna. Taking its title from the Greek mythological creatures who lured sailors to their deaths, Goldin's sixteen-minute found footage film is a meditation on both the euphoria of drug-induced altered states and the seduction of the cinema. *Sirens* begins with Luna's *Salomè*, as she performs the Dance of the Seven Veils for Herod Antipas. Composer Mica Levi's score, as well as Goldin's removal of the dialogue, emphasize not only Luna's otherworldly presence but also her rigorously stylized gestural performance. *Sirens* also includes Luna's appearance in photographer William Klein's fashion industry satire, *Who Are You, Polly Maggoo?* (1966).[10] Dressed in impossible designs made of layered sheet metal, Luna uses her movement to accentuate minimalist, abstract form. And once again, Luna's Oenothea gazes across the fires of her sanctuary. Later, a clip from Luna's 1969 collaboration with Italian pop star Patty Pravo for a rendition of the Beatles' *Michelle* on the television program *Stasera* has her turning towards the camera, revealing a third eye. *Sirens* then returns to Luna's moments of heightened, ecstatic performance in *Fellini Satyricon* and *Salomè* – Oenothea's tortured birthing of fire and Salomè's frenzied domination of Herod – before concluding with Luna's *Screen Test*, in a series of poses that end with a knowing wink toward the camera.[11]

Rather than leave her as a minor performer, or remember her primarily for her tragic death, in this chapter, I provide a broader context for understanding Donyale Luna's presence in Italian visual culture of the 1960s and 1970s. Capturing the political and cultural currents of the period, from the counterculture to the American and European avant-garde, Luna becomes a significant collaborator and artistic force within the Fellinian constellation, a harbinger for the global media environment to come.

NOTES

1 For critical readings of Fellini in relation to racial discourse and postcolonialism, see Marcus (1992, 2022). See also O'Healy (2009); Luijnenburg (2013); Greene (2020b).
2 Along with her screen tests, Luna appeared in Andy Warhol's *Camp* (1965) and *Donyale Luna* (1967), William Klein's *Who Are You, Polly Maggoo?* (1966), and Otto Preminger's *Skiddo* (1968). After *Fellini Satyricon*, Luna's next performance in an Italian film was Carmelo Bene's experimental adaptation of Oscar Wilde's *Salomè* (1972). Luna also had appearances in *Blow-Up* (Michelangelo Antonioni, 1966), *Tonite Let's All Make Love in London* (Peter Whitehead, 1967), *The Rolling Stones Rock and Roll Circus* (Michael Lindsay-Hogg, 1968), *Soft Self-Portrait of Salvador Dali* (Jean-Christophe Averty, 1970), *Il Festival del proletariato giovanile al Parco Lambro* (Alberto Grifi, 1976), *Fellinikon*, also called *Ciao, Fellini!* (Gideon Bachmann, 1969), as well as various television program appearances.
3 Luna's move may have also been prompted by personal tragedies, such the shooting death of her father (Nathaniel Freeman) at the hands of her mother (Peggy Freeman) in 1965 after a domestic dispute.
4 The quote originates from an Avedon profile featured in the April 1975 issue of *Playboy*, which also featured Luna as photographed by her future husband Luigi Cazzaniga.
5 Luna entered Warhol's arena during a period in which he was establishing the Factory (East 47th Street) and beginning his *Screen Tests*. Coincidentally, like Avedon, Warhol was also using his artistic practice to reflect upon the racial currents on the era, particularly in his silkscreen print *Birmingham Race Riot* (1964), also completed during this period.
6 In Jerome Agel's 1967 article, "The Restless Ones," Luna states that she developed the idea that would eventually become *Snow White*: "I've written a movie that Mr. Warhol will make … The name of my movie is *The Orphans*, a sort of modern-day *Snow White*. The 'dwarfs' will be 13 boys, 13 beautiful boys, very young, very rough, very tough-looking, very hip, just 13 typical New York boys who have been through everything, who know what life is all about" (64).
7 Gary Needham suggests that Nico may have come to the attention of Andy Warhol through her print fashion work and "certainly from *La dolce vita*" (2016, 128).
8 "In quei giorni, tra crisi di governo e delitti misteriosi, una Luna tutta felliniana."
9 "Ma soprattutto, nella folta schiera della indossatrici spiccava la splendida figura dell'americana di colore Donyale Luna, 24 anni … Donyale moriva dieci anni dopo, a Roma. La Luna l'aveva tradita."

10 On the relationship between William Klein and Federico Fellini, see Giuliana Minghelli's chapter in this volume.
11 *Sirens* emerged from Goldin's research for a multi-screen video piece on Salomè. In an interview, Goldin stated: "As I was researching that Salomè piece ... I came across this footage of Donyale Luna in a bizarre version of *Salomè* by Carmelo Bene, which appears at the beginning and ending of *Sirens*. In this footage I could see that she was high, and I got an idea. I was also working on *Memory Lost*, about my own addiction. So I thought wouldn't it be great to show the euphoria of being high, with this beautiful actress as the embodiment of that?" (quoted in Weston 2020). *Sirens* includes clips from over thirty films, including works by Michelangelo Antonioni, Kenneth Anger, Carmelo Bene, Fellini, and Henri-George Clouzot. In recent years, Goldin, a recovering addict, has become involved with advocacy through her organization PAIN (Prescription Addiction Intervention Now), working to address the opioid epidemic and to get art institutions to cut ties with the Sackler family, owners of Purdue Pharma, responsible for the manufacture and distribution of OxyContin.

REFERENCES

Agel, Jerome. 1967. "The Restless Ones." *Status & Diplomat* 18, no. 205 (June/July): 64–5, 79.

Baldwin, James. 2021. *Nothing Personal*. New York: Beacon Press.

Bowman, Manoah. 2015. *Fellini: The Sixties*. Philadelphia, PA: Running Press.

Brown, Elspeth H. 2019. *Work! A Queer History of Modeling*. Durham, NC: Duke University Press. https://doi.org/10.1215/9781478002147.

Burke, Frank. 2020. *Fellini's Films and Commercials: From Postwar to Postmodern*. Bristol: Intellect.

Burke, Frank, Marguerite Waller, and Marita Gubareva. 2020. "Fellini and Fashion, a Two-Way Street: An Interview with Gianluca Lo Vetro." In *A Companion to Federico Fellini*, edited by Frank Burke, Marguerite Waller, and Marita Gubareva, 153–62. Hoboken, NJ: Wiley Blackwell.

Caponetto, Rosetta Giuliani. 2012. "Blaxploitation Italian Style: Exhuming and Consuming the Colonial Black Venus in 1970s Cinema in Italy." In *Postcolonial Italy: Challenging National Homogeneity*, edited by Cristina Lombardi-Diop and Caterina Romeo, 189–202. New York: Palgrave Macmillan.

Cazzaniga, Dream. 2019. "Remembering Donyale Luna, the First Woman of Colour Ever to Appear on the Cover of *Vogue*." *Vogue*, 19 April 2019. https://www.vogue.co.uk/article/donyale-luna-model-vogue.

Cheedle, Janice. 2002. "The Politics of the First: The Emergence of the Black Model in the Civil Rights Era." *Fashion Theory* 6 (1): 61–81. http://doi.org/10.2752/136270402778869145.

Friedman, Vanessa. 2016. "China Machado, Breakthrough Model until the End, Dies at 86." *New York Times*, 19 December 2016. https://www.nytimes.com/2016/12/19/fashion/china-machado-first-non-white-supermodel.html.

Gefter, Philip. 2017. "Why Richard Avedon's Work Has Never Been More Relevant." *New York Times*, 13 November 2017. https://www.nytimes.com/2017/11/13/arts/design/richard-avedon-nothing-personal-pace-macgill.html.

Ghirotti, Gigi. 1969. "Donyale Luna senza Fellini." *La Stampa* 103, no. 2 (October): 3. http://www.archiviolastampa.it/component/option,com_lastampa/task,search/mod,libera/action,viewer/Itemid,3/page,3/articleid,0127_01_1969_0240_0003_4967356.

Greene, Shelleen. 2020a. "Beyond Reality and Fiction: William Demby's *Congo vivo*." *Italian Culture* 3 (2): 151–71. https://doi.org/10.1080/01614622.2020.1846354.

— 2020b. "Racial Difference and the Postcolonial Imaginary in the Films of Federico Fellini." In *A Companion to Federico Fellini*, edited by Frank Burke, Marguerite Waller, and Marita Gubareva, 331–46. Hoboken, NJ: Wiley Blackwell.

Harris, Jessica. 2019. "Una rivoluzione sul piccolo schermo? Le donne afroitaliane nelle fiction televisive italiane contemporanee." *Imago: Studi di cinema e media* 19 (1): 153–64.

La Stampa. 1994. "Una Luna tuta felliniana: Donayle, regina della sfilate di moda." July 1994, 14.

Le Cain, Maximillian. 2002. "Carmelo Bene: A Short Obituary." *Senses of Cinema*, no. 20 (May). https://www.sensesofcinema.com/2002/feature-articles/bene.

Luijnenburg, Linde. 2013. "The Other in Italian Postcolonial Cinema: Pasolini and Fellini: Two Case Studies." *Incontri* 28, no. 1 (July): 34–43. https://doi.org/10.18352/incontri.9142.

Madeo, Liliana. 1973. "Donyale Luna rimane a Roma: Niente espulsione, può lavorare." *La Stampa* 107, no. 178 (July): 7. http://www.archiviolastampa.it/component/option,com_lastampa/task,search/mod,libera/action,viewer/Itemid,3/page,7/articleid,1116_01_1973_0178_0007_16193241.

Marcus, Millicent. 1991. *Filmmaking by the Book: Italian Cinema and Literary Adaptation*. Baltimore: Johns Hopkins University Press.

— 2002. *After Fellini: National Cinema in the Postmodern Age*. Baltimore: Johns Hopkins University Press.

Needham, Gary. 2016. "Warhol and Nico: Negotiating Europe from Strip-Tease to Screen Test." *Journal of European Popular Culture* 7, no. 2 (October): 123–42. https://doi.org/10.1386/jepc.7.2.123_1.

O'Healy, Áine. 2009. "'[Non] è una somala': Deconstructing African Femininity in Italian Film." *The Italianist* 29 (2): 175–98. https://doi.org/10.1179/026143409X12488561926306.

Pendleton, David. 2012. "Inutile: The Cinema of Carmelo Bene." *Harvard Film Archive*, 30 March–2 April, 2012. https://harvardfilmarchive.org/programs/inutile-the-cinema-of-carmelo-bene.

Ponzanezi, Sandra. 2005. "Beyond the Black Venus: Colonial Sexual Politics and Contemporary Visual Practices." In *Italian Colonialism: Legacies and Memories*, edited by Jacqueline Andall and Derek Duncan, 165–89. Oxford: Peter Lang.

Powell, Richard J. 2008. *Cutting a Figure: Fashioning Black Portraiture*. Chicago: University of Chicago Press.

Sisto, Antonella. 2020. "Sounding Out Fellini: An Aural Continuum of Voices, Musics, Noises." In *A Companion to Federico Fellini*, edited by Frank Burke, Marguerite Waller, and Marita Gubareva, 251–66. Hoboken, NJ: Wiley Blackwell.

Time. 1966. "Fashion: The Luna Year." 1 April 1966. http://content.time.com/time/subscriber/article/0,33009,840625-1,00.html.

Villa, Cristina. 2020. "*Fellini-Satyricon*." In *A Companion to Federico Fellini*, edited by Frank Burke, Marguerite Waller, and Marita Gubareva, 483–6. Hoboken, NJ: Wiley Blackwell.

Weingart, Brigitte. 2010. "'That Screen Magnetism': Warhol's Glamour." *October* 132 (Spring): 43–70. https://www.jstor.org/stable/20721276.

Weston, Hillary. 2020. "Feeding the Appetites: Nan Goldin's Movie Obsessions." *Criterion*, 10 September 2020. https://www.criterion.com/current/posts/7094-feeding-the-appetites-nan-goldin-s-movie-obsessions.

Consumer Capitalism, National Identity, and Heterotopia in Fellini's *Le tentazioni del dottor Antonio*

ELEONORA SARTONI

Introduction

In *Le tentazioni del dottor Antonio* (1962), Federico Fellini displays Esposizione Universale di Roma (EUR) as a fictional paradise embodying the economic success of Italy in the 1960s. Yet at the same time, the film reveals the risks and the limits of the economic miracle. In view of this ambivalence, Fellini's use of EUR seems to oscillate between the Foucauldian heterotopia of compensation and the heterotopia of illusion. The new neighbourhood is "a space that is other, another real space, as perfect, as meticulous, as well arranged as ours is messy, ill-constructed, and jumbled" (Foucault 1986, 29). In my reading, Foucault's "ours" represents Italy before the economic miracle as well as those neglected areas of the nation (and beyond) that were not touched by economic advancement and social progress in the 1960s. This kind of heterotopia opposing an imperfect society is one of compensation. However, EUR and the space in front of Anita's billboard are also spaces "of illusion that [expose] every real space, all the sites inside of which human life is partitioned, as still more illusory" (29). This is a heterotopia of illusion.

In analysing the multifaceted symbolism of EUR in *Le tentazioni del dottor Antonio* through Michel Foucault's idea of heterotopia and Guy Debord's analysis of the society of the spectacle, this chapter[1] argues that this short film contains a strong criticism of consumer capitalism by exposing the Western illusion of overcoming disparity among social classes and races thanks to the economic boom. In the film, Fellini alludes not only to 1960s Italy but also to post-unification, Fascism, and colonialism, and he traces the long history of the nation's imperialism and its fascination with the United States. This chapter adds to existing literature (Zambenedetti 2010; Marcus 2013) that has built a parallel between Italy's fascist past and the government led by the Christian

Democratic Party by using a more political approach; it therefore defies the traditional portrait of Fellini as a dreamy artist completely detached from Italian society and its issues.[2]

EUR as a Utopic Social Project

Fellini's choice of EUR as a setting for *Le tentazioni del dottor Antonio* has substantial weight in the creation of meaning in the film. Beyond the director's fascination with the district, which he explained in an interview on Anna Zanoli's TV show *Io e ...* (1972), EUR still retains a strong fascist identity in its architecture and urban plan. As a result, it helps create a parallel between Italy's fascist past and the oppressive Christian Democratic government of the 1960s, as Alberto Zambenedetti and Millicent Marcus have already pointed out. As Fellini stated in the interview, EUR is "a sort of crazy dream, interrupted and then transformed into something else."[3] Indeed, EUR was born as E42, the Universal Exposition of Rome that Mussolini organized to celebrate the twentieth anniversary of the *Marcia su Roma* and showcase the regime's achievements and magnificence. Architect Marcello Piacentini guided the construction, which started in 1939 and ended in 1942, but he left the project incomplete because of the Second World War. In the 1950s, the municipality resumed construction and finished the monumental, administrative, and residential buildings; at the end of the 1950s, the first inhabitants moved to EUR. As Fellini said in the same interview, the neighbourhood mutated its identity from one that reflected Mussolini's grandiosity to a sophisticated bourgeois residential area; it changed from a fascist utopia to a bourgeois one. In this sense, EUR is not dissimilar from other urban engineering projects, such as the fascist New Towns. Both were "a model of what that world had the potential to become" (Burdett 2000, 19). In particular, EUR – unofficially the *Roma nuova* – embodies the heterotopic characteristic of the mirror transitioning from reality (Rome's city centre) to the utopic space (EUR). In the eyes of the regime, EUR was a better, modernized version of Rome.

In its second life as an administrative and residential neighbourhood, EUR embodied another utopic social project; at the end of the 1950s, it housed the Roman upper bourgeoisie in a new, neutral setting. Indeed, Mia Fuller identifies EUR as a "post-dialectical colonial city, one that operated in a universe where difference had already been overcome ... In EUR there was no longer any mediator [between differences], any fear of contamination" (1996, 413). Unlike the colonies in East Africa, the differences to overcome in the capital were not based on race but on social class. Politicians have consistently expressed concerns about the distribution of the lower classes in Rome ever since it became the new capital in 1870; ideally, it should have remained a symbolic, administrative city, devoid of the visible poverty of the sub-proletariat and the proletariat, especially in the city centre.[4] Mussolini maintained a similar approach through the implementation of regulations incarcerating *oziosi* (the lazy) and *vagabondi* (the vagrants), already practised in Liberal Italy, the discouragement of the migration of Southern Italians to the capital by denying them residence, and the creation of new neighbourhoods on the margins of Rome for families evicted from the city centre and immigrants from rural areas. In relation to other districts of the capital, social "contamination" and social differences were not present in EUR. As a matter of fact, in the mid-1950s, this new neighbourhood "had grown from a deserted collection of grotesque, half-completed buildings and monuments, inhabited by refugees and goatherds, into a *model community*, linked by subway ... to the Termini railway station. Ministries and city offices ... had acquired and built on EUR sites, and private developers were building there one of the most attractive new residential neighborhoods in the city" (Fried 1973, 46; emphasis added).[5]

Contrary to Rome's city centre in the past, where homeless day labourers from the nearby countryside found shelter at night under ancient ruins, the porticoes of Piazza Vittorio, or in the numerous shacks surrounding the marginal area of the capital, during the Second World War refugees and goatherds occupied the incomplete buildings of EUR for a short period.[6] In the mid-1950s, EUR again became a hotspot displaying Italy's modernity.

The same atmosphere of exemplary novelty was still present in 1960s EUR, when Fellini, in the aforementioned interview, underscored that "its inhabitants seem to have such a mindset: aseptic, new, unknown."[7] In the director's words, EUR's upper bourgeois inhabitants were the nation's newest subjects, and for this reason, they were not totally comprehensible. As Robert Fried pointed out, EUR embodied a "model community"– that is, Foucault's heterotopia: an "effectively enacted utopia" (Fried 1973, 24) In this, EUR followed the second principle of heterotopia, where Foucault affirms that "a society, as its history unfolds, can make an existing heterotopia function in a very different fashion" (1986, 26). From a monumental area celebrating Fascism, EUR became a residential and bureaucratic centre exhibiting the levels of wealth, order, and rectitude achieved with the Christian Democratic government in the era of the economic boom.

Anita's Billboard as a Site of Illusion

How does Fellini play with this utopia? How does he use it to represent Italy during the economic boom and its relationship to Western society?

Fellini's *Le tentazioni del dottor Antonio* 133

Image 24. Anita's billboard, from *Le tentazioni del dottor Antonio*.

Throughout the film, Fellini alludes to the victory of consumer capitalism by making the billboard the new focal point of social life in the neighbourhood. Antonio constantly monitors the crowd night and day, and this is as variegated as the masses gathered in front of the billboard when it was assembled – from children to adults, from white Italian people to African-American people, from Turinese to Neapolitan workers, and from the proletariat to the bourgeoisie and the clergy. Consumerism reaches, or at least attracts, every layer of society independent of an individual's age, gender, and social and geographic origin. Indeed, during the day, the area is mainly frequented by families having picnics, young people arriving with campers or lining up their cars as at a drive-in, and children playing "Ring around the Rosie." At night, prostitutes position themselves under the billboard (image 24).

An analysis of the relationship between the people gathered in front of the billboard allows us to understand how the rhythm of everyday life changes with the advent of consumerism and how people relate to one another in this new type of society. Anita and her billboard function as a spectacle attracting viewers; this embodies a society of the spectacle as intended by Debord, a consumeristic society based on appearances and superficiality. Indeed, according to Debord, "the spectacle has its roots in the fertile field of the economy, and it is the produce of that field which must in the end come to dominate the spectacular market" ([1967] 1994, 37). Therefore, Fellini's presentation of Anita's billboard as a cinematic screen has a dual purpose. On a more superficial level, it advances the director's complaints about censorship in Italy, as Marcus (2013), Zambenedetti (2010), and Tullio Kezich (2006) state. On a deeper level, it allows Fellini to display the mechanisms of the consumeristic society and its effects on the nation. If we observe how people interact in front of the billboard, we can see how Debord's description of the spectacle as the model form of modern society precisely fits Fellini's staging of the crowds in front of Anita:

> The spectacle appears at once as society itself, as a part of society and as a means of unification. As a part of society, it is that sector where all attention, all consciousness, converges. Being isolated – and for that reason – this sector is the locus of illusion and false consciousness ... The spectacle is not a collection of images; rather, it is a social relationship between people that is mediated by images. ([1967] 1994, 12)

The gathering scenes in front of the billboard are a metaphor for what was happening in Italy during the economic boom. While Italy was still a fragmented nation – socially and geographically – consumerism appeared as the only thing able to unify the country. As the variegated extras in Fellini's films, Italians felt unified through their participation in the economy – that is, by being part of the spectacle in front of the billboard that, as Debord explains, has to be isolated in order to function. Indeed, the billboard stands in a *terrain vague* in an underdeveloped EUR, and it anticipates the peripheral location of the many malls that will sprout up around the borders of the capital at the end of the 1990s. The billboard attracts all the attention from the inhabitants of the neighbourhood and beyond, and it activates the illusion and false consciousness of being part of the economic change. Moreover, because the billboard is the focus of attention, the relationship among the population changes. People's interactions are always mediated by the billboard, Anita, and the product advertised – that is, by consumerism.

In the film, Fellini also inserts allusions to festivals and fairgrounds, which, according to Foucault, are perfect examples of heterotopias that break traditional time by proposing a totally temporal existence while being located in "marvellous empty sites on the outskirts of cities" (1986, 7).[8] Their presence marks the coronation of consumer capitalism as an Italian national value in the middle of the film. During the scene, Antonio observes the area in front of the billboard and dictates his thoughts to his assistant: "In a few days, the horrific billboard, the monstrous Circe, the new golden calf, has gathered the corruption of the urban world in its entirety."[9] His words underline the billboard's magnetic power on the population together with the people's devotion towards it and, symbolically, consumerism. Indeed, while Antonio speaks, a country festival similar to those connected to saints' celebrations materializes in front of the billboard. With this scene, Fellini affirms that during the economic miracle, consumerism becomes part of Italian traditions. It drastically changes them by attracting the population as a new social focal point (interactions among people are mediated by media and commodities) and modifying traditional values (celebrities are revered like divinities). According to Debord,

> the spectacle is the material reconstruction of the religious illusion ... those cloud-enshrouded entities have now been brought down to earth. It is thus the most earthbound aspects of life that have become the most impenetrable and rarefied. The absolute denial of life, in the shape of a fallacious paradise, is no longer projected to heavens, but finds its place instead within material life itself. The spectacle is hence a technological version of the exiling of human powers in a "world beyond" – and the perfection of separation *within* human beings. ([1967] 1994, 17–18; emphasis added)

The diva Anita is both terrestrial and divine; she bridges earthly materiality to divinity. Anita's clothes and the association with milk in the image is a postmodern elaboration of the *Madonna galaktotrophousa*, the Virgin Mary breastfeeding baby Jesus. Indeed, some of the people gathered in front of the billboard salute Anita with white handkerchiefs as devotees of the Virgin Mary usually do. Moreover, her powder box evokes a reliquary box with its gilded metal rays (image 25). The absence of baby Jesus means that Anita's "holy" milk is meant only for consumers, who by buying it, can aspire to be elevated into paradise: Italy's modern, wealthy side.

The Italian economic miracle is a "religious" illusion that projects paradise within material life: in commodities themselves. Though, it is an illusion; it does not mean that all Italians can afford commodities. Indeed, the heterotopic space in front of the billboard seems accessible to everyone, but it entails exclusion anyway. This is the fifth principle of heterotopia: "Everyone can enter into the heterotopic sites, but in fact that is only an illusion – we think we enter where we are, by the very fact that we enter, excluded" (Foucault 1986, 28–9). In the scene where the billboard is finally assembled, Fellini introduces a parallel with American society by inserting Black musicians among Italians. Even if prostitutes, Southern Italians, the proletariat, and African Americans are free to stand in front of the billboard and even able to buy the commodity advertised, they cannot afford to live in the rich, bourgeois area where the billboard is positioned.

Image 25. Close-up of Anita, from *Le tentazioni del dottor Antonio*.

While I agree with Shelleen Greene's (2020, 338) reading of the presence of the Black musicians as an ironic comment on the racial segregation and hierarchical project embedded in the fascist architecture of EUR, I also see their attendance of a space highly characterized by different Italian regional accents and the presence of lower classes as a warning against the illusory quality of consumer capitalism.[10] Their presence recalls the American socio-economic model that Italian society is eager to follow. In reality, the African Americans' participation in the festive atmosphere in front of the billboard is as unreal as that of the Southern proletariat with whom they share the space; both of them are excluded from the wealth generated by the economic boom. The musicians' attunement to the advertisement jingle when performing means that, like Italians, they conform to the mechanisms of consumer capitalist society. This illusion of participating in the economic miracle alters the perception of reality of the proletariat and the marginal figures of the society; through the possibility of buying the advertised commodities, wealth appears as something within reach.

A Tracking Shot of Italy's Economic History

Le tentazioni del dottor Antonio also offers a reflection on Italy's economic development since post-unification. Fellini transcends the motionless billboard when he gives life to Anita in the oneiric scene. Anita leaves the billboard/screen, and she behaves like Sylvia in *La dolce vita* (1960). For example, Anita echoes Sylvia with similar lines – "Vieni, dottore" (Come, doctor) instead of "Marcello, come here" – and with her feline purring recalls the kitten that Sylvia finds by the Trevi Fountain. As Sylvia guides Marcello (Marcello Mastroianni) along Rome's monuments, Anita leads Antonio – and the inhabitants of the district together with the spectators – into a world bombarded by advertisements. This futuristic space is the result of the dilatation of the billboard. Fellini completes this metacinematic operation thanks to a tracking shot that virtually conducts the spectators to this new world. "If this monster sets its foot in the city, more than two million souls would be lost in one single night,"[11] Antonio says, identifying Anita with consumer capitalism, a relatively new phenomenon that threatens Italian society. Moreover, this line also confirms EUR as a heterotopia. The separation of this utopic and yet real neighbourhood from the rest of Rome is a fundamental characteristic of "places of this kind [that] are outside of all places, even though it may be possible to indicate their location in reality" (Foucault 1986, 25). Fellini underlines Antonio's line by dedicating the shot to two skyscrapers that symbolize Western modernity and wealth, in particular the American model. On her walk in EUR's Viale della Civiltà del Lavoro, which connects the Palazzo della Civiltà Italiana to the Palazzo dei Ricevimenti e dei Congressi, Anita traverses a space that Fellini decorates with various advertisements that deserve a detailed analysis.

In the oneiric scene, the EUR of Antonio's everyday life shows all its potential. In the dream, Fellini unveils the main driving force of the nation since its birth: the mirage of production and consumerism. Indeed, the tracking shot follows the point of view of Anita – embodying consumer capitalism – in her quest along Viale della Civiltà del Lavoro. It is not fortuitous that the vanishing point coincides with the Palazzo della Civiltà Italiana: only by embracing capitalist production and consumerism can Italy reach civilization. The first elements that Anita crosses and that Fellini presents through the tracking shot are a national bank and a gas station – the finance and the petrochemical industry, respectively. Even if they appear on the screen for only a few seconds, both of them hold significant meaning: they both have a fundamental role in the Italian economic miracle of the 1960s, they are both tied to the imperialist project of Fascism, and they both originate in post-unification Italy.

The Banca Nazionale del Lavoro (BNL) has its roots in the early decades of the Italian nation; founded in 1913 as Istituto Nazionale per il Credito alla Cooperazione during Giolitti's fourth government, it was intended to help Italy transform from a rural to a more industrialized country by supporting worker cooperatives (Castronovo 2013). The bank's birth was strictly connected to the nation's desire – and anxiety – to become a strong economic power in the Western world. In 1927, during the fascist regime, the institute became Banca Nazionale del Lavoro. Being a national bank, it financed the major operations of the Italian empire: the colonial wars, autarky, and support for General Francisco Franco in the Spanish Civil War (1936–9). Beyond its contribution to Italian politics, the bank also financed the construction of Cinecittà Studios and E42/EUR, and throughout the 1960s supported relevant factories that were leading the economic miracle. Beyond the cinema industry and FIAT (Fabbrica Italiana Automobili Torino), BNL financed Enrico Mattei's ENI (Ente Nazionale Idrocarburi), founded by Mussolini in 1926 as AGIP (Azienda Generale Italiana Petroli). Beginning in 1935, AGIP conducted searches in Eritrea, Ethiopia, Somalia, and Libya without much success, while it established important sites in Italy, Romania, Albania, and Iraq (Gagliardi 2016). The tracking shot associates BNL with oil production by positioning a gas station right before the bank. This visual combination highlights not only the national propellers for Italy's economic boom but also the overlapping of economy and politics in shaping Italy's modern imperialist society since its unification.

When Antonio reaches Anita in Viale della Civiltà del Lavoro, the chase takes place under the porticoes, which show many advertisements. Some more than others refer directly to consumerism, while one advertises the newspaper *Il Tempo*. In the 1960s, *Il Tempo* was the most read newspaper in Rome. By giving space to both fascist and antifascist intellectuals in the postwar period, it contributed to a constructive dialogue between the two groups (Archidiacono 1974, 143). Indeed, it is under this neon sign that Anita tries to reconcile with Antonio. By reaching a normal height, Anita/consumer capitalism does not seem to be something unattainable for Italy – like the previously framed skyscrapers recalling American metropolises. In fact, the neon signs reading "bar" and "Stock" – to which Fellini adds "Motta" and "Campari" in the same scene – represent the success of specific Italian brands connected to one of the typical Italian commercial activities: the bar. All of these brands were founded around the same time as the birth of the Italian nation or in its early years: Campari in 1860, Stock in 1884, and Motta in 1919. All of them reached their national and international success during the economic boom. So, the label "Made in Italy" not only can compete with American models – represented by skyscrapers and the neon sign "birreria del west" – but also contributes to the construction of national identity through economic success, like these brands and ENI.

Under the porticoes, a metacinematic scene takes place. Here, Antonio urges the spectators to not look at Anita stripping in front of the Palazzo della Civiltà Italiana. By stripping naked, Anita reveals her true diabolic identity. Every shot in this scene contains at least one neon sign; Antonio – like the spectators – cannot get rid of the products or of Anita's sensual allure – that is, as Marcus (2002) explains, the desire to buy and consume. In *Le tentazioni del dottor Antonio*, Fellini stages a similar omnipresence of commercial posters and signs during the economic miracle. As Antonio exhorts the spectators to leave the theatre, his warnings to not look and to protect the children can also refer to the television program *Carosello*, which entered Italian homes from 1955 to 1977 with its short sketch comedies advertising different products. *Carosello* also attracted children because of its large use of cartoons in the advertisements. At the end of the film, Antonio's inability to leave the billboard means that consumerism, through Anita's sensuality, has conquered him. Before entering the ambulance, he whispers "Anita," and the commercial jingle "bevete più latte" (drink more milk) accompanies his trip to the mental hospital.

Conclusions: Nationalism and Consumer Capitalism

In order to seal the overlapping of national identity and consumer capitalism, it is necessary to return to the pseudo-religious country festival happening in front of Anita's billboard. Here, the *bersaglieri* (light infantry soldiers) participate, too, and instead of playing their anthem, they execute the advertising jingle. Fellini had already made an allusion to the *bersaglieri* in *La dolce vita*. In that case, the band playing at the party at the Terme di Caracalla transforms a cha-cha-cha into the *fanfara dei bersaglieri* while Sylvia and her friend dance. It is when Frankie (Alain Dijon) carries her shoulder-high that the famous, recognizable refrain is played; there, Fellini's attention is more on the divinization of American media stars and their incorporation in Italian culture. In *Le tentazioni del dottor Antonio*, the staging of the Royal Italian Army connects consumer capitalism to national identity.

The *bersaglieri* were founded in 1836 to serve in the army of the Kingdom of Sardinia. They were one of the protagonists in Italian unification; they were also the ones who managed to conquer Rome in 1870 through the breach of Porta Pia. By having the *bersaglieri* play the jingle, Fellini states that nationalism has been substituted with consumerism, which was able to unify – at least, superficially – the Italian population. Antonio can do nothing to oppose this victorious force. Even in the oneiric scene when he is worried about Anita entering into the city, the spectators know that his quest is useless.

Anita – and consumerism – bursts into Italian society with the same energy the *bersaglieri* had when penetrating the Roman walls in 1870.

NOTES

1 A previous version of this essay appeared as a section of the chapter titled "Cinematic Rome and the Disillusionment with the Economic Miracle" in Sartoni (2020).
2 For a recent study on the political criticism embedded in Fellini's films, see Minuz (2015, esp. 90–1).
3 "una specie di sogno folle, interrotto e poi tramutato in un'altra cosa." Translations are my own unless otherwise indicated.
4 For example, right-wing party politician Quintino Sella was one of the advocates for the exclusion of industry and the proletariat from Rome. In "Tornata del 27 giugno 1876" Stella states: "I always wished Rome to be inhabited by the ruling class, the intellectual class, I never wanted large gatherings of workers. I would see a significant population of workers in Rome as a real inconvenience, because I believe this is the place where matters need to be discussed intellectually, requiring the efforts of all the intellectual forces in the country, and the passions of the great masses of workers would not be opportune. I believe that an organization of this nature would be dangerous, or at least inappropriate" (Io ho sempre desiderato che sia in Roma la parte direttiva, la parte intellettuale, ma non ho mai desiderato che vi siano grandi agglomerazioni di operai. In una soverchia agglomerazione di operai in Roma io vedrei un vero inconveniente, perché credo che qui sia il luogo dove si debbano trattare molte questioni che vogliono essere discusse intellettualmente, che richiedono l'opera di tutte le forze intellettuali del paese, ma non sarebbero opportuni gli impeti popolari di grandi masse di operai. Crederei pericolosa o almeno non conveniente un'organizzazione di questa natura) (1876, 59–60). Sella believed that politicians and intellectuals contributing not only to Italy's political unification but also to its symbolic affirmation as a modern nation should be separated from the masses of workers who could alter this order with their presence and possible protests.
5 As Michael Ebner reports, "In the early years, between 1926 and 1934, the branch that handled 'common' criminal suspects – 'habitual' criminals, alcoholics, *mafiosi*, pimps, drug dealers and addicts, and vagabonds – grew remarkably. With the introduction of the police code in November 1926, the fascist police immediately exercised its expanded powers in order to restore 'law and order' and 'clean up the streets' rather than merely suppress anti-Fascism" (2011, 109). Both the *borgate* (suburban

housing projects) and the *confino* (internal exile) worked as dumpsters for the "unfitting" to the eyes of the fascist regime – and of the liberal state, previously. To these disposal systems, Fascists also added homeless shelters. During Fascism, the number of homeless shelters increased in order to collect people evicted from the *sventramenti* (urban gutting) and immigrants from the south. Many of these shelters closed because of security and health conditions; so, their existence did not help in resolving the housing situation (Villani 2012, 53).

6 For more details on the history of homelessness in Rome, see Insolera (1962).
7 "la gente che ci abita ti dà l'impressione di avere una psicologia così: asettica, nuova, sconosciuta"
8 While the reference to the fair might suggest a pretext for fun, lightheartedness, and fellow-feeling for the population attending, I would like to recall another scene in the film where Fellini plays ambiguously with joy. In the opening scene, Fellini shows the administrative buildings on the horizon with some little girls jumping while some priests traverse the scene. Even if the scene presents a contrast between the stillness of architecture, the visual composition of the shot, and the movement of the people present in it (Zambenedetti 2010, 202), I believe that this scene is less positive than it seems. Although Zambenedetti highlights how the seminarians bend forward and direct their eyes to the floor in order to negate their own gaze, his words suggest that the movements vitalizing the shot oppose the surrounding oppressive architecture. Instead, I believe that these movements are but an extension of the rigidity of that architecture and of its symbolic, political power. The focus on the little girls who appear as the most ecstatic and animated presence in the scene is fundamental to uncovering this aspect. After a more detailed observation, the little girls seem entrapped for different reasons: their bodies are contained between the row of the seminarians and the railing without a possibility to escape; their movements are limited to small jumps in the same spot; and their gaze is forced in one direction, towards the administrative buildings and the boulevard. Fellini reinforces this idea of a fixed gaze by framing the shot through the two poles in the foreground; in this way, he also influences the viewer's gaze direction and perspective. In more than one case in the film, Fellini criticizes the apparent joy connected to the economic boom.
9 "In pochi giorni, dico, l'orrendo cartellone, la mostruosa Circe, come ai tempi del Vitello d'oro, ha raccolto intorno a sé tutta la corruzione del mondo cittadino."
10 For a recent study on the relation between Italianness, whiteness, and "otherness" in Fellini, see Greene (2020), as well as her chapter in this volume.
11 "se entra in città questo mostro, in una notte sola si perdono due milioni di anime"

REFERENCES

Archidiacono, Nicola. 1974. *Mezzo secolo di giornalismo*. Rome: Volpe.

Burdett, Charles. 2000. "Journeys to the *Other* Spaces of Fascist Italy." *Modern Italy* 5, no. 1 (May): 7–23. https://doi.org/10.1080/13532940050003014.

Castronovo, Valerio. 2013. "BNL: 100 anni da Giolitti al Duce fino ai francesi." *Il Sole 24 Ore*, 14 August. https://st.ilsole24ore.com/art/commenti-e-idee/2013-08-14/anni-giolitti-duce-fino-064152.shtml?uuid=AbbM13MI&refresh_ce=1.

Debord, Guy. (1967) 1994. *The Society of the Spectacle*. Translated by Donald Nicholson-Smith. London: Zone Books.

Ebner, Michael R. 2011. *Ordinary Violence in Mussolini's Italy*. Cambridge: Cambridge University Press. https://doi.org/10.1017/CBO9780511778728.

Foucault, Michel. 1986. "Of Other Spaces: Utopias and Heterotopias." *Diacritics* 16, no. 1: 22–9. https://doi.org/10.2307/464648.

Fried, Robert. 1973. *Planning the Eternal City: Roman Politics and Planning since WWII*. New Haven, CT: Yale University Press.

Fuller, Mia. 1996. "Wherever You Go, There You Are: Fascist Plans for the Colonial City of Addis Ababa and the Colonizing Suburb of EUR '42." *Journal of Contemporary History* 31, no. 2: 397–418. https://doi.org/10.1177/002200949603100209.

Gagliardi, Alessio. 2016. "La mancata 'valorizzazione' dell'impero: Le colonie italiane in Africa orientale e l'economia dell'Italia fascista." *Storicamente: Laboratorio di Storia* 12, no. 3: 1–32. https://doi.org/10.12977/stor619.

Greene, Shelleen. 2020. "Racial Difference and the Postcolonial Imaginary in the Films of Federico Fellini." In *A Companion to Federico Fellini*, edited by Frank Burke, Marguerite Waller, and Marita Gubareva, 331–46. Hoboken, NJ: Wiley Blackwell.

Insolera, Italo. 1962. *Roma Moderna: Un secolo di storia urbanistica*. Turin: Einaudi.

Kezich, Tullio. 2006. *Federico Fellini: His Life and Work*. Translated by Minna Proctor with Viviana Massa. New York: Faber and Faber.

Marcus, Millicent. 2002. "Fellini's *Ginger and Fred*." In *Federico Fellini: Contemporary Perspectives*, edited by Frank Burke and Marguerite R. Waller, 169–87. Toronto: University of Toronto Press.

– 2013. "Boccaccio and the Seventh Art: The Decameronian Films of Fellini, De Laurentis, Pasolini, Woody Allen." *Mediaevalia* 34: 267–79. https://doi.org/10.1353/mdi.2013.0008.

Minuz, Andrea. 2015. *Political Fellini: Journey to the End of Italy*. Translated by Marcus Perryman. New York: Berghahn Books.

Sartoni, Eleonora. 2020. "Spectacular Capital(ist) City: Wandering through Rome from 1870 to the Economic Miracle." PhD diss., Rutgers University. https://doi.org/doi:10.7282/t3-age7-v683.

Sella, Quintino. 1876. "Tornata del 27 giugno 1876." In *Discorso di Quintino Sella nelle Tornate del 26 e 27 Giugno 1876 sulla Convenzione di Basilea e sul Trattato di Vienna pel Riscatto delle Ferrovie dell'Alta Italia*, 57–83. Rome: Tipografia Eredi Botta.

Villani, Luciano. 2012. *Le Borgate del Fascismo: Storia Urbana, Politica e Sociale della Periferia Romana*. Milan: Ledizioni.

Zambenedetti, Alberto. 2010. "Filming in Stone: Palazzo della Civiltà Italiana and Fascist Signification in Cinema." *Annali di Italianistica* 28:199–215. http://www.jstor.org/stable/24016394.

Fellini, Dante, *Il viaggio di G. Mastorna*, and Dreams

MIRKO TAVONI

Authoritative film historians and Fellini scholars claim that Fellini was deeply influenced by Dante, and even that *La dolce vita* (1960) and *8 ½* (1963) must be considered the most important transpositions of Dante's poetry in twentieth-century cinema. The most recent and evident manifestation of this critical trend was the international conference held in Ravenna in 2015 and the subsequent publication of the conference proceedings under the eloquent title *Fellini & Dante: L'aldilà della visione*. The "Premessa" and the "Presentazione" of the proceedings declared, through a widespread opinion among the most attentive critics of Fellini's work, that Dante's vision represents a sort of inspiring subtext of his films. The Fellini and Dante conference brought together Dante scholars and film critics to verify and develop this critical hypothesis.

The Ravenna conference was the culmination of a line of interpretation that started with Barbara Lewalski's observations in "Federico Fellini's *Purgatorio*":

> So pervasive is the Dantean influence in *La Dolce Vita* and *8 ½*, and so explicit are Fellini's efforts to call attention to the Dantean elements especially in the imagery and language of the latter work, as to suggest that Fellini has consciously undertaken in these two films a contemporary *Divine Comedy* in a modern medium, for modern times. In *La Dolce Vita* the characters and situations make obvious allusions to their Dantean prototypes in the *Inferno*. (1978, 113)

Lewalski added that, "in addition to the Dantean elements repeated and reworked from *La dolce vita*, the new film [*8 ½*] adapts other sequences of actions and methods of presentation from the *Commedia* and especially from the *Purgatorio*" (116). The essay ends with the question: "What, one may well wonder, will Fellini's *Paradiso* be?" (120). By that same token, John Welle, in "Fellini's Use of Dante in *La Dolce Vita*," stated that "*La Dolce Vita* works hand in hand with the *Vita nuova* and the parallel and contrasting points between the two works are numerous and tightly drawn" (1993, 115). Welle summarized these parallels, pointing to the fact that both protagonists are writers, weak, undergo a radical change, seek love, and worship women; moreover, both works begin with greeting, present a view of death, as well as the search for a new life. Guido Fink's 2004 essay, "'Non senti come tutto questo ti assomiglia?' Fellini's Infernal Circles," chose as its title a tendentious, suggestive question ("Don't you feel how much all this looks like you?") that Dantist Jacqueline Risset whispered in the ear of her friend Federico to convince him to make a film about Dante's poem, stubbornly ignoring the fact that Fellini, as we shall see, resisted this suggestion with all his might.

The 2015 Ravenna conference also saw Dantist Raffaele Pinto judge that the explanation spread by Fellini himself for the title of the film *8 ½* – that is, that the films shot by the director up to then would be eight and a half, considering also the "half film" that is the episodes of collective films – is "a highly improbable accounting explanation,"[1] and that one must reject this as a nonsensical joke (2016, 25). The title, Pinto argues, actually reveals a Dantesque symbolism in relation to the number 9, the mystical number of Beatrice in the *Vita nuova*: "8 ½ means a little less than 9, to enigmatically and parodically indicate the myth around which the director's new poetics took form"[2] (25). Cinema historian Gian Piero Brunetta chose to qualify Fellini in the most explicit terms in the title of his article: "L'apostolo più rappresentativo del verbo dantesco sullo schermo" (The most representative apostle of the Dantean verb on the screen). Brunetta writes: "I would like to recognize Dante as 'the one who helps him,' more than Freud and Jung, more than Servadio and Bernhard, to make that inner journey that has produced the marvelous result of all his works, which move in a fluctuating dimension between reality, vision and dream"[3] (2016, 11). He continues: "If Dante wrote *La vita nuova*, Fellini, midway upon the journey of his life, made *La dolce vita* and *8 ½*, probably the most Dantean films in the history of cinema, those in which the protagonist finds himself like Dante in a dark forest and moves without guides, first as the subject of the narrative, like the poet, and then as the subject of the action, who has lost the right creative path"[4] (14).

I confess that I am very sceptical of Dante's fundamental importance for Fellini in these terms. The salient themes of this alleged affinity – the "descent into the underworld" of contemporary society, the saving role of a beatific woman, the writer's metaliterary reflection on his work in progress, etc. – are certainly not exclusive themes. Fellini is not an intellectual artist; indeed, he is a programmatically anti-intellectual man of cinema, very opposed to the transfer of contents from "high" literature to the cinema. According to him, "Each work of art resides in the dimension in which it was conceived and expressed; transferring it, moving it from its original language to a different one, means cancelling it, denying it ... The story, situations, characters, in summary a series of materials, opportunities, and occasions that observing everyday reality and reading the newspaper, for example, are capable of supplying with a more generous and stimulating richness and immediacy" (Fellini 1980, 100).

Italo Calvino rightly pointed out that Fellini, before becoming a director, was a cartoonist for popular humour magazines, such as *Marc'Aurelio*, and that he "never lost his popular communicative matrix even when his language became more sophisticated"[5] (1974, xxii). This graphic world of popular print media retains "its special visual authority"[6] in Fellini's career until the end (xxi). The "Giulietta Masina area" of Fellini's imaginary world will remain faithful to the graphics of the humorous cartoons from *La strada* (1954) up to *Giulietta degli spiriti* (1965), which is the film that sinks into oneirism, while maintaining an explicit figurative and chromatic reference to the cartoons of the *Corriere dei piccoli*. In this regard, as documented by Pier Marco De Santi in *I disegni di Fellini* (1982) and *Federico Fellini dai disegni ai film* (1989), there is absolute continuity between Fellini's early work as a cartoonist for satirical newspapers and as a draftsman in preparation for his films of the 1950s. This popular graphic style continued in *Il libro dei sogni*, the diary of Fellini's daily dialogue with his unconscious on which he worked for thirty years, from the time of *La dolce vita* to that of *La voce della luna* (1990). All this graphic imagery does not seem to have much to do with Dante.

Jacqueline Risset, a Dante scholar, French translator of the *Divine Comedy*, and poet, was a staunch supporter of Fellini's alleged Dantism. She was so convinced of how important Dante was for her friend Fellini that she wanted to convince him of it too. Fellini, however, was desperately reluctant to be convinced, thus giving way to a dialogue not devoid of comedic aspects. In the elegant booklet *L'incantatore*, dedicated to Federico and released a year after his death, a conversation is reported in which Fellini said the following about his relationship with Dante:

> The *Divine Comedy* in film, I will never do it, for the simple reason that Dante has already done this film. He is such a brilliant and precise visual

poet, that I don't see what sense it could have adding images to his words. Yes, of course, I could make Dantean special effects, but for what purpose? And besides, it is true that my films are full of them ... what have I done, after all, every time, if not a descent into the Underworld, with some glimmer of Purgatory and Heaven?[7] (quoted in Risset 1994, 109–10)

Fellini perfectly captures the exceptional visual quality of Dante's poem and, at the same time, recognizes that it has only affected his cinema in very general terms.

Poet Andrea Zanzotto had seen something similar, writing that "any reference to Dante can become as obligatory as it is trivial"[8] (1980, 20), while the critic Massimiliano Chiamenti specifies that

> echoes, suggestions, metaphors, clichés, perhaps coincidences or simple cultural matrices in common [between Dante and Fellini] are certainly suggestive, but hardly demonstrable *more geometrico*, [so that] it seems prudent to suspend the judgment on real or presumed macro-intertextual connections, on the maximum systems, to move on safer and verifiable, more localized, minimal areas, namely those of marked micro-intertextual allusions, parodies, quotations, where the hypotextual reference is limited, explicit, intentional, almost a wink at the viewer.[9] (2004, 225)

Tullio Kezich, a great film critic and a great friend of Fellini's throughout his life, arguably knew him better than anyone else from a myriad of personal and professional angles, and yet, in his all-encompassing biography, *Federico Fellini: His Life and Work* (2006), Dante is not even named.

In Lietta Tornabuoni's book, *Federico Fellini*, Fellini tells a hilarious story about American producers who obsess over him, trying to convince him at all costs to make a film about Dante's Hell, complete with terrifying visions. In this story, Fellini represents himself as a puppet manipulated by these producers/persecutors (see Tornabuoni 1995, 75–81). And under their offensive, what does he think? He thinks of Jacqueline (Risset), who speaks with exalted fervour of Dante and of the ethical, poetic, fatal reasons that lie at the root of an enterprise, which he is not allowed to refuse. "Only you can do it!" she says to the puppet, who, disheartened and resigned, repeats his objections for the hundredth time: he does not remember anything about Dante, he did not even like him at school. At the gymnasium in Rimini, "on a column of frozen marble, there was a black bust of Dante, who looked like a spy. We were all convinced that it was him, with those thin lips like blades, who was telling the teachers about everything we were up to during recess,"[10] Fellini recalls (quoted in Tornabuoni 1995, 78–9).

In fact, the only precise traces of Dante in Fellini's films belong to the Dante of school memories, or the Dante of popular culture. In *8 ½*, Guido's father quotes *Inferno* 33.5: "disperato dolor che 'l cor mi preme" (despairing pain that presses at my heart). In *Amarcord* (1973), the lawyer-narrator, located in the centre of the town square, tells us about Rimini and its history and proclaims, with naive rhetorical emphasis, "From the divine poet Dante, to Pascoli, to D'Annunzio, numerous are the high wits who have sung this land."[11] However, his speech is cut off by a raspberry blown by a schoolboy hidden in the shadows. And in the shop of the prosperous tobacconist there is a poster of Dante with his skull open, in the style of Giorgio de Chirico's metaphysical painting, advertising FOSFORIL, pills for the brain.

Fellini has repeatedly stated that the first film he saw, at the age of six, while sitting in his father's arms at the Fulgor cinema in Rimini, was *Maciste all'inferno* (1926), the extraordinary silent muscleman epic directed by Guido Brignone and brimming with Segundo de Chomón's stunning special effects, and that he was struck by it forever (Costa 1996, 53–4). "My entire film catalogue, in essence, refers back to that film,"[12] he would say when interviewed by Italian journalist Enzo Biagi (ACCASFILM 2020, 01:51). The hell that Fellini liked was this extraordinary mixture of grotesque imagery, sentimental turns, expressionism, and comic book aesthetics. This is reminiscent of Calvino's judgement of Fellini's indulgence and Fellini's refrain from harsh moral condemnation: "The province of the *vitelloni* is a circle of hell just like the Rome of cinema, but they're also enjoyable lands of plenty"[13] (1974, xlvi). This is something that cannot similarly be said of Dante's *Inferno*. One could say, however, that from 1965 to the end of his life, Fellini wanted to make a film about the afterlife: *Il viaggio di G. Mastorna*.[14] Fellini never shot it, but for almost thirty years he worked on its screenplay, involving Dino Buzzati and Brunello Rondi in the writing process, but then rewriting it entirely in his own hand – something he never did for any other film. The screenplay was published posthumously in 2008 by Ermanno Cavazzoni, with a preface by Vincenzo Mollica, opening with the words: "It is the most famous film *never* made in the history of cinema"[15] (Mollica 2008, 7; emphasis added).

Fellini was certainly obsessed with this film for the entire second half of his life. It is the story of a cello player, Giuseppe Mastorna, who dies in a plane crash, but who does not realize he is dead and lives an endless nightmare with no escape from a bureaucratic world governed by incomprehensible, persecutory, and exasperating rules. Image 26

Fellini, Dante, *Il viaggio di G. Mastorna*, and Dreams   149

Image 26. Illustration from Milo Manara's *Due viaggi con Federico Fellini* depicting an imagined scene from *Il viaggio di G. Mastorna*.

represents the dreamlike airplane scene where, after being hit during its flight over the Alps by a terrifying storm that portends the imminent catastrophe, the airplane inexplicably manages to make a "contingency" landing (instead of an "emergency" one, as says the flight attendant with an oneiric slip between the assonant Italian words *emergenza* and *evenienza*) in the central square of a city like Cologne, in front of its Gothic cathedral. It is a plate from Milo Manara's comic *Due viaggi con Federico Fellini* (2001), drawn closely following Fellini's instructions and representing the only figurative outcome of the thirty-year work spent *not* making the film about Mastorna. It is obvious that the airplane crashed in the Alps and that the passengers are all dead, but they do not realize it (image 26). Passengers are then transferred to a motel to spend the night, where they attend a belly dance show that ends with the dancer giving birth to a baby.

Well, what is Dantean about Mastorna's voyage in the afterlife? Absolutely nothing. Or rather, just one thing: several "Beatrices," called by this name; benevolent hostesses or assistants who try in vain to help Mastorna get out of the absurd universe in which he finds himself imprisoned. Dario Zanelli, a friend of Fellini's, in his little book *L'Inferno immaginario di Federico Fellini*, brings the idea of Mastorna back "to the years of high school, when Federico already dreamed of 'making a book about the afterlife,' in order to argue, in controversy with Dante, that in the otherworldly realms that perfect order would not exist ... but 'the same mess we have here on earth'"[16] (1995, 14).

Apart from this possible "anti-Dante" high school prehistory of the idea, it is evident that Fellini's afterlife is not a Dantean but rather a Kafkaesque afterlife. *Il viaggio di G. Mastorna* is a clear transposition of Kafka's *The Trial* (1925), which Fellini read in Alberto Spaini's translation (*Il processo*) published in 1933.[17] Cavazzoni, editor of the posthumous Mastorna screenplay, is perfectly aware of this. He takes Kafka's *The Trial* as a salient, though not unique, example in twentieth-century literature of the hypothesis that "if there is an afterlife it can only be identical to our world"[18] (2008, 222), just what Fellini thought when he was a high school student. Cavazzoni continues:

> The afterlife is underway, and it is likely that we are in it; we often don't notice it, then the afterlife shows up, like an inner pain. *The Trial* is a description of the afterlife that has suddenly come this way ... it is something that comes to visit, it can stay forever and erode life, or disappear, deactivate, without reason, like a viral fever ... The afterlife resembles our

world as dreams resemble it. What happens in dreams is the rule of what happens in the afterlife ... So in today's representations of the afterlife there is no clear distinction between a before and an after (between life and death), so much so that the opinion more frequent in writers who have devoted themselves to this topic is that the person concerned does not realize that he is dead.[19] (223–5)

Unsurprisingly, Fellini asked Dino Buzzati, the most Kafkaesque of the Italian writers of the mid-twentieth century, for help in writing the screenplay. Buzzati had already expressed his interest in magical and fantastic themes in his collection of short stories, *I sette messaggeri* (1942), around the same time that Gianfranco Contini was collecting stories for his own anthology, *Italie magique* (1946). Two things, in addition to Mastorna's script, link Buzzati to Fellini: in 1965, while Fellini was working on *Giulietta degli spiriti*, Buzzati's investigation carried out for the *Corriere della Sera* into occult and paranormal phenomena, entitled "In cerca dell'Italia misteriosa" and later published posthumously as a book with the title *I misteri d'Italia* (1978); and Buzzati's *Poema a fumetti* (1969), a rewrite of the myth of Orpheus and Eurydice (and the first Italian example of a graphic novel), which is another output of the idea of the voyage to the afterlife, cultivated for some years in tune with Fellini.

Likewise, it is evident that Mastorna's afterlife, besides being Kafkaesque, is Jungian. Just note the obsessive repetition of the terms "identification" and "individuation," and the constant request that is made to Mastorna – as to the other inhabitants of this odd afterlife – to provide authentic proof of their identity. It is impossible to escape from this afterlife because nobody succeeds in providing valid documents of their *true* "identity." This request, expressed in bureaucratic terms, imitating the language of Kafka's *The Trial*, is the key request of Jungian analytical psychology: the purpose to which the psychotherapeutic path, and, more generally, the inner search for the human being, is protracted throughout life is to get to "identify" oneself.

A direct confirmation that this pair of cultural referents, Kafka and Jung, was decisive for Fellini since the early 1960s comes from Fellini himself in a 1993 interview with Goffredo Fofi and Gianni Volpi, just a few months before his death. This passage on Jung and Kafka deserves to be read in full:

In my almost total, healthy ignorance – and I say this without boasting, without coquetry – Jung represented an encounter, in terms of great cultural emotions, comparable to the impact that Kafka gave me in literature. Kafka's was the reading of an author who has suggested a way of looking at things that before him we could not identify. We had threatening, confused, disturbing, labyrinthine sensations, but we thought they were not moments that belong to existence, or to the attempt to live it consciously or to interpret it, but fleeting moments or moments of malaise, psychic disturbances, unbearable emotions. Kafka, on the other hand, gave a meaning to this sum of emotions, contradictions, fears, hopes, cruelty, and above all a way of "recognizing" it in the most everyday details. Jung, therefore. Jung, whom I have not read in full because so many pieces, I must admit, are just for initiates, seemed to me the author, the philosopher, the thinker, and above all the most pertinent travel companion for the so nuanced, contradictory psychological type which, offhandedly, we define that of the artist: the immature, the one who extends the adolescent state beyond any current reality and manages to coexist with it without too dangerous logical frictions. Jung seemed to me to be able to suggest, like Kafka, a convincing point of view, reasonable rather than rational, but capable of interpreting not so much the dream fairy tale, the symbols, but our contradictions, the suggestions, the spells, the wonders, the memories always recreating on themselves. He seemed to suggest to me such a phantasmatic, initiatory, occult, but truly psychological key, therefore in some way related to reason, while keeping intact the fascination of semi-darkness, of mystery. It was a nourishing reading that I do not claim to have fully interpreted but that helped me, clarified me, encouraged me.[20] (Fellini 2009, 4–5)

Jung, for Fellini, is essentially represented by the book *Ricordi, sogni, riflessioni*, which, "since its appearance (1965), he kept beside himself, rereading it countless times"[21] (Kezich 1996, 139–40). But, on a personal level, Jung means above all the analysis carried out by Fellini with the analytical psychologist Erst Bernhard (see his 1969 book *Mitobiografia*), which lasted for four years, at the rate of three sessions a week, from 1960 until Bernhard's death in 1965. It means a fundamental experience, whose immediate and tangible result is the legendary *Libro dei sogni*, a collection of over 450 large tables written and above all drawn by Fellini that record all his dreams from 1960 to 1990.

Image 27 reproduces the page from *Il libro dei sogni* dated 30 November 1960, which marks the beginning of Fellini's analysis

Fellini, Dante, *Il viaggio di G. Mastorna*, and Dreams 153

Image 27. Image from Fellini's *Il libro dei sogni*. © Comune di Rimini / Francesca Fabbri Fellini, Archivio del Fellini, Museum di Rimini.

with Dr. Bernhard, who invites him to engage in analysis by asking him, "Mr. Fellini, do we want to work seriously?"[22] As Kezich writes, "Meeting Bernhard reinforces Fellini's contention that his dreams, which produce fantasies, must be considered more important than waking activities ... Fellini started keeping his *Libro dei sogni* between *La dolce vita* and *8 ½*. It will mark an important turning point in his work, which after this will be primarily oneiric ... From this point on we can say that for Fellini, life is but a dream" (2006, 227). In other words, Fellini's cinema from then on falls under the sign of the "creative unconscious," as the title of the booklet *L'inconscio creatore* (2009) says, in which the authors Christian Gaillard and Lella Ravasi Bellocchio, two Jungian psychoanalysts, highlight how the analysis, in addition to having been a path of self-knowledge and personal well-being, was above all used by Fellini as an aid for artistic creation.

Precisely this, in my opinion, is one thing that Fellini has in common with Dante: an overbearing dream-visionary vein. In the case of Fellini this is unanimously recognized, even commonplace. But this vein also consists of a stronger psychic phenomenon than commonly believed. In *Il libro dei sogni* there are at least seven "visions," distinct from ordinary "dreams," and at least thirteen "hypnagogic visions" or "hypnagogic images," real hallucinations, dazzling images that occur before sleep. In one of these, dated 25 June 1965, Fellini notes a "very violent sensation of reality. I heard the crash of the glass. I jumped on the bed with the certainty that someone had <u>really</u> thrown a brick against the windshield of my car"[23] (153).

Recent research has shown that Dante, too, has an extremely rich dreamlike-visionary streak (Tavoni 2005; Huss and Tavoni 2019). This oneirism is already perfectly visible in Dante's youthful book the *Vita nuova*, which tells of his love for the Florentine Beatrice that lasted from when she and Dante were both nine years old until she died at the age of twenty-five. Dante's whole life in this long period from childhood to adolescence to youth is dominated by dreams, daydreams, hallucinations, delusions, and mystical visions – so much so that the neurologist Giuseppe Plazzi (2013) finds in Dante's texts serious indications that he may have suffered from narcolepsy, a sleep disorder that causes a strong intensification of dream activity. Dream-visionary phenomena are very important for the young Dante (Tavoni 2019, 53–66), but he does not know how to explain them. He does not understand what sense they make. He fears they don't make any sense. He considers them pathological phenomena, a sign of weakness. And here we find another extremely important connection between Dante and Fellini: both, at a precise point in their respective history, become culturally aware that their dream inclination has a great cognitive value. Without that discovery, their visionary gifts would have remained underused and could not have become a cornerstone of their intellectual and artistic creativity.

Fellini, as we have seen, made this discovery in 1960, thanks to his encounter with the Jungian analytical psychology personified by Dr. Ernst Bernhard. Dante made the analogous discovery, in terms possible within his culture, ten years after writing the *Vita nuova*, when the fact of being exiled from Florence traumatically changed his life and compelled him to abandon all reverie and to immerse himself in the study of philosophy. At that point, between 1303 and 1304, he came across the *Liber de natura et origine animae* by doctor of the Church Albert the Great, as well as the *Liber de anima* by the Islamic physician and philosopher Ibn Sina, known in the Latin world as Avicenna. Reading these texts, Dante became aware that dreams could be messengers of important truths, and that they are not at all a sign of weakness. On the contrary, they are a privileged gift granted only to the strongest and noblest souls. We realize that Dante has made this discovery in a passage from the *Convivio* (2.8.13), where he states that not only do divinatory dreams exist and truly reveal the future to us, but also that their existence is proof that the soul is immortal (see Tavoni 2019, 43–53). At this point, Dante knows – because two *auctores* have revealed and certified it to him – that his dreams have a prophetic value, and so he is ready to begin his journey into the afterlife; that is the dream vision through which God will show him hell, purgatory, and heaven.

The first creative output of Fellini's gained confidence in the value of his dreams as voices of the "creative unconscious" – a confidence that he owes to Ernst Bernhard and Carl Gustav Jung – is the impressive opening sequence of *8 ½*. This sequence shows Guido, imprisoned in the inextricable clogging of cars in a tunnel, eventually freeing himself from it by flying high above the beach and the sea. The first creative output for Dante's confidence in the prophetic value of his dreams, a confidence that he owes to Albert the Great and Avicenna, is his bewilderment in the dark forest. In a fourteenth-century miniature from the opening page of the *Divine Comedy* (image 28), Dante, at the moment in which he abandons the true path, is shown both asleep in his bed and waking from his dream and walking in the dark forest.

Image 28. Page from a fourteenth-century manuscript of Dante's *Divine Comedy*.

NOTES

1 "una improbabilissima spiegazione contabile"
2 "*8 ½* significa un po' meno di 9, per indicare enigmaticamente e parodicamente il mito attorno al quale la nuova poetica del regista ha preso forma."
3 "Mi piacerebbe riconoscere in Dante 'colui che lo aiuta,' più di Freud e Jung, più di Servadio e di Bernhard, a compiere quel percorso interiore che ha dato come meraviglioso risultato l'insieme delle sue opere, che si muovono in una dimensione fluttuante tra realtà, visione e sogno."
4 "Se Dante ha scritto *La vita nuova* Fellini, nel mezzo del cammin della sua vita, realizza *La dolce vita* e *8 ½*, con ogni probabilità i film più danteschi della storia del cinema, quelli in cui il protagonista si ritrova come Dante in una selva oscura e si muove senza guide, prima da soggetto della narrazione come il poeta e poi da soggetto dell'azione, che ha smarrito la diritta via creativa."
5 "Questa matrice di comunicativa popolare Fellini non l'ha mai persa anche quando il suo linguaggio si è fatto più sofisticato."
6 "la sua speciale autorità visual"
7 "La *Divina Commedia* in film, non la farò mai, per una ragione semplice, che è che questo film, Dante l'ha già fatto. È un visivo così geniale e così preciso, attraverso le parole, che non vedo quale senso potrebbe avere il fatto di aggiungergli delle immagini. Sì, naturalmente, io potrei fare degli effetti speciali danteschi, saprei farli, ma a quale scopo? E inoltre, è vero che i miei film ne sono pieni ... che cosa ho fatto, in fondo, ogni volta, se non una discesa agli Inferi, con qualche bagliore di Purgatorio e Paradiso?"
8 "ogni riferimento a Dante può divenire tanto obbligatorio quanto banale"
9 "echi, suggestioni, metafore, luoghi comuni, forse coincidenze o semplici matrici culturali in comune" between Dante and Fellini "sono certo suggestive, ma difficilmente dimostrabili *more geometrico*," so that "abbandonate le reali o presunte connessioni macrointertestuali, appare prudente sospendere il giudizio sui massimi sistemi per muoversi ora su aree più sicure e verificabili, magari più localizzate, minime, ossia quelle della marcata allusione microintertestuale, della parodia, della citazione, infine del pastiche, in cui il riferimento ipotestuale è circoscritto, esplicito, ostentato, quasi una strizzatina d'occhio allo spettatore."
10 "su una colonna di marmo gelato, c'era un busto nero con gli occhi vuoti, spalancati, di ferro, un volto severo da giudice, da spione. Eravamo tutti convinti che fosse lui, con quelle labbra sottili come lame, a far la spia ai professori di tutto quello che combinavamo durante la ricreazione."
11 "Dal divino poeta Dante, a Pascoli e D'Annunzio, numerosi sono gli alti ingegni che hanno cantato questa terra."

12 "Tutta la mia filmografia, praticamente, si riferisce a quel film lì."
13 "Tanto la provincia vitellona quanto la Roma cinematografara sono gironi dell'inferno, ma sono anche insieme godibili Paesi di Cuccagna."
14 About Fellini's *Il viaggio di G. Mastorna*, see the chapters by Marina Vargau, Ottavio Cirio Zanetti, Frank Burke, and Manuela Gieri in this volume.
15 "È il film non fatto più famoso della storia del cinema."
16 "addirittura agli anni del liceo, quando Federico ... già sognava di poter 'fare un film sull'aldilà,' per poter così sostenere, in aperta polemica con Dante, che nei regni ultraterreni non esisterebbe quell'ordine perfetto, quell'infallibile rispondenza fra colpa e castigo, fra virtù e ricompensa celeste, che il Divino Poeta ha immaginato, bensì 'lo stesso casino che abbiamo qui sulla terra.'"
17 Fellini's interest in Kafka can be seen right from the meanders crossed in the opening sequence of *Agenzia matrimoniale*, an episode of the film *L'amore in città* (1953), and lasts until *Intervista* (1987), where Fellini plays himself while at Cinecittà preparing to shoot a film based on Kafka's 1927 novel *Amerika*.
18 "se c'è un aldilà non può che essere identico al nostro mondo"
19 "L'aldilà è in corso, ed è probabile che ci siamo dentro; spesso non ce ne accorgiamo, poi l'aldilà si fa vivo, come una pena interiore. Tutto *Il processo* è una descrizione dell'aldilà venuto improvvisamente di qua ... è qualcosa che viene in visita, può restare per sempre ed erodere la vita, oppure scomparire, disattivarsi, senza ragione, come una febbre virale ... L'aldilà somiglia all'aldiqua come ci somigliano i sogni. Ciò che accade nei sogni è la regola di ciò che accade nell'aldilà ... Quindi nelle rappresentazioni odierne dell'aldilà non c'è quella netta distinzione tra un prima e un dopo (tra la vita e la morte), tanto che l'opinione più frequente negli scrittori che si sono dedicati a questo argomento, è che il soggetto interessato non se ne accorge, non sa di essere morto."
20 "Nella mia pressoché totale, sana ignoranza – e lo dico senza vanto, senza civetteria – Jung ha rappresentato un punto di incontro, sul piano delle grandi emozioni culturali, paragonabile all'impatto che mi ha dato, in letteratura, Kafka. Quella di Kafka è stata la lettura di un autore che ci ha proprio suggerito un modo di guardare le cose che prima di lui non riuscivamo a individuare. Avevamo sensazioni minacciose, confuse, inquietanti, labirintiche, ma pensavamo fossero non momenti che appartengono all'esistenza, o al tentativo di viverla consapevolmente o di interpretarla, bensì momenti passeggeri o di malessere, di turbe psichiche, di emozioni insopportabili. Kafka invece ha proprio dato a questa somma di emozioni, di contraddizioni, di timori, di speranze, di crudeltà, un senso, ha suggerito un significato e soprattutto un modo di 'riconoscerlo' nei dettagli più quotidiani. Jung, dunque. Jung, che

non ho letto tutto perché tanti pezzi, devo ammettere, sono proprio per iniziati, mi è sembrato l'autore, il filosofo, il pensatore e soprattutto il compagno di viaggio più pertinente per il tipo psicologico così sfumato, contraddittorio quale, con disinvoltura, definiamo quello dell'artista. L'immaturo, colui che protrae lo stato adolescenziale al di là di ogni attualità, e con esso riesce a convivere senza frizioni logiche troppo pericolose. Jung mi è sembrato riuscire a suggerire, come Kafka, un punto di vista convincente, ragionevole più che razionale, ma passibile di interpretare non tanto la favola onirica, i simboli, ma le nostre contraddizioni, le suggestioni, gli incantesimi, le meraviglie, i ricordi sempre ricreantisi su se stessi. Mi è sembrato suggerire una chiave così fantasmatica, iniziatica, occultistica, ma davvero psicologica, quindi in qualche modo in rapporto con la ragione, pur conservando intatto il fascino della semioscurità, del mistero. È stata una lettura nutriente che non pretendo di aver compiutamente interpretata ma che mi ha aiutato, mi ha chiarito, mi ha incoraggiato."

21 "fin dalla sua apparizione (1965) si tenne accanto rileggendolo infinite volte"
22 "Signor Fellini vogliamo lavorare seriamente?"
23 "violentissima sensazione di realtà. Ho udito lo schianto dei vetri. Ho fatto un balzo sul letto con la certezza che <u>veramente</u> qualcuno mi avesse lanciato un mattone contro il parabrezza della mia auto."

REFERENCES

ACCASFILM. 2020. "FEDERICO FELLINI intervistato da Enzo Biagi (1)." YouTube video, 8:38. 9 January 2020. https://youtu.be/b9ov1REaYYs.

Bernhard, Erst. 1969. *Mitobiografia*. Edited by Hélène Erba-Tissot. Milan: Adephi.

Brunetta, Gian Piero. 2016. "L'apostolo più rappresentativo del verbo dantesco sullo schermo." In *Fellini & Dante: L'aldilà della visione: Atti del Convegno internazionale di studi, Ravenna, 29–30 maggio 2015*, 11–19. Ravenna: SAGEP.

Buzzati, Dino. 1942. *I sette messaggeri*. Milan: Mondadori.

– 1969. *Poema a fumetti*. Milan: Mondadori.

– 1978. *I misteri d'Italia*. Milan: Mondadori.

Calvino, Italo. 1974. "Autobiografia di uno spettatore." In *Quattro film: I vitelloni, La dolce vita, Otto e mezzo, Giulietta degli spiriti*, by Federico Fellini, ix–xxiv. Turin: Einaudi.

Cavazzoni, Ermanno. 2008. "Purgatori del secolo XX." In *Il viaggio di G. Mastorna*, by Federico Fellini, 207–29. Edited by Ermanno Cavazzoni. Macerata: Quodlibet.

Chiamenti, Massimiliano. 2004. "Effigi di Dante e di Leopardi in Fellini." *The Italianist* 24 (2): 224–37. https://doi.org/10.1179/ita.2004.24.2.224.
Costa, Antonio. 1996. "L'*Inferno* rivisitato." In *Dante nel cinema*, edited by Gianfranco Casadio, 45–57. Ravenna: Longo.
De Santi, Pier Marco. 1982. *I disegni di Fellini*. Rome: Laterza.
– 1989. *Federico Fellini dai disegni ai film*. Pisa: Giardini.
Fellini, Federico. 1980. *Fare un film*. Turin: Einaudi.
– 2007. *Il libro dei sogni*. Edited by Tullio Kezich and Vittorio Boarini. Milan: Rizzoli.
– 2008. *Il viaggio di G. Mastorna*. Edited by Ermanno Cavazzoni. Macerata: Quodlibet.
– 2009. *L'arte della visione: Conversazioni con Goffredo Fofi e Gianni Volpi*. Turin: Donzelli.
Fink, Guido. 2004. "'Non senti come tutto questo ti assomiglia?' Fellini's Infernal Circles." In *Dante, Cinema, and Television*, edited by Amilcare Iannucci, 166–75. Toronto: University of Toronto Press. https://www.jstor.org/stable/10.3138/9781442673700.14.
Gaillard, Christian, and Lella Ravasi Bellocchio. 2009. *L'inconscio creatore: Attorno al* Libro dei sogni *di Federico Fellini*. Bergamo: Moretti & Vivaldi.
Huss, Bernhard, and Mirko Tavoni, eds. 2019. *Dante e la dimensione visionaria tra medioevo e prima età moderna: Atti del Seminario di studio, Freie Universität Berlin, Novembre 23, 2017*. Ravenna: Longo.
Jung, Carl Gustav. 1965. *Ricordi, sogni, riflessioni*. Edited by Aniela Jaffé. Milan: Rizzoli.
Kafka, Franz. 1933. *Il processo*. Translated by Alberto Spaini. Turin: Frassinelli.
Kezich, Tullio. 1996. *Fellini del giorno dopo, con un alfabetiere felliniano*. Rimini: Guaraldi-Associazione Fellini.
– 2006. *Federico Fellini: His Life and Work*. Translated by Minna Proctor with Viviana Massa. New York: Faber and Faber.
Lewalski, Barbara K. 1978. "Federico Fellini's *Purgatorio*." In *Federico Fellini: Essays in Criticism*, edited by Peter Bondanella, 113–20. Oxford: Oxford University Press.
Manara, Milo. 2001. *Due viaggi con Federico Fellini: Viaggio a Tulum – Il viaggio di G. Mastorna detto Fernet*. Milan: Mondadori.
Mollica, Vincenzo. 2008. "Sulla vicenda cinematografica." In *Il viaggio di G. Mastorna*, by Federico Fellini, 7–14. Edited by Ermanno Cavazzoni. Macerata: Quodlibet.
Pinto, Raffaele. 2016. "La dolce vita in Dante e in Fellini." In *Fellini and Dante: L'aldilà della visione: Atti del Convegno internazionale di studi, Ravenna, 29–30 maggio 2015*, 21–8. Ravenna: SAGE.
Plazzi, Giuseppe. 2013. "Dante's Description of Narcolepsy." *Sleep Medicine* 14, no. 11: 1221–3. https://doi.org/10.1016/j.sleep.2013.07.005.

Risset, Jacqueline. 1994. *L'incantatore: Scritti su Fellini*. Milan: Scheiwiller.
Tavoni, Mirko. 2015. "Dante 'Imagining' His Journey through the Afterlife." *Dante Studies* 133:70–97. https://doi.org/10.1353/das.2015.0008.
– 2019. "La visione interiore dalla *Vita nova* al *Convivio*." In *"Vedi lo sol che 'n fronte ti riluce": La vista e gli altri sensi in Dante e nella ricezione artistico-letteraria delle sue opere*, edited by Maria Maślanka-Soro, 43–66. Rome: Aracne.
Tornabuoni, Lietta, ed. 1995. *Federico Fellini*. Milan: RCS.
Welle, John. 1993. "Fellini's Use of Dante in *La Dolce Vita*." In *Perspectives on Federico Fellini*, edited by Peter Bondanella and Cristina Degli-Espositi, 110–18. New York: G.K. Hall & Co.
Zanelli, Dario. 1995. *L'Inferno immaginario di Federico Fellini: Cose dette da F.F. a proposito de* Il Viaggio di G. Mastorna. Rimini: Guaraldi.
Zanzotto, Andrea. 1980. "Ipotesi intorno alla *Città delle donne*." In *La città delle donne*, by Federico Fellini, 19–31. Milan: Garzanti.

Il viaggio di G. Mastorna's Constellation at the Crossroads of Arts and Media

MARINA VARGAU

A Film Project Never Made, or an (Apparently) Unfinished Journey

Federico Fellini was not interested in physical travel. Instead, mental wandering and hearing the stories of other people's journeys gave him a particular satisfaction (Chandler 2020, 172). This way of travelling allowed him to free his imagination and, at the same time, to virtually reconstruct the world according to his unique and unmistakable vision as a demiurge architect. Here, perhaps, is the reason why the three journeys he devised never materialized cinematically, remaining as open spaces for the imagination and inviting one to dream. As such, they continued to have a life of their own, feeding into Fellini's *opera omnia* and the imaginations of different artists, who recreated them according to their own world views.[1]

This chapter aims to investigate the causes and conditions that allowed *Il viaggio di G. Mastorna*,[2] the most famous of the journeys imagined by Fellini, to become the most productive artistic object of his oeuvre. At the same time, it proposes to map the interartial and intermedial constellation[3] that this unfinished project has generated. Paradoxically, it seems that its prolificity was made possible by its cinematic non-achievement. Existing as a project in progress both liberated Fellini's imagination and fecundated that of other artists, allowing a limitless evasion through time, the arts, and the media.

Considering the abilities of this project to adapt and to be adapted, while also manifesting itself in different arts and media, the central questions it raises concern the dynamics (with their movements and forces) that are established between the initial text, the preceding ones, and the following ones, as well as the relationships[4] that develop between them, inviting us to "question the subject"[5] of adaptation, interartiality,[6] and intermediality.[7] How can we therefore explain the prolificity of the

Mastorna project and its ability to cross arts and media, including writing, cinema, comic books, advertising, video, multimedia exhibition, theatre, drawing, and music? How do the transitions from one text to another take place? What relationships are developed between the different art forms within the constellation? What conditions make possible the intersections between media? How can the plurality of relationships between words, images, and sounds be thought of in these contexts? Also, can we consider a "becoming Mastorna," in the sense that Fellini's initial project (making a film) begins to expand, to transform, and to revive itself in a baroque vertex of revivals, transfers, and hybridizations, as a transmedial storytelling, finding another life in the imagination of other artists, materialized in both traditional and new media?

From Script to Comic Book, or Finding the Equivalents of a Film According to Fellini

The path of this Fellini project is sinuous, crossing various arts and media. The initial script written in 1965 with Dino Buzzati and Brunello Rondi was later reprised by Fellini, in various versions, including as a letter addressed to producer Dino De Laurentiis. In 1992, this never-made film was transformed into a comic book entitled *Il viaggio di G. Mastorna detto Fernet*, the result of a collaboration between Fellini and Milo Manara. Among these materializations, the Mastorna project appears as an explicit reference in the documentary *Fellini: A Director's Notebook* (1969) and in *Viaggio a Tulum* (1989), the first comic book made by Fellini with Manara.

Although freely inspired by Dante's masterpiece, a short novel by Dino Buzzati, and Franz Kafka's universe,[8] the plot of *Il viaggio* is obviously Felliniesque. In the initial script, after a mysterious airplane crash, a cellist, who would have been played by Marcello Mastroianni, arrives in an unnamed city, both known and unknown. Under the sign of the *Unheimlich*, the fictitious city invented by Fellini anticipates in its poetry and its immateriality the invisible cities of Italo Calvino. In this city-like mosaic, made up of pieces belonging to real cities (including Rome, Venice, Naples, Rimini, Florence, Cologne, New York, Amsterdam, and Berlin), the Colosseum is shown close to St. Mark's Square, the Fulgor cinema, and the Cologne cathedral, while skyscrapers and Mount Vesuvius are visible on the horizon. After various strange encounters and misadventures, Mastorna realizes that this city is nothing more than the territory of the afterlife, and that he is dead.

In addition to taking notes and rewriting the script, Fellini, as usual, designed its sets and costumes. Deciding to go ahead with the project, he chose the actors and had certain elements of the set design built in the Dinocittà film studios. But everything seems to have stopped there. The misadventures of the most famous unmade film in the history of cinema, as Vincenzo Mollica (2008, 7) defined it, are well known and recounted by Tullio Kezich (2006) in his seminal biography dedicated to Fellini. Gustavo Adolfo Rol's warning,[9] the problems with Dino De Laurentiis, the strange illness that struck Fellini, his inability to work at Dinocittà, and also his fear and lack of confidence in the project (which Mastroianni mentions in *Fellini: A Director's Notebook*) are among the possible causes that impeded the making of the film (see Perryman 2013, 149–57).

However, without abandoning the project, Fellini returned to it, taking other paths to develop it. In the opening sequences of the television documentary *Fellini: A Director's Notebook*, one can see the set design made for the film's incipit, which reproduces the Cologne cathedral, some perspectives of the square, and the airplane's fuselage. The camera films, in a series of panoramic shots, the silhouettes of the unrealized film, "crazy ruins" inhabited by hippies. Immediately afterwards, the only filmed scene of *Il viaggio* is inserted, showing Mastorna (played by Mastroianni) from behind, walking in the square, while Fellini's voice explains:

> These strange, lonely shapes were being for a film that I planned but I never made. It was called *The Voyage of Mastorna*. The settings have remained like this, useless and empty, in a studio near Rome. In this square, a plane would have come down and out of it would have come the hero, a cellist ... dead. And from this square began his voyage through an absurd, nightmare landscape. A little while ago I came back to see all this again. It was more beautiful now, falling down and covered with weeds.

In the next sequence of the documentary, for the first time in his filmography, Fellini puts himself on stage, explicitly adding a meta-cinematographic dimension to his work. The camera films Fellini as an archaeologist, exploring with Marina Boratto, his assistant, the remains of the abandoned sets in a department store, described by the director himself as "the Mastorna cemetery, a kind of elephants' graveyard of sceneries and props."

Towards the middle of the documentary, at the end of the sequence in which Fellini and his collaborators visit Mastroianni in his villa on Via Appia Antica, the director remembers his audition with the actor while playing the cello. At the beginning of the flashback, the camera films Mastroianni – elegantly dressed, as in *La dolce vita* (1960) and *8 ½* (1963) – from behind, the actor's position making the connection between the present and the past.[10] Immediately afterwards, Fellini inserts the audition images into the documentary. In the three sequences dedicated to the *Il viaggio* that showcase the technologically elaborate editing and the symbolic connections of the film, Fellini invariably introduces the temporal confusion between the present of the film and the past that recalls Mastorna, rendering anachronistic images (buildings, objects, bodies, sights, gestures), sounds (the wind, the noise of the airplane), and Nino Rota's music.

The last time Fellini addressed the project directly was in August 1992, when he published the first part of the comic book *Il viaggio di G. Mastorna detto Fernet* made with Milo Manara. According to Gian Piero Brunetta, this comic book is "una parziale reincarnazione" (a partial reincarnation) (2015, 165) of the initial project. Compared to the set design, there are notable changes. Also, the protagonist – the cellist with Mastroianni's appearance – becomes, more than twenty-five years later, a clown resembling Paolo Villaggio whose main trick is playing the cello.[11] Particularly interesting is the position adopted by Fellini in relation to this "comic book becoming" process of the film:

> *The Journey of G. Mastorna nicknamed Fernet* is a movie in the guise of a comic book, but a movie, nevertheless. The pencils, India inks, mezzotints, brushes belonging to my friend Manara are tantamount to the set designs, costumes, fittings, lights, actors' faces I employ to tell my stories when I make movies. (quoted in Mollica 2001, 69)

At the conclusion of the first of the three projected parts of this comic book, the word "End" appears instead of "Continue," like a tragic premonition. As announced by Gustavo Rol, materializing Mastorna, even if disguised in a comic book, would be the last project realized by Fellini, who died on 31 October 1993.

The "Beguiling Ghost" or the "Story Guide" That Crosses Fellini's Cinema

Made of both reprises and anticipations, in a baroque alternation that embraces his cinematic universe to project it again onto his later works, *Il viaggio di G. Mastorna* traverses Fellini's cinema and imagination, showing once again the impressing coherence of his *opera omnia*. On the one hand, in the script, the director recuperates various images, themes, and characters from his films made before 1965.[12] For example, Mastorna, returning to his past, arrives at a certain moment in the *vitelloni's* room (*I vitelloni*, 1953), and his wife is named Luisa, like Guido's in *8 ½*. The flight attendant's way of speaking by mixing languages is similar to that of the dancer (Magali Noël) of the Cha-Cha-Cha Club in *La dolce vita*, while the child's mocking laughter seen on the advertisements scattered around the city where Mastorna arrives recalls that of the Cupidon at the end of *Le tentazioni del dottor Antonio* (1962).

On the other hand, the "fluids" of this project can be found in later works, expressed through different media: film, documentary, book, comics, and advertising. Fellini himself was the first to recognize the productivity of his project:

> At the end of each film its beguiling ghost appears and asks to be brought to life. And each time something happens to submerge it again, a glorious bit of flotsam in the profound depths where it has lain now for some twenty years. And from there it continues to send out prodigious fluids, radioactive currents that have nourished all the films I have made in its place.
>
> I am certain that without *Mastorna* I would not have imagined *Satyricon*, or at least I would not have imagined it the way I made it; nor *Casanova*, nor the *City of Women*. Even *The Ship Sails On* and *Orchestra Rehearsal* owe a small debt to *Mastorna*. The strange thing is that the story, even though it generously nourished so many of my other films, remains miraculously intact in its narrative structure. It has not lost dimension or substance and remains always the most real of all of the stories I have been able to imagine. I don't know how to explain the strange destiny of this film. Perhaps it's not a film at all but an admonition, a stimulus, a story guide; perhaps it serves the same function at those tugboat operators who pull transatlantic liners out of port: something, in sum, born not to be made but to permit others to be made. A kind of inexhaustible creative uranium ... *Mastorna* is the hint of a film, the shadow of a film, perhaps even a film I don't know how to make. (Fellini 1988, 168–71)

Scholars who have analysed *Il viaggio* have highlighted this idea. Peter Bondanella notes that "almost everything he did during the last three decades of his long and eventful career shows some sign that this unrealized film had left a mark on those that followed" (2013, ix). For his part, Antonio Costa observes that this project "has subsequently resurfaced in other works of Fellini, in fragments, quotations, revisitations"[13] (2013, 344–5). Also, according to Brunetta, *Il viaggio* "is a presence-absence that marks Fellini's journey from the mid-1960s until *La voce della luna*"[14] (2015, 163),while Ottavio Cirio Zanetti notes that this film "destined never to appear on screens" has "become a sort of laboratory of ideas and emotions for other films"[15] (2018, 31).

Il viaggio's "prodigious fluids" or "radioactive currents" can therefore be found in all further films of Fellini. Since it is now impossible to deal with all aspects of the issue, I will only mention a few examples. The atmosphere of limbo, of afterlife, specific to *Il viaggio* is also present in *Fellini: A Director's Notebook* as well as in *Fellini Satyricon* (1969), *Roma* (1972), the night sequence of *Amarcord* (1973), *Il Casanova di Federico Fellini* (1976), and *La voce della luna* (1990). In *Fellini Satyricon*, the walk through the lower-class neighbourhood, the earthquake, the suicide of the patrician couple, and the encounter with the Minotaur are all echoes of the unfinished Mastorna project. The sequences of the ecclesiastical parade and of the brothels filmed in *Roma* were already conceived in the script of *Il viaggio*. The motel far from the city where Mastorna is taken corresponds to the hotel where Amelia (Giulietta Masina) is waiting to take part in a TV show in *Ginger e Fred* (1986).

With regard to other media, besides the documentary *Fellini: A Director's Notebook*, the "ghost" of the cursed project appears as an explicit reference in Fellini and Manara's first comic book. In *Viaggio a Tulum*, at the bottom of the Cinecittà swimming pool – which is now as deep as the ocean – lies Mastorna's airplane next to the relics of the mythical ocean liners *Rex* (*Amarcord*) and *Gloria N* (*E la nave va*, 1983). Even in *Il libro dei sogni* (2007), more than one panel recreates, in colour drawings and words, Fellini's nightmares and fears of not being able to make this film. As an implicit reference, the anguished atmosphere experienced by Mastorna is revisited in the advertisement produced for the Banca di Roma where the main character is played, as if to close the circle, by Paolo Villaggio.

The "Radioactive Currents" out of the "Port Fellini," or Mastorna Imagined by Others

This project did not leave Fellini's collaborators indifferent. In his *Poema a fumetti* (1969), Dino Buzzati introduces a Mastorna-like image through the train with multiple levels. For his part, Bernardino Zapponi[16] wrote the poem "Mastorna Blues," which is recited in *Fellini: A Director's Notebook* by a hippie – a modern version of an ancient youth according to Fellini.

Since the director's passing, *Il viaggio di G. Mastorna* has continued to emit its "radioactive currents," the inner constellation being joined by Chelsea McMullan's documentary *Deragliamenti/Derailments* (2011), Marco Mion, Lorenzo Corvi, and Pietro Izzo's experimental film *Il viaggio di G. Mastorna, esperimento di ricostruzione* (2013), the exhibition *Il*

Viaggio di Mastorna: Il sogno di un film messo in scena (2017), Tyto Alba's comic book *Fellini en Roma* (2017), and the theatrical performance *Le voyage de G. Mastorna* (2019), staged by Marie Rémond.

The documentary *Deragliamenti/Derailments* is based on an interview with Milo Manara. In recalling his collaboration with Fellini, Manara talks about his role as a draughtsman, as summed up by the cinema's production team – costume designer, set designer, lighting director. On this occasion, Manara reflects on the close relationship between cinema and comics, the latter being, according to him, a sequential art. Returning to the title of the documentary, the unexpected derailments are all the things, events, and characters that no longer correspond to reality. An example is the dancer who gives birth each night while performing. With regard to the production of the film, McMullan made the choice of putting together a montage of stills and moving images shot on 16mm black-and-white film.[17] Thus, the stills reproducing comic book tables and the photograms featuring Manara working in his studio are mixed with images filmed on the set of Quentin Tarantino's *Inglourious Basterds* (2009),[18] or with the small film in front of the Cologne cathedral.

Il viaggio di G. Mastorna, esperimento di ricostruzione, a self-produced rubamatic edited with images *stolen* from other films, shows that Fellini's project can easily involve new media. In the film, Mion, Corvi, and Izzo describe their storyboard as "a collage of images taken from the net which, mounted together, could give an idea of the atmosphere of the film." The sources of this rubamatic are the script, which is also shown on film at certain moments, and all existing documents on Mastorna, including photos taken by Tazio Secchiaroli (2000) on the set, images from *Fellini: A Director's Notebook*, drawings by Manara, and some drawings by Fellini published in *Il libro dei sogni*. Added to this material are excerpts from almost all of Fellini's filmography, clearly demonstrating how this project recovers images from his earlier films while remaining part of his later work. To complete the story with images, there are also excerpts from films made by other directors (Antonioni, Bolognini, De Sica, Rossellini, Pasolini, Ettore Scola, Méliès, Spielberg, Tim Burton, etc.), documentaries, TV series, and other books. This very interesting experiment that aims to reconstruct Mastorna's story has a particular dynamic resulting from the mixture of stills and moving images, and also from the montage between the parts that present the story and those in which the makers explain and recount once again, while filmed or in voice-over, what they showed before.

In 2017, at the Gallery of Modern Art in Viareggio, Alessandro Romanini and Francesco Frigeri curated an exhibition suggestively titled *Il Viaggio di Mastorna: Il sogno di un film messo in scena* that was produced by

Image 29. Plate from the exhibition *Il Viaggio di Mastorna: Il sogno di un film messo in scena*.

the Centro Sperimentale di Cinematografia in Rome. This time, to pay homage to Fellini and his never-made film, the acting students at the Centro Sperimentale di Cinematografia, as well as the students responsible for the set, costumes, and sound design, inspired by Fellini's set design and other materials, created fifty plates, costume sketches, and a soundtrack for the exhibition. The plates depicted various scenes from Fellini's initial script, recreating its dreamlike and surreal atmosphere and proposing through beautiful colour drawings a static reconstruction of the film never completed (image 29).[19] In this multimedia exhibition, the original materials were joined by an interview with Fellini talking about his project and Mastroianni's audition in the legendary Studio 5 (today, Studio Federico Fellini) at Cinecittà.

Also in 2017, Tyto Alba published the comic book *Fellini en Roma*. The first thirty-nine plates update Manara's comic book. The oneiric and limbo-like atmosphere, the question of death raised by the first panel, the lonely airplane crossing empty spaces or urban areas, and the emergency landing in the middle of a city are signs that a dialogue in time is occurring between the two graphic artists and, implicitly, Fellini. Obviously, Alba brings his own personal touch. For example, replacing a Mastorna in the guise of Paolo Villaggio is an elderly Fellini, dressed in a long coat, with his legendary red scarf and hat. The director is in the airplane about to make a "Fellinian" descent into a city that is no longer Cologne, but Rome, easily recognizable by images of St Peter's Basilica and the Pantheon. With this choice, Alba directly links, from the beginning, the unfinished project dedicated to Mastorna with Rome, the Fellinian city par excellence, and the eponymous film from 1972. Cinematic Fellinian characters from this film, such as the nuns strolling among the pine trees or the burly shirtless gentleman, now on a balcony, inhabit various city spaces. Reality, Fellini's imagination, and the vision of Alba are mixed together in a cinematic-like montage; one can see Fellini walking along his beloved Via Margutta, scenes from *Roma*, or Fellini again, in the middle of a foggy forest, coming upon the legendary Capitoline she-wolf. After suckling the twins Remus and Romulus, the she-wolf turns into the gigantic prostitute from Fellini's same film, *Roma*.

The Mastorna project haunts the other parts of Alba's comic book. After recounting other famous episodes of Fellini's life (his arrival in Rome and Cinecittà, his encounters with Giulietta Masina, Rossellini, and so on), Fellini meets Pasolini, who explains to him that life is also death ("è la vita anche la morte") as he drives past the ancient ruins on the Via Appia Antica.[20] In the final pages, an aged Fellini wakes up in a hospital bed before escaping with the help of Mastorna (image 30). Fellini, always guided by Mastorna, stops at the beach. Among the people sitting silently on the beach, looking at the sea, is his father. Fellini's final meeting, announced but not seen, will be with his mother, whom Fellini identifies among the silent crowd. In Fellini's universe, it is evidently a mythical encounter, a symbolic and psychoanalytic *regressum ad uterum*.

In 2019, at the Vieux-Colombier Theatre, Marie Rémond staged the play *Le voyage de G. Mastorna* from a script written with Thomas Quillardet and Aurélien Hamard-Padis.[21] Rather than adapting the initial text as such for the theatre, Rémond staged the story around the non-realization of Fellini's project. This time, the main protagonist is Fellini himself (Serge Bagdassarian), who prepares the future film while surrounded on stage by the magician Gustavo Rol (Jérémy Lopez), his assistant Liliana Betti (Jennifer Decker), another assistant director, Marcello Mastroianni (Laurent Lafitte) as Mastorna, and the other actors (Georgia Scalliet, Nicolas Lormeau, Alain Lenglet, and Yoann Gassiorowsky) (image 31).

Unlike the other projects dedicated to *Il viaggio* that sought to reconstruct, partially or entirely, its plot, this play places us in front of a mise-en-abyme. The French director, on the trail of Fellini in *Fellini: A Director's Notebook*, proposes a reconstruction, both real and fictitious, of the days when the director worked in the Dinocittà studios. As in reality,

Image 30. Drawing from *Fellini en Roma* by Tyto Alba (Alba, 2017, 73). © Tyto Alba.

accompanied by his assistant, Fellini is always on stage, overflowing with energy – giving directions to his actors and crew, filming with a handheld camera – but also gripped by anxiety. The other characteristic that distinguishes this play from the previous projects is its humour, which is present in various dialogues and situations, especially in the first part of the play (which would not have displeased Fellini). Linking this theatrical performance with Tyto Alba's comic book is Pasolini's statement about life as death. If the other artists already mentioned have recreated the adventures of Mastorna through videos or drawings, Marie Rémond puts us in an almost palpable and emotional proximity with the bodies, the gestures, the voices of the actors, and the sets that combine the classical decorations with the modern projections of a film made on Mastorna's life.

Image 31. Photograph of a scene from the stage play *Le voyage de G. Mastorna*. Directed by Marie Rémond, Comédie-Française, Paris, 2019.

By Way of Conclusion, without Finishing, or from an Unaccomplished Journey to an Endless One

Rather than *más torna* (never returns), Mastorna returns (*ritorna*) with all the projects that bring it back to life. The appearance of these multimedia objects, created half a century after Fellini wrote the script of *Il viaggio di G. Mastorna*, demonstrates not only the ability of the unfinished project to adapt and to manifest itself in different arts and media, but also its vitality as a tantalizing source of inspiration – "inexhaustible creative uranium" – for artists of all genres. The interstellar cartography proposed here has highlighted the fact that each star constituting the constellation of *Il viaggio di G. Mastorna*, although playing its own well-defined role, enjoys other qualities when put in relation with the other stars. Looking at them together, one can see the presence of a synergetic effect emanating from this constellation, greater than the sum of its components which, complementarily, call and respond to each other. Expressing our gratitude in front of all these wonderful artists, let us continue to imagine together the film that was never made – with Marcello Mastroianni or Paolo Villaggio, Totò and Mina, Wanda Osiris and Vittorio De Sica, Franco Franchi and Ciccio Ingrassia, among others – wishing that the "ghost" provokes the birth of other stars. Paraphrasing the title of a recent documentary,[22] let us think of a Mastorna *fine mai*.

NOTES

1 The autobiographical script *Viaggio con Anita*, written in 1957 with Tullio Pinelli and Pier Paolo Pasolini, inspired certain characters and scenes in *8 ½* (1963) and was the source for films such as Mario Monicelli's *Viaggio con Anita* (1979) and Luca Magi's *Anita* (2012). The script *Viaggio a Tulum* (1986) was turned into a comic book in 1989 by Fellini and Milo Manara and suggestively titled *Viaggio a Tulum: Da un soggetto di Federico Fellini per un film da fare* (Trip to Tulum: From a subject by Federico Fellini for a film to be made). In his novel, *Yucatan* (1986), Andrea de Carlo intends to reveal, under the veil of fiction, the true story of this paranormal journey made by Fellini. Between these two projects, chronologically, is *Il viaggio di G. Mastorna*.
2 Mirko Tavoni, Ottavio Cirio Zanetti, Frank Burke, and Manuela Gieri also write on *Il viaggio di G. Mastorna* in their respective chapters in this volume.
3 A constellation, as I first defined it in the context of Fellini's Rome, is as "an apparent configuration, made up of different works that operate and develop a set of common problems, while preserving their specificities. The constellation is a becoming (in the Deleuzian sense of the term), since it can change its form and constituent elements, adding others or reconfiguring in a different way what already existed" (une configuration apparente, constituée par des œuvres différentes qui travaillent et développent un ensemble de problèmes communs tout en préservant leurs spécificités. La constellation est un devenir [au sens deleuzien du terme], puisqu'elle peut changer de forme et d'éléments constitutifs, en ajoutant d'autres ou reconfigurant différemment ce qui était déjà là) (Vargau 2021, 19). Please note that all translations are my own unless otherwise noted.
4 According to Alfonso de Toro, "media relations are always transgressions of boundaries, translations, transformations and reinventions of dialogic and hybrid structures" (2013, 53).
5 Silvestra Mariniello (2000, 8) invites us to ask questions (or, in Heidegger words, to work to a road, to build it) about the subject of intermediality and cinema.

6 I follow Walter Moser, who defines the concept of interartiality as "all possible interactions between the arts that the Western tradition has distinguished and differentiated, the main ones being painting, music, dance, sculpture, literature and architecture" (l'ensemble des interactions possibles entre les arts que la tradition occidentale a distingués et différenciés et dont les principaux sont la peinture, la musique, la danse, la sculpture, la littérature et l'architecture) (2007, 70). In addition to the traditional arts, we could also add more recent ones, such as cinema and comic books. Interartiality is also a concept mobilized by Dishani Samarasinghe's chapter in this volume.

7 Here I follow Silvestra Mariniello, who, in noting the state of progress in the research on intermediality at the University of Montreal, defines this "polymorphous concept" and "new paradigm" as "the totality of the conditions that make possible the crossings and the competition of the media, the possible ensemble of the figures that the medias produce by crossing each other, the potential disposition of the points of one figure in relation to those of another" (2011, 14).

8 Fellini was freely inspired by two texts read during his adolescence from which he developed much imagery related to death: Dante's *Divine Comedy* (especially *Purgatorio*), and "Lo strano viaggio di Domenico Molo" (1938) by Dino Buzzati. The atmosphere and the idea of the journey can be reminiscent of Kafka's *America* (1927), while in the scene in which Mastorna's life is judged and evaluated by the jury, we can recognize Kafka's *The Trial* (1925). Added to these sources, there is also *Bardo Thodol* (*The Tibetan Book of the Dead*), which Fellini read while writing the first version of the script.

9 Kezich (2006, 276) and, later, Tassone (2020, 791) recall the anecdote in which a notice found in Fellini's pocket contains Rol's warning not to make the film as it would be his last project due to the negative energy contained in it. The note even implied Fellini's death.

10 Originally, *Il viaggio di G. Mastorna* was intended to be the third installment of a Mastroianni trilogy that included *La dolce vita* and *8 ½*.

11 The choice of the protagonist, initially to be played by Mastroianni, proves to be complicated. De Laurentiis proposed Laurence Olivier, Paul Newman, Steve McQueen, Enrico Maria Salerno, and Ugo Tognazzi. Later, in the sketches for the comic book, Fellini added the faces of Paolo Villaggio, John Barrymore Jr., and Edgar Allan Poe to the face of an aged Mastroianni. Thus, over time, the protagonist is built up as a mosaic of faces.

12 In this sense, Alessandro Carrera remarkably argues that "Fellini could not make *Mastorna* for the simple reason that he had already made it" (2020, 130).

13 "è successivamente riemerso in altre opere di Fellini, in frammenti, citazioni, rivisitazioni"

14 "è una presenza-assenza che scandisce il cammino felliniano dalla metà degli anni Sessanta fino alla *Voce della luna*"
15 "destinato a non apparire mai sugli schermi"; "diventato una sorta di laboratorio di idee ed emozioni per altri film"
16 Bernardino Zapponi (1927–2000) wrote or collaborated on the scripts for seven Fellini films between 1968 and 1980.
17 McMullan explains "that, visually, by using stills instead of moving images, Manara, as in his collaboration with Fellini, would act as a bridge between comics and cinema" (2016, 214).
18 These scenes, filmed in the Babelsberg Film Studios in Berlin, replaced the lost sets built at the Dinocittà studios.
19 I warmly thank Franceso Frigeri (image 29), Tyto Alba (image 30), and Marie Rémond (image 31) who all sent me images from their wonderful, respective works and allowed me to publish them in this collection.
20 Alba is inspired here by the "dream with Pasolini" that Fellini recounts to De Laurentiis in the famous letter.
21 I warmly thank Marie Rémond who allowed me to see a recording of the show.
22 In 2019, Eugenio Cappuccio made the documentary *Fellini fine mai*, where, among other subjects (Rimini, the comic book *Viaggio a Tulum*), he gets interested in Mastorna.

REFERENCES

Alba, Tyto. 2017. *Fellini en Roma*. Bilbao: Astiberri.
Bondanella, Peter. 2013. "Preface." In *The Journey of G. Mastorna: The Film Fellini Didn't Make*, by Federico Fellini, ix–xi. Translated by Marcus Perryman. New York: Berghahn Books.
Brunetta, Gian Piero. 2015. "Moraldo e Mastorna: due stelle polari." In *L'isola che non c'è. Viaggi nel cinema italiano che non vedremo mai*, 163–80. Bologna: Cinema ritrovato.
Carrera, Alessandro. 2020. "*Il viaggio di G. Mastorna*: Fellini *Entre Deux Morts*." In *A Companion to Federico Fellini*, edited by Frank Burke, Marguerite Waller, and Marita Gubareva, 129–39. Hoboken, NJ: Wiley Blackwell.
Chandler, Charlotte. 2020. *Io, Federico Fellini*. Milan: Mondadori.
Costa, Antonio. 2013. "Dislocazioni a tempo e luogo indeterminati: Buzzati, Fellini e *Il viaggio di G. Mastorna*." *Studi Novecenteschi* 40, no. 86: 341–52. www.jstor.org/stable/43450158.
de Toro, Alfonso. 2013. "En guise d'introduction: Transmédialité – hybridité – translatio – transculturalité: Un modèle." In *Translatio: Transmédialité et transculturalité en littérature, peinture, photographie et au cinema: Amériques –*

Caraïbes – Europe – Maghreb, edited by Alfonso de Toro, 39–80. Paris: L'Harmattan.

Fellini, Federico. 1988. *Comments on Film*. Edited by Giovanni Grazzini. Translated by Joseph Henry. Fresno: Press at California State University.

– 2007. *Il libro dei sogni*. Edited by Tullio Kezich and Vittorio Boarini. Milan: Rizzoli.

– 2008. *Il viaggio di G. Mastorna*. Edited by Ermanno Cavazzoni. Macerata: Quodlibet.

Fellini, Federico, and Milo Manara. (1992) 1995. *Il viaggio di G. Mastorna detto Fernet*. Montepulciano: Edizioni del Grifo.

Kezich, Tullio. 2006. *Federico Fellini: His Life and Work*. Translated by Minna Proctor with Viviana Massa. New York: Faber and Faber.

Mariniello, Silvestra. 2000. "Présentation." *Cinémas* 10, no. 2–3: 7–11. https://doi.org/10.7202/024812ar.

– 2011. "L'intermédialité: Un concept polymorphe." In *Inter Media: Littérature, cinéma et intermédialité*, edited by Célia Vieira and Isabel Rio Novo, 11–30. Paris: L'Harmattan.

McMullan, Chelsea. 2016. "Spotlight on the Artist: Fellini's M: Considering the Tantalizing Unmade Masterpiece." In *Federico Fellini: Riprese, riletture, (re)visioni*, edited by Paola Bernardini, Joanne Granata, Teresa Lobalsamo, and Alberto Zambenedetti, 209–16. Florence: Franco Cesati Editore.

Mollica, Vincenzo. 2001. *Fellini: Words and Drawings*. Translated by Nina Marino. Welland, ON: Soleil.

– 2008. "Sulla vicenda cinematografica." In *Il viaggio di G. Mastorna*, by Federico Fellini, 7–14. Edited by Ermanno Cavazzoni. Macerata: Quodlibet.

Moser, Walter. 2007. "L'interartialité: Pour une archéologie de l'intermédialité." In *Intermédialité et socialité: histoire et géographie d'un concept*, by Marion Froger and Jürgen E. Müller, 69–92. Münster: Nodus Publikationen.

Perryman, Marcus. 2013. "Imagining Mastorna." In *The Journey of G. Mastorna: The Film Fellini Didn't Make*, by Federico Fellini, 137–202. Translated by Marcus Perryman. New York: Berghahn Books.

Secchiaroli, Tazio. 2000. *G. Mastorna, opera incompiuta*. Palermo: Sellerio.

Tassone, Aldo. 2020. *Fellini 23 ½: Tutti i film*. Bologna: Edizioni Cineteca di Bologna.

Vargau, Marina. 2021. *Romarcord: Flânerie, spectacle et mémoire dans la Rome de Federico Fellini*. Toronto, ON: Guernica World Editions.

Zanetti, Ottavio Cirio. 2018. *Tre passi nel delirio: Fellini tra fumetto, circo e varietà*. Venice: Marsilio.

The Genesis of Steiner:
La dolce vita as Authorial Melting Pot

FEDERICO PACCHIONI

The character of Steiner, the apparently serene intellectual figure who suddenly kills himself and his children in Federico Fellini's *La dolce vita* (1960), has been consistently identified as a central but puzzling element of this film. By unveiling the cultural and literary origins of Steiner – encompassing Christian dramaturgy, existential philosophy, musicology, and real historic figures such as Cesare Pavese and Roberto Longhi – this chapter explains the reasons this character, at once serene and heroic, desperate and cowardly, turned into such a complex and contradictory figure. To clarify the character's genesis, we must examine the collaborative exchanges between Fellini and the writers who contributed to the conceptualization of this character, more specifically Tullio Pinelli and Brunello Rondi, and the filmmaker's mediation between their opposing views. The analysis demonstrates how Steiner is the fruit of conflicting literary, philosophic, and authorial spheres of influence as well as a clear example of Fellini's capacity to blend and neutralize contrasting contributions from his screenwriters.

In his correspondence with critic Tullio Kezich, the screenwriter Ennio Flaiano once confessed, with his usual sarcasm: "I admire Fellini's ability to select his nourishment, and his capacity to steal it whenever necessary wherever he finds it … as a way to give order to chaos"[1] (Kezich 1996, 158). The most valuable talent for directors might very well be their flair for choosing the right collaborators at the right time, and Fellini was certainly not lacking in this vital skill, which was coupled with a remarkable openness to ideas and suggestions. It is indeed astounding to consider the voracity and effectiveness with which Fellini's cinema absorbed and metabolized some of the finest Italian writers of the twentieth century.

A model of a successful artistic and personal life in the eyes of the confused Marcello Rubini (Marcello Mastroianni), the intellectual and family man Steiner, played by Alain Cuny, appears in several crucial scenes of La dolce vita. He first appears playing an organ in church and encouraging Marcello to pursue his dream of being a writer; then during a dialectically dynamic party at his own home filled with endearing family moments and both ecstatic and satirical social vignettes; and finally again in his home, this time lifeless on a chair after having shot his children and himself.

In an interview, Pinelli provided an enlightening description of Steiner:

> [Steiner] is an anticipation of what happens every day. This episode is entirely mine. I suggested and wrote it. Unfortunately, the evening at Steiner's house has been rewritten and is completely different from what I had done, resulting in one of the worst episodes of the film. However, I said this to Federico, "Be careful because here you did something that communicates that the person kills himself because of the type of friends he has, and naturally so." At the beginning, though, it was different. Steiner had to kill himself because of the desperation of happiness. Someone who arrives at the apex of happiness, of life's sweetness, with a beautiful, faithful, and loving wife, with his beautiful children, knows that he has reached a dead end and therefore kills himself and his children. It is not an isolated event. It is truly what is happening now on an immeasurably larger scale. This is an exceptional episode in the film; it is not in the same tone as the other parts; it stands out. In my opinion it is one of the most farsighted moments on what is happening now.[2] (Pinelli quoted in Scolari 2008, 172)

Steiner represented for Pinelli the intellectual affected by a "desperation of happiness," who is materially accomplished but spiritually dissatisfied. As Pinelli alluded above, the singularly tragic tone of the episode was undermined by the party scene where Steiner is surrounded by rather shallow friends and intellectuals, an episode that, according to Pinelli, clouds the deeper reasons behind the character's desperate actions and therefore the significance of his crisis.

Most likely, in Pinelli's point of view, a fitting biographical source for Steiner was the suicide of Cesare Pavese (1908–50), a childhood friend of Tullio and his brother, Carlo Pinelli, to whom they had written letters in an attempt to help him find respite from his depression in the Christian faith. Remaining within the textual domain, Steiner is most fruitfully compared to the tragic character of writer Pietro Rovere in Pinelli's play *Lotta con l'angelo* (Struggle with the angel, 1942), who is also dissatisfied with his material achievements and with his failure to properly respond to God's call for martyrdom, and who finally kills himself and his wife. In Pinelli's writings, tragedy is consistently framed within a religious, definitely Christian, perspective, often leading to climactic moments of redemption. The character of Pietro Rovere, for example, can be viewed in a parallel to Steiner as well as other Fellinian characters strongly linked to this screenwriter's imagination, such as Zampanò from *La strada* (1954). However, Steiner's story is deprived of any religiously redemptive tone, which instead can be found in Pinelli's more autonomous writings, such as in the aforementioned play, and in an original first version of the script of *La strada*. Both texts provide clear examples of Pinelli's own rendition of tragic redemption character dynamics, which Fellini metabolized in less explicit Christian terms.

Below is an excerpt from the finale of Pinelli's *Lotta con l'angelo* that presents the dialogue between Pietro, who has just fatally wounded himself after murdering his wife, and his favourite son, Davide, who does not stop believing in his father's capacity to save his soul:

> PIETRO: (*Stares at Davide in silence. Then with a terrible tone speaks.*) So. May this horror remain as your only memory of me. It will help you to overcome the flesh, when you will be tempted to deny martyrdom. (*Pause*) I have rejected it, and I descend to eternal suffering.
> DAVIDE: No. Not yet.
> PIETRO: It is just horrible. But from the bottom of the abyss, I will see you with our brothers' angels, close to Him. My son. (*Pause*) You will see Him by his side for all eternity.
> DAVIDE: (*Murmuring*) God of mercy.
> PIETRO: Glory to Him.
> DAVIDE: Hope. Save yourself.
> PIETRO: It is not right.
> DAVIDE: Do you still love Him?
> PIETRO: I will make hell tremble, singing glory to Him.
> DAVIDE: (*Murmuring*) If you love Him, the enemy cannot pass.
> PIETRO: (*Murmuring*) God the Father! God the Father!
> DAVIDE: (*Almost speaking into his ear*) You are saved. Do you still love Him?
> PIETRO: (*With a whisper*) To death.
> DAVIDE: You are saved. (*Pause. Slowly he stands, his eyes staring at Pietro Rovere, who still lies on the couch with his eyes cloudy, wide open, and turned to the sky.*)[3] (Pinelli 1996, 239)

Let us also consider the finale of the early archival version of *La strada*, another example of Pinelli's teleological storytelling, where Gelsomina functions as a Christ-like figure for Zampanò's deep regret and own spiritual calvary:

> Zampanò has stopped and is listening. He listens to what he has never listened to before: silence. A sudden shiver shakes him from head to toe. It is a shiver of terror. And after the terror comes the fear of a never-before-experienced feeling of emptiness. It is not the fear of hunger or of jail or of another man; it is the fear of emptiness. His knees weaken. Zampanò crouches down on the sand. As if hit by a concrete and terrifying illness, something he had never felt before, Zampanò struggles against something that is being painfully born out of his bestial soul: angst. In the evening, the rustling of the waves repeats itself continuously, and Zampanò, for the first time in his life, cries. A woman was born and has died for this. The dawn on the sea is like the beginning of the world. Zampanò sleeps profoundly on the sand. He does not rest as he always used to, twisted on himself, as if in an animalistic instinctive defense: his limbs rest open and abandoned, with the serene faith of a child's sleep. His face is calm and human.[4] (Fellini and Pinelli 1954, 101–2)

For many years after the making of *La dolce vita*, Fellini would continue to come to terms with the influence of Pinelli's creative contribution, which he increasingly perceived as overly tragic, as demonstrated by the vivid dream that Fellini recorded in the summer of 1963 – a year that marked a decisive break in their collaboration – of the screenwriter's "exaggerated, outdated and not-valid writing" (Fellini 2008, 126, 492) in connection to a blatantly erroneous characterization of Giulietta/Gelsomina (as conflating characters) as a cruel being.

Brunello Rondi, another of Fellini's instrumental screenwriters, must have understood the incompatibility between Pinelli and Fellini when it came to dramatization. For example, in describing the episode of Marcello's father in *La dolce vita*, he spoke of "traditionalist sediment, [an element] belonging to an old dramaturgy ... that remains abstract within the chaotic and aggressive tone of the film[5] (Rondi 1965, 28–9). Furthermore, Rondi acutely explained how Fellini overcomes the literariness of the episode of Marcello's father by releasing a charge of "sympathy and good-hearted fun [that interjects into the film] a sudden *vitellone*-like complicity between father and son"[6] (281).

Pinelli had prepared the scene of the evening party at Steiner's house as a fresco of perfect familial serenity, which was supposed to end abruptly with Steiner's infanticide and suicide, thus raising the ghost of desperation and emptiness that had been lurking beneath an overly rationalized and self-absorbed life. This plan was thwarted by Fellini's

The Genesis of Steiner: *La dolce vita* as Authorial Melting Pot 181

insertion of a collection of questionable artists and intellectuals orbiting around Steiner, which, for Pinelli, had the unwanted effect of assuaging the tragic actions that led Steiner to murder his children and kill himself. Fellini's change, however, was functional to Rondi's own idea of Steiner and bore the mark of the collaborator's particular vision for the character. Rondi's explanation of his interpretation of the Steiner episode provides a number of informative and palpable clues to the way he intended to develop his own philosophic discourse through this character:

> Fellini well understood the idea that Steiner is a character who has intuited a new and original harmony of relationships, almost as the glimmerings of a new world ... Steiner's fate is that of all disarmed prophets ... perhaps he is the only character that endures beyond *la dolce vita* ... Therefore, it quickly seemed necessary to Fellini, and to us, to build in Steiner's home and in his friendships the quality of a positive solitude, one rich in intuition and with a happiness that goes beyond worn-out and conventional terms. We imagined an ambiance of tranquil intelligence, of subtle but not cerebral intimacy, and one not of pretentious culture. Steiner has his guests listen to electronic music and then to the sounds of nature from his record player, evoking around this almost initiatory gathering the strong and sweet face of nature as it manifests itself through its voices, through its presence that can either disperse or elevate man ... In this way we built the "evening at Steiner's home" as a sort of anxious vigil and like the eve of a new world, intuited by individuals who, however, lack the weapons and the concrete instruments necessary to build it; individuals who also reflect, at least halfway, the pale face of decadence ... It was in this twofold sense that we imagined that "rediscovery" of the sounds of nature: as Steiner's act of love for all things and for reality and as his guests' moment of profound awe, as if they had lost, from time immemorial, their capacity to see and listen to the voice and to the concrete and intimate face of nature.[7] (Kezich 1996, 124–6)

In contrast to the idea that Pinelli conceived for the character of Steiner, Rondi envisioned him – using the Machiavellian image of the "disarmed prophet" – as the only one who seems to have found the secret to serenity. He is a martyr but still a tragic yet positive character whose solitude and approaching demise are rendered visible during his attempts to reawaken the party's guests with his poetry about the simple things in life (Rondi 1965, 207). Well before the scathing remarks that the writer Alberto Arbasino made targeting this sequence of the film, Rondi was aware of the helplessness of the intellectual and artistic figures assembled in Steiner's presence, who are overtaken by the desire for a more harmonious life and world but are miserably incapable of creating it.[8] The idea of Steiner as the martyr of Rondi's organic credo, who was supposed to stand out from the mediocre world of *La dolce vita* by pursuing an ideal of fulfillment through relationships, is further clarified during one of Steiner's memorable monologues in the film: "It would be necessary to live outside passions, beyond sentiments, in the harmony and the enchanted order that exists within a successful work of art. It would be necessary to be able to love each other so much, to live outside of time, detached. Detached."[9]

Interestingly, Rondi is also at the root of a musical discourse developed through the character of Steiner, following the specific coordinates of Rondi's own treatises on the evolution of Western classical music and culminating in the praise of electronic music. Rondi interpreted contemporary classical music through an existentialist lens, praising the courage of composers such as Igor Stravinsky (1882–1971), who had faced and voiced the fragmentation, isolation, and disillusionment inherent in modern life (1952, 133–5). To him, as to many others, Arnold Schoenberg's dodecaphonic language and the new forms of orchestral music that disrupted the laws of tonality expressed a sheer waste of the human being's transcendental possibilities and were therefore the highest representation of the crisis of "modern man." As early as 1949, Rondi wrote that contemporary classical music "was the echo of a disjoined society, of a metaphysics that has been consumed and corrupted, of an individuality inscribed within an elevated nucleus of crisis"[10] (1949, 12). Rondi declared his optimistic view that the times were ready and that it was now possible to find a solution to such a crisis. Together with Italian existentialist philosophers such as Nicola Abbagnano (1901–90), Rondi believed that existentialism was now outdated and limiting to the mind, and he applied this idea to the history of music, indicating what, in his opinion, might be the route to the achievement of a new metaphysical harmony. Even though Rondi knew that "Bach's music represents the total victory over time [and that] modern music represents the total defeat under time,"[11] he did not propose a nostalgic resurrection of the glory days of tonal harmony but instead praised the human and cultural potential of electronic music (1949, 32).

Rondi often described the organ as a symbol of the polyphony of the past, the emblem of a bygone harmonious relationship with the cosmos. In the film *La dolce vita*, Steiner meets Marcello in a church and introduces the organ with these words: "We are no longer used to listening to these sounds. What a mysterious voice, it seems to arise from the bowels of the earth."[12] After the playful and painful contrast between the church's sacred space and the chaotic jazz piece that Steiner improvises for a moment, he then dives into Bach's celebrated beginning of the "Toccata and Fugue in D minor." According to Rondi, the notes of this music are "like the gold from a mine: very deep, subterranean, blinding [and assail Marcello's ears with] the sound of a very ancient bell,"[13] highlighting his distance from the solemnity of such holy fullness and at the same time ominously prefiguring his spiritual perdition (Rondi 1965, 207). The final version of the script reads as follows: "Marcello is engrossed as if oppressed by that wave of sound, which is precise and evocative of a mystery that he is not prepared to solve and which fills him with anxiety"[14] (Fellini 1960, 169). Both Steiner and Marcello know that the sacredness that music embodies, arising from the depth of time, does not belong to their world and cannot be sustained for long.

Rondi considered electronic music to be the future of the European classical music tradition and saw it as a possible way to overcome dodecaphonic fragmentation and incommunicability and embody a more vital rapport of human beings with life. For the same reason that electronic music became a means to reconstruct a new modern "duration" and a new foundation on which to rebuild harmonious relationships, Rondi saw electronic music as a new instrument for research into reality. In his essay on electronic music, he stated that

> the opening of the musical soul unto the spaces of electronic sound [consists in] a plunge into pure matter, into the still uncategorized infinitely colored and variegated myriad of noises and pure sounds, where sonority has the objective and foreign richness of an unexplored mine ... The music that is constructed with already known material places the listener into contact with references of reality, with something alive and familiar, while the music built upon new material throws one into a totally unknown and unfamiliar state.[15] (1959, 84)

Unlike in the case of Rondi's electronic selections, the rarefied simplicity of the music that Nino Rota created for Fellini's films did not point to or try to contend with the fragmentation of the crisis of "modern man." Rota's isolation within the learned musical scene of his time, as well as the marginalization of his music by critics, was due to the apparent backwardness of his compositional style. Rota's music did not reject tonality, and his sensibility did not share the sense of existential disorientation expressed by most of the composers of his time. The universal and timeless virtues of Rota's music can be attributed to the composer's affinity for early sacred music and fervent interest in esotericism. Rondi's influence on the musical discourse of Fellini's films was likewise oriented towards a quest for a harmonious relationship with the world – not through a nostalgic adherence to the harmonic tradition but by embracing the experimental developments of contemporary Western music and going beyond the realm of tonal harmony and traditional sounds.

During the scene at the party at his house in *La dolce vita*, Steiner shyly discloses his secret experiments with music to recapture the perfection of Bach's cosmic harmony by recording the sounds of nature – thunder, rain, birds, and wind – and reorganizing them in a new manmade electronic order. The entire scene of Steiner's experiment with sound is absent from the shooting script, a fact that further testifies to the major changes this part underwent during filming, when Rondi was working as the screenwriter on set. In his description of Steiner (quoted earlier in this chapter) and this scene, Rondi explicitly spoke of electronic music using sounds from nature (Kezich 1996, 126). Steiner's sound experiments recall Pierre Schaeffer's (1910–95) aesthetic experiments with sound recording and tape manipulation. Schaeffer started the movement referred to as Musique Concrète; it became known in France and the rest of Europe in the 1950s and influenced electronic composers such as Tod Dockstader, whose creations were later employed in the soundtrack of *Satyricon* (1969). Steiner, with his own tape manipulations, is enacting Rondi's program and attempting to find a new synthesis between man and nature: "Far from being an intellectual trick, it is a moment of obscurely religious emotion. The noises and the sounds of pure objectivity (almost as manifestations of the pure Being of which Heidegger speaks) pass – as if through astral distances – on the faces of these creatures lost in their abstract and personal mythologies"[16] (Rondi 1965, 279).

Whereas Pinelli's Steiner originated from his Christian dramaturgy, Rondi's extended to the films he himself directed. In fact, Rondi employed Alain Cuny for the role of Conte Davide, a depraved matchmaker who is deeply aware of the philosophic tenets of his work, in his *I prosseneti* (1976, The ruffians). The same year, in his film *Velluto nero* (1976, Black Emmanuelle/white Emmanuelle), we find an example of Rondi's search for a hybrid form of electronic and natural music and the first example of his artistic struggle within the erotic genre. *Velluto nero* revisits the community at Steiner's house in the 1970s. A group of women and men, moved by a desire for a fuller and freer life experience, finds itself in Egypt, seeking more vital mystical and sexual bonds through the re-enactment of pharaonic myths. A sequence from this film depicts an initiatory ritual in which a group of aspiring artists and intellectuals is attempting to achieve a sense of harmony among itself and the world through music and nature but also, and much more explicitly than in *La dolce vita*, through sex. For *Velluto nero*, Rondi likely had the composer (Alberto Baldan Bembo) incorporate in the banal ambiance music that was typical of the erotic genre a mélange of electronic sounds, voices, and folk songs that could suggest the mixture of past and present, human and nature.

To make matters even more interesting, Pier Paolo Pasolini also wrote his version of the sequences involving Steiner, whom he named Mattioli, making him originally from Romagna, as Marcello also is, and a former student of the art historian Roberto Longhi, as Pasolini himself was (2001, 3198–9). The few pages that Pasolini dedicated to his version of Steiner remain marginal to the film because they are not integrated into the final screenplay; however, they do suggest that Steiner inspired Pasolini as another example of an urbanized young man from Romagna who, differently from Marcello, finds in Rome financial success (he owns land in Romagna, and his beautiful house with a panoramic view of Rome is decorated with important works of art), stability (he lives an idyllic life with his family), and cultural prestige (he is an accomplished author and professor). In light of Pasolini's subtle character development, Mattioli/Steiner's horrific final demise can be interpreted as the capitulation of a highly sensitive individual, whose carefully guarded purity eventually can no longer withstand the mediocrity and pessimism of society.

The authorial interplay behind Steiner explains the complex and at times contradictory nature of this character, who was presented as a lost soul, in line with Pinelli, and as a martyr, in line with Rondi. As this chapter argues, the character of Steiner was actually the centre of authorial conflict between not only Fellini and Pinelli but also Pinelli and Rondi. This might explain why, in a letter to Rondi about Steiner, Fellini failed to mention Pinelli's original ideas (Kezich 1996, 27–8). Fellini's comical directorial hand portrayed the community of clueless and somewhat superficial artists around Steiner in his usual caricaturist manner. Fellini inserted Rondi's artistic community and ideals but with a touch of ridicule that Rondi had not envisioned, shifting – much to Pinelli's dislike – the cause of the suicide away from Steiner and to the superficiality of his social world. In fact, in choosing the cast for this scene, the director selected artists such as Anna Salvatore and Leonida Rèpaci who had been fixtures of the social life of postwar Italy (Minuz 2012, 54–5). At the same time, Fellini kept Pinelli's tragic ending, thus questioning and undermining, to Rondi's dislike, the prophetic stance of Steiner's credo.[17]

In conclusion, Fellini modified the party at Steiner's house to neutralize the unwanted influence of both writers, simultaneously softening the inexplicable tragedy that Pinelli conceived and undermining through ridicule the heroic intellectual figure that Rondi conceived. The puzzle of Steiner's genesis is indeed a telling example of the way Fellini cunningly employed differing contributions, thus offsetting the qualities he appreciated less in his writers. This is an ability that plays an important role in much of the poignancy of his cinema. Steiner's case also shows how Fellini's authorial vision developed through and because of contrasting collaborations, and shows that differences in sensibilities and interests were factors that lent an extraordinary complexity and completeness to many of Fellini's more acclaimed films, of which *La dolce vita* is only one example.

NOTES

1 "Io ammiro in Fellini la capacità di scegliere il suo nutrimento, e di saperlo rubare, se occorre, dove lo trova … è un tentativo di mettere ordine nel caos"
2 "È [Steiner] un'anticipazione di ciò che succede ogni giorno. È proprio un episodio tutto mio, l'ho suggerito e scritto io. Purtroppo, la serata in casa di Steiner è stata poi riscritta ed è tutta diversa da quella che avevo fatto, risultando uno dei peggiori episodi del film. Però, questo l'ho detto a Federico. 'Guarda che qui hai fatto una cosa che si capisce che quello si suicida se i suoi amici sono di quello stampo lì. Per forza.' All'inizio, invece, era un'altra cosa: Steiner si toglieva la vita per la disperazione della felicità. Uno che arriva al massimo della felicità, della dolcezza della vita con la bella moglie fedele e innamorata, i bellissimi figli, sa che oltre questo non può più andare e quindi per disperazione uccide se stesso e i bambini. Quindi non è un fatto di per sé. È veramente un'anticipazione di quello che sta succedendo adesso su scala infinitamente più vasta. Questo è un episodio eccezionale del film, non è nel tono degli altri episodi, proprio esce. Secondo me è uno dei punti più anticipatori di quello che sta succedendo adesso."
3 PIETRO: (*Fissa Davide in silenzio. Poi, terribile*) Così. Di me ti resti soltanto questo orrore. Ti forzerà a vincere la carne, quando sarai tentato di negargli il martirio. (*Pausa*) Io l'ho respinto, e scendo al martirio eterno.
DAVIDE: No. Non ancora.
pietro: Orribilmente giusto. Ma te, dal fondo dell'abisso ti vedrò con gli angeli nostri fratelli, vicino a Lui. Mio figlio. (Pausa) Vederlo dappresso, per tutta l'eternità.

DAVIDE: (*Mormorando*) Dio di misericordia.
PIETRO: Gloria a Lui.
DAVIDE: Spera. Salvati.
PIETRO: Non è giusto.
DAVIDE: Lo ami ancora?
PIETRO: Farò tremare gli inferni, cantando gloria a Lui.
DAVIDE: (*Mormorando*) Se Lo ami, il nemico non può passare.
PIETRO: (*In un mormorio*) Dio Padre! Dio Padre!
DAVIDE: (*Quasi parlandogli all'orecchio*) Sei salvo. Lo ami ancora?
PIETRO: (*In un soffio*) Da morire.
DAVIDE: Sei salvo. (*Pausa. Lentamente si leva in piedi, lo sguardo fisso su Pietro Rovere che, gli occhi vitrei, sbarrati, volti al cielo, giace immobile riverso sulla poltrona.*)

4 "Zampanò si è fermato e ascolta. Ascolta quello che non ha ascoltato mai: il silenzio. Un brivido improvviso lo scuote da capo a piedi. È un brivido di terrore. E al terrore succede lo sgomento per questa non mai provata paura del nulla. Non la paura della fame, o della prigione, o di un altro uomo: la paura del nulla. Le ginocchia gli mancano. Zampanò si accoscia sulla sabbia. Come colto da un male sensibile e terrificante, un male non mai provato, Zampanò si dibatte contro qualcosa che faticosamente nasce nella sua anima di bruto: l'angoscia. Nell'ombra si ripete all'infinito il fruscio delle onde, e Zampanò, per la prima volta nella sua vita, piange. Una donna è nata ed è morta per questo. L'alba sul mare è come il principio del mondo. Luminosa, nuova e innocente come il principio del mondo. Zampanò dorme profondamente sulla rena. Non come sempre rannicchiato e contorto quasi in istintiva animalesca difesa: le sue membra giacciono aperte e abbandonate, con la serena fiduciosità di un sono infantile. Il suo volto è pacato ed umano."

5 "sedimento tradizionalistico," an element "da vecchia drammaturgia … che rimane un po' astratto nel piglio disorganico e aggressivo del film"

6 "simpatia e bonario divertimento" that interjects into the film "un'improvvisa complicità vitellonisca tra padre e figlio"

7 "Fellini aveva ben chiara l'idea che Steiner è un personaggio che ha intuito una nuova, originale armonia di rapporti, quasi le avvisaglie di un mondo nuovo. Ma è un'idea senz'armi … la fine di Steiner è quella dei profeti disarmati … forse il solo personaggio al di là della "dolce vita" … Ora, a Fellini e a noi parve ben presto che occorresse costruire in Steiner, nella sua casa, nelle sue amicizie, questo aspetto d'una solitudine positiva, ricca di intuizioni, d'una felicità che sfugge a termini consunti e convenzionali. Immaginammo un ambiente di tranquilla intelligenza, di sottile ma non cerebrale intimità, di non ostentata cultura. Steiner fa ascoltare della musica elettronica, poi dal suo nastro registratore i rumori della

natura, quasi adunando così, attorno a questa riunione un po' iniziatica di persone, proprio il fronte compatto e dolcissimo della natura, quale appare e si manifesta nelle sue voci, nella sua presenza che può disperdere l'uomo o anche elevarlo … Così costruimmo la "serata in casa Steiner" come una specie di ansiosa veglia e vigilia d'un mondo nuovo, intuita però da gente che non ha armi e mani concrete per costruirlo; gente, inoltre, che partecipa almeno per metà alla faccia esangue del Decadentismo … Immaginiamo quella "riscoperta" dei rumori della natura proprio in questo duplice senso: per Steiner è un atto d'amore per le cose, per la realtà; per gli intellettuali invece è un profondo momento di stupore, come se avessero disimparato da sempre a vedere e ascoltare la voce e il volto concreto e intimo della natura."

8 For different reasons, Alberto Arbasino has criticized these characters as "ridiculous figures." See Conti (2008).
9 "Bisognerebbe vivere fuori dalle passioni, oltre i sentimenti, nell'armonia che c'è nell'opera d'arte riuscita. In quell'ordine incantato. Dovremmo riuscire ad amarci tanto. A vivere fuori del tempo, distaccati. Distaccati." Although this essay incorporates a discussion of Rondi's organic philosophy in relationship to music, more pertinently to the strong musical references linked to the character of Steiner, a discussion of Rondi's poetic work, as well as additional context around Fellini's collaboration with Pinelli, can be found in Paccioni, *Inspiring Fellini: Literary Collaborations Behind the Scenes* (2014). Passages from *Inspiring Fellini* contained in this chapter are reprinted with permission of the publisher.
10 "è l'eco di una società disgregata, d'una metafisica bruciata o corrotta, d'individualtà iscritta ad un altissimo nucleo di crisi"
11 "la musica di Bach rappresenta la estrema vittoria sul tempo" and that "la musica moderna rappresenta la estrema sconfitta nel tempo"
12 "Sono suoni che non siamo più abituati ad ascoltare, eh? Che voce misteriosa, sembra venire dalle viscere della terra."
13 "come l'oro da una miniera: profondissime, sotterranee, abbaglianti" and assail Marcello's ears with "il suono di una campana antichissima"
14 "Marcello è assorto, come schiacciato da quell'onda sonora, precisa ed evocatrice di un mistero che non lo trova preparato alla soluzione che gli si ripresenta quasi angosciosamente"
15 " … l'apertura dell'anima musicale agli spazi del suono elettronico … " consists in "un tuffo nella materia allo stato puro, nella miriade infinitamente colorata e variegata, ma non ancora gerarchizzata e suddivisa, dei rumori e dei suoni puri, dove la sonorità ha l'oggettiva e estranea ricchezza d'una miniera inesplorata … La musica costruita nel materiale consueto dà all'ascoltatore il modo di aver a che fare con riferimenti del reale, con qualcosa di vivo e di rapportato, mentre la

musica costruita sul materiale nuovo piomba in un'aria totalmente ignota e priva di questi riferimenti."
16 "È un momento di emozione oscuramente religiosa, al di qua di quella che potrebbe sembrare la più intellettualistica delle trovate. I rumori e i suoni della pura oggettività (quasi manifestazioni del puro Essere di cui parla l'ultimo Heidegger) passano – come da astrali distanze – sul volto di queste creature perse nelle proprie astratte mitologie personali."
17 Both collaborators expressed dissatisfaction with the final result. See Scolari (2008, 272) and Rondi (1965, 28–9).

REFERENCES

Conti, Paolo. 2008 "E Arbasino stronca *La dolce vita*." *Corriere della Sera*. Last modified 26 December. www.corriere.it/cultura/08_dicembre_21/arbasino_dolce_vita_conti_eb4c9ecc-cf44-11dd-9e84-00144f02aabc.shtml.
Fellini, Federico. 1960. *La dolce vita di Federico Fellini*. Edited by Tullio Kezich. Rocca San Casciano: Cappelli.
– 2008. *The Book of Dreams*. Translated by Aaron Maines. Milan: RCS Libri Spa.
Fellini, Federico, and Tullio Pinelli. 1954. *La strada*. Script archived at Library of Rare Books, Indiana University Bloomington (Pinelli MS. 7, IIA).
Kezich, Tullio. 1996. *Su La dolce vita*. Venezia: Marsilio.
Minuz, Andrea. 2012. *Viaggio al termine dell'Italia: Fellini politico*. Soveria Mannelli: Rubbettino.
Pacchioni, Federico. 2014. *Inspiring Fellini: Literary Collaborations Behind the Scenes*. Toronto: University of Toronto Press.
Pasolini, Pier Paolo. 2001. *Pasolini per il cinema volume. 2*. Edited by Walter Siti and Franco Zabagli. Milan: Mondadori.
Pinelli, Tullio. 1996. *Tullio Pinelli*. Rome: Editori & Associati.
Rondi, Brunello. 1949. *Il ritmo moderno*. Rome: Petrignani.
– 1952. *La musica contemporanea*. Rome: Edizioni dell'Ateneo.
– 1959. *Il cammino della musica d'oggi e l'esperienza elettronica*. Padua: Rebellato.
– 1965. *Il cinema di Fellini*. Rome: Bianco e Nero.
Scolari, Giovanni. 2008. *L'Italia di Fellini*. Rieti: Edizioni Sabinae.

Amarcord: Fascism, Nightmares, and the Spectator's Autobiography

EMILIANO MORREALE

Translated by Giovanna Caterina Lisena

In the mid-1960s, Federico Fellini experienced a mental and physical breakdown. While in hospital, memories of Rimini would often return to Fellini's mind. These memories, along with the ironic yet terrified description of the hospital, constitute the seed for texts he wrote during his convalescence and immediately published in a volume titled *La mia Rimini* and edited by Renzo Renzi (Fellini 1966). It's a collection of scattered images that will return in subsequent films, from the mentally ill to the Gradisca, to the childhood escape with the circus. From there, the return to Rimini starts: caressed in *I clowns* (1970) and at the beginning of *Roma* (1972), it will explode in *Amarcord* (1973). At the root of the latter there is, therefore, a sort of hallucination accompanied by funereal signs, born on the ashes of *Il viaggio di G. Mastorna*, a film about the afterlife, whose production Fellini interrupts due to illness.[1] *Amarcord*, read as a nostalgic and reconciled film, as the bittersweet summa of Fellini's world, is in truth inseparable from this nightmare dimension.

The title translates to "I remember" in Romagnol dialect, but with an almost magical-sounding connotation, reminiscent of Fellini's magic formula "Asa Nisi Masa" from *8 ½* (1963). Memory and dream, the quintessential elements of "fellinism." "Amarcord," therefore, would become in Italy a word indicating a nostalgic indulging ("we made an amarcord"), just as in that same year the term "graffiti" began to be used with the same meaning (a usage that was born from a misunderstanding of *American Graffiti*, the 1973 film by George Lucas that was released in Italy a few months before Fellini's).

The use of "fellinism" as a synonym for memory, dream, and remembrance had only begun to emerge during the 1960s. Memory and fantasy appear almost simultaneously in the director's films, and indeed the second is only slightly ahead of the first. The first explicitly dreamlike sequence in Fellini's cinema is in *Le tentazioni del dottor Antonio*, an episode in *Boccaccio '70* (1962). In this episode, Peppino De Filippo imagines a gigantic Anita Ekberg emerging from an advertising poster.[2] Yet the "new phase" of Fellini's cinema begins with the first sequence of *8 ½* and the emergence of childhood memories from the famous scene of the magician who recognizes the words "Asa Nisi Masa." It is significant that memory emerges during a magic "circus" scene that is Gothic in tone. Indeed, the re-emergence of the past almost always occurs in conjunction with nightmarish images, even in Fellini's 1960s cinema. This memory-nightmare pairing will be even more explicit in the subsequent *Giulietta degli spiriti* (1965). However, many reviews of the time saw in *Amarcord* the elegy, a bittersweet and gentle sentiment, the passing of the seasons opened and closed by the poplar seeds dispersed by the wind in spring: "affable and nice" (Leo Pestelli in *La Stampa*), "something delicate and modest" (Ugo Casiraghi in *L'Unità*), but even in more recent years, the film has been defined as "one of the happiest and most airy in the history of cinema" (Gianni Celati)[3] (Giacovelli 2019, 33–4).

This misunderstanding is superimposed on the more general theme of autobiography, as if *Amarcord* were indeed a reconciled version of the ghosts of *8 ½*. Fellini feared it: "Precisely what needed to be avoided was an autobiographical reading of the film. *Amarcord*: a bizarre little word, a music box, a phonetic somersault, a cabalistic utterance, or even a brand of aperitif, why not? Anything other than the irritating association with '*je me souviens*'" (Fellini et al. 2015, 244). In fact, strictly speaking, Fellini is not in the film. Not only and not so much because the protagonist's family is not his own, but rather that of his friend Titta Benzi, but above all because at that point the director has already arrived, from the initial evocation of individual visions and memories, to a complete objectification of the "I remember" as a product not of an individual mind but of a kind of collective spirit that dwells deep within the artist. If in *8 ½* and *Giulietta degli spiriti* there is a point of view that is basically solid even in its apparent passivity and confusion, a mediator beween a chaotic world and the viewer, as the contents become more intimate and profound the director eliminates this intermediary figure. If, in the 1960s, "full" scenes always centred on a lost observer-protagonist (the arrival of guests in Juliet's house, Toby Dammit surrounded by guests), in the 1970s these images developed without an internal observer. From a structural point of view, *Amarcord* should be read, more than to *I vitelloni* or even to *8 ½*, together with the now completely archaeological, archetypal explorations of *Satyricon* or the future *Casanova*.

To the fragmented construction, which already in *I clowns* and in *Roma* marked the triumph of the objectification of the past, *Amarcord* adds emphasis on the cyclical time of the seasons (the film opens with the *"manine"* [puffballs, or poplar seed pods] that mark the arrival of spring). However, despite the title, there is no real "I" who does the remembering, and there is no sense of the individual's growth that has as a counterpoint the regret of a lost time. The significant thing is that, upon closer inspection, Fellini is in no way identifiable with the dimension of nostalgia. On the contrary, the past is first charged with a disturbing and even horrifying connotation, and then it is staged as an authentic repertoire. Thus, his cinema cannot be considered *strictu sensu* a nostalgic one that relishes in the (re)presentation of the past through detail.

This peculiarity emerges even further as Fellini finds himself being contemporary, in Italy and abroad, with authentic poetics (and fashions) of nostalgia, starting with the revival of the 1930s. This phenomenon also involves other countries, from the United States to France. In Italy, where it begins with *Il conformista* (1970) by Bernardo Bertolucci, such revival has eminently ambiguous features: the decade of the New Deal and the Popular Front is, in Italy, that of triumphant Fascism, and turning nostalgically to it has apparent problematic features (Morreale 2009, 101–48).

I clowns, *Roma*, and *Amarcord* are progressive explorations of the power and paradoxes of memory. The three films do not evoke an era, but rather how the era represented itself; that is to say, the origins of mass culture, which took its first steps in a substantially rural and provincial Italy. More than indulging in nostalgia or using the past as a repertoire of images, Fellini shows us the obscene proximity to the soul that Fascism represents psychologically and iconographically (but which can also be recreated, always on a "1930s" basis, in ancient Rome or the eighteenth century). *Amarcord* is not a rêverie, but rather a search for the historical referent of archetypal images, and at the same time the amused observation of how the historical detail, even (or even more so) if laughable, can become an archetype. It is the dream of the country's soul seen through the twenty years (the fascist *ventennio*) that has been revealed to itself.

In his interviews, Fellini heavily insisted on the acrid tones of the film:

> The film is comic, it contains funny characters and ridiculous situations, but some of those who saw *Amarcord* were also touched by it, perhaps because of the nostalgia for past youth, or the things that once pertained to us, the

tenderness, mutual understanding & sympathy for a lost world it can be sweet to identify with. It's natural that it moves us and makes us sigh. But I also maintain the impression that in the microcosm portrayed in *Amarcord* there's also something repellent. I felt a slightly fetid air, an imperceptible, intoxicating, maniacal fervor circulating through its folds, and it should instill us with a disconcerting feeling that encourages us to reflect and leaves us with a sense of embarrassment. (Fellini et al. 2015, 245–6)

Tullio Kezich summarized: "If a sociologist were trying to study Italy between the two wars using only *Amarcord* as a source, what would he find? Tribal families, horrible schools, sexual repression, prisonlike asylums, fascism" (2006, 312). The director himself claimed the same: "Fascism & adolescence continue to be, to some extent, permanent historical seasons of our lives. Adolescence, of our individual lives; Fascism of our national lives" (Fellini et al. 2015, 242). However, Fellini has at least one thing in common with the "nostalgic" attitude. The past no longer serves as a leg on a journey, as a moment in which, through a *continuum*, the roots of the present are reconstructed. It is fixed there, once and for all, as a repertoire of images and situations. And yet it is also, an entirely *fellinian* choice, *the caricature of himself* and the caricature of the present. As Francesco Cataluccio summarized in his essay on images of immaturity:

> Fellini represents well both the seduction of immaturity and the nostalgia for it. It is a world populated by squalid and vulgar parties where people try to exorcise the passing of time (*Satyricon, Giulietta degli spiriti, 8 ½*). His films, in any era they are placed, are representations of the descent into the underworld of human immaturity, of the circuses of fools. His maturity lies in his films.[4] (Cataluccio 2004, 149; cf. Stubbs 2006)

The political role entwined within the theme of immaturity is also addressed by Peter Bondanella in his essay on *Amarcord* entitled *Politics and Nostalgia*. It emphasizes the ambivalence between "remorse and nostalgia" (2002, 130). These two unavoidable themes in the film represent a typical oscillation within films that evoke the Fascist period, and in *Amarcord*, it is almost the object of the film itself. But above all, he points out that there is also a further metafilmic plane. Not only for the strong presence of cinema (especially American) in the lives of the characters, but precisely through the use of Cinecittà:

> Titta approaches Gradisca in a cinema; the Rex is an evident stage construction; the Fascists visit what an attentive observer notes to be the main

building of Cinecittà! Fellini used the studio built in the Fascist style as a ready-made scenography, since his architecture ... was so typical of the architectural style of the regime that he needed very few sets to complete the sequence. (Bondanella 2002, 135)

Ultimately, with Fellini, we are faced with one of the greatest and most complete examples of how nostalgic sensitivity towards the past, typical of modernity, can be subjected to a critical twist, an authentic disassembly, and the ambiguity towards the past bought to levels of paroxysm. Fellini derives the tools for his operation precisely from the "low" forms of communication. For this reason, a cinema of memory and the influence of comics in his work manifest and develop simultaneously.

Paradoxically, it was precisely through this increase in the hallucinated and farcical dimension that Fellini produced one of the most revealing films on Fascism and its relationship with national identity. As Kezich noted, the film has slightly contrasting chronological references (the action can be placed between 1933 and 1937), as if to underline that the four seasons depicted not only those of a specific year but of an era (2006, 309). The story flows as a myth, circular, with the times of adolescence, but also of the province: "The province in *Amarcord* is one in which we're all recognizable, director included, in the great ignorance that blinded us. That said, I don't want to downplay the economic and social causes of fascism. What I mean to say is that what interests me is the psychological, emotional manner of being fascist: a sort of blockage, stopping development at the adolescent phase" (Fellini et al. 2015, 242).

Fellini precisely describes the past as a prison but also makes a strong point to demystify the present. Obviously, Fellini can only be understood as an artist who shapes his own vision of Italy, entertainment, culture, and sex *under Fascism*. It is by remaining obsessively faithful to his past that Fellini manages to demystify it; it is by remaining faithful to his self-representation, indeed by moving his "lowest" expressions against it like a lapsus, that he produces, through a circus-like somersault, a profound historical interpretation of such a past. It is no coincidence that an essential book on Italian cinema under Fascism is subtitled *The Passing of the Rex* (an apparently meta-historical, archetypal image) and uses *Amarcord* as an accurate compass for orienting oneself in the relationship between Fascism and modernity (Hay 1987). However, at the time of its release, some writers, more or less the same age as the director, would grasp Fellini's film's historical and anthropological dimension.

The first to foresee this, even prior to the film's release, is Pier Paolo Pasolini. Reviewing the book of the script penned by Fellini and Tonino

Guerra in September 1973, he expressed his fears of a neorealist and late-Zavattinian revival and dares to say: "If I were a producer, I would not let anyone make a film out of this story"[5] (1999, 1897). (For the same reason, screenwriter Bernardino Zapponi chose not to collaborate on the film, fearing yet another return to Rimini, but he would regret his decision years later; 1995, 79–82). Fellini's main sentiment, Pasolini says, is "the mysteriousness of a world based on nothing, [but his petty-bourgeois sentimental upbringing] implies first of all a fear of feelings and even more of expressing them"[6] (1999, 1896). In *Amarcord*'s script/novelization, then, laughter intervenes to correct and mystify feelings: "But it is a strident laugh, often with infernal wrong notes. A nervous laugh, the one prostitutes have when they speak of dirty stuff, or the masochists when they speak of whips."[7] What will Fellini-director do with this material full of neorealist elegy tempered by a shrill laugh? Pasolini predicts Fellini will bring it to its own extremes: "He will not have any hesitation to be an extremist in turning all his little characters, good for a poem in dialect by the town's pharmacist, into vulgar, atrocious, repulsive monsters, human stumps, deprived even of reason. Their utter lack of humanity – which is completely atrophied – brings the embellished narrative material back to its original tragedy"[8] (1999, 1898).

Pasolini comes to fantasize in detail about this fellinian "method" that he foresees, inferring it from previous films (*Roma*, above all):

> Considering reality as a whole as inexpressible and unrepresentable; then choosing a part of it, an element, a shape, a reduction; making sure this "sample" of reality ... is as close as possible to the common, public, even conventional idea; on this piece of reduced and conventional reality (this is the crucial moment), operating an excessive semantic and formal dilatation without reservations; presenting this little piece of reality, with a massive enlargement that transforms its meaning, to an audience who: a) will be shocked by its expressionistic enormity; b) will recognize its current and familiar value.[9] (1999, 1898)

After seeing the film, Pasolini wrote a long, twisted piece in the Italian edition of *Playboy*, in which it seems that viewing *Amarcord* definitively put him in turmoil rather than providing clarity. Above all, he notices the immobility transmitted by the film: the non-evolution of the characters, the surprising immobility of the camera, the poetry constantly and solely present in the bodies, "clumsy bags filled with innocence and guilt, with impulsiveness and obsession"[10] (1999, 2636).

Pasolini is not alone in being uncomfortable imagining, filming, or watching *Amarcord*. There is a class of viewers for whom the film is immediately something special. A class to be also understood at a biographical level: those who grew up under Fascism. The "class of butter," as defined by one of his members, Oreste Del Buono (born three years after Fellini and his faithful exegete over the decades): "They presented us with the dilemma: butter or cannons, and, why, we chose"[11] (1979, 476). For them, *Amarcord* has an equivalent value to that of a self-analysis session, both individual and historical; an epiphany, a trauma, which is intertwined within the biographies of fifty-year-olds lost in the post-1968 era. This, starting with Del Buono himself, who saw "a lie hiding a truth …, a civil movie that no other author of our cinema had attempted before the anarchist, unengaged, stubborn, intimist, absent-minded author of *La dolce vita*"[12] (1979, 59). The older Moravia saw a rather a-historical dimension in the film, compared to the description of the years of Fascism in the previous *Roma* (2010, 959–61). Natalia Ginzburg, four years older than Fellini, left the film as if from a revelation and wrote about it in the newspaper *La Stampa*: "It had never happened to me to see the years of my youth and of Fascism evoked with such truth and such horror. Suddenly I remembered how horrible that age was for me. I knew it, but suddenly I remembered it with my eyes"[13] (1987, 561–7). However, the most striking case is that of Italo Calvino, who in 1973 was commissioned to write a preface to Fellini's screenplays for Einaudi; he delivered "A Spectator's Biography," an essay that is in truth the tale of one's distant past as a cinema lover, understood as the Hollywood one of the 1930s, as a pleasure of escape and *distance*, which is interrupted when cinema becomes an adult, like our lives, closed.

Of Fellini's film, Calvino underlines, amongst other things, the precision of the historical reconstruction even within a baroque style that "in the direction that goes from the caricatural to the visionary":[14]

> For those of us from his generation; in Fellini, however grotesque the caricature may be, they always have an element of truth. In the course of twenty years, fascism had lots of different psychological climates, just like the uniforms changed year to year: and Fellini always puts the right uniform & the right psychological atmosphere for the years he's depicting.
>
> The faithful representation of reality shouldn't be a criterion for aesthetic judgement, and yet I can't help but suffer upon seeing the films of young directors who like to reconstruct the fascist era indirectly as a historic-symbolic landscape. Especially in the most prestigious of young filmmakers,[15] everything that that has to do with fascism is regularly out of place, perhaps justifiable conceptually but false on the level of the images,

as if it couldn't hit the mark even by chance. Does it mean that the experience of an age isn't transferable, that a thin web of perceptions inevitably becomes lost? Or does it mean that the images through which the younger imagine fascist Italy and that are above all the ones that writers have provided them (we provided), partial images that presupposed an experience that pertained to everyone, are no longer capable of evoking the historical insight of an era now that this common reference has been lost? (2015, xiv)

But there is more. At the time of his "Autobiography," Calvino lived in France; he would frequent the Oulipo and Tel Quel; he was fascinated by combinatory arts, by allegories, and he was about to create his doppelgänger, Palomar, who from the very title aspired to be "pure gaze." But *Amarcord* revealed to him the impossibility of distance by presenting him with a proximity, or better with an obscene promiscuity, to which the writer surrendered. The logical and disembodied Calvino, the Parisian, is sutured by the film to his own Italianness; he discovers that inside of him, lying dormant, and ready to be diabolically invoked, was a Fascist in short trousers, a groper of "Gradiscas":

> For this reason Fellini manages to disturb you deep down: because he forces us to admit that what we'd like to distance ourselves from the most is intrinsically close to us.
>
> Like when analyzing neurosis, past and present mix their perspectives, like when breaking out in a fit of hysteria they manifest themselves in spectacle. Fellini makes cinema the symptomatology of Italian hysteria, that distinctive, well-known hysteria that was primarily represented as a southern phenomenon before him, from his Emilia-Romagna, that site of geographic mediation, in *Amacord* he redefines it as the true unifying element of Italian behaviour. (2015, xlvi–xlvii)

In the final sentences, having come into contact with Fellini, Calvino's style becomes very different from its usual clarity; it becomes almost baroque, dazed:

> The cinema of distance that nurtured our youth is definitely overturned in the cinema of absolute proximity. Everything remains there, distressingly present, during our limited lifetimes; the first images of eros and premonitions of death reach us in every dream; the end of the world started with us and it doesn't show signs of ending; the film we deceived ourselves into thinking we're just the spectators of it the story of our lives. (Calvino, xlvii)

It may be surprising that *Amarcord* is seen as a political and generational film and that viewers of Fellini's age underline its peculiar reading of Fascism. Nevertheless, this reminds us how much Fascism can appear as a past that was believed to be closed but which instead disturbingly returns or persists and flows underground – particularly in Italy where youth movements were already in crisis, thwarted by the strategy of tension and the economic crisis (those are years in which institutions and laws are still burdened by the fascist legacy, years of neo-fascist plots, of links between subversive movements of the extreme right, politicians, and the state). It is perhaps no coincidence that, after *Amarcord*, the two significant occasions in which there will be a public debate of writers and intellectuals around two films will be *Novecento* (1976) by Bernardo Bertolucci and above all *Salò o le 120 giornate di Sodoma* (1976) by Pier Paolo Pasolini. The two films are set, with very different purposes, during Fascism: and even if in the latter the historical epoch is essentially an allegorical background, Pasolini's operation will be read simultaneously as the quasi-voluntary testament of the author and as a dazed vision of an era of abjection that also returns as a metaphor for the present.

NOTES

1. The chapters by Marina Vargau, Mirko Tavoni, Frank Burke, and Ottavio Cirio Zanetti in this volume all offer different interpretations of *Il Viaggio di G. Mastorna*'s relationship with the afterlife.
2. For counter-readings of this film, see Eleonora Sartoni's and Dishani Samarasinghe's chapters in this volume.
3. "Affabile e simpatico" (Leo Pestelli, in *La Stampa*), "qualcosa di delicato e di modesto" (Ugo Casiraghi in *L'Unità*), "uno dei più felici e ariosi della storia del cinema" (Gianni Celati).
4. "Fellini rappresenta bene la seduzione dell'immaturità, ma anche la nostalgia di essa. È un mondo popolato di feste squallide e volgari dove si cerca di esorcizzare il tempo che passa (*Satyricon, Giulietta degli spiriti, 8 ½*). I suoi film, in qualsiasi epoca siano collocati, sono delle discese agli inferi dell'immaturità umana, dei circhi di bambocci. La sua maturità sta nei suoi film."
5. "Se io fossi un produttore non farei fare a nessuno un film da questo racconto."
6. "l'enigmaticità di un mondo fondato sul nulla," but his petty-bourgeois sentimental upbringing "implica prima di tutto la paura dei sentimenti e ancor più della loro esprimibilità"

7 "Ma si tratta di un riso stridulo, che spesso ha stecche infernali. Un riso nervoso, quello che hanno le puttane quando si parla di cose sporche, o un masochista quando si parla di fruste."
8 "Non avrà la minima esitazione ad essere estremista nel realizzare tutti quei suoi piccoli personaggi da poesia dialettale di farmacista di paese, in volgari, atroci, ripugnanti mostri, veri e propri monconi umani, privi del bene dell'intelletto. La totale mancanza di umanità – completamente atrofizzata – riporterà la materia imbellettata del racconto alla sua originaria tragicità."
9 "considerare la realtà nel suo insieme come inesprimibile e irrappresentabile; sceglierne dunque una parte, un elemento, una forma, una riduzione; fare in modo che questo "campione" di realtà ... sia il più vicino possibile all'idea comune, pubblica, addirittura convenzionale; su questa fetta di realtà ridotta e convenzionale operare (è il momento essenziale) una dilatazione semantica e formale eccessiva senza riserve; presentare questo pezzettino o frangia di realtà, dilatata in una gigantografia che ne trasforma il senso, a uno spettatore che: a) resta sconvolto di fronte alla sua espressionistica enormità, b) ne riconosce il valore corrente e familiare."
10 "sacchi goffi e gonfi di innocenza e di colpa, di sventatezza e di ossessione ..."
11 "Ci posero il dilemma: burro o cannoni, e insomma, scegliemmo"
12 "una menzogna che nasconde una verità ..., un film civile che nessun altro autore del nostro cinema aveva tentato prima dell'anarchico, del disimpegnato, del refrattario, dell'intimista, dello svagato autore della *Dolce vita*"
13 "Mai mi era capitato di vedere evocati gli anni della mia giovinezza, e il fascismo, con tanta verità e tanto orrore. Di colpo mi sono ricordata che quell'epoca era per me orribile. Lo sapevo, ma d'un tratto l'ho ricordato con gli occhi."
14 "nella direzione che dal caricaturale porta al visionario"
15 In this sentence, Moravia is clearly alluding to Bernardo Bertolucci's *Il conformista* (1970).

REFERENCES

Bondanella, Peter. 2002. *The Films of Federico Fellini*. Cambridge: Cambridge University Press.

Calvino, Italo. 2015. "A Spectator's Biography." In *Making a Film*, by Federico Fellini, xvi–xlvii. Translated by Christopher Burton White, New York: Contra Mundum Press.

Cataluccio, Francesco. 2004. *Immaturità*. Turin: Einaudi.
Del Buono, Oreste. 1979. *Il comune spettatore*. Milan: Garzanti.
Fellini, Federico. 1966. *La mia Rimini*. Edited by Renzo Renzi. Bologna: Cappelli.
Fellini, Federico, Italo Calvino, Liliana Betti, and Christopher Burton White. 2015. *Making a Film*. Translated by Christopher Burton White. New York: Contra Mundum Press.
Giacovelli, Enrico. 2019. *Tutto Fellini*. Rome: Gremese.
Ginzburg, Natalia. 1987. *Vita immaginaria*. Turin: Einaudi.
Hay, James. 1987. *Fascism and Popular Film Culture: The Passing of the Rex*. Bloomington: Indiana University Press.
Kezich, Tullio. 2006. *Federico Fellini. His Life and Films*. New York: Farrar, Strauss & Giroux.
Moravia, Alberto. 2010. "L'Espresso. 23 dicembre 1973." In *Alberto Moravia. Cinema italiano. Recensioni e interventi 1933–1990*, edited by Alberto Pezzotta and Anna Gilardelli. Milan: Bompiani.
Morreale, Emiliano. 2009. *L'invenzione della nostalgia. Il vintage nel cinema italiano e dintorni*. Rome: Donzelli.
Pasolini, Pier Paolo. 1999. *Saggi sulla letteratura e sull'arte. Volume II*. Milan: Mondadori.
Stubbs, John C. 2006. *Federico Fellini as Auteur: Seven Aspects of His Films*. Carbondale: Southern Illinois University Press.
Zapponi, Bernardino. 1995. *Il mio Fellini*. Venice: Marsilio.

Spectres of Venice: Gothic Apparitions in *Il Casanova di Federico Fellini*

MARCO MALVESTIO AND
ALBERTO ZAMBENEDETTI

This chapter discusses the presence of Gothic themes, tropes, images, and atmospheres in *Il Casanova di Federico Fellini* (1976). A multifarious concept, the Gothic had a troubled history within Italian culture: discarded as something foreign and opposed to the perceived values of "Italianness" when it first was imported in the nineteenth century, the Gothic as a literary and cinematic form never gained a great reputation among Italian intellectuals. Nevertheless, the Gothic, and more in general an interest for the occult and the macabre, can be found in various cultural milieus in twentieth-century Italy, most notably in the short-lived, but stylistically innovative *filone* of Gothic films in the late 1950s and 1960s. We argue that Fellini, always animated by great curiosity for popular culture and eccentric characters, was influenced by Gothic imagery in his lunar rendition of Giacomo Casanova's autobiography.

We do not investigate the Gothic in *Casanova* as a form of the return of the repressed (as codified in David Punter's influential *The Literature of Terror*, 1996) or as a *negative aesthetics* (the Gothic's reaction to Enlightenment culture, which leads to a preference for the irrational over the rational, chaos over order, decadence over construction, uncontrolled passion over harmony and balance; Botting 2014). Rather, we set out to identify a set of tropes and images (often inspired by contemporary Gothic Italian cinema) that enhance the mortuary dimension of Fellini's film. The adoption of these imagery and tropes, we argue, structures Fellini's interpretation of Casanova. The Gothic genre's preoccupation with the dangers of artistic creation and its tendency to metafiction influence Fellini's portrayal of Casanova as a postmodern, fragmented subjectivity. At the same time, hints to the genre's insistence on morbid sexuality (especially in Italian cinema) contribute to Fellini's extensive critique of Italian masculinity, from *I vitelloni* (1953) to *La città delle donne* (1980).

Fellini and the Gothic Genre

Before considering how the Gothic surfaces in *Casanova*, we should account for Fellini's often overlooked relationship with the corresponding *filone* in Italian cinema. Belonging to the semantic field of mining, the Italian word *filone* (lode) suggests that the history of Italian horror and gothic cinema is underpinned by a series of imitative practices and remediating processes. Screenwriters and directors "dug" independently but in the same "vein," working within a defined set of sources, models, tropes, narrative situations, themes, and atmospheres. The films belonging to the Gothic *filone* were often penned by the same writers, most notably Ernesto Gastaldi, and featured the same performers – English actress Barbara Steele, who also appears in *8 ½* (1963), being the undisputed protagonist of the whole subgenre. While Fellini's films could hardly be considered genre films, undoubtedly there is a strong connection between his work and the Gothic film industry, at the very least at the level of personnel.

One key figure constituting a veritable trait d'union between these two worlds was author and screenwriter Bernardino Zapponi (1927–2000). Fellini asked him to write *Toby Dammit* (1968), after reading his collection of supernatural stories *Gobal* (1967).[1] Zapponi had previously published *Nostra signora dello spasimo* (1963), a non-fiction book about the Inquisition and witch hunting, and he would proceed to write five more Fellini films: *Fellini: A Director's Notebook* (1969), *Fellini Satyricon* (1969), *I clowns* (1970), *Roma* (1972), and, of course, *Il Casanova di Federico Fellini* (1976). While working with Fellini, Zapponi also penned the screenplay for Dario Argento's *Profondo rosso* (1975) a seminal work in the Italian *giallo filone*. Crucially, Zapponi was also one of the key figures of the magmatic and multifarious diffusion of occultural interests in 1960s and 1970s Italy (see Camilletti 2018). "Occulture," a term coined by Christopher Partridge, designates the circulation of occult themes first into subcultures, and their eventual absorption into the mainstream. As defined by Partridge, occulture is "a meaningful confluence of competing spiritual and paranormal discourses, many of which appeared to be related in some way to everyday life through popular culture and the media" (2015, 10). In short, Partridge continues, "there is evidence for an influential culture of enchantment, which encompasses the marginal and the mainstream, the deviant and the conventional, and which circulates ideas, creates synergies, and forms new trajectories, all of which are driven by wider cultural forces, particularly those of popular culture and the media" (11). This was definitely the case for Fellini, who, beginning with *8 ½*, paid increasing attention to the world of the occult; for instance, during the preparatory stages of *Giulietta degli spiriti* (1965), the director travelled across Italy in search of "sorcerers, clairvoyants, witches, possessed people, mediums, astrologists, metapsychical operators, people with occult powers,"[2] as writer and Fellini collaborator Dino Buzzati reported (1978, 39–40). Zapponi's expertise in eccentric topics such as witchcraft and horror fiction is what elicited Fellini's curiosity and his desire to collaborate with him on the script for *Toby Dammit*. As Pacchioni writes, "Zapponi's lowbrow status as a writer and his proficiency in the popular genres of horror, science fiction, mystery, and eroticism appealed to Fellini's increasingly dominating authorial and psycho-analytical interests and galvanized his already natural inclination for popular culture" (2014, 79).

Toby Dammit is a clear example of the merging of Fellini's authorial approach and the Gothic *filone*. An adaptation of a story by Edgar Allan Poe, "Never Bet the Devil Your Head" (1841), Fellini's film appeared in the omnibus *Tre passi nel delirio* alongside the segments *Metzengerstein* (Roger Vadim) and *William Wilson* (Louis Malle). The idea of adapting short stories by Poe for a collective project originated from French producer Raymond Eger, who was riding the wave of a revival of sorts. In fact, Poe was quite a popular source for Gothic cinema at large, at least since Roger Corman's influential adaptations (the first one being *House of Usher*, 1960). For instance, in Antonio Margheriti's *Danza Macabra* (1964), the American writer is not only credited as the source of the story (which has, however, nothing to do with anything Poe ever wrote) but also appears as a character. It is worth noting, moreover, that the foreigner who visits Italy and finds himself captured in a web of intrigues and mysteries is a recurring trope of Italian gothic and *giallo* cinema alike (including Zapponi's own *Profondo Rosso*), as well as television (as in the hugely popular five-episode mini-series *Il segno del comando*, 1971).

The film stages the arrival of British actor Toby Dammit (Terence Stamp) in Rome to participate in a "Catholic Western." Possibly due to his alcoholism, Dammit is tormented by the vision of an uncanny little girl (Marina Yaru), who, in the last scene, causes the protagonist's beheading. The portrayal of the devil as a child with angelic, if sinister, features is borrowed from Mario Bava's *Operazione paura* (1966), in which the ghost of a blond girl terrorizes the inhabitants of a Carpathian village in the early twentieth century. The similarity is so clear (Fellini even adopts camera angles and a saturated colour palette that recall Bava's work) that the great genre director himself complained with Giulietta Masina about her husband's putative intellectual theft (Curti 2015, 189). However, this small "homage" is only partly Fellini's fault. In fact, the choice of representing the devil as a spectral apparition is likely attributable to Zapponi, who, as Roberto Curti suggests, "admired Bava to the point that, at the time when he was editor of the magazine *Il Delatore*, he announced a special issue entirely dedicated to the director – a project which was shelved due to the mag's folding" (2015, 188).

Toby Dammit brims with references to the Gothic stories of Edgar Allan Poe, to the extent that it can be considered a rumination on Poe's legacy rather than the (loose) adaptation of a single story (Sharrett 2002). Curti provides a succinct list of these instances:

> the shot of a hostess' face in a monitor at the Fiumicino terminal is a technologized version of "The Oval Portrait"; the television interviewer … asks Toby whether he has seen the devil in the shape of a black cat; the actor is introduced to his own stunt double …, just as "William Wilson's" *doppelganger* shows up in a cowboy hat and boots; … last but not least, the red Ferrari which is Toby's object of desire is an up-to-date version of the "fiery colored horse" in "Metzengerstein" [which Roger Vadim adapts in *Tre passi nel delirio*]. (2015, 190–1)

Of course, all these factors (Fellini's interest in occulture; his homage to, or plagiarism of, Bava's work; his several references to Gothic fiction; his enduring collaboration with Zapponi) do not mean that Fellini's work belongs to the Gothic *filone*. It is more appropriate (and cautious) to argue that Fellini was working *alongside* this industrial and commercial phenomenon, and that he was absorbing it into his own cinema much like he assimilated comic books, the circus, and other popular art forms – albeit to a much lesser extent. Nevertheless, *Toby Dammit* proves Fellini's knowledge of and interest in certain stylistic and thematic features of the Gothic that would return in his sumptuous but melancholic adaptation of Casanova's memoirs.

The Mortuary Dimensions of *Il Casanova di Federico Fellini*

Venetian writer and philosopher Giacomo Casanova (Venice, 1725–Duchcov, 1798) is remembered primarily as an adventurer and a seducer; unquestionably, his name has become synonymous with a generic idea of "Latin lover" at home and abroad. Despite belonging, at least in part, to the century when the Gothic developed and spread across Europe (Horace Walpole's *The Castle of Otranto*, which is considered the genre's first novel, was published in 1764), Casanova is not usually associated with the themes and atmospheres that characterize the genre. Nor are his many cinematic portrayals, from Riccardo Freda's 1948 *Il cavaliere misterioso* to Lasse Hallström's *Casanova* (2005), which tend to emphasize (and embroider on) the more salacious episodes of his massive memoirs rather than his much touted encounters with many of the principal artistic and political figures of the eighteenth century. Zapponi, however, underscores the rather contradictory tensions that haunt the century of many revolutions. He writes:

> The eighteenth century was the century of Sadism, the expression of a caste of oppressors furious about their lost privileges, and of oppressed that could finally express their repressed aggressiveness. Two great revolutions stand out: one is political, the other is sexual. Casanova expressed through thousands of gallant adventures the inability to love, the Marquis de Sade reached new extremes with his summa of perversions: an encyclopedia more lasting than Diderot's. And Robespierre revealed a new civilization with the purity of the guillotine.[3] (1963, 16)

In the hands of Fellini and Zapponi, the popular lothario becomes a sinister figure, a corseted melancholic prone to disquieting sexual voracity (if not predation) rather than a free-spirited pursuer of joyous libertinage. According to the director, in reading his memoirs "you are faced with a giant, endless cemetery; all that ever was is gathered here, but it is dead, without judgements, without emotion"[4] (quoted in Angelucci and Betti 1977, 22). For these reasons, *Il Casanova di Federico Fellini* is replete with references to Gothic imagery, some of which are central to understanding Fellini's critique of Italian traditional masculinity as embodied by notions of *casanovismo*.[5] Unlike Mario Monicelli's *Casanova '70* (1966), Fellini does not remove his protagonist from the eighteenth century, nor does he update his exploits to favour the taste of a contemporary audience accustomed to the many licentious comedies that circulated in the 1970s. His film remains anchored to the contradictions of Casanova's century, the era of rationalism and neoclassicism, of democratic revolutions, but also a period marked by the emergence of the interest in the occult that characterized the Gothic. Rather than emphasizing the Enlightenment and its empiricist foundations, the director opted for the mysteries of a literary genre that turns decidedly away from the light and embraces what hides in the shadows. Much of *Casanova* unfolds in enclosed spaces (rooms, palaces, carriages, theatres), and when it opts for outdoor settings (albeit studio-bound), they are often clad in darkness and/or impenetrable fogs. In his own production notes from 10 April 1974, Fellini writes:

> CARRIAGES – ROOM – CELLS – BEDS
> ALL IS NARROW – CRAMPED
> ALL ENCLOSES HIM
> HOLDS HIM CONFINED – PINNED – BURIED AS IN THE WOMB
> OF THE MOTHER – PLACENTA – COFFIN.[6] (quoted in Copioli and Morin 2017, 48)

The imagery in these notes hardly evokes the merry sexual romps generally associated (and perhaps wrongly so) with the figure of Giacomo Casanova. Rather, the words seem to conjure up the many characters buried alive in the tales of Edgar Allan Poe (*The Premature Burial, Berenice, The Cask of Amontillado, The Fall of the House of Usher, The Black Cat*), returning here as a major influence after *Toby Dammit*; in fact, Poe is directly referenced in the London tavern scene, where Casanova runs into his friend Egard[7] while looking for the Giantess. Moreover, rather than emphasizing its power to conceive life, Fellini casts the uterus as a space of entombment, and Casanova as buried inside this confining, crystallized, oppressive organ. Consistently then, Fellini's film rejects the idea of Italy as a land of rational thought and classical harmony, turning instead to the vocabulary of the Gothic genre and its strangely populated imagery – obscure settings, esotericism, witchcraft, and artificial creatures. This rendition of the eighteenth century is indebted to nocturnal and satirical painters such as Pietro Longhi, Giacomo Ceruti, and William Hogarth (the latter is particularly clear in the London sequence). But Fellini's film also gestures to Romantic and Symbolist painters such as Arnold Böcklin, as well as to the metaphysical landscapes of Giorgio de Chirico (Aldouby 2013, 111–30).

Fellini's choice is particularly significant if one considers the problematic reception of the Gothic genre in Italy. As Alessandra Aloisi and Fabio Camilletti argue, discourses on Italian identity tend to configure "Italianness" as "the encounter between the legacy of Classical antiquity, Catholic religion, and philosophical rationalism," which had the effect of "rooting cultural identity in the worship of aesthetic 'measure,' the refusal of superstition, and philosophical/theological rigour" (2019, 2). This scepticism towards the genre can be traced back to the late eighteenth and early nineteenth century, at the time of the "Classical-Romantic quarrel," when Italian intellectuals debated the merits of Classicism and Romanticism (which includes the Gothic), dismissing the latter as alien to Italian sensibilities. In a famous letter sent by Alessandro Manzoni to the Marchese D'Azeglio in 1823, the author expresses disdain for these manifestations of Romanticism. He labels them as "an unimaginable muddle of witches, specters, a systemic disorder, an extravagant research, and an abjuration of common sense. In short, a kind of Romanticism that one would have much reason to reject and forget, had it ever in fact been proposed by anyone"[8] (Manzoni 1965, 886). This suspicion would continue throughout the twentieth century as well: in the 1980s, when critics and authors such as Gianfranco Contini and Italo Calvino debated on the presence of the fantastic (in the Todorovian sense) in Italian literature, most of them tended to regard it as a minor occurrence in Italian letters and culture (see Lazzarin et al. 2016). By portraying Casanova's eighteenth century not as an age characterized by stylistic Classicism and Enlightenment culture, but one populated by macabre undertones and esoteric curiosities, Fellini explicitly contradicted a popular critical view of Italian culture as immune to the excesses of the Gothic – albeit one where home-grown superstitions and mysticism continue to permeate the mainstream.

As mentioned, the film's sepulchral atmosphere is certainly relatable to Zapponi's sensibility.[9] As Pacchioni argues, "the 'infernal' atmosphere that is perceivable in Fellini's cinema from 1968 to the end of the 1970s … owes much to Zapponi's leanings for 'horror genre, Poe's tales, ghosts, gothic, and dark and sinister atmospheres,' which characterized his writings …, but at the same time satisfied Fellini's longing for the unrealized hereafter of *Il viaggio di G. Mastorna*" (2014, 86). The film's first scene is set in a nocturnal Venice entirely built in Cinecittà, or rather signified by means of scaffoldings and painted backdrops vaguely resembling iconic Venetian buildings (the Rialto Bridge, the façade of Santa Maria della Salute, a bell tower) and its principal waterway, the Grand Canal. From the start, the eighteenth century is portrayed as a dark, cemeterial space, crowded with remnants of a fading civilization and two-dimensional or hollow simulacra. It is, as Fellini put it, "a Venice with more water, with water everywhere, … an imprisoning amniotic sac, a wet blister where Casanova lives his imaginary life"[10] (quoted in Angelucci and Betti 1977, 32). On the night of Shrove Thursday (the last Thursday before Ash Wednesday, when the forty-day period of Lent begins), Venice's inhabitants are celebrating the beginning of Carnival with the traditional *volo dell'angelo* (flight of the angel). In typical fellinian fashion, the historical ritual is modified to accommodate an image from his dreams; as Gérard Morin reports, "a night in June, Fellini dreams of a large head of a woman surface from the water and then descend back into it and never reappear"[11] (quoted in Copioli and Morin 2017, 62).

Casanova is introduced as this massive head of Venusia fails to be born out of the amniotic Venetian waters. A tall figure clads in a flowing white sheet topped by an undersized red tricorn, our protagonist resembles a carnivalized ghost emerging from a crowd partly made up of papier mâché masks and puppets. Himself a marionette in the hands of Fellini, as the director frequently remarked, Casanova is barely a sketch, an idea, a prelude to his own mythologization created out of wigs, heavy make-up, and costumes: as Morin noted, "numerous wigs and about thirty extravagant costumes make up this 'zombie' who will travel the world seeking for an inner peace that only death will bring him"[12] (quoted in Copioli and Morin 2017, 56). Once disrobed, or rather unveiled, his physical appearance is not rendered as a sensual, machoistic Latin-lover type, but as a cadaverous and manneristic individual. Donald Sutherland's face is disguised by prosthetics, with Casanova's pronounced nose and wide forehead made even bigger and wider; his blue eyes are rendered cold and watery. As Fellini explains:

> The true motive of my choice is precisely the "lunar" face of Sutherland, totally estranged from the conventional image that people have of Casanova: the Italian with dark, magnetic eyes, raven hair, swarthy complexion, the classic type of the Latin lover, in short, his archetype. And therefore the operation that I want to perform with Casanova, of estrangement, or overturning the traditional model, is precisely this. (quoted in Marcus 1980, 20)

According to Zapponi, the Casanova created by him and Fellini is "a character who lives permanently in a mortuary dimension, made of beds that resemble coffins of funereal apparitions, of old women, in the putrid greenish colour of Venice" (quoted in Pacchioni 2014, 86).

In the quote above, Morin describes him as a zombie, but these features also resemble another popular character in Italian gothic cinema: the vampire (see Guarneri 2020). While the first literary depiction of the vampire was produced in 1819 by John Polidori (*The Vampyre*), the vampire, like Casanova, is a creature of the previous century – an age when Eastern European folklore about the undead travelled across the continent raising the interest and curiosity of intellectuals and even of governments (see Groom 2018a, 2018b). Like a vampire, Fellini's Casanova seems to be active almost exclusively at night, his complexion is pale, and his predatory sexuality is not procreative. Of course, the release of the Hammer Film Production of Terence Fisher's *Dracula* (1958) prompted a cinematic revival of the undead (pun intended), including several comedic and satirical titles. For instance, in Steno's *Tempi duri per i vampiri* (1959), the male vampire functioned as a commentary on Italian sexual mores and addresses traditional depictions of masculinity.

Lucio Fulci's *Il cav. Costante Nicosia demoniaco, ovvero: Dracula in Brianza* (1975) also addressed the rapidly changing sexual mores of the post-1968 era. Similarly to the way Steno and Fulci employed the sex appeal of the vampire to satirize the stereotypical sexual prowess of the Italian male, Fellini's depiction of Casanova's troubling sexuality aimed to subvert traditional notions of Mediterranean masculinity. In this light, we argue that Fellini's Casanova is both unborn (as the failed emersion of Venusia suggests) and undead (as hinted by his sexual vampirism). A crepuscular figure at the tail end of an era and at the cusp of a new one, Casanova belongs anywhere and nowhere, travels the world but remains confined to Cinecittà, is neither fully alive nor does he ever die. Like an insect trapped in amber, he is forever crystallized in our culture; Casanova simply *endures*.

Automata and Mannequins

The Gothic genre is profoundly concerned with the seductions and dangers of storytelling, and metanarration has been a feature of the genre since its inception: in *The Castle of Otranto*, Horace Walpole used the topos of the old manuscript, which would become ubiquitous in the genre (Hogle 2002); more than a century later, Bram Stoker chose the epistolary form for his *Dracula* (1897). Moreover, the Gothic tends to exaggerate its own fictionality, emphasizing the sensational nature of its plots and adopting narrative tools that enhance the textual elements of story. If letters, books, notes, secret messages abound in Gothic stories, so do paintings, portraits, sculptures, and (later on) photographs. The presence of doubles, mannequins, and automata highlights the fragmentation of the modern self and the fear inspired by machines in the wake of the Industrial Revolution. Unsurprisingly, the same themes and figures are central to Fellini's understanding of Casanova and of the dangers of such imitative artistic practices. In fact, Casanova walks through life as if in a simulation, performing his mannered persona both privately and publicly. Theatricality and affectation are, for him, more real than reality itself, the simulacrum substituting the real. In his speech, Casanova is always reciting, as Millicent Marcus notes:

> Casanova does in fact recite. He recites Ariosto before an irreverent public toward the end of his days at the Castle of Dux. He recites Tasso as he is about to jump to his death in the river Thames. He recites Petrarch as a prelude to the seduction of the mechanical doll, Rosalba. Often he is pictured self-consciously seeking the proper pose for the creation of a desired theatrical effect, such as his entrance into his mother's box in the opera

house of Dresden. And it is by no means coincidental that the one woman he professes truly to love, Henriette, is herself a performer – a cellist of some talent. (1980, 24)

Furthermore, down to his very underwear, Casanova is always costumed, not simply dressed; his body striking a pose, but never reposing; and he is often surrounded by imitations of human figures. For instance, in a crucial scene, when Henriette leaves him, he finds himself alone in a room full of mannequins.

As mentioned, Fellini transforms Casanova into a figure oscillating between life and death; similarly to a sculpture, a doll, or a mannequin, he is "life-like." He is deprived of any real interiority; even when reciting poetry, his constant goal is the exhibition of his erudition and wit, and is therefore mechanical, much like his lovemaking. In fact, almost all of Casanova's sexual encounters are not only performative, as they have and are aimed at an audience, but they are also accompanied by the fluttering on a portable mechanical bird – an effective solution that allows Fellini to suggest his erection without showing it. Much like the rest of the film's supernatural iconography, the bird is inspired by the images printed in the *Enciclopédie de la Divination* (1965), which Fellini received in 1967 from Ernesto Ugo Gramazio (quoted in Copioli and Morin 2017, 107). As Rosita Copioli observes, the bird

> becomes a blasphemous symbol of the holy ghost, the Trinity's dove with spread wings, in the ostensory of the altar of a new (and ancient) religion, personally reinterpreted by Fellini as the rigid projection of a metal and ice. As every Christian identifies in the Christ on the altar as embodied by the host, so Casanova identifies with the idol of his body part that is the instrument of pleasure.[13] (Copioli and Morin 2017, 111)

Evoking the early mechanical toys contemporary to Casanova, his bird blurs the line between the organic and the inorganic, the animate and the inanimate. In fact, Jacques de Vaucanson's famous *Canard Digérateur* (Digesting duck, 1739) *appeared* to eat food, process it, and excrete waste; similarly, Wolfgang von Kempelen's *Turk* (1770) *appeared* to play chess. Of course, neither did what it purported to do. And yet these examples are paradigmatic of automata's enduring appeal, which resides not in their impressive cogs and wheels, but in the belief that they actually work. Faith, or at the very least suspension of disbelief, is what makes them compelling. It is not coincidental that when Casanova first encounters Rosalba, the dancing doll, at the court of the Duke of Württemberg, he mistakes her for a real person.

In this, he echoes Nathaniel, the hero of E.T.A Hoffman's story *The Sandman* (1816), who falls in love with the beautiful automaton Olympia. Believing she is real, Nathaniel is driven to madness (and eventually his own death) upon discovering the truth. The basis of Sigmund Freud's famous essay *The Uncanny* (1919), Hoffmann's tale is predicated on Luddite fears of technology superseding life; yet, as Stanley Cavell notices, it is not Freud but Ernst Jentsch who "attributes the sense of the uncanny to the recognition of an uncertainty in our ability to distinguish the animate from the inanimate" (1983, 155). But this uncertainty does not lead Casanova to madness, quite the contrary; as Zapponi writes in the film's novelization, Casanova almost wishes to be like Rosalba: "To become an automaton, thinks Casanova, what a wonderful thing! No death, no life, no feelings, only movement, incessant movement – what else has his existence been but the incessant movement of a mechanical doll?" (177, 198). Her ambiguous, undead status is the source of his attraction to her and leads him to serenade her with Petrarch's "Sonnet XXIV" of the *Rime in morte di madonna Laura* before he makes passionate love to her – without the help of the mechanical bird.

Conceived by Fellini and Zapponi as undead, Casanova meets his match in Rosalba, the dancing automaton strangely equipped with a vagina. As Marguerite Waller wrote, "She leaves no inconveniently organic leftovers (she does not eat, sweat, defecate, grow old, or give birth) and brings with her the blessing of uncomplicated patrilineal authority. With her, Casanova can enjoy the ecstasy of complete colonial mastery, and, indeed, he weeps with happiness after engaging in "sexual intercourse" with "her" (2020, 317). And it is to the memory of this encounter with another being oscillating between animate and inanimate that his thoughts return in his final hours. In their last dance on the frozen Venetian waters that still enshrine Venusia, the two become, as Copioli writes, "a beautiful bisque porcelain couple, a Sèvres statue on a music box, as Fellini asked Leda Lojodice, their heads joined forever in the same immobile pose. Casanova has become a decorative statuette, his transformation into her has become definitive; they become something strange, an allusion to a work of art or perfect craftsmanship"[14] (quoted in Copioli and Morin 2017, 103). In this last dream, other figures from Casanova's life appear and disappear, revealing their spectrality; conversely, Casanova and Rosalba, clasped in their revolving embrace, endure. In textual and historical term, they are fixed in place, once again reprising imagery from less erudite cinema, such as Giorgio Ferroni's seminal horror *Il mulino delle donne di pietra* (1960) in which women are petrified and turned into mannequins.

Conclusions: Metatextual Spectres

The act of creation (of bestowing a soul onto previously inanimate matter) and its inherent dangers are a recurring topos of Gothic fiction, at least since Mary Shelley's *Frankenstein* (1818), and become especially prominent in the postmodern Gothic. Similar to Fellini's critique of masculinity in his *Casanova*, the Gothic tradition is profoundly concerned with the lack of boundaries between reality and representation, which leads to the evanescence of identity and social norms. This ambiguity is greatly emphasized by the quintessentially postmodern schizophrenic separation of the text and the referent, embodied here by Casanova himself, which leads to a crisis of social and personal identity that is characteristic both of Gothic and postmodern literature. This is also coherent with Fellini's choice to treat Casanova not as an historical subject, but as a literary construct, as Marcus has noted (1980, 20).

The film is not based on a biography, but on Casanova's own memoirs, a text that is, by definition, performative. The autobiography is the literary space where a subject narrates their own life in order to give it meaning by means of emplotment. More importantly, it is a solipsistic text in which even reproachable actions find justification and exculpation – the Catholic ritual of confession being a close comparison, if not necessarily a model. It is a literary space, in other words, where we can find a project of the subject constructed with narrative tools, rather than the subject itself. Fellini exploited this double cone device to its richest representational possibilities, as the film's title suggest: *Il Casanova di Federico Fellini*. The use of the definite article in "*Il*," as if Casanova was a character of the *commedia dell'arte* (e.g., "l'Arlecchino"), means that Fellini's creation emerges from a literary character rather than a historical figure, whereas "di Federico Fellini" highlights the director's ownership of this transformation. From a hauntological perspective, then, we can say that Casanova (the historical figure) is haunted by the ghost of his own notoriety, while Fellini's film is haunted, in a rather Gothic fashion, by the spectre of Casanova's literary character.

NOTES

1 On Zapponi's stories, see Camilletti (2018, 161–9).
2 "maghi, indovini, streghe, invasati, medium, astrologi, operatori metapsichici, depositari di occulte potestà"
3 "Il settecento fu il secolo del sadismo, espressione di una casta di oppressori furenti per i privilegi perduti, e di oppressi che potevano

finalmente sfogare l'aggressività repressa. Vi campeggiano due grandi rivoluzioni: l'una politica, l'altra sessuale. Casanova espresse attraverso migliaia di avventure galanti l'incapacità di amare, il marchese de Sade trasse le estreme conseguenze con la sua "summa" delle perversioni: un'enciclopedia più durevole di quella di Diderot. E Robespierre rivelò la civiltà nuova con la purezza della ghigliottina."

4 "ti trovi davanti a un enorme, immenso cimitero, tutto ciò che è stato si raccoglie qui, ma morto, manca il giudizio, l'emozione"
5 For more on Fellini's take on the toxicity of *casanovismo*, see Zambenedetti (2020).
6 CARROZZE – STANZE – CELLE – LETTI
TUTTO È STRETTO – ANGUSTO
TUTTO LO RINSERRA,
LO TIENE RINCHIUSO – INCHIODATO – SEPOLTO COME DENTRO LA PANCIA DELLA MADRE – PLACENTA – CASSA DA MORTO.
7 The film's published screenplay identifies this character, who is made up to look like Edgar Allan Poe, as "Egard," the anagram of the author's first name (Angelucci and Betti 1977, 151).
8 "non so qual guazzabuglio di streghe, di spettri, un disordine sistematico, una ricerca stravagante, una abiura in termini del senso comune; un romanticismo insomma, che si sarebbe avuta molta ragione di rifiutare, e di dimenticare, se fosse stato proposto da alcuno"
9 We should also note that Zapponi might be responsible for the increasingly episodic and fragmentary narrative structure of Fellini's 1970s films. This approach is mirrored in Zapponi's own work, as the introduction to *Nostra signora dello spasimo* confirms: "Vogliamo dare un consiglio ai lettori: non leggete questo libro tutto di seguito, ma cominciate pure nel punto dove vi incuriosisce di più. Non è un trattato a rigida architettura, ma un *collage* impressionista, o, se preferite, un documentario. E un documentario lo si può vedere anche a proiezione iniziata" [We have a suggestion for the readers: do not read this book from cover to cover, but start at the point that is of most interest for you. This is not a pamphlet with a rigid architecture, but rather an impressionistic collage, or a documentary, if you will. And a documentary can be seen even after the screening has begun] (1963, 21). While the definition of "collage impressionista" could be applied to films such as *Amarcord* and *Roma*, the narrative of *Il Casanova di Federico Fellini* is best described as the accumulation of chronologically organized, but geographically dispersed, and not necessarily interrelated episodes from his life.
10 "una Venezia con più acqua, con acqua dovunque, ... un imprigionante sacco amniotico, un'umida vescica dentro la quale Casanova vive la sua vita immaginaria"
11 "una notte di giugno, Fellini fa un sogno dove vede un'enorme testa di donna uscire dall'acqua e poi inabissarsi senza apparire più"

12 "numerose parrucche e una trentina di abiti più agghindati l'uno dell'altro finiscono di costruire questo 'zombie' che percorrerà il mondo alla ricerca di una pace interiore che solo la morte gli darà"
13 "diventa un blasfemo simbolo dello spirito santo, la colomba ali aperte della Trinità, nell'ostensorio dell'altare di una religione nuova (e antichissima), reinterpretata in chiave personale dalla proiezione in rigidità di metallo e ghiaccio di Fellini. Come ogni cristiano si identifica nel Cristo esposto sull'altare sotto le specie dell'ostia, così Casanova si identifica nell'idolo della parte del proprio corpo che è strumento di piacere."
14 "una bellissima coppia di bisquit, un gruppo di Sèvres sul carillon, come aveva chiesto Fellini a Leda Lojodice, le teste accostate per sempre l'una sull'altra nella medesima immobile posa. Casanova si è trasformato in una statuina di decoro, è avvenuta la trasformazione definitiva di Casanova in lei, e in qualche cosa di strano, di allusivo a un'opera d'arte o di perfetto artigianato."

REFERENCES

Aldouby, Hava. 2013. *Federico Fellini. Painting in Film, Painting on Film.* Toronto: University of Toronto Press.
Aloisi, Alessandra, and Fabio Camilletti. 2019. "Introduction." In *Archaeology of the Unconscious: Italian Perspectives*, edited by Alessandra Aloisi and Fabio Camilletti, 1–12. New York: Routledge.
Angelucci, Gianfranco, and Liliana Betti, eds. 1977. *Il Casanova di Federico Fellini*. Bologna: Cappelli Editore.
Botting, Fred. 2014. *Gothic*. New York: Routledge.
Buzzati, Dino. 1978. *I misteri d'Italia*. Milan: Mondadori.
Camilletti, Fabio. 2018. *Italia lunare. Gli anni Sessanta e l'occulto*. Oxford: Peter Lang.
Cavell, Stanley. 1983. *In Quest of the Ordinary. Lines of Skepticism and Romanticism*. Chicago: University of Chicago Press.
Copioli, Rosita, and Edgar Morin, eds. 2017. *Il Casanova di Fellini ieri e oggi. 1976–2016*. Rome: Gangemi Editore.
Curti, Roberto. 2015. *Italian Gothic Horror Films, 1957–1969*. Jefferson, NC: McFarland.
Groom, Nick. 2018a. "*Dracula*'s Pre-History. The Advent of the Vampire." In *The Cambridge Companion to Dracula*, edited by Roger Luckhurst, 11–25. Cambridge: Cambridge University Press.
– 2018b. *The Vampire: A New History*. New Haven: Yale University Press.
Guarneri, Michael. 2020. *Vampires in Italian Cinema, 1956–1975*. Edinburgh: Edinburgh University Press.

Hogle, Jerrold E. 2002. "Introduction: The Gothic in Western Culture." In *The Cambridge Companion to Gothic Fiction*, edited by Jerrold E. Hogle, 1–20. Cambridge: Cambridge University Press.

Lazzarin, Stefano, Felice Italo beneduce, Eleonora Conti, Fabrizio Foni, Rita Fresu, and Claudia Zudini, eds. 2016. *Il fantastico italiano. Bilancio critico e bibliografia commentata (dal 1980 a oggi)*. Florence: Le Monnier Università.

Manzoni, Alessandro. 1965. *Opere*. Edited by Lanfranco Caretti. Milan: Mursia.

Marcus, Millicent. 1980. "Fellini's Casanova. Portrait of the Artist." *Quarterly Review of Film & Video* 5, no. 1: 19–34. https://doi.org/10.1080/10509208009361028.

Pacchioni, Federico. 2014. *Inspiring Fellini. Literary Collaborations behind the Scenes*. Toronto: University of Toronto Press.

Partridge, Christopher. 2015. "Introduction." In *The Occult World*, edited by Christopher Partridge, 1–14. New York: Routledge.

Punter, David. 1996. *The Literature of Terror. A History of Gothic Fictions from 1765 to the Present Day*. 2nd ed. London: Routledge.

Sharrett, Christopher. 2002. "Toby Dammit,' Intertex, and the End of Humanism." In *Federico Fellini. Contemporary Perspectives*, edited by Frank Burke and Marguerite Waller, 121–36. Toronto: University of Toronto Press.

Waller, Marguerite. 2020. "'Il Maestro' Dismantles the Master's House: Fellini's Undoing of Gender and Sexuality." In *A Companion to Federico Fellini*, edited by Frank Burke, Marguerite Waller, and Marita Gubareva, 311–28. Hoboken, NJ: Wiley Blackwell.

Zambenedetti, Alberto. 2020. "*Il Casanova di Federico Fellini (Fellini's Casanova)* in the Age of #MeToo." In *A Companion to Federico Fellini*, edited by Frank Burke, Marguerite Waller, and Marita Gubareva, 491–4. Hoboken, NJ: Wiley Blackwell.

Zapponi, Bernardino. 1963. *Nostra Signora dello Spasimo. L'inquisizione e i sistemi inquisitori*. Milan: SugarCo.

– 1967. *Gobal*. Milan: Longanesi.

– 1977. *Fellini's Casanova*. New York: Dell Publishing.

Sense of Place and "Placelessness": Fellini's Rome

ANDREA MINUZ

Translated by Giovanna Caterina Lisena

Introduction

Within Fellini's oeuvre, *Roma* (1972) occupies an eccentric position. On the one hand, with *La dolce vita* (1960) and *Satyricon* (1969), *Roma* is considered the final episode of a "trilogy on Rome" (although the film is significantly less studied and celebrated compared to the prior two). On the other hand, the film is viewed as a "prequel" to *Amarcord* (1973), and it is overshadowed by the notoriety of the latter for both its recollection of Fascist-era education within the Italian school system, and because *Roma* depicts an urbanized version of the melancholic province from *Amarcord*. In addition, and as argued by several critics, *Roma*, along with *I clowns* (1970) and *Amarcord*, forms an "ideal trilogy of memory"[1] (Tassone 2020, 528). Memory, however, as is well known, constitutes one of many themes that permeates almost all of Fellini's works. The same may also be stated for the metropolitan city of Rome. As Alberto Moravia wrote, "Fellini's cinema always had Rome as a protagonist, as opposed to simply a background or setting"[2] (2010, 878). In regard to this profound connection, celebrated since Fellini's debut, one that functions as a symbiosis that equates Fellini with Rome, much has been written and said.[3] Together with autobiography and the circus, Rome is a massive commonplace of Fellini's cinema and the scholarship devoted to it.[4] We find ourselves facing a paradox: Fellini's cinema surrounds itself in large part with Rome, but *Roma* is, among his films, less known by the public, less analyzed, and rarely included among the major films by Fellini (*La dolce vita*, 8½ [1963], *La strada* [1954], *I vitelloni* [1953], *Amarcord*). *Roma* is seldom called to mind, even when "Fellini's Rome" is evoked. Nevertheless, *Roma* boasts numerous admirers, above all those who appreciate Fellini's most experimental phase. It is a film whose appeal has grown with time. Shortly after the film's debut,

Pier Paolo Pasolini presciently wrote, "*Roma* is Fellini's masterpiece. It is a film where he had the courage to destroy even the last non-trivial, irrelevant or minimal element of reality, which is to say the character"[5] (2006, 247–8). Elements of the film that, for Pasolini, were strong points, were considered main limitations by Italian critics. *Roma* was not structured (if not in part) within the myth of Fellini's autobiography. Moreover, the film may not be considered a "survey of Rome," as Fellini attempted to suggest in various interviews.[6]

It was a film without a plot, without stars, without a protagonist. It was episodically constructed and lacked a proper central thread. A series of fantastic *views of Rome,* that flow forward and back in time: an apocalyptic traffic jam on the Grande Raccordo Anulare highway, a gloomy catwalk of ecclesiastic fashion, the remains of a Roman house that crumbles among the underground excavations, the invasion of a gang of motorcyclists wandering in a deserted city, immersed in the darkness, as if escaped from a nuclear catastrophe. It was also a troubled film that Fellini had a difficult time completing. At the time, it was also obscured by the release, the following year, of *Amarcord*, which quickly became one of the director's most acclaimed films. Viewed today, *Roma* is instead an inventory of themes of Fellini's cinema: memory, remembrance, dreams, but also anthropological investigations, Italian folklore, chronicle, and an incredible mix of languages – *cinéma-vérité*, investigation, *avanspettacolo*, self-portrait, mockumentary (with which he had previously experimented in *Fellini: A Director's Notebook* [1969]). In addition to the film encapsulating the relationship between Rome, Italy, and Italians, and the archetypes of Western culture the city embodies, *Roma* is also, in my opinion, a decisive film to understand Fellini's sense of place at the moment when this begins to weaken, gradually giving way in his cinema to placelessness. As observed by John Agnew (2020),[7] who views Fellini's cinema through the lens of cultural geography, sense of place, so strong within his opera, enters into crisis concomitantly with the disintegration of the sense of community. In later films, the bewilderment towards Italy's 1980s cultural transformations reverberates in the construction of neutral spaces (*E la nave va* [1983]), or is reduced to an essential evocation, made up of a few recognizable signs (the province in *La voce della luna* [1990]). In short, Fellini translates into images the idea of an irreparable loss of the relationship between places and communities. The city, reinvented in *Roma*, with its distressing, hyperbolic, abstract spaces, is at the origin of this path. In this sense, attempting to reread the film in the light of the so-called Italian *mondo-movie* is of great interest.

"Like a Documentary about the Amazon"

La dolce vita recounted the city at the dawn of the 1960s, when it was at the centre of fashion and the international jet-set. *Satyricon* ventured into a pre-Christian *Roman-ness*, imagined more through science fiction and psychedelia than from Petronius's fragments. *Roma* is a crazy and impossible synthesis of everything that the word "Rome" evokes: the one encountered by the director on his arrival in the city at the end of the 1930s, and that of the early 1970s, of traffic, of protests, of overcrowding, of the interminable construction of the subway, the one loved by tourists and hated by many Italians. While beginning his work on *Roma*, Fellini suffered a massive creative and productive failure: *Il viaggio di G. Mastorna*, a decisive watershed in his career. However, Fellini was also enjoying the great international success of *Satyricon*, a film that, together with *Toby Dammit*,[8] opened the second period of his filmography. Towards the end of the 1960s, the director approached the world of television documentary with *I clowns* (co-produced by Rai Radio, and broadcast on Rai Due (Rai Radio 2) on 25 December 1970), and with *Fellini: A Director's Notebook*. Made for the series *NBC Experiment in Television*, the latter aired on the American network in March of 1969, and was a sort of dress rehearsal for *Satyricon*, containing many ideas that would return in *Roma*, as well as a precious account of the preparations for *Mastorna*. In fact, it opens on the remains of the sets of an elusive, ghostly Cologne Cathedral, rebuilt in Dino De Laurentiis's studios on Via Pontina, towards the Roman coast, for a film that will never be made but "like the relic of a sunken ship at the bottom of the sea, would nurture all my movies that came after" (Kezich 2006, 280).

The first news of a film project on Rome dates back to the shoot of *La dolce vita*. Fellini was going to make a series of twenty-four television documentaries on Italy and especially on Rome: "My job will be to get Romans to know Rome, and Italians to know Italy"[9] (quoted in *La Stampa* 1959). Of this unlikely didactic-documentary turn, halfway between the reports by Guido Piovene and Rossellini, there is no trace in *Roma*. Immediately following *Satyricon*, other news circulated regarding various investigative projects that Fellini was supposed to make with an American television company – eight films for television that he never made. However, they are worth mentioning as they give insight on Fellini's ability to promote himself as a "documentary filmmaker" immediately attuned to the political climate of 1969:

> The project includes a portrait of Mao, a reportage on Tibetan monks, an investigation into the Ford factories. America has given him free rein. If

Fellini does not reconsider it, he will leave, with two collaborators, as soon as the new film is finished, for a trip to China and Tibet. "It may be that I will not arrive in China – says Fellini – as I may stop in the country's orbit" … Wouldn't Fellini do something for Italian TV? "Without a doubt, but would our television give me free rein, that is, the possibility of making what interests me? For example, I would like to shoot a day in the life of a Cardinal, or of a politician, or a day in the Vatican for TV. I would like to spend a week in overalls, inside Fiat or Pirelli, and report on these Italian factories, as I see them, beyond any ideology."[10] (Acconciamessa 1969, n.p.)

Exotic journeys, portraits of Mao, investigations on factories, a week in a metalworker's overalls: projects unrelated to Fellini's habits and interests but offered as possible options by virtue of the spell of being able to *fellinize* everything, including Fiat and Pirelli. Fellini continued: "Ultimately, I think that a film about China and about Mao can also be made by taking a trip from Rome to Ostia"[11] (Acconciamessa 1969, n.p.). In the same way, according to Fellini, a film on Rome should be carried out like a documentary about a distant continent, like a report from an exotic country. Launched several times during production, the idea of an inquiry into Rome generated misunderstandings and betrayed expectations (and disoriented much of the Italian criticism of the time).[12] Like Xavier De Maistre in *Voyage autour de ma chambre*, Fellini launched into an explorative journey around Rome. A Rome that did not resemble the city in De Sica's or Rossellini's films nor did it venture into Pasolini's *borgate*. It neither resembled the carefree destination of *Roman Holiday* (1953) nor the space of the *commedia all'italiana* (also because it was a Rome largely rebuilt in the studio, including five hundred metres of ring road set up in front of Cinecittà). At the same time, *Roma* gathered around itself a repertoire of commonplaces and tourist stereotypes, accompanying the viewer among the clichés of a cinematographic city built in the image and likeness of Federico Fellini. But upon closer inspection, the film does look like a "documentary about the Amazon" (Kezich 2006, 304). As Fellini stated:

> Right after *La dolce vita*, certain Italian films about exotic travels became popular, *Magia verde* (*Green Magic*, 1953) and other similar movies. So then I maintained, in part because I love polemics and also because I thought there wasn't any need to travel to come upon the unusual, the strange, and the unexpected, that also and above all, things close by can present unfamiliar aspects, or rather, it's precisely in your own home among friends that certain new openings suddenly appear, certain mysterious fissures, to stare at in dismay. And so since then I'd thought about a Rome scrutinized

as if by a foreigner, a city both extremely close and far away like another planet. (Fellini 2015, 231–2)

Fellini confused the dates. *Magia verde* (1953), a documentary that recounts the trip to South America of explorer, philanthropist, tennis champion, and husband of 1930s diva Clara Calamai, Count Leonardo Bonzi and his troupe, was released seven years before *La dolce vita*. The film was presented at both the Cannes and Berlin film festivals with great success, thanks to the dazzling cinematography in "Ferraniacolor," the pride of the Italian film industry, which had just entered circulation at the time. Nevertheless, beyond the mistaken dates, *Magia verde* is considered one of the founders of the exotic documentary, which, after the success of the film *Mondo cane* (1962), initiated the cycle of the *mondo-movies*, one of the longest-lived, most successful, most profitable, and most popular genres of Italian cinema.[13] It is probable that Fellini was alluding to this phenomenon.

Mondo-Movie

Behind the apparent form of reportage, of ethnological interest and travel diary, the *mondo-movie* relied on the exhibition of nudity, on the morbid description of exotic rituals and customs, on shocking, crude, violent imagery, in a crescendo of monstrosity and sensationalism that eventually saturated the curiosity of the spectators around the end of the 1970s. In his analysis of popular Italian cinema, Vittorio Spinazzola described a progression of the phenomenon in three stages: the initial exoticism is layered with eroticism and eventually with sadism, followed by the "third reincarnation of the sensational documentary, [that is to say] the gratuitous search for horrifying or disgusting effects in large part connected to the manifestation of a deviant sexuality"[14] (1985, 321). Initially, when the figure of eroticism prevails, the phenomenon also acts as a counterweight to the folkloric provincialism of our popular comedies, in that "the local colour of Trastevere or Boscotrecase may be substituted with those of Tahiti or Perù"; however, these films had the advantage of being able to show "splendid female nudes on which censorship does not speak, since they are women of colour"[15] (Spinazzola 1985, 318). The epic emphasis of the commentary brings back the parade of religious ceremonies, bucolic scenes, tribal rites, and orgiastic parties in the frame of an idyllic setting, with the Polynesians being "mythologized in the same way as the peasants of Abruzzo and Calabria or as the Sardinian shepherds in the pages of Corrado Alvaro, Gabriele D'Annunzio and Grazia Deledda" (Pezzotta and Gilardelli

2010, 870).[16] Fellini reverses the process: *Roma* demonstrates how much Tahiti o Peru there can be in Trastevere, among the prostitutes of the Appia Antica, in the underground excavations from which, not surprisingly, a giant mammoth tusk emerges. This is a type of exoticism that becomes threatening, alienating, and more and more unknowable as we advance in the account of the city. The narration is that of a myth and, at the same time, the staging of its construction; an operation different from films such as *I misteri di Roma* (1964), a reportage coordinated by Cesare Zavattini that recounts the intimate physiognomy and life of the city, based on the teachings of *cinéma-vérité*, the theory of shadowing subjects and Zavattini's conception of inquiry as a key to understanding reality. Nothing could be more distant from Fellini's *Roma*.

After the overwhelming success of *Mondo cane*, the exotic documentary stabilized in a whirlwind of spectacular moments in which the attraction for the unusual, the bizarre, and the monstrous and an excitement bordering on morbidity prevail. However, critics recognize, at least at the onset of the phenomenon, the innovations introduced by Gualtiero Jacopetti, Francesco Prosperi, and Paolo Cavara: the overcoming of the novelistic form through a fragmented structure, the montage used for contrasts, rhymes, visual associations, the irreverent and unscrupulous use of the voice-over, the general prevalence of the visual over the narrative. *Roma* employs many of these elements: the idea of the film as a *compilation* of sensational moments arising not from a character or plot but from the mysteries of a place, the celebration of the spectacle and the monstrous, the use of the sometimes pedantic voice-over, which in *Roma* mocks educational documentaries, *cinéma-vérité* and reportage.[17] If the initial models of *La dolce vita* were magazines and newsreels, if *Satyricon* abandoned the knowledge of the ancient world promoted by the classical world to cross over into psychedelia, then *Roma* is a visionary and fantastic expansion of the fashion of exotic reportage: a *mondo-movie* that moves through time and memory rather than the geography of the continents. It is a journey around *planet Rome*, constructed with the same harmonious interconnectedness of truth, fiction, and improbability of the classic *mondo-movie* (see also Zanelli 1969). The tagline chosen for the launch of the film in the Italian distribution also evokes the erotic allusions typical of the *mondo-movie*, transferred from exploitation to the heights of Fellini's authorship: "The murky, gluttonous Rome of the 1970s in Federico Fellini's masterpiece."[18]

Roma thus finds its monstrous and sensational poetics in the animalistic gluttony of the trattorias, in the binges of sauces, *pajata* snails, in the *Camp* crowd of Trastevere, in the dismal parade of prostitutes, the launching of dead cats on the theatre stage, in the nocturnal raid of motorcyclists (pure *mondo-movie*).[19] To obscure religious rituals and processions, Fellini favours a sparkling ecclesiastical fashion catwalk. One may also note that *Amarcord* too has an episodic format and is based on a fragmented narrative structure. However, there are no time leaps. The moments of pure entertainment do not prevail over the story, and the film relies heavily on the dialogues by Tonino Guerra. In *Roma*, there are at least four main narrative blocks: the Grande Raccordo Anulare highway; the subway; the Vatican fashion show; the motorcyclists' night-time race – established largely through music and sound design. Ultimately, as David Forgacs (2016) noted, *Amarcord* is less radical and experimental than *Roma*. In *Roma*'s story, Fellini returns to the idea of *the great city as a forest*, a theme dear to the surrealists and to Walter Benjamin's explorations of urban memory. It is an association that, after all, is already present in *La dolce vita*: "I really like Rome [confesses Marcello to Maddalena]. It's like a *lukewarm, peaceful jungle*. It's easy to hide in it."[20] However, in *La dolce vita* the urban corresponds to the modern, to the Italy of the economic boom, to a fleeting experience made up of encounters, seductions, randomness, and erotic adventures. *Roma*, on the other hand, is a return to the state of nature. A jungle that has now taken over the city, as in the famous Piranesi engravings with the vegetation enveloping the monuments and growing uncontrolled among the ruins of Rome. Finally, another element underlines this dimension of Rome, and how the sense of place borders on placelessness: the film's poster.

Donyale Luna[21]

Roma was screened at the competition at the Cannes Film Festival on 14 May 1972. The film was met with a good reception; however, in those days, it made the news for the protests triggered by what Tullio Kezich defined as an "unfortunate poster, which showed a naked woman on all fours with three breasts – a staging of the lupa capitolina, the she-wolf symbol of Rome" (2006, 307). Shortly before the film's screening, a group of American feminists gathered in front of the Carlton Hotel, where there stood a large poster promoting *Roma* and threw cans of red paint onto the poster – Fellini, as is known, was a great forerunner of fashions and costume revolutions, including those that throw paint against symbols of patriarchy. Led by writer, screenwriter, and activist Eleanor Perry, the group held a sit-in chanting slogans and holding signs that read: Women Are People, Not Dirty Jokes. This marked the beginning of a tumultuous relationship between the feminist movement and Fellini that, by the end of the decade, would result in the kind of playful settling of scores that is *La città delle donne* (1980). However, at Cannes, the outrage for the *Roma* manifesto was widespread. Angelo Maccario, a critic sent to the Festival by the newspaper *Corriere della Sera*, observed: "As an Italian, I do not appreciate feeling represented by a work that, to attract spectators, needed to flaunt a three-breasted wolf-woman, especially since this image does not exist in the film"[22] (1972, n.p.).

The poster initially selected by United Artists for the film's launch can be seen only as cheap, offensive, sexist eroticism. Nevertheless, other traces and meanings can be discovered. These meanings are lost in the *Roma* poster designed by Rinaldo Geleng, featuring a gigantic prostitute with a proud look that breaks through the night mists of the Appia Antica – a scene at the beginning of the film. The she-wolf displayed on the poster at Cannes instead has dark skin. The image was inspired by the figure of Donyale Luna (see Le Votro 2015), the first Black model of international fame, the first ever to end up on the cover of a magazine not specifically marketed to an African-American audience. In a 1965 feature by Richard Avedon, her appearance in *Harper's Bazaar* marked a radical revolution in the world of fashion and a decisive watershed in the history of African-American visual culture (see Powell 2008). The following year, Luna's fame reached such heights that her figure was reproduced as a fibreglass mannequin by Adel Rootstein. Tall, thin, with an oval face and two very large eyes, Donyale Luna was born Peggy Ann Freeman in Detroit in 1945. "Luna" was her father's nickname for her, or at least that is how the story goes. Certainly, a perfect name for a woman who looked like a sphinx, a mysterious creature from a distant planet. In those years, Donyale Luna, who dreamed of acting and had Anna Magnani as her model, was one of the muses of Andy Warhol's creative studio known as the Factory (she appears in *Screen Tests* and in the 1965 film *Camp*). She subsequently moved to Europe and soon became an icon of Swinging London, and was photographed with the Rolling Stones, the Beatles, and the Who. Manly also began speaking of her in Italy at the end of the 1960s. *L'Unità* presented her to their readers thusly:

> "Someone calls her the gazelle. Salvador Dalí even called her: 'Nefertiti resurrected.'" Her name is Donyale Luna, a black model from Detroit, to whom the fashion magazine "Harper's Bazaar" has ensured a dazzling career in the world of haute couture. The long-limbed Donyale (1.79 m) points to her face as the source of her success, saying: "I have a perfect head: Egyptian profile, Indian eyes and black woman's mouth. It is a great mix and I am extremely pleased with it."[23] (1968, n.p.)

In 1969, Fellini hired Luna to play the sorceress Oenothea in *Satyricon* – the character who should have restored Encolpius's virility. We are at the last stage of the journey, at the height of the wanderings of Encolpius and Ascyltus, who have now arrived in an increasingly exotic, alienating, mysterious world: in the house of Oenothea "Menhirs appear, as they do in Celtic Brittany, but also a statue covered with nails recalling works from Central Africa"[24] (Slavazzi 2009, 77; see also Gaggetti 2009). Though she had a small part, Donyale Luna is featured on the cover of *Epoca* (16 January 1969) as a symbol of the contamination of styles, imaginaries, ethnicities of Roman science fiction staged in *Satyricon*, a film that under the pretext of the ancient world built a kaleidoscopic game of mirrors between the pre-Christian world of Petronius and the libertarian culture of 1968. Immediately following *Roma*, we find her naked and completely shaven in *Salomè* by Carmelo Bene, in her first and only role as a protagonist. Luna became a glamorous icon of the world of art, fashion, counterculture; she lived most of her years in Rome in a whirlwind of an unruly bohemian lifestyle and intense LSD use. In Rome, Luna would die of an overdose before turning thirty-five in 1979.

It may be that the poster for *Roma* was only intended to leverage the erotic imagery that had attracted audiences to Fellini's films since *La dolce vita*. However, the idea of an African she-wolf, from which Romulus and Remus have also been removed, very well exemplifies the exotic and mysterious elements of the film and underlines an imagery distant from the oleographic cliché of the Magna Mater and the Roman matron of the Italian poster. It is the she-wolf of Rome, the symbol of its foundation, one of the archetypes of Western culture, but it could also be a Polynesian Venus, a pre-Colombian idol, an Indian deity.

Conclusions

On the back cover of the film script published by Cappelli in 1972, Fellini and Zapponi are immortalized as they travel up the Tiber aboard a boat, but rather than a director and a screenwriter scouting locations they look like two explorers travelling to distant lands, with Fellini wearing a life jacket and a wool cap, like an old sea dog. Various passages of the text underline the project's exotic appeal: the Palace of Justice in Rome, known to Romans as *il Palazzaccio*, an insane Umbertine building where Orson Welles shot some scenes of his adaptation of *The Trial* by Franz Kafka, thus became a "Temple of the Law," a "Pagoda of Justice," and a "Pharaonic Palace of the Law"[25] (Zapponi 1972, 14). Here, Fellini was supposed to shoot a sequence that seems to have sprung out of a *mondo-movie*:

> It seems that when it was inaugurated, Palazzo di Giustizia was invaded by gigantic sewer rats, which arrived underground from the nearby river: As they devoured papers and shelves, it was decided to fight them off with a battalion of cats. However, the mice devoured the cats, smaller than them; after much thought, it became the Zoological Garden. All available leopards were mobilized and scattered in the basements and finally made the rats disappear.[26] (Zapponi 1972, 14)

This long-cherished sequence was not shot because the necessary permits were not received. Nevertheless, it undoubtedly expresses the register and tone sought by Fellini, the exotic, animalistic, alienating feeling of *Roma*. In *Roma*, the popular city is not idealized in any communal or identity utopia, let alone traced back to authenticity, genuineness, or folklore. The large, festive meals in open-air trattorias, a consolidated topos of the popular Roman oleography of neorealist cinema, are on the contrary reversed in a ferocious caricature, as in an unlikely neorealist version of Bosch's *Last Judgement*. Thus, Bernardino Zapponi, the film's screenwriter, described the preparation of the set for the long sequence. Fellini's fascination with Rome did not in any way cancel in him the annoyance for *romanità* or the repulsion for ignorance, coarseness, superficiality, rudeness, or chronic infantilism of its inhabitants. ("Here there are no neurotics, but there are no adults either. It's a city of idle, skeptical, ill-mannered children; they're also a little deformed psychologically, since impeding growth is unnatural"; Fellini 2015, 227). It is an aspect that is little considered when celebrating the idyll between Fellini and the city. An idyll that *Roma* itself helps to question. Not surprisingly, when reviewing the film, Oreste Del Buono did not hesitate to ask: "But does Fellini truly like Rome?"[27] (1972).

Finally, in *Roma*, we find the early affirmation of a *tourist imagination*[28] modelled upon cinematic memory, projected onto a multiplication of screens, signs, and devices transforming historic cities into media environments. With great anticipation, Fellini imagines the shift of archeology and antiquity towards the forms of permanent spectacle, of sensorial seduction, between phantasmagorias, installations, attractions, light effects, nocturnal visits to monuments, and virtual immersions. From the *sightseeing* of the final sequence of the motorcyclists to the *seeing-through* of virtual reality, Fellini's fantastic reworking of the myth of Rome is a crucial node in our collective imagination and in the contemporary narration of large metropolises.

NOTES

1 "ideale trilogia della memoria"
2 "il cinema di Fellini ha sempre avuto Roma come protagonista piuttosto che come sfondo e ambiente." An observation that we also find in Antonello Trombadori's review: "Si può dire che non vi sia film di Federico Fellini dove Roma non appaia come protagonista" (One may declare that there is not one Fellini film that does not have Rome as its protagonist). See *Quella vecchia baldracca che è la Roma di Fellini*, "Giorni," contained in the file *Informazioni Cinematografiche*, edited by the Ufficio Stampa dell'Italnoleggio Cinematografico, a volume devoted to the film *Roma*: a collection of cinematographic criticism published by the Italian press, November 1972, 6.
3 Among the most recent contributions, see Di Biagi (2014) and Carrera (2018).
4 I borrow the expression from Giori (2006).
5 "*Roma* è il capolavoro di Fellini, il film dove ha avuto il coraggio di distruggere anche l'ultimo elemento irrisorio, irrilevante o minimo della realtà, cioè il personaggio"
6 For an example of this, see Tornabuoni's interview "La grande madre sciattona" (1971).
7 For a broader analysis, see Agnew (2002).
8 *Toby Dammit* is Fellini's episode in the three-part film anthology *Tre passi nel delirio* (1968); the other two episodes are by Louis Malle and Roger Vadim. For more on this, see the chapters by Frank Burke, Marco Malvestio, and Alberto Zambenedetti in this volume.
9 "Il mio compito sarà quello di far conoscere Roma ai romani, l'Italia agli italiani." Note that the interviewer is anonymous.
10 "In progetto ci sono un ritratto di Mao, un reportage sui monaci del Tibet, un'inchiesta sulle fabbriche Ford. L'America ha dato carta bianca. Se Fellini non ci ripenserà partirà, con due collaboratori, appena terminato il nuovo film, per un viaggio in Cina e nel Tibet. "Può darsi che in Cina non ci arrivi – dice Fellini – che mi fermi nella sua orbita" … Non farebbe Fellini qualcosa per la Tv italiana? 'Naturalmente sì, ma mi darebbe la nostra tv carta bianca, cioè la possibilità di realizzare quello che mi interessa? Io vorrei, per esempio, fare per la Tv la giornata di un cardinale, o di un uomo politico, o una giornata in Vaticano. Vorrei passare una settimana in tuta, dentro la Fiat o la Pirelli, e realizzare un reportage su queste fabbriche italiane, viste da me, al di fuori di ogni ideologia.'"
11 "In definitiva," Fellini continued, "penso che un film sulla Cina e su Mao, si possa realizzare anche facendo un viaggio da Roma a Ostia."
12 On the film's reception, see Tassone (2020). For particular reference to Italian criticisms, see Minuz (2020).

13 For a general reconstruction of the phenomenon, see Francione and Fogliato (2016) and Godall (2008).
14 "terza reincarnazione del documentario spettacolare," that is to say, "la gratuita ricerca di effetti raccapriccianti o disgustosi, per larga parte connessi alla manifestazione di una sessualità deviata"
15 "al colore locale di Trastevere o Boscotrecase si sostituisce quello di Tahiti o del Perù"; "splendidi nudi femminili su cui la censura non fiata, in quanto si tratta di donne di colore"
16 "mitizzati allo stesso modo dei contadini abruzzesi e calabresi o dei pastori sardi nella pagine di D'Annunzio, Grazia Deledda, Corrado Alvaro." See Moravia's review of Folco Quirici's documentary *Oceano* (1970) in Pezzotta and Gilardelli (2010).
17 On the reworking of the lexicon of reportage in Fellini's cinema and on his specific parody of the forms of the television documentary see Warren (2003).
18 "La torbida, ingorda Roma degli anni Settanta nel capolavoro di Federico Fellini."
19 At the dawn of the seventies, in the wake of an irrepressible production, the word "mondo" had become synonymous with sordid, kitsch, extravagant, shocking. Pauline Kael, in one of her usual, contemptuous pans of European auteur cinema, did not hesitate to define *Satyricon* as "Mondo Trasho di Fellini (Fellini's Trasho World)" (Kael 1970). The reference is to the eponymous film by John Waters made in 1969.
20 "A me Roma piace," confesses Marcello to Maddalena, "è una specie di *giungla tiepida*, tranquilla, dove ci si può nascondere bene." Italics for emphasis are my own.
21 For more on the career of the magnetic model-turned-actress, see Shelleen Greene's essay in this volume. Greene expounds on her fashion career in parts 1 and 2, positioning Luna's dazzling rise in the context of the Civil Rights movement, Swinging London, American Pop Art, and Italian experimental cinema of the 1970s.
22 "Come italiano, non gradisco sentirmi rappresentato da un'opera che per richiamare spettatori ha avuto bisogno di esibire una ragazza-lupa tripopputa, tanto più che poi nel film quest'immagine non esiste." The title of Maccario's 1972 article references Fellini's failure to arrive at Cannes, preferring to remain in Rome at the last moment: "Fellini snobba il Festival di Cannes. Applausi a Marx (il comico) e a Peck" translates as "Fellini snobs the Cannes Festival. Applause for Marx (the comic) and Peck."
23 "Qualcuno la chiama la gazzella. Salvador Dalí l'ha addirittura definita: 'Nefertiti risorta.' Il suo nome è Donyale Luna, fotomodella negra [sic] di Detroit, alla quale la rivista di moda 'Harper's Bazaar,' ha assicurato una carriera folgorante nel mondo della haute couture. La longilinea Donyale (m. 1,79) indica come fonte del suo successo il viso, dicendo: 'Ho una

testa perfetta: profilo egiziano, occhi di indiana e bocca di negra [sic]. È un'ottima mescolanza e ne sono estremamente soddisfatta.'"
24 "compaiono dei menhir, come nella Bretagna celtica, ma anche una statua ricoperta di chiodi che ricorda opere dell'Africa centrale"
25 "Tempio della Legge"; "Pagoda della Giustizia"; "Reggia faraonica del Diritto." The full quotation reads: "'Fellini mi fa notare che tutta piazza Cavour ha un aspetto orientale,' prosegue Zapponi. 'Il Tempio di Palazzo di Giustizia, la Chiesa Valdese che sembra una Moschea, le grandi palme nel mezzo. È vero, non me n'ero mai accorto; pare di stare a Bangkok'" ("'Fellini points out to me that the whole of Piazza Cavour has an oriental aspect,' continues Zapponi. 'The Temple of the Palace of Justice, the Waldensian Church that looks like a mosque, the large palm trees in the middle. It's true, I had never noticed it; it's like being in Bangkok'") (Zapponi 1972, 15).
26 "Pare che quando fu inaugurato, Palazzo di Giustizia fosse invaso da giganteschi topi di chiavica, che arrivavano nei sotterranei dal vicino fiume: divoravano carte e scaffali, si pensò bene quindi di combatterli con un battaglione di gatti. Ma i sorci divorarono i gatti, più piccoli di loro; allora, dopo molto pensare, ci si rivolse al Giardino Zoologico. Tutti i gattopardi disponibili furono mobilitati e sparsi negli scantinati, e finalmente fecero scomparire i topi."
27 "Ma davvero Roma piace a Fellini?"
28 The notion of the tourist imagination, which originates from Brooks's (1995) original formulation of *melodramatic imagination*, is discussed in Crouch et al. (2005).

REFERENCES

Acconciamessa, Mirella. 1969. "Su Mao e sul Vaticano le telecamere di Fellini?" *L'Unità*. 2 November.
Agnew, John. 2002. *Place and Politics in Modern Italy*. Chicago: University of Chicago Press.
– 2020. "Fellini's Sense of Place." In *A Companion to Federico Fellini*, edited by Frank Burke, Marguerite Waller, and Marita Gubareva, 117–27. Hoboken, NJ: Wiley Blackwell.
Brooks, Peter. 1995. *The Melodramatic Imagination. Balzac, Henry James, Melodrama and the Mode of Excess*. New Haven: Yale University Press.
Burke, Frank, Marguerite Waller, and Marita Gubareva, eds. 2020. *A Companion to Federico Fellini*. Hoboken, NJ: Wiley Blackwell.
Carrera, Alessandro. 2018. *Fellini's Eternal Rome: Paganism and Christianity in the Films of Federico Fellini*. London: Bloomsbury.

Crouch, David, Rhona Jackson, and Felix Thompson, eds. 2005. *The Media and the Tourist Imagination*. New York: Routledge.
Del Buono, Oreste. 1972. "Roma 1972 D. F. (Dopo Fellini)." *L'Europeo*, 23 March.
Di Biagi, Flaminio. 2014. *La Roma di Fellini*. Genoa: Le Mani.
Fellini, Federico. 2015. *Making a Film*. Translated by Christopher Burton White. New York: Contra Mundum Press.
Forgacs, David. 2016. "*Roma*: Rome, Fellini's City." The *Criterion Collection*, 14 December. www.criterion.com/current/posts/4349-roma-rome-fellini-s-city.
Francione, Fabio, and Fabrizio Fogliato. 2016. *Jacopetti Files. Biografia di un genere cinematografico italiano*. Milan: Mimesis.
Gaggetti, Elisabetta. 2009. "La percezione dell'antico. I romani di Fellini-Satyricon tra musei capitolini e 'Harper's Bazaar.'" In *Fellini-Satyricon. L'immaginario dell'antico*, edited by Raffaele De Berti, Elisabetta Gaggetti, and Fabrizio Slavazzi, 166–252. Milan: Cisalpino.
Giori, Mauro. 2006. "8½ and the Cinema as an Institution. Il film "difficile" di Fellini e la cultura italiana del suo tempo." In *Federico Fellini: Analisi di film, possibili letture*, edited by Raffaele De Berti, 75–101. Milan: McGraw-Hill.
Godall, Mark. 2008. "Mondo Roma: Images of Italy in the Shockumentary Tradition." In *Cinematic Rome*, edited by Richard Wrigley, 97–108. Leicester: Troubador.
Kael, Pauline. 1970. "Fellini's Mondo Trasho." *The New Yorker*, 14 March. www.newyorker.com/magazine/1970/03/14/fellinis-mondo-trasho.
Kezich, Tullio. 2006. *Federico Fellini: His Life and Work*. New York: Faber and Faber.
La Stampa. 1959. "Fellini televisivo dopo la dolce vita." 5 September 1959.
Lo Vetro, Gianluca. 2015. *Fellini e la moda. Percorsi di stile da Casanova a Lady Gaga*. Milan: Mondadori.
L'Unità. 1968. "La gazzella." 5 April 1968.
Maccario, Angelo. 1972. "Fellini snobba il Festival di Cannes. Applausi a Marx (il comico) e a Peck." *Corriere della Sera*, 15 May.
Minuz, Andrea. 2020. *Fellini, Roma*. Soveria Mannelli: Rubbettino.
Moravia, Alberto. 2010. "D'Annunzio sulla piroga." In *Alberto Moravia. Cinema italiano. Recensioni e interventi 1933–1990*, edited by Alberto Pezzotta and Anna Gilardelli, 869–71. Milan: Bompiani.
Pasolini, Pier Paolo. 2006. "Federico Fellini e Tonino Guerra, Amarcord." In *Pier Paolo Pasolini: Descrizioni di descrizioni*, edited by Graziella Chiarcossi, 247–8. Milan: Garzanti.
Pezzotta, Alberto, and Anna Gilardelli, eds. 2010. *Alberto Moravia. Cinema italiano. Recensioni e interventi 1933–1990*. Milan: Bompiani.
Powell, Richard J. 2008. *Cutting a Figure: Fashioning Black Portraiture*. Chicago: University of Chicago Press.

Slavazzi, Fabrizio. 2009. "L'immagine dell'antico nel Fellini-Satyricon." In *Fellini-Satyricon. L'immaginario dell'antico*, edited by Raffaele De Berti, Elisabetta Gaggetti, and Fabrizio Slavazzi, 59–92. Milan: Cisalpino.

Spinazzola, Vittorio. 1985. *Cinema e pubblico. Lo spettacolo filmico in Italia: 1945–1965*. 2nd ed. Rome: Bulzoni.

Tassone, Aldo. 2020. *Fellini 23 ½. Tutti i film*. Bologna: Edizioni Cineteca di Bologna.

Tornabuoni, Lietta. 1971. "La grande madre sciattona (intervista)." *La Stampa*, 21 March.

Warren, Paul. 2003. *Fellini ou la satire libératrice*. Montreal: VLB.

Wrigley, Richard. 2008. *Cinematic Rome*. Leicester: Troubador.

Zanelli, Dario. 1969. "Dal pianeta Roma." In *Fellini Satyricon by Federico Fellini*, edited by Dario Zanelli, 11–79. Bologna: Cappelli.

Zapponi, Bernardino. 1972. *Roma*. Bologna: Cappelli.

Framing Women in Fellini's Films and Drawings

DISHANI SAMARASINGHE

As is well known, Federico Fellini turned to his dreams for inspiration to overcome his creative blocks, much like several of his characters, most notably Guido in *8 ½* (1963).[1] After the 1960s, a great part of his cinema derives from his dreams, from *Le tentazioni del dottor Antonio* (1962) to *8 ½* (1963), from *Giulietta degli spiriti* (1965) to *Fellini Satyricon* (1969) and *La città delle donne* (1980). Fellini's dreams are transformed into images, in turn feeding his cinematographic universe (Aimé 2012, 7). Indeed, in 1960, Ernst Bernhard, a Jungian psychoanalyst, introduced Fellini to Jung's theories, based on analytical psychology – the study and investigation of the unconscious, more precisely of the individual psyche. The central concept of analytical psychology, to which Fellini was very sensitive, was individuation – the lifelong psychological process of differentiating the self from the conscious and unconscious elements of everyone (Adler 1957).[2] Fellini was attracted to Jung's work on dreams and the treatment of symbols. Between *La dolce vita* (1960) and *8 ½* (1963), Bernhard and Fellini met for therapy sessions three times per week (Aimé 2012, 13). Bernhard guided Fellini and encouraged him to keep a dream journal that later became *The Book of Dreams*, which he drew on throughout his career (Aldouby 2013, 19–20). This diary was a way to openly explore his creativity and elaborate on his ideas that at times are brought to life in his films (Hayes 2005, 6). Through the creative processes of the cinema – which for Fellini included dreaming, writing, storyboarding, shooting, and editing – the images from his dreams are transformed, modified, metamorphosed. This chapter explores the representations of women in two films: *8 ½* (1963) and *La città delle donne* (1980), films Fellini made while devoting himself to the study of Jung. First, I analyze the bodies of the women in his dreams and those in his films in relation to Fellini's framing. Second, under the prism of interartiality, I turn to the relationship between cinema and painting.[3]

Interestingly, many of his drawings share a fundamental common thread: they represent and typify women. Indeed, Fellini was both fascinated and distressed by women throughout his life: everyday women, the women in his dreams, his own wife. Women occupied an important place in his dreams and this can be seen in his drawings and notably in his films. In *The Book of Dreams* (2007, 107, 202, 376), Fellini wrote imaginary dialogues directly influenced by Picasso; it is very clear that the filmmaker admired the painter. The two did cross paths on a few occasions, but Fellini also dreamt about several other possible encounters with him. These dreams would have occurred to Fellini in periods of doubt and artistic crisis. The influence of Picasso's paintings also seems to be embodied by the different types of female bodies that appear in the *The Book of Dreams*, from the curvy and voluptuous ones to the deconstructed forms (Mollica 2003, 33). There are interesting particularities surrounding the features and shapes of women's bodies in some of Picasso's paintings that seemed to have inspired Fellini. The pictorial quality of Fellini's films reveals this connection. This intermediality,[4] or more precisely, the interartiality – which is a branch of intermediality dealing with the particularity of the exchanges that exist in several mediums, especially in art, from a more aesthetic point of view[5] – is perceptible in Fellini's works. In fact, Fellini introduces interartiality through his way of framing the shapes of those women's bodies, which demonstrate the influence Picasso had on the director.

From Unconscious Images to Moving Images of Women

Aside from his cinematographic universe, Fellini managed to express his world, his visions, and his emotions through his drawings, which were sometimes the source of his filmic production. His drawings were fundamental for the creation of his cinematographic characters. Indeed, some of his characters display common features such as the outrageous caricature of women's bodies and faces. In his more spontaneous drawings, where the erotic aspect comes into play, we can see darker curves and his strokes are thicker and loosened. Moreover, in those drawings, women possess attributes that are sometimes completely disproportionate comparatively to men, who in turn feel crushed by their immensity. Several women in his films follow this pattern: they appear as grotesque, strong, and overwhelmingly immense, such as Saraghina in *8 ½* and the motorcyclist in the *La città delle donne*. Indeed, the framing of these bodies highlights their size and attributes, making them imposing and dangerous.

In *8 ½*, the character Saraghina is a woman with seductive charms who embodies certain vices and sins in the eyes of the priest who welcomes Guido as a child into his confessional. In the famous sequence, the children summon her and, in exchange for some money, she dances for them. Her generous forms, which are framed to appear almost disproportionate, hypnotize the eyes of these children who observe her in raptured silence. At first, upon exiting her shack, her shadow is projected on the walls. As she leaves her shack, her shadow is projected on the walls. She is shown in a low-angle shot with a close-up of her back and then a close-up of her breasts. Tight inserts of her eyes underscore her heavy make-up, emphasizing the importance of her facial expressions. Then, the camera alternates close-up shots of her face and buttocks. These low angles stress the difference in size between the children and the woman. The Saraghina character, as she appears in *8 ½*, and her facial expressions, are clearly reminiscent of a drawing in *The Book of Dreams* of a large-breasted dark woman, framed in profile in a medium close-up (Fellini 2007, 354). She poses like an Egyptian sphinx. In front of this gigantic statue of a dark woman there are two human-sized people (we can suppose that one is Fellini and the other a woman). The facial features of this sphinx are recognizable in Saraghina. Her black eyes are heavily made up, her lips emphasize her smile, and she takes hold of the children's attention, who observe her dancing in silence. The statue in the drawing and Saraghina in *8 ½* are imposing in their size when compared to the smallness of two adult characters and the children, respectively.

In his drawings, the buttocks, breasts, and genitals have an imposing size, and these are replicated in *La città delle donne*, particularly in the scene in which Snàporaz's childhood and young adult memories are displayed. Snàporaz finds himself in a brothel waiting for his prostitute. When she arrives, she is introduced by the sound of her footsteps, which becomes louder and louder as she approaches the waiting room. This woman is tall, scantily dressed, her generous breasts and hips on display. The camera is fixed on her in shoulder shot at first, then when Snàporaz meets her, he follows her. In a subjective shot, the camera frames her buttocks as she walks, leading the protagonist to a tiny room, disproportionate to her imposing size. Snàporaz is crushed under her and almost disappears. The whole scene revolves around the size of her buttocks, enveloping at the same time the body of Snàporaz but also of the prostitute herself. This image refers to one of Fellini's drawings in *The Book of Dreams*, which depicts several women from both front and behind (Fellini 2007 , 303, 385). They are corpulent, the contours of their bodies are rather thick, and their backs are clear and borderline white and red. But their buttocks are round, and red tints have been added to accentuate their size. These links between drawings and film images are echoed repeatedly. Fellini attempts to draw them through his camera, to reproduce these types of effects.

Another example of this technique is the motorcyclist in *La città delle donne*, who helps Snàporaz get out of the hotel. She has the particularities of the dominant woman, the woman of power, or the sadomasochistic woman. At first, she seems completely surreal, enlarged by shadow play, just as the drawing of Fellini where we see a naked woman from behind revealing her posterior to the light of a candle (Fellini 2007, 299). Here, the shadow of the motorcyclist reveals her greatness and when she comes out of the shadow, her position as a dominatrix stands out through her clothes, her perspiration, and her sweat that has turned black from having worked with fire. These elements of fire, perspiration, and her layered attire are reminiscent of Fellini's drawings in which we see several women dressed in sadomasochistic accessories and whipping two men in front of them (Fellini 2007, 87).

On the contrary, the portraits and caricatures of relatives are made with softer, finer, less imposing pencil strokes, evoking a sense of trust. They have more childish features, especially the ones depicting Fellini's wife, Giulietta Masina (Fellini 2007 , 54, 67), or Marcello Mastroianni – as we can see in some loose drawings from the storyboard of *Intervista* (1987) (Hindry 2008). The same approach is followed in his films through the casting of actresses like Anouk Aimée, who plays Luisa Anselmi (Guido's wife in *8 ½*), or Anna Prucnal, who plays Elena (Snàporaz's wife in *La città delle donne*). These women are both childish and maternal, and seem to accompany the protagonist without being of significant help in his quest; they are both a burden and a vital component in their husbands' lives. In *8 ½*, Luisa is regularly framed in profile and shoulder-facing shots. At times, in close-ups of her face, her facial expressions are frozen and left open to interpretation. In *La città delle donne*, Elena appears halfway through the film, in Dr. Sante Katzone's house. In this extended sequence, she first remains in the background, then confronts her husband about their relationship, and eventually dances with one of Katzone's guests. The framing in this scene focuses primarily on her face, moving to full shots of her body when she dances.

Other types of female characters can be observed in these two films, and may be described as the accompanying women – those who will help the male protagonist move further in his quest, attempting to reposition him. These women are more angelic, seductive, and irresistible to the eyes of the protagonist. Most of the camera's framing of them is done in close-ups on their eyes and faces, sometimes with a few medium shoulder shots to emphasize their décolletage. There is an interest depicted through the eyes of these women. In *8 ½*, when Claudia Cardinale's character is first introduced at the spa, the scene starts with a wide shot encompassing her whole body, then a close-up of her face in profile, with a smile. Her beauty is underscored in these images, a formidable beauty seen through the eyes of the director and the protagonist. Then suddenly, when she holds out the glass of mineral water, smiling kindly, she is framed in a high angle. The music (Rossini's overture to *Il barbiere di Siviglia*) pauses for a second, as to emphasize Guido's rapture before her beauty.

Finally, there are also those women who obsess over the protagonist in a maternal but also in a sensual, sexual way. These are framed in a fragmented fashion: sometimes body parts are cut off from these women that haunt the protagonist's mind. In *La città delle donne*, the character of Donatella is one such figure. She helps Snàporaz more in a maternal way. Yet her physical attributes become much more important than her own face, especially in the scene where she dances with a partner in a light, sequined dress. The shots are tightly focused on her breasts, buttocks, and hips, the female body parts that Fellini captures from his dreams (Fellini 2007, 59) where the shapes of his women emerge visually. This kind of fragmentation of women's bodies and faces from his childhood, and the memories of youth are apparent in the films. For instance, when Snàporaz slides down the "memories and fantasies" slide, the first shot is a close-up of Rosina from Verucchio's legs. Then a shot of her hips as they swing while she irons, then finally the camera tilts up to reveal her face. The second woman is the fishmonger from San Leo, who is first shown in a close-up on her face, but then a pan up and down on her body lingers on her décolletage and her hands as they suggestively stroke a bunch of squirming eels. Her full body is never shown.

In *The Book of Dreams*, Fellini transposes these women from his dreams onto paper, the images becoming fixed. But in second instance, by means of cinematic techniques, these bodies are brought back to life and become moving images (Deleuze 1983, 87). This creates a perfect fusion between his dreams, his drawings, and the cinema, through a process of interartiality.

Intermedial Cinema-Painting of Women

It is through the intermediality of his process that Fellini travels from dream to drawing, from drawing to film, and from film to painting. The notion of intermediality does not consider media as isolated phenomena but promotes processes where there are constant interactions between them (Müller 2006, 100–1). The concept of intermediality is thus necessary and complementary insofar as it supports the processes of production of sense linked to media interactions. According to Jacques Aumont, this intermedial aesthetic of the cinema is called "cinematization" or the "becoming cinema of the painting"[6] (2007, 121–5, 137). With these aesthetic interactions of cinema and painting, Fellini creates these bodies of women as his filmic images. These women's bodies, their features, colours, and forms, are given a painterly treatment, the filmic frame appropriating the pictorial frame. This mashing of film and painting aesthetics characterizes much of Fellini's late work.

Hava Aldouby's remarkable research in her book *Federico Fellini: Painting in Film, Painting on Film* (2013) examines the references, influences, and symbols of painting and painters in Fellini's cinematographic works. The scholar discusses the paintings of Rembrandt and Francis Bacon in relation to *Toby Dammit* (1968), as well as the oneiric allusions to Giorgio de Chirico in films such as *Fellini Satyricon* (1969), *Il Casanova di Federico Fellini* (1976), or *Giulietta degli spiriti* (1965). Moreover, Fellini had an admiration and a fascination for the work and the person of Henri de Toulouse-Lautrec (Mollica 2003, 34). In his films, especially in *8 ½*, he was inspired by the aesthetics and techniques of the painter; this can be observed in the treatment of some female characters, whose bodies are depicted as thin, light forms on the screen. For instance, in Toulouse-Lautrec's painting *At the Moulin Rouge, the Dance* (1890), the eye is led to focus on the centre of the painting, where a dancer is lifting her skirt to reveal her red-stockinged legs. In the foreground is another woman in a pink dress whose posture and clothes betray a higher social class. Her hips and bust are accentuated. There is a marked similarity between this woman and Carla, Guido's mistress in *8 ½*. Indeed, when she arrives at the station, she wears a similar dress, albeit in black, but with a corset that highlights her figure. Her white velvet hat with black veil gives her this very distinguished and seductive air. She appears in a long shot when introduced for the first time, her whole body and gestures on full display. Several shots of Carla focus on her chest. There is also a certain resemblance between the framing of Toulouse-Lautrec's painting *Aux Ambassadeurs: Gens Chic (Fashionable People at Les Ambassadeurs*, 1893), and the scene where Guido and Carla are caught in a long shot at a table in the hotel. Indeed, Guido is positioned facing the camera, while Carla is framed from the side in this empty restaurant room. In the background, some objects fill the emptiness of this space: white tablecloths and black chairs. The influence of Toulouse-Lautrec's paintings can be noticed in the love scene in the hotel room as well.

When Carla drapes herself with the white bed sheet, she is reminiscent of *Woman in a Chemise Standing by a Bed (Madame Poupoule)* (1899).

Fellini is influenced by a certain technicality used in painting, especially in the way he freezes moving images into fixed images, like a picture in a frame. One example of this technique is the scene that follows the lovemaking between Guido and Carla. The camera is fixed, Carla is lying down, and she is draped in the bed, almost like a painter's model. Guido is asleep, lying on his side. A bowl of peaches recalls a still life. Then the light comes to illuminate completely Carla's face, while the shadow comes to rest on Guido's face. This play of light and shadow is based on methods used in painting, which makes it possible to think of these images through a pictorial framework.

As previously mentioned, Fellini had a great admiration for Pablo Picasso. Although these two artists barely crossed paths during their careers, Fellini made sure to engage with him through his dreams. The first dream in which Picasso is present, gave birth the following year to the film *8 ½* (Fellini 2007, 107). The second dream announces another film, *Fellini Satyricon*, in which we find references to the work of Picasso (202). Finally, the third dream evokes the *La città delle donne*, the theme of the woman constituting a real link between the two artists (376). These artists shared many obsessions and themes and displayed similar sensitivities. They both were interested in depicting women in all their facets, the circus, and the mythology from which their characters often emerged. The cinema of Fellini reflects in a sense the art of Picasso, especially in the way the two artists represent women's bodies, from fragmented, hybrid forms, to very sensual and curvaceous figures. As we have seen, the character of Saraghina in *8 ½* and the motorcyclist in *La città delle donne* are more voluptuous than the other female characters in the two films, and the camerawork (through angles and shadow play) enlarges their bodies. Needless to say, it is in *Il Casanova di Federico Fellini* (1976) that his fantasy of the giantess is finally embodied. Similarly, Picasso's Cubist period presents numerous women depicted with generous and distorted proportions. For instance, in Picasso's painting *A Dream* (1932), a woman is sitting on an armchair and her face is split in two, but she also has a sensuous body, and the outline of her breasts is suggested. In his painting *Nude Woman in a Red Armchair* (1932), the subject is, indeed, naked, the shapeliness of her body exaggerated and sensuous, but the atmosphere remains similar to *A Dream* in its ethereality. The curves of the women in these paintings are reflected not only in Fellini's films but also in his drawings. For example, a drawing of a naked woman lying on a field floor presents the usual rounded curves, but they are disproportionate when compared to her small head (Fellini

2007, 289). Finally, the statue embodying femininity in *La città delle donne* references art history as well: on the one hand, it echoes the *Venus of Willendorf* figurine as seen from the angle of a fertility goddess, as the mother-woman; on the other hand, the rounded belly, breasts, and hips recall Picasso's ink and charcoal drawing, *Standing Woman* (1946).

Fellini also literalizes the connection between female characters and paintings in *La città delle donne*. When Snàporaz is at the home of Dr. Sante Katzone, he enters a gallery of portraits; darkened at first, the light-boxes light up with a switch that also plays a recording of the women's voices who are talking while they are engaged in sexual activity. The framing makes them into trophies. They are tight shots of faces, breasts, waists, legs, and so forth. Fellini offers us an interesting metaphor. They are an art gallery, an exhibition of women seen by a man, seen by a male artist who paints them, touches them, manipulates them.

In conclusion, Fellini employed a process that relied on interartiality to create a certain way of visualizing the women that he saw in his dreams. It was rather laborious work of creation that entailed several stages; first, he would transcribe his dreams into a drawing; then he would combine those with references to art history; and finally, the women would be "re-born" as film characters. These women's bodies seen from different angles bring us into the Fellinian universe, a universe where they are captured cinematically, but often as fragmented figures: a face, a chest, a waist, a buttock, an eye. The bodies of these women are revealed to us as Fellini saw them in his imagination. They are visible and alive, with their flesh and bones on display. And yet these women do not exist, they are women of imagination, of a certain utopia typical of the Fellini universe. These interactions between dreams, drawings, and cinema represent Fellini's creative process. Ultimately, Fellini's poetics must be understood as profoundly intermedial.

NOTES

1 This chapter focuses on the period after 1960, a time when Fellini devoted himself to Jungian studies and started to be more interested in his dreams.
2 Individuation is a concept that Fellini uses extensively in his films in which dreams are paramount, such as in *8 ½* and *La città delle donne*. For more on this, see Frank Burke's chapter in this volume.
3 Marina Vargau's chapter in this volume also mobilizes the concept of interartiality in Fellini, especially in relation to *Il vaggio di G. Mastorna*.
4 Müller's full quote reads: "The intermediality operates in a domain that includes the social, technological and media factors, while the interartiality

is limited to the reconstruction of the interactions between the arts and the artistic processes and is rather registered in a 'poetological' tradition" (2006, 100–1).
5 See Moser (2007). The interartiality is interested in the relations between the arts and relations that include the media, but that go beyond being summarized because art is not the sum of its medial components; it is also defined by aesthetic considerations.
6 "le devenir cinéma du tableau"

REFERENCES

Adler, Gerhard. 1957. *Etudes de psychologie jungienne: Essais sur la théorie et la pratique de l'analyse jungienne.* Geneva: Georg.
Aimé, Agnel. 2012. "Jung et Fellini. L'inconscient crée des images, le film reste à faire." *Cahiers jungiens de psychanalyse* 135, no. 1: 7–17. https://doi.org/10.3917/cjung.135.0007.
Aldouby, Hava. 2013. *Federico Fellini. Painting in Film, Painting on Film.* Toronto: University of Toronto Press.
Aumont, Jacques. 2007. *L'oeil interminable.* Paris: Les Essais, Éditions de la Différence.
Deleuze, Gilles. 1983. *Cinéma 1: L'image-mouvement.* Paris: Éditions de Minuit.
Fellini, Federico. 2007. *The Book of Dreams.* Edited by Tullio Kezich and Vittorio Boarini. Milan: RCS Libri Spa.
Hayes, Mark. 2005. "Psychoanalysis & the Films of Federico Fellini." *Honors College Theses Paper* 12. http://digitalcommons.pace.edu/honorscollege_theses/12.
Hindry, Ann. 2008. *Quoi de neuf Federico? Dessins de Fellini. Musée des beaux-arts de Nancy 30 Octobre 2008–28 Janvier 2009.* Lyon: Fage.
Mollica, Vincenzo. 2003. *Fellini!* Rome: Comunicare Organizzando: Skira.
Moser, Walter. 2007. "L'interartialité: pour une archéologie de l'intermédialité." *Intermédialité et socialité: histoire et géographie d'un concept*, edited by Marion Froger and Jürgen E. Müller, 69–92. Münster: Nodus Publikationen.
Müller, Jurgen. 2006. "Vers l'intermédialité: histoires, positions et options d'un axe de pertinence." *Médiamorphoses. L'identité des médias en question*, no. 16: 99–110. https://doi.org/10.3406/memor.2006.1138.

Originals in the Dark, Imitations in the Light: Fellini's *Ginger e Fred*

GIOVANNA CATERINA LISENA

Introduction

Federico Fellini's antepenultimate film, *Ginger e Fred*, released in 1986, is a love story between the film's two protagonists, Amelia Bonetti (Giulietta Masina) and Pippo Botticella (Marcello Mastroianni), who transform into the titular characters, Ginger and Fred. During their prime over thirty years prior, the pair of dancers imitated old Hollywood stars Ginger Rogers and Fred Astaire. Amelia and Pippo are invited to perform one final dance on a "container"[1] Christmas special set to air on a commercial television network. It is through the eyes of Amelia and Pippo that Fellini expresses his opinions on commercial television and its destructive effects on televised films and audiences, while calling to mind the nostalgic memory of *avanspettacolo* and the dying art of cinema. Italian film scholar Millicent Marcus has described the film as portraying "the struggle between the cinematic past and the televisual present as a battle between good and bad, between innocence and decadence, between memory and oblivion" (2002, 185). Although the term "the anti-television movie" has been applied to the film (Kezich 2006, 367), Fellini was not entirely against this mass medium. At first, he had seen it as an opportunity to enter into the intimate space of people's homes, and in some ways, believed that it allowed more freedom in comparison to the confines of the cinema industry.[2] After his experiences with both American and Italian television networks, creating *Fellini: A Director's Notebook* (1969) and *I clowns* (1970), respectively, the author's perspective changed drastically.

Television's main focus "was no longer, as it was in the sixties, to educate and inform but to capture viewers and keep hold of them with their remote-control devices" (Minuz 2015, 171).[3] Fellini recognized that with the growing interest in television, audiences no longer took part in the ritual of cinema – meaning physically going to the movie theatre to be surrounded by other spectators to view a film on a big screen *without* interruptions. The new television culture also pushed audiences to be *impatient* and have a reduced attention span, making spectators more inclined to use the power of a remote control to find other programs that would attract their attention. As opposed to the ritual of cinema, televised movies removed artistic control by placing it in the hands of spectators who could potentially view multiple programs at a time with the simple click of a button. The world of commercial television lives on the premise of capturing the consumer's attention. If commercial breaks were the main focus, then the spaces "in-between" had to be filled with content that would keep the viewer entertained for long enough to see the next commercial, levelling all forms of entertainment to a specific time slot. The medium's interest was, therefore, inextricable from commercial interest. The point was *not* to convey a message about humanity through an art form but to *fill in the gaps* between commercial advertisements. In Fellini's view, this produced "insignificant" messages (Bondanella 1992, 223).[4] It is for this reason that the author comes to severely criticize many aspects of commercial television, including the television culture of moral levelling – that is to say of reducing "everything it presents to the same mass level of insignificance" (Bondanella 1992, 225) – along with its anti-cultural use of imitations. Fellini heavily criticized the interruptive nature of advertisements and their effects on both televised movies and spectators, as they break the film's artistic rhythm while rendering audiences impatient. Fellini's 1986 film addresses these ideas by creating a caricatured version of commercial television; by showing the backstage production of a grotesque rendition of the variety show *Ed ecco a voi …*; and by placing the protagonists in the centre of this chaotic new world. This chapter analyzes how Fellini, in *Ginger e Fred*, uses his protagonists to provide a prophetic warning about the effects of television in 1980s Italy, while at the same emphasizing his nostalgia for the dying art of cinema and *avanspettacolo*.

Distinguishing Real from Fake

The film is told through the point of view of the two protagonists, who together embody the nostalgic memory of the *avanspettacolo* and cinema – an art form that was viewed as dying with the onset of commercial television in the 1980s (Gallippi 2016, 221). Through their participation in the commercial television world of *Ed ecco a voi …*, Fellini demonstrated how the old and new begin to clash. Fellini emphasizes three criticisms of commercial television, which are contrasted with his nostalgia for cinema and theatrical variety shows, making his characters represent the old cinema culture. In many ways, Amelia and Pippo are reminiscent of the mother/wife figure of Melina Amour, and the irresponsible, childlike adult, Checco Dal Monte, from Fellini and Lattuada's 1951 film *Luci del varietà* – another film that centres on Fellini's nostalgia for the *avanspettacolo*, for which he cared deeply (Bispuri 2003, 174). Both Amelia and Pippo seem to arrive from the *Luci del varietà* stage, much older and thus belonging to a different generation than their *Ed ecco a voi ...* fellow performers. The protagonists are not only continuations of his earlier films as an "ongoing creative project" (Marcus 2002, 182) but also represent Fellini's point of view towards postmodern mass television culture.

As the film progresses, it becomes evident that the qualities of Amelia and Pippo together form Fellini's self-portrait (Kezich 2006, 371). On the one hand, as Tullio Kezich explains, "Amelia in the beginning of the film, trying to feel her way through a world that doesn't belong to her, is a self-portrait of Fellini: shy, curious, vulnerable, impatient, angry, determined" (2006, 371). Her shyness and curiosity are best exhibited through one of the film's earlier scenes, where Amelia looks between the blinds in her hotel room window at the extraterrestrial-looking television tower. Fellini begins with an establishing shot of Amelia looking out the window, cutting to a close-up of her eyes peering between the blinds with curiosity and uncertainty, almost in awe of this object that is seemingly foreign to her. The camera pans from the bottom of the television tower to the top, taking the point of view of Amelia's eyes. Once the camera pans to the top of the tower's circling spotlight, the scene cuts to a close up of Amelia's eyes looking in the same direction the camera was fixed on, all the while accompanied by a piece of non-diegetic eerie music to emphasize the sentiment of an unknown world. This scene shows how Amelia is foreign to this new world, and that her eyes and those of the camera are the same, implying that her role represents the author's point of view – that of a sense of estrangement in the postmodern world (Minuz 2015, 173).[5] Her vulnerability is represented through the belief that she will be able to restore the romantic and nostalgic world of the past with her partner Pippo (Bispuri 2003, 175).[6] At its core, the nostalgic element through this film is best defined through the words of Svetlana Boym, who stated: "Nostalgia is a sentiment of loss and displacement, but it is also a romance with one's own fantasy ... A cinematic image of nostalgia is a double exposure, or a superimposition of two images – of home and abroad, past and present, dream and everyday life. The moment we try to force it into a single image, it breaks the frame or burns the surface" (2001, xiii–xiv).

Amelia's impatience, anger, and determination are a consequence of the clash between the old and new worlds. In her mind, Amelia hopes this experience will magically recreate the memories of her youth dancing with her lover, Pippo. Boym defines this attitude towards the past as "Reflexive Nostalgia," which emphasizes the *algia* (pain) of nostalgia as it "dwells on the ambivalence of human longing and does not shy away from the contradictions of modernity" (2001, xviii). Amelia is willing and somewhat excited to embark on this new journey into the televisual world. In fact, she admits that she accepted the invitation to perform not only for her grandchildren who insisted heavily on her participation but also for the "myth of television that fascinates everyone"[7] (Guerrini 1986, 153). At the same time, Amelia also embodies the *nostos* aspect of nostalgia – "Restorative Nostalgia" – in her attempt to recreate a lost home, hence, the stage of *Luci del varietà* (Boym 2001, xviii). This type of nostalgia "does not think of itself [as] nostalgia but rather as truth and tradition" (xviii), meaning it "manifests itself in total reconstructions of monuments of the past" (41). Amelia's oscillation from "Reflexive" to "Restorative Nostalgia" is seen in her frustration with the *Ed ecco a voi ...* production staff and cast. Their lack of care, professionalism, and art, that she was used to earlier in her career, hinders her ability to reconstruct her past. As a result, Amelia symbolizes "Fellini's ambivalence toward television ... [as she] admits to an irresistible fascination for the medium ... but who is scandalized by the tacky and unprofessional preparations for the show" (Marcus 2002, 184).

On the other hand, Amelia's partner Pippo "represents the director's most conciliatory qualities: lucidity, self-irony, and tolerance" (Kezich 2006, 371). Although Amelia is the film's focalizer (Marcus 2002, 184), Pippo displays the synthesized characteristics of the "Mastroianni" character throughout Fellini's oeuvre. He continues to represent the author's alter-ego and perpetual male infantilism, exhibiting the constant need for a mother/wife figure while desiring a lover figure at the same time, both of which he finds in Amelia (Rohdie 2002, 83–4).[8] In addition to Pippo's function as the author's alter-ego, his costuming is intended to reference the same outfits worn by Fellini.[9] Just the same, Amelia's costuming coordinates with Pippo's, not only making them look like they belong to the 1940s but also resembling the plaid coat and cape worn by Melina in *Luci del varietà* (Stubbs 2006, 168). This aspect of the mise-en-scène reinforces how the pair should be regarded as Fellini's self-portrait, and a continuation of Fellini's past works, as opposed to merely being an imitation of old Hollywood stars. Such a distinction leads to the author's first major criticism: distrust for television as a result of its simulated reality and moral levelling.

Criticism: Distrust for Television and Cultural and Moral Levelling

Throughout the film, Fellini inserts a flood of bizarre characters to take part in the container show, including imitators of famous poets and singer-songwriters, cross-dressers, little people, and so on. The viewer's first encounter with imitations is when the van transports Amelia and other cast members to the hotel. Amelia steps into the van and notices two Lucio Dalla look-a-likes. She takes a moment to analyze them and is in awe of how closely they resemble the *original*. In the same sequence, the scene cuts to a monitor inside the van showing a puppet version of Dante Alighieri. While reciting the opening lines of the first *canto* of *Inferno*, where Dante finds himself lost in the *selva oscura*, the puppet modifies the lines to promote a compass watch that helps him find his way. The television commercial, therefore, appropriates and distorts Dante's masterpiece, ignoring the message of his literary pilgrimage while creating a reduced simulation, or better, *simulacrum*.

Jean Baudrillard explains the concept of the *simulacrum* stating: "Simulation is no longer that of a territory, a referential being, or a substance. It is the generation by models of a real without origin or reality: a hyperreal" (1994, 1). In *Ginger e Fred*, Fellini recreates this conceptualization of the *simulacrum* through the constant images of impersonators and imitators. These *simulacra* emphasize how commercial television is a "new reality" for the Italian society of the 1980s – not deriving from any previous version of itself. This reveals how this new type of reality lacks the humanistic, fantastic, dreamlike elements that play an essential role throughout Fellini's films. In his article "Fellini's Ginger and Fred: La Dolce Vita of the 1980s?," Franco Gallippi discusses how and why Fellini attempts to mythologize commercial television as to detoxify its soullessness:

> In the 1980s, Fellini is dealing with a society that is more than ever prone to succumb to the subtle but powerful requirements of the simulated reality of commercial television. It is a society that can be described as a demythologized world lacking effective rituals that initiate people into their societies through the phases of life. When a society loses its sustaining mythology, and Western society has been viewed as such, no longer depending on its rituals, what is the result? Part of it is represented in Fellini's *Ginger and Fred*, where it is clear that the director is attempting to mythologize commercial television. What this means is that Fellini recognizes the archetypal or universal truth that requires a new metaphor or story for a new time. The function of mythologization is to preserve the essential human element that always risks being suppressed by advances

in technology and science, which often find us vulnerable and prone to be dominated by them and which must, therefore, be mythologized in such a way that they are incorporated into human life. (2016, 234)

In *Ginger e Fred*, Fellini attempts said mythologization of television by inserting Amelia and Pippo into this new world as they embody a generation that has not been completely suppressed by modern technology. The result is that they are able to project the director's estrangement to this new world while successively being ambassadors of the humanistic elements strongly projected throughout Fellini's entire oeuvre. Hence, the contrast between the human component (brought forth by the film's protagonists), and the imitations further emphasizes the element of hyperreality. The hyperreality itself, created through the constant use of impersonations and imitations, invokes moral levelling. Examples of moral and cultural levelling are pronounced through the film's distorted version of the variety show *Ed ecco a voi ....*

Television culture, as Marcus states, "works not only to provincialize but to reduce all its personalities to the same cognitive level" (2002, 186). Fellini includes these strange imitations and characters, giving them all the same two-minute time slots to perform on the same main stage. He essentially mixes the talented with the talentless. Fellini mimics how television networks *fill in the gaps* with diverse content in order to maintain the spectator's attention. As a result, Fellini reduces all performers to the same basic level, including Amelia and Pippo, whose talent to tap dance is reduced to a joke for the sake of entertainment. By doing so, the director communicates his distrust for the use of television for capitalist gain as it does not provide any real communication and serves no purpose. Guy Debord develops this concept of media culture in his book *The Society of the Spectacle*, arguing, "As culture becomes completely commodified it tends to become the star commodity of spectacular society ... The task of the various branches of knowledge that are in the process of developing spectacular thought is to justify an unjustifiable society and to establish a general science of false consciousness" (2014, 104).[10]

Therefore, the simulacrum of the commercial television culture creates a new passive reality, one which no longer desires, nor renders necessary, a conscious transmission of a message other than that related to consumerism. As Rhodie affirms, "Television is crucial for Fellini because of its pretence to [the] truth (when it is false) and its pretence to the genuine (when it is vulgar). To reveal the grotesque of television is to call for something more pure and simple and for which Fellini is nostalgic" (2002, 134). As a result, Fellini's grotesque imitators justify the imitation of reality produced by commercial television while summoning the nostalgic memory of cinema.

As society adopted the new television culture, the medium, in turn, reduced the divide between artists and common people (Minuz 2015, 168). Amelia once again articulates these messages when asking the secretary who oversees transporting the cast to the hotel what relevance the admiral has in the show. "Excuse me, but what is the admiral doing in our show?" The secretary responds, "He is going to perform with you, no?" Amelia, confused, says, "But how could he perform with us? We dance"[11] (Guerrini 1986, 156). The theatrical *avanspettacolo*, with which Amelia was so familiar, would not have ever included such irrelevant acts. Amelia (as Fellini's eyes) grows ever more frustrated and confused as the distance between the old and the new expands. The memory and nostalgia of the old variety show are distorted through the insertion of irrelevant acts. This creates a new type of program designed to serve a different purpose: its concern is no longer to create an artistic spectacle for the *pleasure of viewing*, but instead aims to retain audience's attention in order to promote a greater number of commercial products.

Fellini and Television Advertisements

Throughout *Ginger e Fred*, the author makes clear that his most severe criticism is that directed towards television commercials. It is crucial to note that Fellini's denunciation of television advertisements was not on commercials in general but rather towards their disruptive and destructive qualities to both televised film and television audiences.[12] He was heavily involved with the referendum on television advertising, particularly concerning "commercial breaks in films shown on television" (Minuz 2015, 162). Such a referendum was formulated to abolish the previous policy that limited advertisements *entr'acte*. This gave television networks free rein to insert unlimited advertisements throughout programming as opposed to inserting them in between the end of one program and the start time of the next (see Marcus 2002, 187).[13] Fellini despised how they would chop up films shown on television, including his own. He states,

> The continuous interruption of films shown on private networks are an outrage; it not only hurts the director and his work, but the spectator as well, who becomes accustomed to this hiccupping, stuttering language, and the suspension of mental activity, to a repeated blood clot in the flow of his attention that ends up turning the spectator into an impatient idiot, unable to concentrate, reflect, make intelligent connections, look ahead;

he loses the sense of musicality, harmony, and balance that are integral to storytelling … This disruption of syntax can only serve to create a race of illiterates on an epic scale. (quoted in Kezich 2006, 367–8)

Fellini further delineated the major differences that distinguish cinema and television as two distinct worlds with two distinct purposes. In doing so, he expressed the difficulty audiences have with concentrating on important messages within the storyline. He demonstrated this through Amelia's second phone conversation with her daughter. The sequence begins with a medium shot of Amelia holding the phone to her ear, expressing her immense frustrations, which had risen from the few hours of being at the hotel. The scene cuts from the same medium shot to a full screen displaying a sexualized advertisement about pizza. At the same time, the diegetic sound of the television has a notable increase in volume, so much so that it just overpowers Amelia's voice. This is an explicit narrative cue of the author's argument of the television's disruptive nature and how commercial interruptions make it difficult to concentrate on what is being presented (in this case, what is being presented are Amelia's emotions). Moreover, the overshadowing of Amelia's voice by the sound emitting from the television makes it difficult for the viewer to discern the sounds of the film itself (representing the *real world*) from the sounds emitting from her TV set (representing the *imitation of the real world*). By doing so, the author recalls his distrust with television as being unable to distinguish between the real and the imitation, while signaling his nostalgia for art and meaningful messages – what is lacking.[14] Consequently, such an editing decision supports the argument that television commercials take precedence over the programming itself.

In this scene, Fellini also demonstrates how the protagonist's emotions are interrupted to replicate, in a more tangible essence, the disturbing impact commercials have on televised films and beyond. He does this through invasive crosscutting during Amelia's discussion with her daughter, cutting to various commercials on the television screen. The spasmodic cuts are used to emphasize the same disruptive flow that television presents and that the author heavily criticized. The scene draws attention to Fellini's argument on how commercial interruptions lead viewers to suspend mental activity and become in many ways, as Pippo describes, mindless *pecoroni* (sheep).[15] As she is concluding the phone conversation with her daughter, Amelia expresses how she is going to relax by watching television, and to try to forget everything that made her upset – especially Pippo not showing up to the hotel on time. The narrative affirms that television does not require undivided attention nor active participation from the audience, whereas the opposite is true for the cinema.

The author does not convey his message surrounding the destructive effects interruptions have on cinema exclusively through literal advertisements. Interruptions to the love story's narrative are also demonstrated through the show's chaotic, circus-like preparations. This is particularly evident during the parking-lot scene. Amelia and Pippo share brief moments updating each other on the portion of their lives not lived together amidst the confusion of the acts scattered around the parking lot, shown through the camera's pan of the area. It is as though they must reduce their story to a brief summary so as not to be cut off by the camera, which cuts to other discussions and goings-on throughout the chaotic scene. Once again, the disjointed editing reduces Amelia and Pippo's few moments to the same level of importance as the image of provincial dancers hopping around as a cow with eighteen teats is displayed in the background. It also interrupts the love story's narrative, leaving little to no room for a storyline. The author mimics the commercial television culture as theorized by Marshall McLuhan in his work *The Medium Is the Message*, in which he writes: "Most often the few seconds sandwiched between the hours of viewing – 'the commercials' – reflect a truer understanding of the medium. There simply is no time for the narrative form, borrowed from earlier print technology. The storyline must be abandoned" (McLuhan and Fiore 1967, 126). Fellini thus replicates the style of television by rendering it difficult for audiences to follow along with the love story's narrative by breaking traditional cinematic continuity. Consequently, while Fellini makes his nostalgia for the dying art clear by showing what television is lacking, he criticizes consumer television culture for its inability to transmit a meaningful message, and thus "one that can signify" (Marcus 2002, 193).

The signifying message is transmitted through the performance of Amelia and Pippo's final dance. During their performance, there is a moment where cinematic elements are made present, and the nostalgia of the past is restored. The dance scene is incredibly significant as it symbolizes a return to the memory of theatrical variety shows while embodying past cinema. It is crucial to note that Amelia and Pippo's onstage performance, as Ginger and Fred, is shown in its entirety, whereas the director only shows selected moments the other acts. Fellini's decision to give Amelia and Pippo's dance considerably longer screen time is symbolic as it breaks the culture of moral levelling and hyperreality of television, expressing the importance and significance of their performance. Through this scene, the director reclaims control of what the audience sees by abolishing such moral levelling and the confines of television culture, finally allowing the audience to experience the emotions invoked by their performance – and the reunion in general. Sam Rohdie explains:

> When Ginger-Amelia and Fred-Pippo take the stage at the vulgar, indifferent television spectacular to dance the tap dance of their past and the past of dance and the past of cinema, they transform the ugliness and superficiality of the television stage on which they find themselves by a perfect rendering of these pasts ... Ginger [Amelia] and Fred [Pippo] in the midst of the horrors of television through which they navigate, the sublime is touched and another world sensed. As Ginger-Amelia and Fred-Pippo dance they go beyond the television stage into that other and precious world ... Their dance is a dance in cinema with the qualities of cinema: its luminosity and clarity and the grace of its movements transcend, transform *reality*. (2002, 139)[16]

It is through this dance that Fellini achieves the mythologization that Gallippi discusses (referenced above). He transforms the hyperreality of the television program into a cinematic exhibition, bringing the human element, once lost to commercial television, back to life.

Of course, during Amelia and Pippo's performance, there is a power outage, causing yet another interruption. However, this time, the interruption is "anti-commercial." As opposed to breaking the story into even more pieces, it unites them (Marcus 2002, 195).[17] The world of television ceases to exist for a few minutes allowing the love story between the two old lovers to reach its long-awaited climax (Bispuri 2003, 177).[18] Just before returning to the pair's dialogue, the director begins with an establishing shot of the television studio's exterior, darkened by the power outage, cutting to the same camera pan of the television tower mentioned earlier. Holding the shot for an extra moment, the director emphasizes that the circling light at the top of the tower, that was once rotating, has now gone quiet. The tower that powers the hyperreal society is now powerless. In comparison to the earlier hotel room scene, where Amelia gazes upon the foreign structure, the diegetic sound in this scene is quiet and natural, including a couple of barks emitted from an off-screen dog far off in the distance, all accentuating a transition to a different reality, one which signals a return to life before the invasion and eventual takeover of commercial television.

Cutting back into the building, a crane shot shows Amelia on the stage in a silent studio. Although the studio is dark, there is a small light that emits just enough luminescence to call attention to Amelia's white outfit, while the camera operators and television staff all look like silhouettes.

This prompts the audience to see and acknowledge the transition from the television world to the nostalgic world of cinema, where the ghosts of the past come to life in the dark. Cutting to a medium shot of Amelia slowly walking forward with caution, she calls out to her partner, Fred, with a loud whisper. Addressing her partner as *Fred*, instead of *Pippo*, is a subtle yet crucial discernment as it signifies both her professionalism and not wanting to break character. More importantly, it is in contrast with a shot/reverse-shot of Pippo beginning to laugh and calling her *Amelia*, as opposed to *Ginger*. As such, Pippo's choice to address his partner by her name marks their transformation back to *Amelia* and *Pippo*, and ignites the complete entry into the "real" world, represented by cinema, alive only in the dark. It is during this black-out that Pippo transfigures into the strongest rendition of the director's alter-ego. He exhibits both the director's criticism toward the television organization and proceeds to create a fantastic storyline fit for a film, embodying the screenwriter and director *personae*. After explaining to Amelia that the lights are not going to come back, he gives his reasoning, stating,

> First, because this organization is shit ... the famous giant with steel feet. And then, who's to say it's not an act of terrorism, one of the usual attempts? I don't exclude that at one moment or another, pam, everyone will be in the air ... Ah! Amelia, it would be a fantastic story ... Imagine the title! "They broke up thirty years ago and are reunited to die together."[19] (Guerrini 1986, 261)

Pippo exemplifies Federico Fellini's disgusted attitude towards the aspects of commercial television mentioned throughout this chapter, while playing upon his own self-irony by inventing a concept fit for a film, filled with the director's typical fantastical elements – befit for Fellini's cinema. Pippo goes on to explain that he feels comfortable in the darkness that surrounds them in the studio, "Far from everything, like in dreams"[20] (Guerrini 1986, 261). This statement that invokes the idea of dreams, echoes the line "True life is that of dreams"[21] from Fellini's 1952 film *Lo sceicco bianco*. "Fellini therefore attempts to lead his viewers back to reality through the dream of cinema" (Gallippi 2016, 237). The darkness reveals what would be considered as grotesque in a television-centered world, the nostalgia for cinema through the dimly lit faces of Amelia and Pippo. In its essence, the dance on stage is "a successful prank" (Kezich 2006, 372) because the televised stage is unable to produce art. However, the emotions rendered from their performance are a direct message of what cinema is capable of doing. Amelia and Pippo are set apart from the commercial television world; therefore, they can

Originals in the Dark, Imitations in the Light: *Ginger e Fred* 251

only truly exist as *originals in the dark,* as opposed to the imitations living in the light.

NOTES

1 Kezich explains that "containers" from the Italian *contenitori* is the term used to describe "new-generation variety shows" (2006, 658).
2 Kezich explains that Fellini "suddenly takes to the idea of working for television; he's attracted to the notion that he won't have to bother with extensive preproduction and the organizational hurdles of the cinema industry" (2006, 298).
3 One may recall the 1960s television program *Non è mai troppo tardi*, which was a program intended for illiterate adults. Critic Aldo Grasso comments on this program: "Nata nell'ambito di *Telescuola* e varata in collaborazione con il ministero della Pubblica istruzione, si propone di facilitare il processo di scolarizzazione di massa e consentire agli adulti analfabeti di conseguire la licenza elementare" (Born during the era of *Telescuola* and launched in collaboration with the ministry of public education, it proposed to facilitate mass education and consent uneducated adults to obtain an elementary diploma) (2004, 93).
4 Minuz also adds that "because revenue of private channels came solely from commercials, … its programs where therefore designed as platforms for the commercials" (2015, 172).
5 Minuz adds that Fellini's "parody of television is shown by [the] oscillation between incredulity and invective, the inability to understand a wold without magic and poetry" (2015, 173).
6 Ennio Bispuri furthers this point: Amelia "crede veramente di poter rivivere forse per l'ultima volta nella sua vita i piccoli fasti dell'avanspettacolo, con l'applauso di un pubblico capace ancora di emozionarsi e di apprezzare l'esibizione di due attempati ballerini di tip-tap" (Amelia truly believes that she can relive, maybe for the last time in her life, the little splendours of the *avanspettacolo*, with the applause of an audience that is still able to be moved emotionally and appreciate the two elderly tip-tap dancers) (2003, 175).
7 "mito della televisione che ci affascina tutti"
8 Sam Rhodie explains how Marcello Mastroianni possesses three identities in Fellini's imaginary world. For the purpose of this essay, the "Marcello" in quotes is of greater importance. Moreover, the mother/wife figure, as represented through Giulietta Masina's characters throughout Fellini's oeuvre, further develops the point on how Pippo and Amelia resemble Checco and Melina from *Luci del varietà*, respectively (2002, 83–4).

9   In an interview conducted by Gideon Bachmann entitled "FMM: Fellini, Mastroianni, Masina. Interviste sul set di Ginger e Fred," Bachmann asks Federico Fellini "is it a film that is biographical in any way because Marcello is playing in it?" While being asked the question, Fellini jokingly points to Mastroianni and responds, "because we have the same hat?" then proceeds to exchange hats with Mastroianni who is sitting next to him. The comment on costuming is further solidified through this interview as both director and actor, in addition to their hats, wear a white shirt, mahogany vest, red tie and blazer. Essentially matching in every aspect of their outfits.
10   About Fellini and Debord, see also the chapters by Veronica Pravadelli and Eleonora Sartoni in this volume.
11   "Scusi sa ... ma l'ammiraglio che ci fa nel nostro programma?" The Secretary responds, "Passa con voi, no?" Amelia, confused, says, "Ma come con noi? Noi balliamo."
12   Similar to his work produced for television networks, Fellini also worked on a handful of advertising projects for major Italian brands including, Barilla, Campari Bitter, as well as three commercials for Banca di Roma. See Kezich (2006 643–4, 696).
13   Marcus discusses the program "Carosello," which was a ten-minute segment devoted exclusively to commercials. It aired on RAI from 1957 to 1977. Grasso, *Storia della televisione italiana*. According to Aldo Grasso, "[Carosello] introduce il telespettatore nel ghetto dorato della pubblicità. Tutta l'Italia, bambini compresi, attende le storie più incredibili, i personaggi più suggestivi incorniciati da gioiosi e cortesi consigli per gli acquisti" (Carosello introduced viewers to the gilded ghetto of advertisement. The entire country, including children, expected the most incredible characters, gently framed by shopping suggestions) (2004, xx). With the referendum releasing controls over advertisements, Grasso explains that the state-owned television network RAI Radiotelevisione Italiana provided advertising time through *Carosello* to no more than 500 networks, a major contrast to the 2000 plus companies who had been given access to commercial time on privately-owned networks, like Silvio Berlusconi's *Fininvest*. Fininvest is the same company which had overrun RAI's advertising company Sipra. See also Minuz (2015, 163, 171).
14   Maurizio Nichetti will adopt a similar tactic in his film *Ladri di saponette* only three years later in 1989, specifically when the protagonists from the televised film are introduced into commercials themselves, and vice versa where an actor in a commercial enters the black and white film in colour.
15   The use of the term *pecoroni* may also be viewed as a reference to television mogul Silvio Berlusconi. Fellini will also make a reference to Berlusconi in *La voce della luna* depicted on the door opening to a restaurant's kitchen which is constantly swung open, hitting the adjacent wall on which is a mural of the A.C. Milan soccer team, owned by the same Berlusconi.

16 The reality to which Rhodie refers is a postmodern reality adopted by 1980s Italian society (2002, 139).
17 Marcus adds that, "The blackout sequence provides a moment of stylistic repose in a film otherwise governed by the audiovisual techniques of television" (2002, 195).
18 Bispuri adds: "In quei pochi minuti, al buio, Ginger e Fred sembrano finalmente dirsi le uniche cose importanti che non sono ancora riusciti a darsi nel clima demenziale in cui è avvenuto il loro incontro" (In those few minutes, in the dark, Ginger and Fred seem to finally say the only important things that they were not able to give to each other in the crazy climate in which their encounter took place) (2003, 177).
19 "Primo perché questa è un'organizzazione di merda ... il famoso gigante dai piedi di argilla. E poi, chi ci dice che non sia un'azione terroristica, uno dei soliti attentati? Io mica escludo che da un momento all'altro, pam, zompiamo tutti per aria. ... Ah! Amelia, sarebbe una storia fantastica ... Pensa che titolo! 'Si erano lasciati, trent'anni prima e si ritrovano per morire insieme.'"
20 "È come nei sogni, lontano da tutto"
21 "La vera vita è quella del sogno"

REFERENCES

Baudrillard, Jean. 1994. *Simulacra and Simulation*. Translated by Sheila Faria Glaser. Ann Arbor: University of Michigan Press.
Bispuri, Ennio. 2003. *Interpretare Fellini*. Rimini: Guaraldi.
Bondanella, Peter. 1992. *The Cinema of Federico Fellini*. Princeton, NJ: Princeton University Press.
Boym, Svetlana. 2001. *The Future of Nostalgia*. New York: Basic Books.
Debord, Guy. 2014. *Society of the Spectacle*. Translated by Ken Knabb. Berkeley: Bureau of Public Secrets.
Gallippi, Franco. 2016. "Fellini's Ginger and Fred: La Dolce Vita of the 1980s?" In *Federico Fellini Riprese, riletture (re)visioni: Atti della North American Conference on the Italian Master of Cinema*, edited by Paola Bernardini, Joanne Granata, Theresa Lobalsamo, and Alberto Zambenedetti, 219–38. Florence: Franco Cesati Editore.
Grasso, Aldo. 2004. *Storia della televisione italiana*. Milan: Garzanti.
Guerrini, Mino. 1986. *Ginger e Fred: Rendiconto di un film*. Milan: Longanesi.
Kezich, Tullio. 2006. *Federico Fellini: His Life and Work*. New York: Farrar, Straus and Giroux.
Marcus, Millicent Joy. 2002. "Ginger and Fred: Fellini after Fellini." In *After Fellini: National Cinema in the Postmodern Age*. Baltimore, MD: Johns Hopkins University Press.

McLuhan, Marshall, and Quentin Fiore. 1967. *The Medium Is the Message: An Inventory of Effects*. Toronto: Bantam Books.
Minuz, Andrea. 2015. *Political Fellini: Journey to the End of Italy*. Translated by Marcus Perryman. New York: Berghahn Books.
Rohdie, Sam. 2002. *Fellini Lexicon*. London: British Film Institute Publishing.
Stubbs, John C. 2006. *Federico Fellini as Auteur: Seven Aspects of His Films*. Carbondale: Southern Illinois University Press.

"The Tyrant Spectator": Intermediality, Spectatorship, and Subjectivation in Fellini's Work

GIACOMO TAGLIANI

Criticizing the Spectacle

> I think that cinema has lost authority, consideration, mystery, magic ... a tyrant spectator is born, an absolute despot who does whatever they want and is more and more convinced of being the director – or at least the editor – of the images they are watching. Will it still be possible for cinema to seduce such a spectator? (Fellini 1988, 217–18)

Federico Fellini famously expressed these bitter considerations during the production of *E la nave va* (1983). Even though this is a famous quote, these words may still cast a new light on a peculiar aspect in Fellini's work: the diagnostic gaze into the role of images in contemporary society, making the director one of the most insightful anthropologists of the evolution of the forms of spectatorship in modern Italy (see also Bertozzi 2021, 123–44). Fellini's view on the transformations involving the relationship between spectators and images is quite drastic. The playful attitude of spectators expressing their sheer belief in the images turns into a cynical and disenchanted approach vaguely recalling Pier Paolo Pasolini's claims about the "anthropological mutation" as an outcome of capitalistic society:

> Spectators get used to a whimpering and stammering language, to the suspension of mental activity, to several little ischemiae of attention that eventually will make them impatient dummies, incapable of mental links, previsions, and even that sense of musicality, harmony, and eurhythmics always sustaining what is narrated.[1] (Fellini 1985, 12)

This chapter deals with the peculiar "intermedial critique" developed by Fellini's works, particularly focusing on the progressive changes of

Italian modes of spectatorship that increasingly attracted the director's attention during the 1970s.[2] From the photo-novel (*fotoromanzo*) in *Lo sceicco bianco* (1952)[3] to *La voce della luna* (1990), Fellini has always sketched a caricatural portrait of the spectacle and its ceremonies.[4] From this point of view, his works could be considered a continuous reflection about the "relationship with reality that media promise"[5] (Volpi 2019, 34) developed by remediating different media within a cinematic framework.[6] Fellini always inquired the "spectacle" from the inside, trying to find tactics of counter-spectacle able to criticize contemporary society. Thus, generalizing what Frank Burke specifically refers to with regards to Fellini's commercials, his entire body of work can be considered an "opposition from within that which one seeks to criticize" (Burke 2020, 283).

The following paragraphs aim to outline the transformation of Fellini's view about the forms of spectatorship from the late 1960s to the end of the 1980s by analyzing key moments of his films, from *Toby Dammit* (1968) to *La voce della luna*. These sequences testify to the shift from a positive and playful depiction of the complex relationship between subject and media to a pessimistic and eventually harsh representation of this very relation and the forms of subjectivation it produces. Such a shift is also reflected in the director's role staged by Fellini in his final films, especially when directly or indirectly compared to the televisual landscape. Through this analysis, I propose to identify Fellini's unique political approach as peculiarly rooted in the critical employment of intertextuality (Aldouby 2013) and then intermediality, once television fully becomes that "'alien species' that brings about a new regime of social subjection" (Ravetto-Biagioli 2020, 301).

"Prosumer Culture": The Spectator as Bricoleur

In Fellini's works, every spectacle encompasses two sides: the performer making it, and the spectator attending it. Usually, it was the latter that interested Fellini the most. This twofold dimension always leaves the exclusive realm of the spectacle to fill everyday life and turn it into spectacular situations. Eventually, it even moves beyond the limits of cinematic representation, as proven by the growing importance of direct addresses to the spectator that, from the ending of *Le notti di Cabiria* (1957) onwards, characterize his films. Throughout the 1960s, the relationship between these two aspects remains balanced and positive, always being represented as a suspension of the ordinary that preserves the mystery and *wonder*[7] of any spectacle as such.

However, with *I clowns* (1970) and *Roma* (1972) something happens: "The problems connected to production, audience, distribution, acting, as well as the violence of themes Fellini wants to address and solve, the moments of difficulty and uncertainty demand new reflections"[8] (Manganaro 2014, 268). But what exactly has changed? A possible answer could be the foreshadowing of what Alvin Toffler (1980) called "prosumer culture,"[9] inserting the performance of himself as a director to make visible his role as manipulator of images, to reaffirm that task that later would have been endangered by the appearance of a new tyrant-spectator created by television.

In *I clowns*, Fellini establishes an explicit confrontation with television for the first time. However, the changing relationship between the spectacle and its spectator completely emerges as a problem within a self-reflexive frame, one in which Fellini appears as himself while dictating to his assistant the goals of the film:

> Can that exhilarating and agitated big noise still entertain? Sure enough, the world to which it belonged and of which it was expression no longer exists. The theatres turned into tracks, the bright and naïve scenarios, the audience's childish credulity no longer exist. Few thin and poignant traces survive in current circuses: this is the object of our research.[10]
> (Fellini 1972, 112)

Fellini is clear on this: *I clowns* is a real investigation into the current condition of spectatorship that he is unable to fully understand anymore. And if this exploration produces a melancholic outcome, it still leaves room for the old-fashioned spectacle's magic to be displayed. The investigation is further developed in *Roma*.[11] Here, in the traffic-jam sequence on Rome's Grande Raccordo Anulare, the director (as himself) marks the transition from the staging of the past to an inquiry into the current image of the city. Contemporary Rome is a giant spectacle that tourists wish to take possession of by compulsively photographing themselves while taking pictures. Facing the new problems of the present day – such as the technical reproducibility for anyone or the pushing demands in taking an explicit ideological stance – the narrative of *Roma* returns to the past, staging the world of *avanspettacolo* and its audience. Such an audience is surely mocking, even offensive sometimes, but intimately connected to that moment of suspension of disbelief that constitutes a threshold to access another world, whose magic is shattered by a traumatic event: war.

"Rome is the city of illusions," Gore Vidal says in a sequence at the end of the film aimed to recover the remnants of the *dolce vita* ten years after the 1960 masterpiece was released. Not by chance, *Roma* begins in a theatre (staging the death of Caesar) and in a movie theatre (screening a gladiators' fight), that is, two spectacles that must produce illusions to be effective and tell the same story: the survival of the traces of a mythical past in the present-day city that are accessible only through media narratives.[12] Tears pour from wide eyes, mouths are open: here are the irrefutable signs of the wonder these forms of representation manage to produce in spectators. However, these signs belong to the past, and with *Amarcord* (1973), and especially *Il Casanova di Federico Fellini* (1976), investigations into the forms of spectatorship take the shape of an archaeological enterprise.

At the end of the decade, Fellini cast his look back on the present. In *La città delle donne* (1980), his investigation takes a crucial turn. In a multilayered oneiric scenario, the voyage of Snàporaz (Marcello Mastroianni) through the imagery projected by his outdated chauvinist fantasies climaxes in a sequence of meta-representations encompassing different forms of spectacle. Among these sequences, one is particularly relevant. Laying down on a giant bed, children and grown-ups watch a mock 1920s-style movie while masturbating together, creating an eerie and disturbing performance. However, such a way of interaction with these images has nothing to do with a cynical or predatory appropriation by spectators – different from what will be staged in *La voce della luna*, for instance, as I will explore below. Instead, it embodies the playful, yet respectful attitude made possible by specific environmental conditions, such as the dark room and the partition between spectacle and spectator, as underlined also by the musical score. This sequence is clearly located in the past, looking like a memory gone for good and recalled with nostalgia.

Conversely, another sequence displays the new forms of interaction with images of the present day, where the relationship between spectator and spectacle is portrayed under a completely different light. After being welcomed at Katzone's (Ettore Manni) house, Snaporaz finds an uncanny section of the house catching his attention: a gallery looking partly like a mausoleum and partly like a cabinet of wonders, with dark framed surfaces covering its walls. As soon as Snaporaz pushes a button below a frame, an audiovisual "picture" is revealed: the image of a woman coupled with her own voice while having sex with Katzone. Fascinated by this grotesque collection, Snaporaz turns on these pictures one by one, thus creating a kind of personal movie, until he discovers that his wife is sitting there, waiting for him. With a gesture, she makes all the pictures turn on simultaneously, producing a bizarre "total work of art" made up of sexual relics.

Snaporaz's playful attitude is contradicted by the funereal setting. Underneath an illusory euphoria, the overlapping of producer and consumer as the trademark of prosumer culture causes the death of the spectacle as known so far. Losing its magical distance as a detached and oneiric world, the spectacle of the future needs to find other ways to enchant its spectators: "To see four films at the same time might seem like the work of a great mind, someone with some kind of extraordinary powers. In effect, it is only the inability to pay a minimum amount of attention to those who are talking; the inability to be seduced, enchanted by a story" (Fellini quoted in Ravetto-Biagioli 2020, 302). The risks are great, as Fellini shows: Katzone is a grotesque, fascist-like character (the word "Dux" appears in writing on the road for a brief moment just before arriving at Katzone's house), whose interaction with others is based on exploitation. Leaving the production of images to such a character paves the way to those dystopic scenarios that Fellini represents in his last movies.

More generally, *La città delle donne* is Fellini's attempt to reflect on the possibilities for the spectacle to continue to enchant a spectator in the time of prosumer and screen cultures. In fact, he pays great attention to new media practices, foreshadowing what will become clear only years later. For instance, at the very beginning of the film, sunglasses and train windows create further frames within the image, thus turning into surfaces of projection that serve as alternate screens. This reflection finds its final step in 1985 with "Che bel paesaggio," a commercial Fellini produced for Campari that also takes place in a train compartment. A bored girl looks out of the main window, which is, in fact, a television screen; compulsively using the remote control, the girl browses through pictures of landscapes as if they were television channels, trying to find one that will retain her attention, until another passenger takes control of this editing practice and finally selects the desired image: the Leaning Tower of Pisa with a giant bottle of Campari beside it. Accompanying this image, a voice-over says, "Una favola moderna" (A modern fairy tale) as the commercial ends. This ironic depiction of the prosumer culture retains that playful attitude previously highlighted. However, one must notice that the spectator-bricoleur has now become a real director, able to edit their own movie and thus radically change the forms of media experience. This transformation would have been a major concern for Fellini, who, at the time, had already begun investigating the drifts of these new practices.

Cinema and Television: The Disenchanted Spectator

Signs of a progressive lack of understanding in the direction taken by the present audiovisual scenario intersect most of Fellini's works from the 1970s. His retreating to the past, his turning away from the present day, and his unfolding self-reflexivity made him a target of accusations of conservatism. Starting from *La dolce vita* (1960), cameras and recording devices gain a major role in his movies, making explicit that reality has become a spectacle that maintains a closer relationship with the entertainment business than it did in the past. This topic is at the core of *Toby Dammit*, where an alcoholic actor agrees to perform in a Western movie on the condition that he is given a Ferrari; he subsequently takes part in a television interview explaining his choice. The resemblance of the television studio (where the interview is shot) to an operating room is striking; operators wearing white coats manage the procedures, somehow anticipating the setting of the Ludovico Technique and the idea of an audiovisual normalizing therapy, as staged in Stanley Kubrick's *A Clockwork Orange* (1971). Moreover, the interview with the protagonist displays a feature that would have become distinctive of the media system of the following decades – that is, the increasing demand for confession as a specific discursive form.

Years later, *Prova d'orchestra* (1978) elaborated on these elements as a specific televisual problem. Produced by Radiotelevisione Italiana (RAI), the film could be defined as a cinematic reflection on television through a meta-televisual language. Here, television is considered a character: "We have a very special guest: Television"[13] (Fellini 1980, 69), the conductor tells the orchestra – the other characters interacting with the camera as if it were a tangible entity. As the story unfolds, television turns from being a participating witness of the event depicted to playing a more active role in the narrative. This shift is also highlighted by the film's cinematography, which emphasizes direct addresses to the camera at a central part of the film: after having rehearsed, the players begin to talk with the camera, soon moving from the classical interview pattern towards a different discursive model. As Fellini stated, "This little movie stages an environment between the interview and the confession, which seems to me a feature of television language, something immediate, colloquial"[14] (Fellini 1980, 138).

The circulation of a "confessional air" is a key point in this reflection about the new forms of spectatorship. Confession is a complex discursive apparatus that has played a major role in moulding Western subjectivity, recently having become the cornerstone of what, in 1982, Michel Foucault called the "new aesthetic of the self," that is, a different relationship with oneself based on the exhibition of an alleged truth and authenticity of behaviour (2005, 297). Considering how in this new millennium first reality TV and then social media have shaped our idea of (publicly) telling the truth on oneself, we can easily see how confession has become so important in our relationship with media and how Fellini managed to foreshadow future features of audiovisual communication.

From the beginning of *Prova d'orchestra*, the relationship with the technical device is twofold: some characters fulfil the role of narrators, thus directly addressing the camera, while others play themselves as members of the orchestra, thus trying to avoid looking directly at the camera. "Careful, there is a television crew, but try to act normal"[15] (Fellini 1980, 63) one player says to another while setting up their instruments. Evidently, the sheer presence of the recording equipment is sufficient to provide drastic behavioural modifications, as someone points out later: "When you are in front of the camera you turn into an asshole, you start chatting away"[16] (94). As a matter of fact, when the camera approaches and players start talking, "acting normal" becomes a difficult task. "Are you filming?"[17] (95), the bartender asks before singing a popular song. As it occurs in reality TV, spectators are now ready to transform themselves into the spectacle. More precisely, every character in front of the camera makes their subjectivity the real topic of the program, feeling the uncontrollable need to express their inner truth and making it the core of the documentary. Mischievous smiles, exaggerated statements, words of (trite) wisdom, cynical reflections, futile secrets, and bitter revelations outline a set of postures evidently well known to any disenchanted spectator familiar with the language of modern television. This is a powerful tool to guide behaviour, and it is able to create a subjectivity moulded on the rules of the spectacle – that is, uniqueness, extraordinariness, and visibility. Not by chance, the harsh demonstration against the conductor is organized after everybody's close encounter with the TV crew, after each of the orchestra players has shown off for a few seconds in front of the camera.

Prova d'orchestra's political stance thus belongs to the field of a critique of visuality rather than sociology, making the film "a broader investigation of the new forms of 'direct appeal' on television and the fake intimacy of television talk shows' live recording appeal" (Minuz 2015, 158). From this point of view, the enigmatic figure of the orchestra conductor should be literally intended as a (film) director: someone who has the ultimate responsibility of assembling different parts to create a whole. The "despotic director" could be therefore identified with Fellini himself, who intends to reaffirm his creative role against that "despotic spectator" who is convinced of being the director – or at least the editor – of what is screened and demands to take control of the images. While investigating the side of image production and industry, the film also questions image consumption. "Nowadays the audience is very different"[18] (Fellini 1980, 62), the old copyist says at the beginning, addressing the camera and therefore the empirical spectator who is watching the movie at home; Fellini's concern could not be expressed more explicitly.

The research about the forms of spectatorship continued two years later with *La città delle donne*, but it is *E la nave va* that developed these elements in a new direction that would eventually open the way to the third part of Fellini's reflection. This film stages a nostalgic and intimate portrayal of early cinema, yet it could be considered an "anachronistic" depiction of present-day audiovisual consumption. Themes such as the display of the self, the possibility of editing and manipulating images, and the focus on the private sphere are now framed by a dream-like dimension, elaborating what partially emerged in the two previous films in a melancholic scenario. The end of the world staged in the film – 1914 and the beginning of the First World War – is quite clearly the end of a peculiar relationship with images that, until then, had characterized the history of cinema.[19]

The wonder and curiosity shared at the very beginning by both the young and elderly characters in front of the recording devices – embodied by the fleeting and smiling camera-look – turns into disenchanted self-awareness as soon as they become actors in the performance, consisting of the arrival of the ashes of the late soprano, Edmea Tetua. Direct addresses to the camera now attest to their desire to be filmed and their lost reverence towards the mystery of cinema as a spectacular apparatus. The transition from sepia to colour marks this sudden change, expressing the broad temporal ellipsis that occurs in just a matter of seconds. As part of the spectacle, spectators now show their urge to insert themselves into the foreground and pose narcissistically, resulting in a parodic challenge among the singers who take any opportunity to show off.

However, this grotesque competition ceases due to two distinct events. On the one hand, the reverence towards the mythical dead singer contaminates the passengers, who progressively express their wonder for her extraordinary skills by watching old reels and pictures, or by listening to memories about her mesmerizing power over her audiences. On the other hand, the rescue of Serbian refugees fleeing their country after the declaration of war allows the illustrious guests to perform in front of a new audience. As the first sequence after their embarkment shows, the refugees assist with the guests' lunch through the windows of the dining room, until the waiters let the curtain fall both literally and metaphorically. The embarrassment soon ends: artists and refugees fraternize, at first for the compassion felt by the former, then because the latter become performers at their turn, switching roles with the opera singers. The mutual admiration for respective artistic skills displays once again the force of the spectacle when it manages to create a community. Contrary to any prediction, the two communities merge through a dance performance, creating a bond that does not loosen even when an Austrian battleship demands the immediate delivery of the Serbs. Singing in chorus, the high-ranking guests oppose an irrevocable refusal: "No, we won't give them up!"[20] (Fellini 1983, 125).

Things did not go this way, the narrator says, even though the actual course of the events remains unclear. However, the film makes it plausible by showing it. If this possibility may be false in the actual historical world, it is true in the cinematic world, as the narrative implies by revealing the backstage soon after. When the world becomes fake, the only real experience is cinema that embodies a specific means of image production that is able to reimagine history and the present. The director does not appear as himself this time, portraying cinema as a collaborative effort: *it is not Fellini, it is cinema*, the movie suggests.

The possibility for a spectator to be enchanted by images is once again expressed by Fellini's choice to display the huge machinery and the illusory nature of any film production. Fellini keeps a door open for a hopeful attitude to emerge, a "ray of sunshine," as the last words of *Intervista* (1987) affirm. Here and there, recalling the memory of past experiences is the way to renew the wonder of spectatorship: for instance, watching library pictures of the late diva in *E la nave va*, or re-enacting one of the most famous sequences in film history at Anita Ekberg's home in *Intervista*. In this latter scene, a cross-dissolve overlaps the shadow play between Ekberg and Mastroianni with the actual footage of *La dolce vita*'s episode at the Trevi Fountain: this clearly states the continuity between forms of representation linked by the same relationship they keep with their audience.[21] This nostalgic yet euphoric feeling deeply connects these movies with past films. Here, television is depicted with sympathetic irony by showing "two directors working in that medium who both possess the same kind of authoritarian personalities as the directors working in the cinema" (Bondanella 2002, 154), or Indigenous Americans wielding TV antennas instead of the stereotypically offensive lances and bows. However, times are ready for the director to lead his work on to a harsher field.

Television and the Display of the Self: The Spect-actor

"Fellini's television is too much, all of it. It is not drawn by Daumier nor Grosz; it is painted by Hieronymous Bosch"[22] (Eco 1986). This is how Umberto Eco famously commented on the release of *Ginger e Fred* (1986), highlighting a major shift in Fellini's approach. With this film,

Eco suggests, Fellini definitively left caricature – the favourite form of expression of a lifetime – for the grotesque as a different way of representing reality. The political dimension becomes explicit, not just for the content but also for the form he adopted. As a matter of fact, the grotesque had been the most distinctive feature of Italian political cinema of the 1960s and 1970s,[23] and, perhaps for the first time, Fellini resorted to established patterns to question the present world, however filtered by his unique vision. By referring to Bosch, Eco's claim also makes clear another aspect: Fellini's gaze is no longer lenient with his subjects. These two changes in his look upon reality summarize the third step of his relationship with the present-day forms of the spectacle.

Television was now the only target of Fellini's investigation into that relationship with reality that media promises, as the roofs filled with TV antennas or the giant TV as an environmental background in *La voce della luna* demonstrates. Somehow, television had managed to conquer and colonize all the other media that played such an important role in his previous films, signalling a crucial turning point in the history of spectacular forms as well as in Fellini's work. As a matter of fact, for Fellini, the relationship between the different media was never conflictual: media could coexist and overlap, creating a thick web of intermedia exchanges and mutual loans.[24] In its infancy, television shared this common ground, as exhibited by *Fellini: A Director's Notebook* (1969), *I clowns*, and *Prova d'orchestra*, with the critical aspects previously highlighted. However, with the rise of what Eco (1983) defined as "neo-television," the situation drastically changed.

The reason for this metamorphosis in the media landscape finds its core precisely in the different relationship that spectators now maintained with this new media, in the framework of a rapid transformation of society between the 1970s and the 1980s (see Crainz 2009; Debord 1990). That reversibility of spectacle and spectator as a distinctive feature of Fellini's work assumes pathological outlines: the spectator is now the spectacle, and the difference between them is no longer distinguishable. *Ginger e Fred* deals precisely with this major turn: beyond the grotesque portrayal of the vulgarity and senselessness of 1980s television, the film focuses on the complete elision of boundaries between the space of representation and that of the audience by setting the narrative in the framework of a mock television program, *Ed ecco a voi*. This variety show aims to represent modern society as well as the survival of the past into the present, in this sense maintaining some twisted continuity with Fellini's poetics. Different characters take turns on the stage, creating a freakish gallery of ordinary individuals. However, the show finds its climax when another character is picked directly from the studio audience: Pietruzza Silvestri, the woman who survived without watching television for a whole month. While recalling that painful experience about the forced impossibility of being a spectator, the TV host suddenly remarks how he has the impression that she has a studied voice. Without further incitements, she immediately looks in the camera, singing soprano "Nevermore!" Her quick transformation perfectly embodies the new questions that have arisen from this new media: in just one highly self-reflexive sequence, she turns from being a denied remote spectator to a live spectator and, finally, an actor.

Different from all the other forms of spectacle, this new television therefore defines a double place for the spectator, one internal and one external. Circus and theatrical realms were limited to the physical space where the performance took place, and even when the spectacle crossed its threshold of pertinence, these spaces remained distinct; cinema happened at a distance, regardless of any direct addresses to the camera or continuity between film and everyday life. On the contrary, neo-television mixed the two previous spectacular apparatuses, thereby making the two spaces indistinguishable. Here, the audience in the television studio completely becomes part of a spectacle broadcast for audiences sitting in front of their own televisions. In fact, this internal audience is the real spectacle. In turn, the audience at home, continuously addressed by the TV host, only exists in the projection of their desire to be part of the show, "to perform as the model of desire, to stand as the paragon of perfection that advertisements promise us we will become once we accept their messages to consume" (Marcus 2002, 175). This dialectic is crucial to *Ginger e Fred*, as the two parts of the film prove. The first part is still based on the models of popular spectacle, with everyday life being based after these very models and television keeping the right distance by letting the enchantment emerge. The second part, however, absorbs this enchantment, turning it into the cynicism of show business, making each one's life a spectacle to be sold. Still, the symptoms of this economy of life through the media are spread everywhere: screens obsessively filling any environment exercise a sort of telecontrol through commercials that are the literal transformation of dreams, desires, and expectations into money, cinema's "most indispensable enemy" (Deleuze 1989, 77).[25]

Such a pathological drift is at the core of *La voce della luna*. The film begins with a monetary transaction to attend a show, with the creepy sneer of the manager making explicit Fellini's point of view. The show is a spectacle of everyday life, perceived through a window that is no longer on the world but rather on a domestic interior: here an old woman improvises a striptease in front of a television that ironically has no signal. This commodification of the body – and by extension, of life – is the principle of the new spectacle, and such a principle is so rooted in the modern subjectivity that the woman is performing without being aware of the audience spying on her. The spectators are part of the spectacle even though they are excluded from its space. The new spectacle created by neo-television has definitively lost that enchantment and invisibility at the core of Fellini's idea, as embodied by Wanda, Gelsomina, or Gradisca – just to name a few. As a matter of fact, Ivo Salvini (Roberto Benigni) attempts without succeeding to take a picture of the "small discs departing from the bell." "But soon it will be possible to also photograph things others cannot see,"[26] he concludes (Fellini 1990, 41).

Famously, the point of arrival of this pathological condition is represented by the capture of the moon, which – together with stars – historically and mythologically has always constituted the quintessential natural spectacle and the greatest wonder for humankind. Being seized by the Micheluzzi brothers, the heavenly body is now tied up within a farm, losing its distance with the Earth that made that very enchantment possible. Broadcast live, this extraordinary historical event is clearly a "media event" (Dayan and Kazt 1992): a ritual that has already transformed society and exists only in its mediated dimension. This is proven by the sort of trial quickly staged in the main square, surrounded by giant screens duplicating the live event. The town has now become a single television studio.

Conclusions: Visual Traces of a New Subjectivity

"Yes, it is true, the moon watched and spied on us from above, but we still need someone who watches us"[27] (Fellini 1990, 124). The spectator's urge to be part of the spectacle is clearly expressed by the words of one of the Micheluzzis, summarizing the critical course Fellini has developed since the end of the 1960s. The caging of the moon and its live broadcast are a point of no return for the forms of spectatorship and – this is a direct consequence in Fellini – subjectivation; as Kriss Ravetto-Biagioli convincingly argues, "commercial television represents a transformation from older narrative forms of subjectivity (and with them sovereignty) to newer affective modes of sensationalism" (2020, 305). That overlapping of world and spectacle that made Fellini's poetics so peculiar progressively assumes a bitter turn. This eventually results in a harsh critique of the widespread symptoms of the "drift of imagery,"[28] the complete and pathological superimposition of reality and its images (Grande 2003, 71) that endangers the very nature and cultural function of the spectacle as the privileged form to give the world a shared meaning.

Fellini's works stage a complex reflection on Italian society that resulted in a broad critique of modern visual culture foreshadowing "the ongoing mutations of the media and society"[29] (Bertozzi 2021, 141). Commercial television is not the cause but rather the effect of such a transformation. For Fellini, television and cinema should not be opposed; instead, they need to respect their mutual limits and domains of pertinence. The films analyzed in this chapter display a diagnosis of the new forms of relation connecting subjects and images, anticipating the changes that would have wholly occurred at the beginning of the twenty-first century. As I have tried to show, traces of this reflection can be found in Fellini's films at least since the late 1960s, thus considering his last films as the final stage of a long, critical course consisting of "a sort of ironic anticipation, even cynical, of what will be television programming"[30] (Daney 1999, 307). Besides helping us in casting a more insightful look over our present-day forms of subjectivity, these films also help us reassess Fellini's political stance, which has often been sought in the hidden folds of his stories when it has always been at the forefront of his images.

NOTES

1 "lo spettatore, lo si abitua a un linguaggio singhiozzante, balbettante, a sospensioni dell'attività mentale, a tante e piccole ischemie dell'attenzione che alla fine faranno di lui un cretino impaziente, incapace di concentrazione, di riflessione, di collegamenti mentali, e anche di quel senso di musicalità dell'armonia, dell'euritmia che accompagna qualcosa che viene raccontato." All translations are my own unless otherwise indicated.
2 After the release of *La città delle donne* (1980), Fellini even decided to lead field research on the topic. In a letter to Dino De Laurentiis, who lived and worked in Los Angeles at the time, he wrote: "Did you know that people don't go to the movies anymore here? There's no audience, and we don't know where they went. Are they all over there? If so, will you please send them back here to visit our movie theatres every once in a while too?" (quoted in Kezich 2006, 347).
3 For more, see Parigi (2020, 50–3).
4 About interartiality in Fellini, see the chapters by Marina Vargau and Dishani Samarasinghe in this volume. The chapters by Veronica Pravadelli, Eleonora Sartoni, and Giovanna Caterina Lisena collected here also

address Fellini's understanding and response to Guy Debord's theory of the rise of the society of the spectacle.
5 "rapporto con la realtà che i media promettono"
6 Intermediality is here considered as an overt comparison between different media within a certain medium (see Montani 2011).
7 *Wonder* has been identified as a peculiar response to Fellini's film-making developing productive effects: "Fellinian wonder, eluding clichés of Western visuality and spectatorship, powerfully draws spectators toward a level of perception characterized by constantly shifting relations and interconnections" (Burke and Waller 2020, 6).
8 "I problemi legati alla produzione, al pubblico, alla distribuzione, alla recitazione degli attori, come alla violenza delle tematiche che Fellini intendeva affrontare e risolvere, i momenti di difficoltà e di dubbio richiedono delle nuove riflessioni."
9 Despite having coined the term "prosumer" only in 1980, Toffler already anticipated the fusion of producer and consumer in his 1970 book *Future Shock*.
10 "Quel grande chiasso esilarante e spasmodico può ancora divertire? Certo il mondo a cui apparteneva e di cui era espressione non c'è più. I teatri trasformati in piste, gli scenari luminosi e ingenui, la credulità infantile del pubblico non esistono più. Restano delle tracce sottili e struggenti negli attuali circhi: è questa la nostra ricerca."
11 For more on the relationship between *Roma* and (cinematic) spectacle, see Andrea Minuz's chapter in this volume.
12 Without a media framework that is able to make meaning of the past, the latter vanishes, as it happens during the sequence where the frescoes are discovered during subway construction.
13 "Abbiamo un ospite molto speciale: la televisione."
14 "Nel filmetto circola un'aria fra l'intervista e la confessione che mi pare una delle caratteristiche del linguaggio della televisione, un che di immediato, di colloquiale."
15 "Attenta, fa' finta di niente, c'è la televisione."
16 "Quando c'è la telecamera davanti diventi subito stronzo, chiacchieri, chiacchieri …"
17 "So' inquadrato?"
18 "Oggi il pubblico non è più così."
19 Not by chance, most of Fellini's pessimistic considerations about the transformation of Italian spectators were released right before or during the production of this movie.
20 "No, noi non ve li diamo!"
21 For an affective analysis of this scene, see Zambenedetti (2023).
22 "La televisione di Fellini è tutta troppo. Non è disegnata da Daumier, neppure da Grosz, è dipinta da Hieronymus Bosch."

23 This topic has been extensively addressed by Maurizio Grande (1995) and Roberto De Gaetano (1999).
24 On intermediality and interartiality in Fellini's oeuvre, see Marina Vargau's and Dishani Samarasinghe's chapters in this volume.
25 For an extensive comment on Gilles Deleuze's reflections about the relationship between money and cinema in Fellini, see Ravetto-Biagioli (2020, 305).
26 "Però presto si potrà fotografare anche le cose che gli altri non vedono."
27 "Sì, è vero, da lassù ci guarda e faceva la spia, ma qualcuno che ci guarda ci vuole."
28 "deriva dell'immaginario"
29 "il mutamento mediale, e sociale, in atto"
30 "una sorta di anticipazione ironica, perfino cinica, di quello che sarà la programmazione televisiva"

REFERENCES

Aldouby, Hava. 2013. *Federico Fellini. Painting in Film, Painting on Film*. Toronto: University of Toronto Press.
Bertozzi, Marco. 2021. *L'Italia di Fellini. Immagini, paesaggi, forme di vita*. Venice: Marsilio.
Bondanella, Peter. 2002. *The Films of Federico Fellini*. Cambridge: Cambridge University Press.
Burke, Frank. 2020. *Fellini's Films and Commercials: From Postwar to Postmodern*. Bristol, UK: Intellect.
Burke, Frank, and Marguerite Waller. 2020. "Introduction." In *A Companion to Federico Fellini*, edited by Frank Burke, Marguerite Waller, and Marita Gubareva, 3–12. Hoboken, NJ: Wiley Blackwell.
Crainz, Guido. 2009. *Autobiografia di una Repubblica: Le radici dell'Italia attuale*. Milan: Feltrinelli.
Daney, Serge. 1999. *Ciné Journal*. Rome: Fondazione Scuola Nazionale di Cinema.
Dayan, Daniel, and Elihu Katz. 1992. *Media Events: The Live Broadcasting of History*. Cambridge, MA: Harvard University Press.
Debord, Guy. 1990. *Comments on the Society of the Spectacle*. New York: Verso.
De Gaetano, Roberto. 1999. *Il grottesco nel cinema italiano*. Rome: Bulzoni.
Deleuze, Gilles. 1989. *Cinema 2: The Time-Image*. Translated by Hugh Tomlinson and Robert Galeta. Minneapolis: University of Minnesota Press.
Eco, Umberto. 1983. *Sette anni di desiderio: Cronache 1977–1993*. Milan: Bompiani.
– 1986. "La bustina di Minerva." *L'espresso*, 2 February 1986.

Fellini, Federico. 1972. *Fellini TV: Block-notes di un regista/I clown*. Edited by Renzo Renzi. Bologna: Cappelli.
– 1980. *Prova d'orchestra*. Milan: Garzanti.
– 1983. *E la nave va*. Edited by Gianfranco Angelucci. Milan: Longanesi.
– 1985. "Italiani ribellatevi a queste TV." *L'Europeo*, 7 December 1985.
– 1988. *Comments on Film*. Edited by Giovanni Grazzini. Translated by Joseph Henry. Fresno: The Press at California State University.
– 1990. *La voce della luna*. Edited by Gianfranco Angelucci. Turin: Einaudi.
Foucault, Michel. 2005. *The Hermeneutics of the Subject: Lectures at the Collège de France 1981–82*. Translated by Graham Burchell. New York: St. Martin's Press.
Grande, Maurizio. 1995. *Eros e politica. Sul cinema di Bellocchio, Ferreri, Petri, Bertolucci, P. e V. Taviani*. Siena: Protagon.
– 2003. *Il cinema in profondità di campo*. Rome: Bulzoni.
Kezich, Tullio. 2006. *Federico Fellini: His Life and Work*. Translated by Minna Proctor with Viviana Massa. New York: Faber and Faber.
Manganaro, Jean-Paul. 2014. *Federico Fellini: Romance*. Milan: Il Saggiatore.
Marcus, Millicent. 2002. "Fellini's *Ginger e Fred*: Postmodern Simulation Meets Hollywood Romance." In *Federico Fellini: Contemporary Perspectives*, edited by Frank Burke and Marguerite R. Waller, 169–87. Toronto: University of Toronto Press.
Minuz, Andrea. 2015. *Political Fellini: Journey to the End of Italy*. Translated by Marcus Perryman. New York: Berghahn Books.
Montani, Pietro. 2011. *L'immaginazione intermediale: Perlustrare, rifigurare, testimoniare il mondo visibile*. Rome: Laterza.
Parigi, Stefania. 2020. "Neorealism Masked: Fellini's Films of the 1950s." In *A Companion to Federico Fellini*, edited by Frank Burke, Marguerite Waller, and Marita Gubareva, 43–58. Hoboken, NJ: Wiley Blackwell.
Ravetto-Biagioli, Kriss. 2020. "Remote Control Politics: Federico Fellini and the Politics of Parody." In *A Companion to Federico Fellini*, edited by Frank Burke, Marguerite Waller, and Marita Gubareva, 295–308. Hoboken, NJ: Wiley Blackwell.
Toffler, Alvin. 1970. *Future Shock*. New York: Bantam Books.
– 1980. *The Third Wave*. New York: Bantam Books.
Volpi, Gianni. 2019. "Media, grottesco, fine del mondo." In *L'Italia secondo Fellini*, edited by Goffredo Fofi, 32–54. Rome: Edizioni E/O.
Zambenedetti, Alberto. 2023. "Locating Fellini: Affect, Cinecittà, and the Cinematic Pilgrimage." In *Screen Tourism and Affective Landscapes: The Real, the Virtual, and the Cinematic*, edited by Erik Champion, Christina Lee, Jane Stadler, and Robert Peaslee, 64–80. London: Routledge.

Imaginary Worlds and Startling Creatures: Fellini and Popular Culture

MANUELA GIERI

Fellini ... has lived to redeem the cinema from what is external to itself, that is, from the pre-filmic, or to demonstrate that the pre-filmic, with everything it borrows from physical reality, practices an art that is a reconstruction of interior worlds, no matter how private.

– Umberto Eco (1993, 294)[1]

In 1993, with these words, Umberto Eco commented on Federico Fellini's ability to promote a cinema that would enable one to go beyond physical reality and into the inner spaces of the human soul. The previous year, Peter Bondanella had aptly stated: "More than any other director of the postwar period, Fellini's public persona ... projected the myth of the director as creative superstar, as imaginative magician" (1992, xix). Indeed, Federico Fellini was not only a masterful director, but a true alchemist of spectacle who forever changed the relationship between the world and its iconic representations in movies; and yet, he also contributed to the thorough transformation of the spectator's rapport with the filmic image that took place in the very heart of the twentieth century, with the 1960s Modernist "revolution." Moreover, over the decades, we have witnessed a true "cannibalism" of the Fellinian filmic body whose images and sounds, light and movement have been constantly appropriated and repurposed as icons or myths of popular culture; Fellini's cinema has thus been progressively emptied and incessantly replicated as an unrestrained and exciting *simulacrum* of itself and of the very culture it fed upon. In time, Fellini's own name has become more frequently associated to wild imagination and exuberant creativity, and his images have thus penetrated contemporary Western culture to the point that almost thirty years after his untimely death, Fellini and the *felliniesque* are recognized even by those who have never seen his films.

While over time I have reflected on Fellini and his contribution to Italian and world cinema, the purpose of my chapter is to investigate the ways in which the development of Fellini's unique and "authorial" discourse was variously and profoundly influenced by multifarious forms of popular culture, Italian and otherwise – from comic strips and cartoons, paper and audiovisual advertising, to radio and television, and so on.[2] In particular, I will analyze the ways in which various and diversified forms of Western popular culture not only entered, but truly shaped the process of Fellinian communication, signification and, ultimately, narration.

In "Autobiografia di uno spettatore," his introduction to the 1974 edition of *Quattro film* published by Einaudi and collecting the screenplays of four early Fellini films, Italo Calvino discusses the intricate relationship the director entertained with popular culture and writes, as quoted here from the 2015 edition of *Making a Film*:

> The power of the image in Fellini's films, so difficult to define because it doesn't conform to the rules of any figurative culture, comes from the inflated, disharmonious aggressiveness of journalistic art. That aggressiveness is capable of imposing cartoons and strips all over the world which become more communicative on a mass level the more they appear marked by an individual style. (Calvino 2015, xliii)[3]

Thus, in spite of their unquestionable enunciative violence, the inexhaustible reservoir of dysphoric images (Barthes 1994, 516)[4] present in satire, comic-strips and advertising which were all prevalent in the years of his youth, offered Fellini an alluring route towards the construction of an increasingly seductive filmic image charged with expressive and narrative power as well as communicative energy. Such awareness sheds a new light on Fellini's pre-cinematographic beginnings, such as the series of roughly forty articles published in the satirical magazine *Marc'Aurelio* in 1939, under the title *Il raccontino pubblicitario*. In those pieces, Fellini offered an exhilarating, and yet quite revealing parody of popular print and radio advertising of the time (Bondanella 1992, 3–29),[5] and they constitute the beginning of Fellini's long and ineffable relationship with the advertising image.[6]

Then again, the history of Federico Fellini's relationship with the various forms of spectacle and popular culture can be defined as an unexhausted and indefatigable itinerary of appropriation and remediation, but also of sheer seduction, which produced diversified outcomes during the director's magical journey in the *imaginary*. One can speak of a fatal attraction, a true temptation with not only different forms of spectacle, but also – and surely towards – *the spectacular*. Such an approach was at first merely internal to the narrative as a founding element of the plot – as in his directorial collaboration with Alberto Lattuada, *Luci del varietà* (1950), but also in the many inserts scattered throughout his early films, such as in *I vitelloni* (1953), *La strada* (1954), and *Le notti di Cabiria* (1957). Yet such powerful attraction towards the spectacular eventually became unquestionably and permanently woven into the fabric of the Fellinian filmic image itself, as it occurs from *8 ½* (1963), or rather from a short that immediately precedes it, *Le tentazioni del dottor Antonio* (1962), all the way up to his last film, *La voce della luna* (1990).

The journey leading to the apocalyptic, and yet prophetic vision of *La voce della luna*, lasted over fifty years. During this fascinating journey, the relationship between Fellini and the various forms of spectacle, or rather with the whole process of "spectacularization" of reality in its multifarious cultural expressions – from comic strips and cartoons, to variety shows; from the circus to advertising and television – experienced various stages of development. Indeed, as his cinema moved from an initial proximity to the neorealistic mandate to a decisive move away from it, the startling world of popular culture contributed to the construction of Fellini's personal and idiosyncratic filmic narratives. What is intriguing, however, is to comprehend how the multifarious forms of popular culture at first became intertwined with his unconscious life, and then came to truly participate in his creative process. Furthermore, it is necessary to understand the ways in which, and by which, those forms came to be remediated by the artist, first in his oneiric experience and then in his imaginary worlds. In short, the questions this chapter seeks to answer is: What is the channel through which these forms entered the process of communication, of signification, and then of narration? What is the appropriate methodological tool that would allow one to identify such a channel, such a venue? My hypothesis is that such tool may be found in Paolo Fabbri's insightful reading of Algirdas Julien Greimas's (1987) interpretation of the process of communication and signification.

According to the semiotic approach developed by Greimas, it is necessary to reflect upon aesthesia and empathy, as well as on the aesthesic processes in both communication and narration. If we assume that the communicative process grows with, and is a constitutive part of the text, one must note that at the foundation of both signification and communication (which, in semiotic terms, are essentially the same thing) one finds an "aesthesic" articulation, an empathy. Thus, we may speculate that signification originates from a connection with the world that pre-exists it, and that such a world may be defined as "aesthesic." In this perspective, empathy and aesthesia imply the articulation of feeling and thinking, and they are articulated and textualized dimensions, rather than mystical or transcendental ones. An accurate semiotic approach to a text must, thus, focus on such articulations and their networks. Within the given framework, the notion of communication, even though still fundamentally represented by texts, acquires a further dimension: it is no longer merely a process of interrelation and negotiation of meaning in view of a connection to be, but it is a founding dimension of the signifying processes. We signify and communicate because we experience an articulated aesthesia with the world, with ourselves, and with others. In this regard, in an interview given in 1991, Paolo Fabbri stated that the various articulations of the communicative process are thus inspired by, and move from, aesthesic or sinaesthesic articulations (quoted in Franceschetti 1999). Thus I suggest that such an approach may open new and unforeseen territories in the study of the relationship between Fellini and popular culture, as well as of the ways in which the various forms of such culture were insinuated into his creative process.

In a famous interview given to Renato Pallavicini and published in the daily paper *L'Unità* on Sunday, 26 July 1992, the director declared: "My name is Federico and my cinema was born from the comics"[7] (Pallavicini 2020, n.p.). It is thus Fellini himself who indicates the way for a correct interpretation of his creative process. In that interview, Fellini focuses on *Il viaggio di G. Mastorna detto Fernet*,[8] Milo Manara's comic based on the project for a film that Fellini had worked on since the 1960s but never completed. In the same interview, he also recalls the days of his youth:

> My love for comic strips is lost in the dawn of time. It was my initial contact with an imaginary world that expressed itself through pencils, quills and colors: something that had nothing to do with school, church and family. I remember that Sunday was a weekly appointment filled with gayety, when – coming back from the station where one could find Rimini's biggest newsstand – my father would bring us the *Corriere dei Piccoli*.
>
> What fascinated me was the way in which comic strips frame images, their narrative rhythm, the way they jump from one scene to the other, as well as the way in which they let the reader fill the voids, and the manner in which they mobilize stillness. I believe that cinema, especially the early

one, the short silent comics by Chaplin, Harry Landton, Buster Keaton, Fatty, Max Linder, Ben Turpin owe much to comic strips. I am thinking of Krazy Kat's tables by Herriman. After all, those early animated films are nothing but animated comic strips, and everything in them refers back to comic strips' technique: from perspective to specific cut in each shot, that which stops at the ankle and would later be called "plain américain."[9] (Pallavicini 2020, n.p.)

Thus, comic strips served as a process of alphabetization to the world of the moving images, as well as a venue for the construction of Fellini's own universe; the rich and multifarious world of paper cartoons combined with that of early silent comedies, the multicoloured world of the circus, advertising and, later on, even of television, all contributed to shaping the director's imaginary worlds, populating it with startling creatures inspired by Western popular culture, and yet immediately translated into a personal and idiosyncratic language.

In the first stage of Fellini's filmography, advertising is mostly exemplified by comic-strip images and paper representations of heroes belonging to an already mythical cinematic world, and they offer the director new and unforeseen possibilities in the creation of his characters. At the level of *récit*, the advertising image contributes to a widening of the narrative space in a metaphoric direction: the famous juxtaposition of the image of Gelsomina onto the poster of a religious procession in honor of the Virgin Mary in *La strada* clearly adds a metaphoric surplus to the already complex parable of the text. In this film, as in most of Fellini's early movies, advertising remains mostly confined to wall posters, and contributes to the narrative development by adding a vertical signification that is simultaneously beneficial and menacing. On the one hand, one can think of the wall posters placed all around the town square in the nocturnal opening sequence of *I vitelloni*: they play a limiting function on an already circumscribed and claustrophobic *space*. On the other hand, the large film posters that stand as a backdrop to the return of Fausto and Sandra from their honeymoon in Rome, Africa, and America, refer back to the dream/desire of the journey/escape that haunts the "vitelloni" throughout the entire story and ultimately leads one of them, Moraldo, to leave, in a fairly modern "opening closure" of the film.

While in the director's early filmography the syntax of wall messages remains mostly caged in a prosaic, documentary, and linear tension, in later efforts the intrinsic ambiguity of the poster gradually comes to be emphasized, as Fellini becomes increasingly aware of the kind of enunciation and communication such a message foresees and generates:

> the poster participates in the elaborate magic of the wall, which is both an obstacle and a support, a screen that conceals and receives, a space that obstructs and projects ... Different from the familiar, almost domestic gesture, through which we "consume" the advertising messages in print and radio, the gesture subtended to the wall poster brings us back, in a more enigmatic form, to the very act because of which we exist, and which, irreducible to an act that precedes it, consists in the tracing of a difference.[10] (Barthes 1994, 509)

Poster advertising of the early 1960s is the core around which there develops, for instance, the complex narrative of *Le tentazioni del dottor Antonio*. In the short film, Fellini reflected on such "difference," on the irreparable gap existing between paper advertising and audio-visual commercials – and thus between two diverse ages of our life, and of our experience of reality.

In 1962, while he was hopelessly trying to find the lead actor for one of his films, Fellini accepted to contribute to *Boccaccio '70* (1962), a four-episode film he made with Luchino Visconti, Vittorio De Sica, and Mario Monicelli.[11] He considered this movie as a trifle, a little tale like those he used to write for *Corriere dei Piccoli*. In the title itself, Fellini displays his true intention since *Le tentazioni del dottor Antonio* is most likely a parody of *La Tentation de Saint Antoine* (1874), the haunting text Gustave Flaubert worked on for his entire adult life, and in which the author narrates the many temptations faced by Saint Anthony the Great in the Egyptian desert.

Fellini wrote the screenplay in collaboration with Goffredo Parise, Brunello Rondi, and Tullio Pinelli, but also with Ennio Flaiano, whose contribution seems crucial to the making of this little film. At the time, Flaiano was working with Fellini on the screenplays for *Le tentazioni del dottor Antonio*, *La dolce vita*, and *8 ½*, while he was simultaneously writing his most famous and yet unfortunate tale, *Un marziano a Roma* (1983) – a reworked version of a short story first published in *Il mondo* on 2 November 1954, and then included in *Diario notturno* (1956). The text was adapted to the stage by the Compagnia del Teatro Popolare Italiano, which was founded by Vittorio Gassman in Milan, on 23 November 1960, and was then republished by Einaudi in 1971. Flaiano's tale displays unexpected synergies with *Le tentazioni del dottor Antonio*, even though on a metaphorical level and by operating a significant and unforeseen reversal. *Un marziano a Roma* tells the story of Kunt, a blond and gentle Martian who, one day, with his yellow spaceship, lands on the lawns of Villa Borghese, and brings to terrestrials/Romans the wisdom and culture of a superior race, ready, as he is, to disseminate far more advanced science and philosophy than our own. At first, the Scandinavian-looking alien is welcomed and admired, but then, his spaceship is barricaded and becomes, together with the poor Martian, a freakshow, the object of public mockery. The gentle and beautiful Kunt undergoes a progressive debasement, and the tale becomes yet another one of Flaiano's biting satires of contemporary Italian society as represented by a particular type of humanity that populated Roma, and, most of all, Via Veneto; this consisted of intellectual circles, social salons, journalists, beauty queens, and even the Pope. Kunt's ultimate attempt to write and disseminate his memoirs remains unheard.

Numerous appear to be the connections between this famous and extremely unfortunate tale by Flaiano and Fellini's own cinematic stories – with the most notable resemblance in *Le notti di Cabiria*, *La dolce vita* and, obviously, *Le tentazioni del dottor Antonio*, in which, with an intriguing overturning,[12] Kunt becomes "Anitona" (Anita Ekberg), a blond and gentle woman. An agent of Venus, Anitona is the unconscious bearer of a new and dangerous message of love and desire, one that finds a perfect metaphor of maternal nourishment and life-giving in the billboard advertising for milk. However, such a message would undermine a socialized life grounded in falsehood, a thoroughly fake and distorted self-image that Dr. Antonio Mazzuolo (Peppino De Filippo) defends to the bitter end and is showcased at the close of the film when Anita is "killed" by Antonio, who throws ink bombs against the billboard until the woman's body is completely covered. Ultimately, Antonio and his followers celebrate Anita's funeral in an ironic, or rather, humoristic vein, when an enormous coffin is brought in front of the gigantic billboard. At this point, the coffin is emptied of her body, and thus of an obscure object of desire. Due to the meta-discursive, self-reflexive, and more generally ironic temptations internal to the text, Fellini's film generates interest in the viewer more for the complex structure of its *récit* than for its content. The tale begins at a fairly spectacular pace in which one finds a constant shift in register – from high to low and back, while we are introduced to the main character, a punctual, and yet almost crazed, censor of contemporary Rome. The Capital, however, is a place of magical and amusing make-believes, as we are soon to discover in this meta-discursive *divertissement* in which Fellini amuses himself in showing the very heart of cinematic make-believe by taking us "inside" cinema, in its becoming the very embodiment of our own imaginary.

278 Manuela Gieri

Dr. Antonio Mazzuolo is a condescending bespectacled little man, always dressed in black and with short whiskers *à la Chaplin*, but with an unmistakable drive to the ironic shift that leads him to resemble a more "domestic" and "domesticated" version of Adolf Hitler. Since its *incipit*, the movie places in the foreground not only the main character, but also the actor that gives him body and voice, and thus declares his centrality to the narrative. Indeed, as soon as the opening titles fade, Peppino's face is shown in a closeup shot as a yielding and expressive mask that immediately establishes an accessory, and yet slightly censoring relationship with the viewer. The film continues by exhibiting Dr. Antonio as he deals with and tries to contain numerous infractions to common morals; indeed, the tale seems to be initially structured as a familiar satire, typical of the ones published in *Corriere dei Piccoli*, and yet it promptly assumes the more severe tones of Jonathan Swift's parables, and most relevantly *Gulliver's Travels* (1726), bringing to the viewer's memory the filmic versions of King Kong. The parallel appears particularly evident in its most climatic sequence, which closes with a fabling tirade. This segment of the story is set at the EUR (Esposizione Universale Roma), with a *décor* that is strikingly reminiscent of the Fascist regime, and in which the skyscrapers stand out against a paper sky[13] – they are nothing more than saturated reflections of the mythical New York buildings.[14]

The shifting signifier – man/woman – coincides with intriguing shifts of a signified meaning in the construction of a parable that needs to establish sound alliances with a shared popular tradition, and thus to operate in its primary satirical intention: the sharp and merciless critique of Western civilization, with its false mythologies and its papier-mâché icons. Obviously, in order to provide such an efficient satire of middle-class and catholic morality, Fellini needed an exceptionally clever actor, capable of a medium-like acting: indeed, he found one in Peppino De Filippo, who manages to perform a true expressive miracle and embodies perfectly the depraved mechanisms of self-repression, typical of those spurious catholic morals that enslave human beings and irreparably make them unable to fulfill their dreams and dialogue with their own desires.

With *8 ½* Federico Fellini declared the urgency of a thorough severance of representation by freeing the narrative of both *discourse* and *story*. Indeed, this little filmic tale that comes two years after *La dolce vita* and one year before *8 ½* unveils the lucid self-awareness with which Fellini was slowly but surely abandoning the reasons of representation, testimony, and faithfulness. He did so by unraveling not only the reasons of his life-long fascination with advertising images and messages, but also the internal transformations experienced by the long and unexhausted loving dialogue he entertained with the world of the *Imaginary*. The plethora of critical analyses on *Le tentazioni del dottor Antonio* may display diverse evaluations of its aesthetic value, and yet, they all agree on granting it a central position in the development of Fellini's cinema. It moved from an initial "objectifying" and representational stance to a more subjective and figurative one in its progressive appropriation of a thoroughly fragmented and surreal *récit*, one of memory and dream, and also of seduction and desire. It is indeed starting with the mise en forme, or rather the mise-en-scène of Dr. Antonio/Fellini's "temptations" that, in a most evident and explicit manner, the advertising discourse, for instance, becomes a true internal "temptation" of the Fellinian image. In and with this filmic text, we witness the passage from a prosaic representation of reality to the ineffable form of an oneiric imaginary; this new path is similar to the syntax and morphology of desire, a passage within which Anita is contemporarily object and subject of the *récit*. The acquisition of movement allows her to leave the territory of reification and to invade the space and time of the grandest of all narrations: History. Yet, once she achieves her place in History, she is already the myth and icon cinema has made her into. While Anita leaves the street poster and, as a gigantic phantom-like image takes the miniscule Dr. Antonio in her hand, she gives body and form to the fears and desires of a collective male imaginary. In that very instance, in the open quote of the King Kong metaphor, we witness one of the several meta-discursive moments one finds scattered in Fellini's filmography. Furthermore, in the non-secondary inversion of large body/little body, woman/man, one may detect a humoristic shift, and the expression of an ironic appropriation of the larger filmic body, the one that has built the most powerful myths of our times. Thus, the sign becomes doubly "signic," and Anita's image, from being icon and myth of our civilization, becomes a true simulacrum.

Nevertheless, as indicated by Roland Barthes, to appropriate the advertising message and its subversive usage and turning it into an ironic reflection on reality is the only possible response the artist may give to the aggressiveness of the advertising message:

> to appropriate it, to falsify it, to combine, in a new form, the units that at first sight seem to make up [such a message] naturally. Such copy, such plagiarism is a sign of freedom, as it represents an act of profound irony and constitutes the only means at our disposal to speak the language of mass communication.[15] (Barthes 1994, 516)

By consciously identifying in Anita/Sylvia of *La dolce vita* the perfect iconography of desire, at first Fellini transforms her into a billboard/ screen of the erotic projections of a repressed male imaginary embodied by Peppino De Filippo's body and voice; emptied of its essence and then filled with milk/products/goods, Anita's body becomes an advertising image. Yet, once in touch with Antonio/Peppino's "sensoriality," the body/phantom is first emptied of the goods and then becomes a "doubly-signic sign"; no longer simply a sign that refers directly to what it denotes, but also a sign that identifies itself with the veritable product that is at last called to designate desire itself; ultimately, the body/phantom becomes a simulacrum of desire.

No longer a goddess, Anita becomes a modern nymph as she completes her fall, not only by descending out of the poster, but also by assuming Dr. Antonio's proportions and, in the final climactic sequence, becoming "accessible," so to speak, and thus creating a complex and self-referential iconographic structure. At an iconic level, since his first appearance, Peppino/Dr. Antonio proposes the representation of a censoring middle-class normality that progressively displays its frailties and instability, especially when it is called to confront the seductive discourse of a long-repressed desire. The undermining of the character ultimately takes place when such a bourgeois subject, whose normality is saturated by erotic drives that produce an extraordinarily censoring discourse, undergoes an overturning, a true shift in meaning, so that those erotic obsessions come to be embodied in Anita Ekberg's sensual body as presented in its most lunar and oneiric dimension.

Unquestionably, then, *Le tentazioni del dottor Antonio* is one of Fellini's most self-reflexive texts, one in which the director frees his fervid imagination, and yet traces, with self-awareness, an expressive path that was to lead him further away from the realistic and representational requirements that motivated his early works. In order for the journey to continue, the large Fellinian body had to free itself from the demands of both narration and History, a kind of discourse that was clearly characterized by linearity and monologuism, and thus by fundamentally "hysterical" forms of enunciation and signification. Beginning with this little filmic tale, for an entire decade that culminates with the Roman trilogy – *Fellini: A Director's Notebook* (1969), *Fellini Satyricon* (1969), and *Roma* (1972) – Federico Fellini definitively liquidates the demands of representation, testimony, and faithfulness; he leaves the time of the city and enters that of the metropolis. His vision then becomes motivated by the flaneur's gaze, and his image definitively acquires the presence of desire, in a perpetual transit from one present time to another.

Over time, not only have I reflected on the relationship Fellini entertained with comic strips and advertising, but I also pondered on his meditation over the rapport between cinema and television, as well as their many differences as means of expression and communication: such reflection began with *Fellini: A Director's Notebook* in 1969.[16] The feelings of attraction and repulsion the director experienced towards television are therefore familiar to most of us: on the one hand, he was attracted to the potential for synthesis and immediacy inherent in TV story-telling, and to the possibility of a higher degree of intimacy with the TV spectator. On the other, he became increasingly aware of the power of fragmentation over the *récit* played by channel-surfing, but also by constant and obtrusive commercial interruptions. Furthermore, over time he grew aware of the progressive "lowering" of the relationship between spectacle and spectator, deprived as it was and is of any kind of magic and seduction in the stifling familiarity of the domesticated environment of a mass mediatic house. In a long interview Fellini granted to Charlotte Chandler, the director synthesized with eloquence what is, I believe, his conclusive position on the medium of television while commenting on his decision to shoot *Prova d'orchestra* (1979):

> For me, however, the decision to work on the small screen went beyond a question of morals, technical limitations, or aesthetics. I had done television twice before, *A Director's Notebook* and *The Clowns*, but each time it meant walking into a fog of blurred, confused images. I felt ambivalent about contributing again to the jumble of images with which TV fills our minds every second of the day and night. Insidiously, it seduces us, obliterating every vestige of discernment, substituting an alternative, synthetic world to which we must adjust. Worse yet, we *want* to adjust to it. I see TV and its viewer as two mirrors facing each other, reflecting between themselves an infinite void, endlessly monotonous. The question we must keep asking ourselves is, Do we believe what we see or do we see what we believe? (Chandler 2001, 194)

Such a question somewhat aids us in the effort to map and interpret Federico Fellini's journey in the multifaceted universe of Western popular culture insofar as its characters, places, and phantasmatic images are replicants of mental and imaginary worlds: they become progressively familiar as they appear over and over, helping the director in the construction of the alchemical objects of his possible worlds. Fellini's journey was, indeed, nothing but a long and uninterrupted itinerary in the world of possibility, in the mysterious and ineffable universe of an imagination that follows the enveloping and alluring coordinates of memory, dream, seduction, and desire. It is perhaps by travelling that magic itinerary, by pursuing such paths of inquiry, that one shall better understand the mysterious, at times disquieting, and yet, always seductive presence of spectacle and of the spectacular in the long and uninterrupted film Fellini crafted during his lifetime.

The relationship was not unilateral, as countless are the cases of true "cannibalism" exercised by audiovisual and paper forms of spectacle on the large and sensuous Fellinian filmic body made of images and sounds, light and movement. That body has been repeatedly appropriated and re-purposed as an icon or a myth of Western culture and has been progressively emptied and incessantly replicated as an unrestrained and exciting *simulacrum* of itself and of that very culture. Thus, on screens and telescreens, on billboards and tabloids, the phantasmatic forms of Anita and Marcello in the Trevi Fountain of *La dolce vita*, or the beaches enveloped in cerulean lights and magic atmosphere, materialize and disappear in an incessant motion, in an eternal transit. These images offer us fragments of *I vitelloni*, *Amarcord* (1973), and maybe even of *Fellini Satyricon* and *Il Casanova di Federico Fellini* (1976); frozen in an eternal present time, and thus becoming the "traces" of that which was, for many of us and for a long the time, the "world."

In an unstoppable process of simulation, the Fellinian filmic body annuls itself in the obliteration of the border between the real and the imaginary. As Jean Baudrillard once stated, in our time the principle of simulation wins over both the reality principle and the pleasure principle (Baudrillard 1985, 152). This is the apocalyptic and yet, not iconoclastic atmosphere that dominates the last filmic vision generated by Federico Fellini, *La voce della luna*, the poem of those great simulators which are the lunatics, the fools.[17] And yet at the end of this last film, it is Fellini himself who seems to be proposing a way out of the labyrinth: through Ivo Salvini's/Roberto Benigni's[18] request for silence as the only possibility to acquire access to meaning and signification Fellini is undoubtedly calling for the sensoriality of experience. It is thus by activating an "aesthesic," and not aesthetic, circuit (141) that one could better understand both Federico Fellini's creative process as well as once again circulate the Fellinian body, an indefatigable producer of oneiric phantasmagoria and seductive objects of desire which are perpetually fluctuating in the universe of possibility.

NOTES

1 Eco (1983), reprinted as "Thoth, Fellini, and the Pharaoh" in Bondanella and Degli Esposti (1993).

2 About the connections between Fellini's films and popular culture(s), see the chapters by Veronica Pravadelli, Ottavio Cirio Zanetti, and Eleonora Lima in this volume.
3 Unless otherwise noted, all translations are mine. The English translation of Calvino's "Autobiografia di uno spettatore" used here comes from Christopher Burton White's 2015 translation of the essay in *Making a Film* (Calvino 2015, xvi–xlvii).
4 Barthes (1994) is referenced throughout. See also Barthes (1973).
5 See also Fellini (2004), Olivieri (1986), and Chiesa (1974).
6 On Fellini and advertising, see also Fabbri and Guaraldi (1997) and Codeluppi (1995, 2020). Over the years Fellini repeatedly commented on the issue of TV commercials; see, for instance, the interviews given to Bruno Blasi (1989) and Charlotte Chandler (1995). For more on this, see also the chapters by Giovanna Lisena and Giacomo Tagliani in this volume.
7 "Mi chiamo Federico e il mio cinema è nato dai fumetti."
8 About Fellini's *Il viaggio di G. Mastorna*, see the chapters by Marina Vargau, Mirko Tavoni, Frank Burke, and Ottavio Cirio Zanetti in this volume.
9 "Il mio amore per il fumetto si perde nella notte dei tempi. È stato il primo contatto con un mondo immaginato che si esprimeva con le matite, con le penne, con i colori: qualche cosa che non aveva a che fare con la scuola, con la chiesa, con la famiglia. Mi ricordo che una data festosa della settimana era proprio la domenica, quando papà, tornando dalla stazione dove c'era l'edicola più fornita di Rimini, ci portava il *Corriere dei Piccoli*.

Mi affascinava il modo, tipico del fumetto, di inquadrare le immagini in una cornice, la sua scansione narrativa, il salto di immagine da un quadretto all'altro, l'affidare al lettore il compito di colmare i vuoti, di rendere dinamica la staticità. Penso che il cinema, specialmente il primo cinema muto, quello delle comiche di Chaplin, Harry Langdon, Buster Keaton, Fatty, Max Linder, Ben Turpin debba molto ai fumetti. Penso a certe tavole di Krazy Kat di Herriman. In fondo quei primi film sono dei fumetti animati, e tutto si richiama alla tecnica del fumetto: dalle prospettive, al taglio dell'inquadratura, quel taglio particolare che si ferma alla caviglia e che prese il nome di 'piano americano.'"
10 "l'affiche participe de la magie complexe du mur, qui est à la fois obstacle et support, écran qui cache et reçoit, espace où l'on s'arrête et projette … Différent du geste familier et comme ménager par lequel nous manions les annonces de la presse et de la radio, le geste impliqué par l'affiche murale nous reporte d'une façon plus énigmatique à l'acte même par lequel nous existons et qui est, irréductible à tout autre précédent, de tracer une différence."
11 Fellini was looking for a forty-year-old Chaplin, an actor that did not truly exist.

12 By reversing the male/female perspective, Fellini activates a sort of "carnivalesque" strategy, according to Michail Bakhtin's reading of Rabelais (1970), of social, political and cultural "overturning."
13 In a rich interplay of cross-referencing, one may here recall the paper sky in Luigi Pirandello's *Il fu Mattia Pascal* (1904): once the paper sky is torn apart, the truth of humanity's frailty is forever exposed, and "Oreste will forever be Hamlet," uncertain and unable to act, tormented with doubts. Such is Peppino De Filippo's character once he is reduced to a little puppet in Anitona's hands.
14 For the direct reference to *King Kong* as a classic filmic representation of male desire, see Bondanella (1992), Rondi (1965), Amengual (1988), and Burke (1996).
15 "à le dérober, à le falsifier, en combinant d'une façon nouvelle les unités qui le composent d'une façon à première vue naturelle. Ce larcin signe d'une liberté, constitue un acte d'ironie profonde, qui est aujourd'hui le seul moyen que nous ayons de parler à notre tour la langue des communications de masse."
16 See Fellini (1972, 209–13).
17 My reading of *La voce della luna* owes much to Millicent Marcus' accurate analysis in her essay "Fellini's *La voce della luna*: Resisting Postmodernism," included in her volume *Filmmaking by the Book: Italian Cinema and Literary Adaptation* (1993). In that essay Marcus indeed suggests that in his last cinematic text, Fellini defines at least the search for a possible resistance to the loss of meaning characteristic of the postmodern universe. My discussion is also indebted to Cristina Degli-Esposti Reinert's study of the neo-baroque aspects of Fellini's last film in her "Voicing the Silence in Federico Fellini's *La voce della luna*," and of course, to Peter Bondanella's groundbreaking contribution to the understanding of Fellini's world with his *The Cinema of Federico Fellini* (1992).
18 Fellini here plays on the ambiguity between the "persona," Roberto Benigni, and the character, Ivo Salvini.

REFERENCES

Amengual, Barthélemy. 1988. "Une mythologie fertile: Mamma Puttana." In *Federico Fellini*, edited by Gilles Ciment, 32–9. Paris: Éditions Rivages.
Bachtin, Mikhail. 1970. *L'œuvre de François Rabelais et la culture populaire au Moyen Age et sous la Renaissance*. Translated by Andrée Robel. Paris: Gallimard.
Barthes, Roland. 1973. *Mythologies*. London: Paladin.

- 1994. "Société, imagination, publicité." In *Ouvres complètes*, vol. 2, edited by Éric Martin, 507–17. Paris: Éditions du Seuil.
Baudrillard, Jean. 1985. *Simulations*. Translated by Phil Beitchman. New York: Semiotext(e).
Blasi, Bruno. 1989. "Spot teppisti: intervista con Federico Fellini." *Panorama* 27 (November 5): 55.
Bondanella, Peter. 1992. *The Cinema of Federico Fellini*. Princeton, NJ: Princeton University Press.
Bondanella, Peter, and Cristina Degli Esposti, eds. 1993. *Perspectives on Federico Fellini*. New York: G.K. Hall & Co.
Burke, Frank. 1996. *Fellini's Films: From Postwar to Postmodern*. Woodbridge, CT: Twayne Publishers.
Calvino, Italo. 1974. "Autobiografia di uno spettatore." In Federico Fellini, *Quattro film. I vitelloni, La dolce vita, Otto e mezzo, Giulietta degli spiriti*, ix–xxiv. Turin: Einaudi.
- 2015. "A Spectator's Autobiography." In *Making a Film* by Federico Fellini, Italo Calvino, Liliana Betti, and Chistopher Burton White. Translated by Christopher Burton White. New York: Contra Mundum Press.
Chandler, Charlotte. 2001. *I, Fellini*. New York: Cooper Square Press.
Chiesa, Adolfo, ed. 1974. *Antologia del "Marc'Aurelio" 1931–1954*. Rome: Casa Editrice Roberto Napoleone.
Codeluppi, Vanni, ed. 1995. *La sfida della pubblicità*. Milan: Franco Angeli.
–, ed. 2020. *Fellini e la pubblicità*. Milan: Franco Angeli.
Degli-Esposti Reinert, Cristina. 1994. "Voicing the Silence in Federico Fellini's *La voce della luna*." *Cinema Journal* 33, no. 2 (Winter): 42–55. https://doi.org/10.2307/1225516.
Eco, Umberto. 1983. "Theut, Fellini e il Faraone." In *Fellini della memoria*, edited by Ester de Miro and Mario Guaraldi, 9–10. Rimini: Guaraldi Editore.
- 1993. "Thoth, Fellini, and the Pharaoh." In *Perspectives on Federico Fellini*, edited by Peter Bondanella and Cristina Degli Esposti, 293–4. New York: G.K. Hall & Co.
Fellini, Federico. 1972. *Fellini TV: Block-notes di un regista/I clown*. Edited by Renzo Renzi. Bologna: Cappelli.
- 2004. *Racconti umoristici: "Marc'Aurelio" 1939–1942*. Turin: Einaudi.
Franceschetti, Massimo, ed. 1999. "L'estesia e la comunicazione *di Paolo Fabbri*." *Parol online*, December. www.parol.it/articles/fabbri.htm.
Gieri, Manuela. 1997. "Fellini, la pubblicità e gli ineffabili oggetti del desiderio." In *Mistici & Miraggi. Mystfest 1996*, edited by Paolo Fabbri and Mario Guarandi, 307–23. Milan: Mondadori.
Greimas, Algirdas J. 1987. *De l'imperfection*. Paris: Editions Fanlanc.
Marcus, Millicent. 1993. *Filmmaking by the Book: Italian Cinema and Literary Adaptation*, 225–48. Baltimore: Johns Hopkins University Press.

Olivieri, Angelo. 1986. *L'imperatore in platea: i grandi del cinema italiano dal "Marc'Aurelio" allo schermo.* Bari: Edizioni Dedalo.

Pallavicini, Renato. 2020. "Mi chiamo Federico e il mio cinema è nato dai fumetti. Fellini story in un'intervista (d'antan)." *BookCiak Magazine. Cinema Meets Literature/Il cinema incontra la letteratura,* 20 January. www.bookciakmagazine.it/mi-chiamo-federico-e-il-mio-cinema-e-nato-dai-fumetti-fellini-story-in-unintervista-dantan/.

Rondi, Brunello. 1965. *Il cinema di Fellini.* Rome: Edizioni di Bianco e Nero.

The Megaphone Ran Out of Battery: The Invitation of Fellini's Voices

GAIA MALNATI

Fellini's *I vitelloni* (1953) begins with five large shadows, representing the film's protagonists, occupying an entire wall of an old building in a piazza, coming forward in a row with bold, buoyant movements. Even preceding their shadows, however, are the men's voices. They sing in a chorus: "Open the doors so they can pass, so they can pass,"[1] a popular alpinist tune that perfectly introduces the friends as a united gang. First, the chorus of the *vitelloni* resonates, then the shadows enter the scene; only after the figures of the men arrive on-screen does the chorus end, opening the space for the title to appear and the music to begin. While the opening titles roll, the music accompanies the five men, who, still arm in arm, cross the square and then turn the corner, gradually vacating the space of their voices and bodies. Together with the music, the chorus of voices aims to establish the presence of the five friends on the screen as a compact herd.[2]

The group's unity is fractured when Moraldo breaks away from its limited reality at the end of the film. More specifically, the event that dismantles the group is not Moraldo's departure per se but the new note in his farewell to the young friend Guido. Repetitively questioned by Guido on his destination and the reason for his departure, in fact, Moraldo replies twice – with a faint voice – that *he does not know*. Thus, Moraldo alone is not determined enough to act subversively. The moment of rupture happens only when Fellini takes possession of Moraldo's character by personally dubbing him through the words: "Good-bye, Guido."[3] The change of Moraldo's voice in the farewell implies that the old character has left, irrevocably, turned into a stranger to the *vitelloni*'s life. The transition of Moraldo's voice, which progressively becomes subdued by the noise of the train's engine, allows Fellini to introduce his voice as a substrate layer and himself as a new subject in the film. This verbal act – the first instance of Fellini's voice being utilized in his oeuvre (Di Cola 2005, 244) – engages the author and the spectator in a complicit way.

In this chapter, I investigate the function of Fellini's voice, which, starting from such a minor interference in *I vitelloni*, becomes an absolute protagonist in later films such as *Fellini: A Director's Notebook* (1969), *I clowns* (1970), *Roma* (1972), and *Intervista* (1987). The analysis of Fellini's voice across these films draws from some fundamental studies that have emphasized the importance of the voice as theory and practice in critical debates and film studies, such as Roland Barthes's (1977) essay on the grain of the voice, Mladen Dolar's (2006) study of the voice as an ethical space, and most importantly, Mary Ann Doane's (1980) theory on the articulation of voice in cinema. On this theoretical ground, I link Fellini's voice in his films with the creation of the director as an authorial figure, but ultimately my analysis reveals that his voice is a tool for establishing a connection with the spectator.

The voice is a physical yet intangible agent. It easily slips in the crevices between objects and bodies, covering distances and unexpectedly forging connections. As Dolar observes, the voice enables an ethical dimension; it "appears as the non-signifying, meaningless foundation of ethics" (2006, 98). Dolar clarifies that the voice, however, does not belong to anyone; in fact, "the ethical voice is not the subject's own, it is not for the subject to master or control it ... But it does not pertain simply to the Other either, although it stems from it" (102). According to Dolar, investigating the voice means to situate its enunciation with respect to both subjectivities implicated in the exchange. The voice can be better thought of as a statement identifying each subjects' positionality relative to the other.

The voice is also a substantial body that interacts with the involved subjectivities by outlining unknown spaces. These spaces are empty, filled with yet unformed words. Barthes, indeed, evokes a place of "displacement" as the space engendered, that is, by "the encounter between a language and a voice" (1977, 181). Similarly, Dolar observes that the ethical voice inhabits a place of absence, as the ethical voice "can be located at the juncture of the subject and the Other, ... circumscribing a lack in both" (2006, 100). Notably, according to both critics, the vocal act is a place of intersection between the subject and its counterpart, but also of "displacement" and "lack." The study of the voice in cinema allows us to explore how the voice moves in spaces, anchored in places of absence and forming relationships between author and spectator.

Doane's (1980) study on the voice in film particularly focuses on how the voice's body affects the representation of spaces in the cinema and the relationship of dominance between film and spectator. Doane observes that the voice can recreate for the spectator the pleasure of the unified body (47) and yet it can also disrupt this "imaginary cohesion" (48) of the body by playing with the spaces of cinema. Doane defines this latter option as an alternative politics of the voice, based on "an erotics" (48). The *erotics* of the voice allows us to view cinema "as a series of spaces including that of the spectator-spaces which are often hierarchized or masked, one by the other, in the service of a representational illusion" (50). Doane's theory brings up questions that are specific to Fellini's case. For example, how do Fellini's voices occupy in his cinema the spaces of the author as auteur and that of the author as man, and do they establish with the spectator relationships of dominance, intimacy, or solidarity?

Fellini's voice acquires a special significance when confronting the vocal landscape typical of his oeuvre. Critics have, in fact, often highlighted that in his films, Fellini measures himself against a polymorphous body of voices. For example, Alma Mileto defines Fellinian voice as "a multi-voice" and notes that Fellini wrestles with it by oscillating between "the creative impulse and the perfectionist obsession to revise these dialogues until the last syllable"[4] (quoted in DASS Cinema Sapienza 2021). According to Michel Chion, Fellini "plays to the hilt the freedom cinema gives him to mix together voices and accents" and "throws them into a great cauldron of voices, shouts, snickers, sighs and murmurings in various languages" (1999, 86). As Chion adds, however, this cauldron cannot be mastered, not even by the author. Conversely, Elizabeth Alsop thinks that this "cauldron" functions to strengthen Fellini's authorial mark, specifically in contrast to the "impression of amplitude and solidarity" of Neorealist *coralità* (2014, 28). Alsop adds that Fellini's vocal chaos "appears to dialogically produce groups only to showcase their collapse" (38). Despite differences, all these critics suggest that the crowd of voices is auxiliary to the definition of Fellini's role as author. Either in control or overpowered by the vocal element, Fellini needs to mingle *and* stand apart by finding his own voice as the author. Fellini's voice is a key element in the representation of the figure of Fellini as auteur.

Scholars Frank Burke and Peter Bondanella mention Fellini's voice to support their opposite views with respect to this figure's subsistence in Fellini's films. Burke theorizes that Fellini's identity as the author is represented as fragmented from *I clowns* onward. He observes, for example, that in *Roma*, "the most important yet subtle way in which representation is undercut lies in the fact that the narrator in both the Italian and the English film versions is not Fellini, even though the narrator himself is presumably representing Fellini's opinions and Fellini's flashbacks" (1996, 192). By contrast, Bondanella analyses Fellini's voice-over in *Intervista*, when he commands the light to turn on. The critic affirms that "this heroic image of a film director attempting to create something from nothing in an empty film studio cannot but help recall the definition of God in the Creation Story of Genesis" (2002, 161). Burke and Bondanella, then, associate the voice of Fellini to the debunking or consolidation of Fellini's self-representation as auteur. It remains to be assessed whether Fellini himself had ever any intention to use his voice to say anything definite in favour of or against the creation of such a figure.

Fellini himself is self-conscious about the specificity of the crowd of voices in his oeuvre and about his privileged role in directing them. In an interview with film critic and journalist Tatti Sanguineti, Fellini notes that during the work of post-synchronization, he had always wanted to be immersed in the same chaotic vocal landscape that he would reproduce in his films, "a babel of idioms, languages, dialects, of people reciting numbers, others saying prayers, and above everyone my voice that suggests, exhorts, reproaches, shouts, yells"[5] (quoted in Sanguineti 2005, 12). Remarkably, the director here both underlines and ironizes the contribution of his own guiding voice, with a crescendo of verbs from the kind and respectful ("suggest") to the excessive and tyrannical ("yell"). Thus, Fellini ambiguously evokes both his authorial command over its creation and his willingness not to take this power too seriously, to allow himself to be incorporated into the vocal disorder of his own production. Stepping down from his role as author, Fellini enters the diegetic space of the film, a more proper place of encounter with the spectator.

Reconsidering now *I vitelloni*, it is possible to see how Fellini creates a first direct contact with the spectator through his voice. Supposing it is true that the Fellinian *coralità* in this film suggests the character of "moral lassitude" of the five men (Alsop 2014, 38), the chorus, in the beginning, may be seen then to represent the concept of a group shelter, where the men can take refuge from the responsibilities of adulthood. During the party sequence following this opening scene, the narrator introduces the five characters, each of them with a stable role, but together forming a whole, "a sort of multiple character"[6] (Pecori 1974, 43). Even when Moraldo and Fausto speak over the narrator and are thus identified as the main protagonists, they do not betray their role in the group. On the contrary, they follow their assigned parts, Fausto as the seducer and Moraldo as the dreamer.

The unity of the gang remains untouched by age and events. Only the intervention of Fellini's voice puts an end to the group's security.

Fausto's marriage and new job position do not affect his role as the playboy of the group, while Moraldo's will still vacillates, despite his decision to leave town. Then, right when Moraldo departs, Fellini's voice brings a stranger into the group and provokes the final rupture. Little does it matter whether Moraldo represents "the most secret part of the author's aspirations"[7] (Pecori 1974, 44), or if Moraldo's "alienated escape has little in common with Fellini's one" (Burke 1996, 286). The vocal interference of Fellini neither affirms nor refutes the autobiographic connotations of Moraldo. Instead, it offers a commentary on the film as apparatus.

Fellini's voice crucially diminishes the distance between author and spectator. Entering the picture makes the production process more explicit and reveals the director behind the camera. First, Fellini's voice abruptly tears Moraldo away from his precedent representation as a dreamy *vitellone* and creates a sudden fracture between the image of Moraldo and its sound. Consequently, it breaks the unity between visual and acoustic senses that, according to Rick Altman (1980, 71), is present in humans and that cinema mirrors to disguise the production process. Then, after forcing the spectator to acknowledge this pretence, Fellini introduces a new layer of representation. The soundtrack adds "a secondary representation" (Belton 1999, 379) to the one created by the images; Fellini's voice, adding a layer to the already existing soundtrack, creates not a secondary but a tertiary representation. This third imaginative space coincides paradoxically with the spectator's reality now hearing the director's voice. Thus, Fellini personally encourages the spectator to meet him in the fictional space, where image and sound on-screen intersect with the director and spectator off-screen.

Fellini: A Director's Notebook is constructed upon the exploration of this spatial dimension of possible dialogue. Unlike *I vitelloni*, Fellini's voice is in the main soundtrack of *Fellini: A Director's Notebook*, where another in-between layer of diegetic narration does not exist. In the film, notably shot for an American television network (NBC), an English-speaking voice-over follows and interviews Fellini on the abandoned set of his never-completed film *Il viaggio di G. Mastorna*. This voice is what Chion defines as a complete *acousmêtre*, a voice whose origin is not to be seen and that "invites the spectator to *go see*" (1999, 24). When Fellini addresses other characters in the film, he makes clear that the dialogue with the unseen interviewer was only a device for Fellini to call the spectator in and start his own personal conversation with them. Once started, this conversation can now continue with or without the interviewer, as Fellini gradually introduces the spectator into his world of production, at times even letting them enter his intimate sphere.

In *Fellini: A Director's Notebook*, during the scene at Marcello Mastroianni's villa, for example, Fellini recalls his failed attempt to transform the actor into his Mastorna. At first, Fellini directly addresses the viewer with a pensive and confidential tone. However, while showing to the viewers how he tested the actor for the role, the scene slowly exhibits characteristics of a nightmare. At first, Fellini plays the stereotypical part of the whimsical director, but then, the closer he comes to Mastroianni, the more his voice becomes enmeshed with the distorted sound of the violin played by the actor. When Fellini's figure is towering above the seated actor, the film's soundtrack likewise threatens the spectator by forcing on them Fellini's voice mixed with the distorted violin. This closeness violates the spectator's boundaries. Opposed to delivering an intimate confession, Fellini's voice provokes a moment of disunity and fails to establish any intersubjective relation either with Mastroianni or with the spectator. When the sequence ends, and Fellini's voice returns to the neutral space of the documentary, the spectator – who for a moment had hoped to be introduced to Fellini's intimate sphere – is left wounded and estranged.

With his voice, Fellini in *I vitelloni* leads the spectator into the middle of the diegetic space and then, abruptly unmasking the diegesis, brings them back into the extra-diegetic space; in *Fellini: A Director's Notebook*, he invites the spectator into his private world and then casts them out. In *I clowns*, Fellini accompanies the spectator in the crossover of different diegetic spaces, ultimately to share with them the position of the listener. The film starts with opening titles on a red background, Nino Rota's music, and extremely close, guttural voices speaking almost unintelligible words. Once the titles end, the frame opens on a child's room at night, and the same voices are now coming from afar, as the spectator assumes the child's perspective. As the child goes to open the window, the faraway voices become more intelligible. While the tip of a tent is rising magically, it becomes clear that the voices belong to the clowns who are building the circus' tent and chanting "Up! Up!"[8] Later, the child goes to the circus with his mother, but he is then forced to leave. Fellini's voice enters the scene when, after the show, the child gazes again upon the circus from his bedroom window. Revealing himself as the child, Fellini explains the reason of his leaving the show: "The clowns didn't make me laugh. On the contrary, they had scared me. Their faces made of plaster, with their indecipherable expressions."[9] Fellini's initial intercession as narrator functions here to guide the disoriented spectator in the chaotic vocal landscape of his memory.

A new diegetic layer takes over these past episodes through Fellini's narration. This transition occurs gradually. First, Fellini's voice-over explains how the clowns reminded him of the "freaks" of the province: "The clowns didn't make *me* laugh ... they reminded *me*"[10] (my emphasis). Then it describes the clown-like figures that the picture is presenting through some anecdotes: "A quiet type, *we said*, of Giudizio. The madness would take him suddenly, the day after he watched a war film"[11] (my emphasis). The narration initially exhibits a first-person singular perspective, then a first-person plural one. This shift suggests a transformation of the individual experiences into an indefinite collective memory. In so doing, it prepares the spectators for the following documentary component.

The scene transitions from the past to a modern interior, and Fellini's voice is suddenly replaced by that of the typist, Maya. It is now revealed that Fellini was not simply performing the voice-over narration; he was, in fact, dictating his memories as part of the film's screenplay. Maya reads aloud the continuation of Fellini's speech from a paper and asks, "Where are the clowns of back then, when I was a child? Do they still exist?"[12] After correcting Maya's mistakes, Fellini continues dictating his aureate narrative, his voice grave and severe, interrupted only by the noise of the typewriter. In *I clowns* Fellini's voice first invites the spectator into the space of seemingly personal memories, then makes them the addressees of his commentary on his current research on the circus. However, Fellini's voice is constrained by Fellini's role as director, and it turns out to be inadequate to bring to life for the spectator these old memories and the circus' stories.

Throughout the film, Fellini's voice is juxtaposed with voices. The analysis of three physical aspects of the voice – namely, duration, rhythm, and grain (Châteauvert 1992, 67) – can help us understand the nature and the effect of this juxtaposition. As for duration, Fellini's voice invades the picture pervasively, as the director introduces his collaborators himself instead of letting them speak on their own behalf, narrates events and visits, and comments on the findings and conclusions of their trips. In terms of rhythm, one may note that Fellini's cadence is here homogenously slow and measured, without the fast-paced and disordered beats typical of his spoken and improvised speech. By contrast, the voices of the clowns, the child's mother, and other villagers from the opening sequence emerge in the picture episodically and thus have a brief duration. Their voices, moreover, move faster and with a more spontaneous rhythm. Hence, Fellini always lags behind the characters inhabiting his memories and the circus. He comments on their beloved worlds, but his voice follows the script, incapable of grasping their ephemeral happenings, which the camera only can catch with immediacy. Consequently, Fellini's voice is distant from the material of his film, and its performance is inadequate to the storytelling.

Another essential characteristic of the voice is the grain, which connects voice and identity (Châteauvert 1992, 68). Moreover, the grain recalls what Doane (1980, 48) defines as the *erotics* of the voice. As in Barthes's famous essay, it is the most visceral aspect of the voice, it "is directly the cantor's body, brought to your ears in one and the same movement from deep down in the cavities, the muscles, the membranes, the cartilages" (1977, 181), and it "bears along directly the symbolic, over the intelligible, the expressive" (182). In *I clowns*, Fellini's voice has two grains, which correspond to two distinct personas of Fellini on-screen.

One grain belongs to the voice of Fellini during the narrations. In these sequences, Fellini's voice merely carries over the task of describing memories and events, and the grain is neutral, empty of any physical or symbolic meaning. Again, it differs from the distinctive grains of his past characters and the circus. The clowns and freaks evoked in the beginning, for example, have rough and grotesque voices tinted by the local dialect. Anita Ekberg, standing in front of the circus' caged panthers, uses her voice to give an animalesque representation of herself, laughing from deep inside her body and roaring louder than the panthers themselves. The Augusto clowns, conversing with the scholar Tristan Rémy, speak while moving their bodies and greatly modulating their voices, contrasting Rémy's more measured speech. Throughout this episode, Fellini reports most of the scholar's and the clowns' words. However, Fellini sounds detached and counterfeit, as when he narrates memories and events. On top of that, in this episode more than ever, Maya's flat reading of his words amplifies the artificiality of Fellini's narrative, adding a parodic effect. While clowns, women, and freaks all evoke effortlessly through their bold and physical voices the past and the lively world of the circus, the grain of Fellini's voice in the narration highlights the distance of the director from these realities.

The other grain emerges in the finale when Fellini directs the scene of the death of the clown Fischietto. In this case, Fellini's voice expresses authority, and its grain symbolizes the power of Fellini as auteur. In a similar fashion to the Mastroianni episode in *Fellini: A Director's Notebook*, the authority of the director's voice is here also undermined. However, in *I clowns*, Fellini himself silences his voice as director. In fact, Fellini leaves the narration of two important stories in the film, Jimmy Guyon's death and the reunion of the two clowns in the finale, to other characters. Burke sees in this last episode the auteur's self-dismissal, as Fellini "disappears, never to reappear, and Fumagalli's words materialize as images without apparent authorship on Fellini's part" (1996, 185). Yet, this finale may also suggest that the author shares the act of storytelling to create what Fellini himself termed "a way of storytelling that is drier, more immediate, relaxed, maybe even more slovenly and cheeky"[13] (quoted in Zanelli 1987, 53). Having realized his voice cannot quite capture the worlds of memory and fantasy to which he does not belong anymore, Fellini shows, as Francesco Dorigo would call it, his "affectionate participation"[14] (quoted in Fava and Viganò 1981, 133) in these lost worlds by enabling the person next to him to take over his voice as a storyteller. Thus, he leaves his director's chair and joins the spectator in the act of listening.

In *Roma* (1972), the voice of Fellini as director loses the assertive tone that it exhibited in *Fellini: A Director's Notebook* and *I clowns*. The voice of the auteur in this film at times flattens, only rarely stands out, and most often disappears, leaving an absence. In the beginning, the film is set in rural Romagna and then narrates the story of a young man leaving the province and starting a new life in chaotic Rome. Fellini's voice only enters the scene later, in the sequence dedicated to the Grande Raccordo Anulare (GRA). This scene is introduced by a voice-over commentary, which, tying in with the story of the young man's arrival in Rome, asks: "What about the Rome of today? What impression does it make on the visitor arriving for the first time?"[15] Among the cars, Fellini appears in the role of the director getting out of his vehicle with two other collaborators. His voice is clearly audible when he gives instructions to a crew member. Yet, it soon becomes clear that it is just one – and certainly not the most remarkable – of the many acoustic elements composing the cacophony of the highway. Later, as the traffic's noises intensify – cars racing, motors rumbling, car horns, human voices, loud utterances – Fellini is inside his automobile again, and his voice struggles to be heard, thus necessitating the use of a megaphone: "Can you hear me? Raise the boom now, as high as you can."[16] Hence, from the very beginning, the director's voice blends in with the surrounding soundscape, almost flattened by it. It will not take long before it completely vanishes.

After the sequence of the GRA, Fellini and his crew meet some journalists to discuss his new film on Rome. In this scene, Fellini's voice briefly exhibits the forceful grain of the auteur, but soon this nuance dies out. Questioned by a group of young students and activists on whether his film will engage with political actualities of the city, Fellini vehemently replies that anyone should do "only what is true to their own nature." Then, his voice turns more tender, and Fellini states: "Here's what I'd like to film, for example: a variety show at the Barafonda Theatre, as it was thirty years ago, at the beginning of the war."[17] Thus, the director introduces another sequence about the young man going to a show at the old theatre, letting the spectator assume that the narrated episode is a personal memory. Surprisingly, however, Fellini's voice does not narrate. On the contrary, it silences itself and disappears.

Fellini's voice does not even introduce the third and last episode narrating the young man's visit to a brothel in Rome. In its place, an external voice-over comes in, further reconfirming the impersonal tone of this narration. The commentary in Fellini's *Roma*, partly constituted by the voice-over narration – external to the diegetic space – and partly voiced by Fellini himself, both an insider and outsider with respect to the diegesis, is, therefore, hybrid. While, according to Doane, the commentary's "radical otherness with respect to the diegesis … endows this voice with a certain authority" (1980, 42), the mixed source here has an opposite effect on the voice of the director: it highlights the inadequacy of the authorial voice of Fellini to take possession of these memories and diminishes its authority.

The director's voice returns to the stage in the last sequence, when, luring in the off-screen, it attempts for the last time to command the space. But there, it fails again, does not belong, and ultimately goes missing. At the beginning, Fellini's off-screen voice counts to coordinate the chorus of the crew singing the popular Roman song "La società dei magnaccioni" while they all go to the Festa de' Noantri on a wagon. Thereafter, however, the director's voice disappears, leaving as the absolute protagonist of the scene the celebration with its crowds, voices, and songs in the streets. Fellini's voice comes back only when the celebration is over to address Anna Magnani and declare her as the symbol of the city: "a Rome seen as a she-wolf and a vestal virgin, aristocratic and tattered, gloomy, clownesque, ghostly."[18] Similar to the description of the circus in *I clowns*, Fellini's ceremonious declamation here fails to integrate and participate in the events and the figures so alive in his films. His voice is rich with high-sounding adjectives, but the effort eventually flattens the grain and renders it empty of any *erotics*. Magnani, in fact, scornfully puts him off: "You better go home and get some sleep, Federì."[19]

While the voice of Fellini as auteur is cut off, the voice of Fellini as man resounds silently and insistently. Once Fellini has compelled the spectator to witness his past through the voice that is more personal than authorial – that one time of the Barafonda – now this voice is summoned, and it haunts the memories. Its absence makes it even more tangible. While, according to Burke (1996, 192), this absence suggests the dissolution of Fellini as an authorial figure, it may be true that the withdrawal of Fellini's voice could also serve to intensify the myth of the author's biography. In the words of Franco Pecori, in fact, with *Roma* Fellini achieves "the annihilation of an existence through a ritual existence"[20] (1974, 121). The spectators expect to hear the voice of Fellini the man as a way for the author to authenticate these memories through his body. However, this voice remains buried under the thick layers of the past and invites the spectator to construct a "ritual biography" instead. Fellini does not bombard spectators with solely subjective experiences; rather, he invites them to explore an ambiguous space of autobiographical possibilities, only to show the impossibility of tracing back to the real autobiographical roots. In the same way that mosaics underground disappear if revealed, so Fellini excavates but does not retrieve his voice. Around the lack of Fellini's voice, author and spectator can imagine a shared and common memory.

In *Intervista*, the voice of Fellini as man emerges, prevailing decisively over the authorial voice.[21] In fact, although the film partly depicts Fellini in his role as director, his voice as auteur is in several occurrences interrupted. At the beginning, for example, the megaphone suddenly runs out of battery, while later Fellini delegates parts of the interview to his collaborators, claiming that they know better than him. In another moment – strongly reminiscent of *Fellini: A Director's Notebook* – as Fellini instructs a young actor about how to play his young self, his authoritative explanations are continuously disturbed by the noise of the radio. Burke claims that *Intervista* finalizes the "effacement of the film-maker," and that nonetheless the finale still bespeaks/shows the "valorisation of the film-maker as auteur" and the re-establishment of Fellini's agency (1996, 275). Accordingly, the auteur's voice also conspicuously vacillates, constantly on the verge of effacement but still powerful.

However, as in earlier films, this voice is merely descriptive and cannot reach the immediacy of figures and events. It only becomes effective when it takes on another grain, signalling the advent of a different persona from that of the director. Describing the setting to the interviewers, Fellini starts with the usual pedantic tone: "That's it, you see, over there it [the camera] needs to be higher than those pines' crown," and then, "That's it, you see, on that crane we mounted lights to create the general effect of moonlight."[22] Fellini's voice only warms up when he explains, directly addressing his interlocutors' experience, that they are shooting "the beginning of this little film that I thought to open with a dream, the classic dream where we feel like we're flying, I guess you have dreams like that in Japan as well, don't you?"[23] Fellini's voice is still detached and ironic here but has become slightly more intimate in the effort of sharing his vision. Finally, when the megaphone runs out of battery, the director's voice dries out completely. Then, Fellini's directorial voice silences and makes room for the voice of Fellini the man.

At this point, the narration becomes more spontaneous and familiar. Taken by his vision, Fellini starts to describe the landscape of his dream:

> The darkness was deep, and my hands touched a wall that was endless ... I was struggling a lot to get off the ground. Finally, I managed to do so, and I found myself hovering very high in the sky, ... and the landscape I glimpsed below through gaps in the clouds, what was it? The university? The municipal hospital? It looked like a prison, a fallout shelter. At last, I recognized it, it was Cinecittà.[24]

The voice has transformed itself. It is intimate, its body light. It rises closer to the spectator, dreamy yet clear. Now its cadence is less sustained, less pedantic. The rhythm is varied, it lingers slowly, or it runs faster, as if taken by a sudden vision, an emotion. Fellini has disappeared, and the camera gropes in the darkness of his dream and then moves higher in the air with him, finally framing the buildings of Cinecittà. After Fellini has abandoned the role of the director, his voice detaches from him, enchants the ears of the spectators, and invites them on a journey in the sky to admire Cinecittà from above. Now the grain of the voice has become that of a man speaking to an old companion.

As for the actual memories of Cinecittà, again, the voice of Fellini falters or seems buried under places that have already disappeared. As in *Roma*, Fellini refuses to acknowledge the past with his own voice. Although the autobiographical lens is here unambiguous, Fellini is cautious when it comes to committing his words to the truth: "Of course, I would be embarrassed if I had to swear that the trip to Cinecittà was exactly like that back then, but who knows, maybe in reality it was even more adventurous, more exciting, I don't remember well."[25] Admittedly, Fellini's refusal to remember is a renunciation to try to bring to life the past through his voice. Memories speak with their own voices, and by now, Fellini understands that he cannot capture or reproduce them.

Consequently, the voice of Fellini as a man, when the film goes back in time, is missing. Fellini evokes other voices to talk for him, the usual grotesque voices that are the only ones able to colour these departed moments. For instance, Sergio Rubini, the actor playing the young Fellini, has a distinct voice – exaggeratedly awkward, ungainly, shy. The unwillingness of Fellini to account for the past is juxtaposed to the forceful descriptions of his present and future visions when his voice is light and the grain so resonant with calls of intimacy. When the film ends, Fellini's off-screen voice asks for "light." The light turns on and illuminates an empty place, where author and spectator may only imagine together the past – whose contours remain mythical – but also envision new possibilities of encounter in the present.

This chapter analysed how Fellini's voices move across layers of representation. The focus on the interplay between these voices shows that Fellini, film after film, gradually, cautiously, introduces the spectator to a space of intimacy. Because the voice of Fellini as director cannot perform the storytelling, it becomes an invitation for others to speak. However, when it comes to letting the spectator enter a personal memory, this same voice deceives and threatens instead of warmly getting close. In *Roma*, the director's voice starts to subside. Then, the voice of Fellini the man emerges ephemerally, if only to sink immediately after, buried under the thick layer of fictionalized memory. The lack created by the voice of Fellini as a man enables the spectator to intimately imagine its sound, thus sharing with Fellini the act of memory-making. Finally, a voice emerges that meets the spectator directly. While Fellini still chooses not to speak for the past, his voice now shows the gratitude of someone who has found a companion for life with whom to share stories and voices.

NOTES

1 "Aprite le porte, che passano che passano."
2 The title does not actually refer to a herd of calves. It may derive either from the Riminese word *vidlò*, used by working people to define idle middle-class young men who did not have to earn their living, or, according to screenwriter Ennio Flaiano, from the Marchigiano *vudellone*, which means big intestine, and therefore someone who is good just for eating (Kezich 2002, 131).
3 "Addio, Guido."
4 "una multi-voce"; "lo slancio creativo e l'ossessione perfezionista di ritoccare questi dialoghi fino all'ultima sillaba"
5 "una babele di idiomi, di linguaggi, di dialetti, di gente che recita i numeri, di altri che dicono le preghiere e su tutti la mia voce che suggerisce, esorta, rimprovera, grida, sbraita"
6 "una specie di personaggio multiplo"
7 "la parte più segreta delle aspirazioni dell'autore"
8 "Suu! Suu!"
9 "I pagliacci non mi avevano fatto ridere, al contrario mi avevano spaventato. Quei volti di gesso, dall'espressione indecifrabile."
10 "non *mi* avevano fatto ridere . . . *mi* ricordavano"
11 "Un tipo tranquillo, *dicevamo*, di Giudizio. La botta da matto lo prendeva all'improvviso, il giorno dopo che aveva visto un film di guerra."

12 "I clown di allora, di quand'ero bambino, dove sono adesso, esistono ancora?"
13 "una maniera di raccontare più asciutta, immediata, disinvolta, magari anche più trasandata e cialtronesca"
14 "affettuosa partecipazione"
15 "E la Roma di oggi, che effetto fa a chi arriva per la prima volta?" On *Roma*'s peculiar rhetorical strategies, see Andrea Minuz's chapter in this volume.
16 "Mi senti? Alza la gru adesso, più alto che puoi."
17 "solo ciò che ti è congeniale"; "Ecco per esempio cosa mi piacerebbe raccontare, uno spettacolo di varietà al teatrino della Barafonda, com'era trent'anni fa, i primi tempi della guerra."
18 "una Roma vista come lupa e vestale, aristocratica e stracciona, tetra, buffonesca, spettrale"
19 "A Federì va a dormì va."
20 "l'annientamento di una esistenza nei termini di una biografia rituale"
21 Similarly to *Intervista*, in the film *Prova d'orchestra* (1978), Fellini's voice signals his intention to withdraw from his role as the film's director. Fellini becomes a listener and leaves the pleasure and the responsibility of the storytelling to the voices and instruments of the musicians and the orchestra conductor. In fact, in *Prova d'orchestra*, Fellini's voice mingles with the crowd of voices and sounds as if Fellini was just an interested observer who happened to pass by.
22 "Ecco vedete laggiù deve oltrepassare la chioma dei pini"; "Ecco vedete su quella gru abbiamo invece montato le lampade per dare un effetto di luce lunare a tutto l'insieme."
23 "L'inizio di questo filmetto che pensavo di cominciare con un sogno, il classico sogno dove ci sembra di volare, immagino che anche voi in Giappone fate dei sogni così, no?"
24 "L'oscurità era profonda, e le mie mani toccavano una parte che non finiva mai ... Facevo una gran fatica a sollevarmi da terra, infine ci riuscivo e mi trovavo librato a grandissima altezza ... e il paesaggio che vedevo tra squarci di nubi laggiù in fondo, cos'era? La città universitaria? Il policlinico? Sembrava un reclusorio, un rifugio antiatomico, alla fine la riconoscevo, era Cinecittà."
25 "Certo sarei imbarazzato se dovesi giurare che il viaggio verso Cinecittà fu proprio così quella volta, ma chissà forse nella realtà fu anche più avventuroso, più emozionante, non mi ricordo bene."

REFERENCES

Alsop, Elizabeth. 2014. "The Imaginary Crowd: Neorealism and the Uses of Coralità." *The Velvet Light Trap* 74: 27–41. https://doi.org/10.7560/VLT7404.

Altman, Rick. 1980. "Moving Lips: Cinema as Ventriloquism." *Yale French Studies* 60: 67–79. https://doi.org/10.2307/2930005.
Barthes, Roland. 1977. *Image, Music, Text*. Translated by Stephen Heath. London: Fontana Press.
Belton, John. 1999. "Technology and Aesthetics of Film Sound." In *Film Theory and Criticism: Introductory Readings*, edited by Leo Braudy and Marshall Cohen, 376–84. 5th ed. New York: Oxford University Press.
Bondanella, Peter E. 2002. *The Films of Federico Fellini*. Cambridge: Cambridge University Press.
Burke, Frank. 1996. *Fellini's Films: From Postwar to Postmodern*. Woodbridge, CT: Twayne Publishers.
Châteauvert, Jean. 1992. "Il faut trouver la voix." *Cinémas* 3, no. 1: 64–77. https://doi.org/10.7202/1001180ar.
Chion, Michel. 1999. *The Voice in Cinema*. Translated by Claudia Gorbman. New York: Columbia University Press.
DASS Cinema Sapienza. 2021. "Convegno Fellini, l'Italia, il cinema." Facebook video, 23 June 2021. 00:53:10–01:12:53. www.facebook.com/dasscinema/videos/330116998573586.
Di Cola, Gerardo. 2005. "Filmografia delle voci di Federico Fellini." In *Voci del Varietà/Federico delle voci: I direttori di doppiaggio di Fellini*, edited by Tatti Sanguineti, 239–82. Rimini: Fondazione F. Fellini.
Doane, Mary Ann. 1980. "The Voice in the Cinema: The Articulation of Body and Space." *Yale French Studies* 60: 33–50. https://doi.org/10.2307/2930003.
Dolar, Mladen. 2006. *A Voice and Nothing More*. Cambridge, MA: MIT Press.
Fava, Claudio, and Aldo Viganò, eds. 1981. *I film di Federico Fellini*. Rome: Gremese Editore.
Kezich, Tullio. 2002. *Federico Fellini, la vita e i film*. Milan: Feltrinelli.
Pecori, Franco. 1974. *Fellini: Federico Fellini*. Florence: La nuova Italia.
Sanguineti, Tatti, ed. 2005. *Voci del varietà/Federico delle voci: I direttori di doppiaggio di Fellini*. Rimini: Fondazione F. Fellini.
Zanelli, Dario. 1987. *Nel mondo di Federico: Fellini di fronte al suo cinema (e a quello degli altri)*. Turin: ERI.

Watch Out! Flashback! Fellini's Memory Films

RUSSELL J.A. KILBOURN

Fellini and the Flashback

This chapter surveys Fellini's post-1960 films in the light of a narrative technique often overlooked in Fellini scholarship: the flashback. Combining flashback studies with memory theory, alongside close analyses of representative sequences in key films, I examine the variations in Fellini's approach to the objective representation of the past, or rather of subjective memory, while investigating the nature of subjectivity in a cinematic context.[1] I also shed light on the Italian director's significant contribution to the formal, thematic, and mythographic development of the filmic flashback more broadly, as narrative cinema adapts to changing sociocultural conditions in the postwar period and beyond. I will touch on a number of Fellini's memory films, culminating with *8 ½* (1963), the first in which something like a flashback occurs, at the point when Fellini had moved beyond his neorealist roots towards his self-reflexive, pseudo-autobiographical, artificial, studio-based, "Fellinian" style. This shift is signalled by key formal innovations, including Fellini's distinctive use of the close-up combined with long takes, a mobile camera, and the exploitation of the mise-en-scène as the setting for memory's performance. The latter I call the *mnemic chronotope*, in contrast to the conventional flashback, built from specific editing patterns and transition techniques.

In the second decade of the twenty-first century, cinema continues to mediate our experience of time and space, which together constitute the primary axes of modern subjectivity.[2] In the Kantian humanist tradition, time and space are *distinct* categories of knowledge (epistemology) and of representation (aesthetics). In practice, however, things are not so neat. Anticipating posthumanism, Mikhail Bakhtin gave "the name *chronotope* (literally, 'time-space') to the intrinsic connectedness of temporal and spatial relationships that are artistically expressed in literature" (1981, 84). I appropriate this term here in the context of cinematic memory by way of contrast with the flashback in its classic form.[3]

According to Maureen Turim,

> the term *flashback* was first used in its sense of narrative returns to the past in reference to *film*, rather than other forms of storytelling ... Cinematic renderings of storytelling and memory processes may have borrowed from literature and sought to reproduce human memory mimetically, but originally, the cinematic presentation of the flashback affects not only how modern literature is organized ... but perhaps also how audiences remember and how we describe those memories. (1989, 4–5)

The claim that cinema "reproduce[s] human memory mimetically" only really makes sense when one recognizes that, historically, memory is always already conditioned, if not determined, by available media technologies, from writing onwards (see Erll 2011). This becomes clearer when one considers alternatives to the classical flashback. According to Turim, "in its classic form, the flashback is introduced when the image in the present dissolves to an image in the past, understood either as a story-being-told or a subjective memory. Dialogue, voice-over, or intertitles that mark anteriority through language often reinforce the visual cues representing a return to the past" (1989, 1). According to David Bordwell and Kristen Thompson, "in the classical continuity system, time, like space, is organized according to the development of the narrative. We know that the plot's presentation of the story typically involves manipulation of *time*. Continuity editing seeks to support and sustain this temporal manipulation" (2004, 245).

Temporal or chronological shifts are represented in classical film narrative, in which the emphasis is on the maintenance of spatial and temporal coherence: "Usually the flashback is motivated by the plot, as when a character ... recalls a memory. Flashbacks typically emphasize important causal factors in a film's *fabula* [story]" (Pramaggiore and Wallis 2011, 206). Of all Fellini's films, *Amarcord* (1973) displays the most conventional use of the flashback as an embedded micro-narrative. In an early scene, for instance, teenage Titta (Bruno Zanin) is at confession, where the priest, Father Balosa (Gianfilippo Carcano), asks him if he ever "touches" himself. As he hesitates, Titta, complicit with the viewer, recounts in voice-over an afternoon the previous summer when he encountered Gradisca (Magali Noël), the woman of his dreams, alone in the town's cinema watching Gary Cooper in *Beau Geste* (1939). A cut to the main street hazy with summertime heat; in long shot, Gradisca enters the cinema, followed by Titta, whose arrival, despite the colour film stock, is sped up, mimicking the often incorrect projection speed of silent films. He sidles up to Gradisca in the darkened theatre, putting his hand on her knee, which is as far as he gets. Back in the diegetic present, he tells Father Balosa that he touched himself once, "just a little, but that I regretted it immediately."[4] Titta's voice-over "confession," one of numerous embedded narratives, is addressed to the viewer alone. The shifting back and forth in time, with the action returning to the same diegetic moment, is classic in form.

This is also true of *Amarcord*'s other flashbacks, including the sequence in which the lawyer (Luigi Rossi) recounts to the camera how Gradisca got her nickname ("Whatever you desire"), a local "memory" prompted by the lawyer's annual visit to the town's Grand Hotel. In this case, the madeleine-object[5] or mnemic precipitant is the location itself, the hotel as one of the film's principal mnemic chronotopes, organizing the on-screen performance of collective memory filtered through the film-making process. That the lawyer questions the veracity of his own story underlines the slippage in this film among diegetic "truth," subjective fantasy, and objectively presented past events. The lawyer is the on-screen narrator even within the flashback, playing a role while also standing back to comment on it, in Brechtian *gestic* manner (Brecht 1977, 42). In this long sequence both Gradisca and Buscein (Gennaro Ombra) address the camera, like Giudizio (Aristide Caporale) in the following scene in which the whole town turns out to watch the *Rex* passenger liner sail past. This episode, as much as any other, accentuates the ironically elegiac quality of the film's engagement with memory as malleable, trans-subjective, and dependent for its existence upon the medium in which it is expressed.

As the foregoing suggests, Fellini's most "conventional" flashback scenes demonstrate that the classical understanding of the technique is inadequate to conceptions of memory and the subjectivities that emerge in the postwar period. According to Turim,

> both earlier and later in film history, other forms of flashbacks occur that are less obviously marked. We therefore need a more general definition for the flashback that includes all types of flashbacks. In its most general sense, a flashback is simply an image or a filmic segment that is understood as representing temporal occurrences anterior to those in the images that preceded it. The flashback concerns a representation of the past that intervenes within the present flow of film narrative. (1989, 1–2)

The flashback, "in its most general sense," is dependent upon editing or montage. But there are other ways to return to the past cinematically. What André Bazin prizes in postwar Italian film realism – deep focus, deep space, long takes – is tantamount to the spatialization of time: the mnemic chronotope. As Gilles Deleuze (1989, xii), following Bazin, reminds us, the postwar European art film privileges the shot over montage, allowing time to reveal itself, in contrast to the artificial manipulation of time (and therefore space) via the cut. This form of the flashback, based in the spatial extension of time, has proven to be the defining mode for the postwar art film and its contemporary instantiations, with Fellini as a leading figure in this development.

Fellini's Performative Memory

In Cosetta Gaudenzi's view, "Fellini uses language to recount and reinvent his own memory" (2002, 155). She quotes Tonino Guerra's 1973 poem "A m'arcord" (I remember):

> I know, I know, I know,
> That when a man is fifty
> His hands are always clean.
> I wash mine several times a day.
> But when I see my hands are dirty
> It's [only] then that I remember (Che me a m'arcord)
> My carefree boyhood days.[6]   (quoted in Gaudenzi 2002, 157)

In her gloss, Gaudenzi makes explicit the Proustian echo: "Only when his hands are dirty can he remember his youth, the time when he was a [boy]. Just as in Marcel Proust's *À la recherche du temps perdu* the little madeleine cake, when dipped in tea and tasted by the narrator, calls up a whole train of reminiscences about Combray, so does the sight of dirty hands evoke in Tonino Guerra his boyhood" (2002, 157). As for Guerra, so Fellini: "In *Amarcord* the director portrays the childhood and adolescent recollections mentioned by the poet. Guerra needs improper and imperfect dirty hands to recall his childhood memories; Fellini seems to require the expressions and inflection of Romagnolo to mediate the narration of his recollections" (158). An analogy may therefore be made between Fellini's – or any film-maker's – use of linguistic dialect to tell their story, and their use of a non-standard visual style for the same purpose; a cinematic "dialect," signalling not a singular and personal but a non-standard, idiomatic language. And, while the economic class distinctions marked by verbal dialects do not apply in this analogy, it is the case that the decision to use an alternative cinematic language – as in the emergence of Italian neorealism – makes a clear political statement against hegemonic structures, whether those of capitalist Hollywood film-making, or of Italian Fascism (see Gaudenzi 2002, 162, 165). For, just as (borrowing Deleuze and Guattari's terminology) the function of the Romagnolo dialect in *Amarcord* "becomes that of a minor literature refusing to submit to an external entity that would dictate the choices, tastes, and life of its people" (Gaudenzi 2002, 164), in the equivalent manner, Fellini's evolving mid-period style is like a "minor literature," in a sense, "opposed not to 'major' but rather to something more like 'national'" (Waller 2002, 15) – a counterhegemonic art film style.

While memory may be "the fundamental structure in Fellini's films," as Gaetana Marrone (1993, 240) asserts, Fellini consistently denied his films' autobiographical basis:

> It is not memory that dominates my films. To say that my films are autobiographical is an overly facile liquidation, a hasty classification. It seems to me that I have invented almost everything: childhood, character, nostalgias, dreams, memories, for the pleasure of being able to recount them. In the sense of the anecdotal, there is nothing autobiographical in my films … I could easily make a film composed of memories and nostalgias on Turkey, a country that I do not know at all. (quoted in Waller 1990, 127)[7]

Marguerite Waller analyzes *La dolce vita* (1960) in relation to Fellini's claim that, in her words, "his project does not stand in any hierarchical, mimetic relation to memory" (1990, 127). In the light of contemporary memory theory, however, one need not look for mimetic correspondence between Fellini's life and his films; from this perspective he is not lying when he claims to have "invented almost everything" because this is how "personal" memory works. As neuroscience has known for some time, a given memory is never simply summoned up with each instance of recall but is fashioned anew in a present-tense performative act (Plate and Smelik 2013; van Dijck 2007). Memory in its "natural" state and "memory" as reflected in its cultural constructions are not mutually exclusive. Things get complicated, though, when this logic of memory in its ever-present reinstantiation is applied on the transcultural level on which narrative cinema operates. The second-order representation of memory in film presents a highly persistent counter-narrative of memory as fixed cinematic image, always the same every time it is revisited, but this is not the same thing as either the willed or accidental return of the past *in itself* – as seen in the narrator's experience at the climax of *Swann's Way* (see Proust [1923] 1996, 53–4). As

Turim puts it, speaking of Proust's *Recherche*, "the work of fiction is also a work of formal structure, which cannot be taken directly as a personal memoire that chronicles introspection as a theoretical example in a phenomenology of memory" (1989, 66).

In contrast to a psychoanalytic theory of memory (Freud), or a memory theory rooted in the body (Proust) – each of which privileges the involuntary basis of mnemic recall – contemporary memory theory privileges the agential "present-tenseness" of memory; its emergence out of action or reaction in the present rather than the return of some authentic or inauthentic past; its performance or construction; its malleability and productivity. Richard Terdiman defines memory as "the past made present" (quoted in Rothberg 2009, 3); as Michael Rothberg makes clear, the notion of memory as a "making present" means that memory is not "strictly separable from either history or representation," and yet it "nonetheless captures simultaneously the individual, embodied, and lived side and the collective, social, and constructed side of our relations to the past" (2009, 3–4). Liedeke Plate and Annette Smelik likewise emphasize memory's performative dimension: "Memory is work – creative work – doing or carrying out the act ... [It is] an embodied act grounded in the here and now, generating memory in the act of performing it" (2013, 2–3). Such an approach, however, must be accommodated to memory's ongoing archival function, conditioned by its mediatic form. Memory emerges at the intersection of present-tense performance (whether conscious, or agential, or not) and the archival function, because there is no memory without the materiality of a medium (Erll 2011, 114). Cinematic mediality takes precedence over the categories of memory, dream, or the past in itself. It is even possible for the mediated and fictionalized memory-representation to completely supplant the actual memory of the past in its authenticity. As Fellini recalled of his childhood reconstructions: "Now I can't distinguish what really happened from what I made up. Superimposed on my real memories are painted memories of a plastic sea, and characters from my adolescence in Rimini are elbowed aside by actors or extras who interpreted them in my films" (quoted in Bondanella 1992, 283).

As an example of Fellini's self-reflexive formalization of the process of mnemic creation, Marco Vanelli cites the conclusion of *E la nave va* (1983), in which the camera pulls back, revealing the film's crew shooting the final scene on a soundstage at Cinecittà:

> [Fellini] wants the viewer to realize what he is doing, to take note of it, to enter and become familiar with another dimension that is no longer the simple realm of being told a story, but the experience of putting oneself in

the shoes of the storyteller (or in the position of one who no longer knows how to tell the story, or no longer wants to tell it) … mak[ing] us feel the vertigo of the *mise en abyme* of story within story within story. (2020, 208)

Fellini's intra-diegetic "performance" of his own memories, combined with cinema's inherently archival function, is also exemplified in an early scene in *Intervista* (1987). Seeking locations for a *Roma*-like autobiographical film-within-the-film, Fellini's crew fabricates the hotel in which Fellini stayed in 1940, before his first-ever visit to Cinecittà. In a few minutes of screen time, the crew erects period streetlamps and a hotel façade with "Casa del Passeggero" emblazoned above the door. The result proves eminently more suited to a representation of Fellini's memories, reinforcing the fact that comparable cinematic sleights of hand are behind many of the mnemic set pieces in films like *I clowns* (1970), *Roma* (1972), and *Amarcord*, in a manner identical to the often obviously artificial settings of his films from *Giulietta degli spiriti* (1965) onwards. This means of course that the material of memory – Fellini's autobiographical content – is subjected to the same process of cinematic recreation, which is also always an "original" creation.

The central role played by memory – in all its complexities – in Fellini's mid to late works must be balanced against the director's consistent denial of the putatively autobiographical nature of some of his more famous films, as well as the critical reception of these films in light of their engagement with memory, both thematically and formally, as (in some cases) the subject of the story and also as structuring device. Although scholars have analysed the significance of memory in Fellini's films from a variety of approaches (Deleuze 1989; Marrone 1993; Burke 1996; Gaudenzi 2002), the comprehensive *Companion to Federico Fellini* (published in 2020, to coincide with his centenary) has no index entry for "flashback." Outside of Italian film studies, Fellini is largely overlooked in the scholarship on the flashback and the cinematic representation of memory. "Fellini" is absent from the index of Maureen Turim's (1989) seminal *Flashbacks in Film: Memory and History*, for instance.[8] In *Cinema 2*, by contrast, Gilles Deleuze identifies Fellini's singular postwar contribution to the "slackening of the sensory-motor connections" of the movement-image and the consequent emergence of the new time-image, of which the Fellinian "recollection-image" is exemplary (1989, 7–8). Deleuze does not apply the term "flashback" to Fellini, reserving it for the cinema of the movement-image, in comparison to the time-image in its distinctive function (1989, 48–55). While the marked absence of Fellini in the critical literature on the flashback is surprising, it is also important to not overlook the innovative nature of Fellini's stylistic relationship to the cinematic representation of memory more broadly.

The Mnemic Chronotope

What is the filmic flashback, and why is it so rare in postwar European or international modernist art film narrative, despite the constitutive *modernity* of each?[9] Or rather: What is it about the postwar cinema that makes it unconducive to the flashback as narrative device? Part of the answer is that the conventional flashback and modernist cinema are not "modern" in the same sense: the former is symptomatic of a film style that arose first in Hollywood to define narrative cinema as the mass art form of the first half of the twentieth century; the latter is an expression of cinema's own proper modernist phase, which came some fifty years after literary modernism. The analogy with literature extends also to the consideration of modernist cinema's engagement with memory.

As Turim acknowledges, "the term flashback was first used in its sense of narrative returns to the past in reference to film, rather than other forms of storytelling ... This term for a return to a narrative past inserted in a narrative present is apparently derived from the speed with which cinematic editing was able to cut decisively to another space and time" (1989, 4). Hence, the emphasis on the magic of the cinematic transition to effect the shift from present to past and back again, from one shot to the next. In literary terms, *analepsis* is

> a scene that interrupts the present action of a narrative work to depict some earlier event – often an event that occurred before the opening scene of the work – via reverie, remembrance, dreaming, or some other mechanism. The term may be used to refer to the scene itself or to its presentation. Flashback has its origins in the ancient epic tradition of beginning a work *in medias res* (in the middle of things) and then moving back in time to tell the beginning of the story. (Murfin and Ray 1997, 130)

The transformation of the flashback in the postwar period is linked to its conceptual association with psychology and psychoanalysis; as with memory more generally, the flashback starts out being compared to specific mental processes and ends up providing a new term for scientists to apply to mental phenomena. In 1916, Hugo Münsterberg introduced the new technique of the "cut-back," which would eventually give way to the more popular term "flashback," as an "objectification" of the "mental act of remembering" ([1916] 2002, 90; see also Turim 1989,

1–20). My point of view is that the discourses of psychology or psychoanalysis reflect changes in technologies and media, such as cinema, and not the other way around. The shift from the flashback proper to the mnemic chronotope is the shift from a psychoanalytic model to a kind of posthumanist allegorical model, in which the (gendered) psyche follows a trajectory that does not appear to be predetermined. The significance of death broadens out to encompass a wider affective register, from melancholia and mourning to the elegiacally nostalgic sensibility often encountered in Fellini's later films.

Fellini's *La città delle donne* (1980) is a rare cinematic allegory where the allegorical nature of the story is right on the surface, evoking the flashback's distant origins in the medieval dream vision, in which the protagonist travels to a spatiotemporal zone equivalent to the underworld or land of the dead, as in the epic *katabasis*. Greek for "a going down, a descent," *katabasis* refers to an underworld journey undertaken by a hero in quest of special knowledge (Holtsmark 2001, 25). Major premodern examples include book 11 of Homer's *Odyssey*, book 6 of Virgil's *Aeneid*, and Dante's *Inferno*.[10] After a lengthy itinerary – including Milton and Joyce, for instance – the *katabasis* narrative has remained a persistent model in the secularized, psychologized – and irreducibly ironic – form so familiar in European literary modernism's peculiar Judaeo-Christian convergence. Modernist cinema provided a fresh audiovisual framework for the cinematic perpetuation of the secularized *katabasis* narrative, in which the return to or of the past is a form of mild psychic torment inducing regret. Fellini's trajectory, from his early "Christian humanism" to a postrealist, increasingly self-reflexive style in the post-1960s films, is emblematic of the supposed shift in the later twentieth century from modernism, with its vestiges of faith "shored against our ruin" (in T.S. Eliot's phrase) to a secular, proto-posthumanist vision based around the individual subject of modernity. Fellini remediates the medieval dream-vision *katabasis* in spectacularly cinematic manner in *La città delle donne*'s final sequence, in which Snàporaz (Marcello Mastroianni), sailing down a seemingly interminable amusement park slide, is granted glimpses of stylized tableaux re-enactments of his memories of the women in his life. This bravura sequence exemplifies Fellini's uniquely Brechtian, multiform updating of the classic flashback.

This transmedial narrative subgenre – what I have elsewhere called the *psycho-katabasis* (Kilbourn 2010, 31) – is also the basis of what András Bálint Kovács (2007) names the postwar modernist "mental journey film," exemplified by Ingmar Bergman's *Wild Strawberries* (1958). Kovács does not include Fellini's *8 ½* in this category, although it is arguably an even better example. *Wild Strawberries'* protagonist's physical journey is paralleled by his sojourn through the spaces of memory and dream, precipitated by his encounter with the wild strawberry patch, his "madeleine-object," outside the house of his formative early memories, a mnemic chronotope overlapped (via a dissolve) with the actual space in which events unfolded.[11] Guido Anselmi's (Mastroianni) "journey" in *8 ½*, engaging both dream and memory, is entirely mental, which is to say self-reflexively cinematic, and a realist register becomes untenable.[12] For Kovács,

> *8 ½* was an important milestone in the development of modern cinema [because] it was the first film to include virtually all the important innovations of newborn modernism. First of all, here Fellini sheds entirely the neorealist tradition and makes a film in which "reality" can be interpreted only as an object of auteurial fantasy. Three years had passed since the release of *Hiroshima, My Love* and it became common practice, almost compulsory, for a modern filmmaker of the time to merge past and present and make reality and fantasy indiscernible. (2007, 320–1)

Alain Resnais's 1959 film established the new paradigm of modernist memory-film, analysing a French woman's traumatic experience of taking a German soldier as lover – he is killed and she is ostracized – against the background of the aftermath of the atomic bombings of Hiroshima and Nagasaki in August 1945. Highly novel at the time, the film includes single frames from the back story (occupied France) in the present-tense diegesis in postwar Japan. Famously, Resnais cuts in close-ups of the woman's dead lover's hand – in a scene where she is shown looking at her Japanese lover as he lies sleeping, his hand extended beside him. A rapid succession of close-ups, shifting back and forth in time, solidifies the impression of watching the woman's thought process unfold, as the association between past dead lover and present living one manifests on-screen, unbidden by the subject.[13]

As in *Hiroshima, My Love*, the links between episodes in *8 ½* are looser than in *Wild Strawberries*; after each dream or flashback or fantasy sequence, the narrative action continues in a new setting, in what Deleuze calls the "false movements" of a modernist discontinuity style (1989, xi).[14] In this sense, *8 ½*'s health spa location, as mnemic chronotope, operates less like Isak Borg's (Victor Sjöström) childhood summer house and more like that other spa hotel setting in Resnais's next film, *Last Year at Marienbad* (1961), although in the earlier film the difference between present and past action, or real and imaginative space, is always already effaced.[15] The self-reflexivity in *8 ½* is, rather, emblematic of the kind of postwar art film that David Bordwell, chiming with Kovács's auteur-based survey of modernist cinema, calls "authorial expressivity" (2019, 776). The obvious danger of an auteur-centred view, however, is that it can obscure a given film's contribution to our understanding of how the representation, and therefore the constitution, of memory changed in the postwar period and beyond.

Fellini and the Recollection-Image

Fellini holds a special place for Deleuze, for whom the flashback is ultimately a function of the action-image and the "recollection-image" as a heightened instance of the time-image cinema (1989, 47–55), largely because of the latter's dependence on on-screen spatial depth over cutting. *Cinema 2*'s third chapter, "From Recollection to Dreams: Third Commentary on Bergson," illustrates Deleuze's combination of Bergson and Bazin in his rethinking of the cinematic representation of time and memory. For Deleuze, what links the images in the time-image cinema is not movement but memory, via the "recollection-image" (1989, 44–6). For Deleuze, then, the conventional flashback epitomizes the movement-image:

> We know very well that the flashback is a conventional, extrinsic device: it is generally indicated by a dissolve-link, and the images that it introduces are often superimposed or meshed. It is like a sign with the words: "watch out! recollection." It can, therefore, indicate, by convention, a causality which is psychological, but still analogous to a sensory-motor determinism, and, despite its circuits, only confirm the progression of a linear narration. (48)

Deleuze lays bare the bankrupt psychologism of the movement-image and the genre-bound, redemptive narratives it supports. In terms of the flashback, the shift to the time-image means the disruption of memory recuperated in the service of narrative telos, reaching a height of ironically elegiac nostalgia in Fellini's post-1960 films. Significantly, Deleuze (1989, 82) attributed his notion of the time-image to Proust, grounding his theory in one of the key texts for modern memory theory.

The distinction between conventional flashback and mnemic chronotope – between movement and recollection-image – is well illustrated in *8 ½*, in which Guido's subjective memory content – including himself as Catholic schoolboy, and Saraghina (Eddra Gale), the avatar of the "monstrous" feminine/sexual temptress – manifests. This is triggered in an instance of cinematic Proustian involuntary memory by the sudden appearance of a nameless woman, a worker, whose entire function in the film is to prompt this unforeseen memory in Guido as he sits with the cardinal at the hotel spa. Guido's past obtrudes into the physical spaces of his present experience, whether in memory, dream, or fantasy, in a manner that diverges from the classic flashback (see Deleuze 1989, 8). It does, however, correspond in general to the focus on the mnemic chronotope. Fellini repeatedly denied having ever read Proust, which may or may not be true. Not that it matters: the madeleine-image is too fundamental to be limited to a simplistic account of authorial influence. In true intertextual fashion, Fellini invokes the Proustian trigger of involuntary memory because it is a key aspect of a modern(ist) understanding of memory.

If the treatment of memory in *8 ½* does not correspond to the parameters of the classic flashback, Turim's more general definition – "a flashback is simply an image or a filmic segment that is understood as representing temporal occurrences anterior to those in the images that preceded it. The flashback concerns a representation of the past that intervenes within the present flow of film narrative" (1989, 1–2) – seems to fit. More than one major sequence in the film represents an occurrence temporally anterior to preceding events in the diegesis. The problem, if it is one, is that these sequences may not always look like flashbacks. "Flashbacks typically hide their formal function ... by being presented as memories, dreams, or confessions" (6). The latter is true especially of *Amarcord* and *8 ½*. It appears that the designation of flashback for a specific narrative sequence – for a "flashback" to make sense as a flashback – depends on the presence of certain formal features of an ostentatiously artificial nature. In their absence one is left with a return to or of the past, but of a different nature and value. Where the often self-reflexive formal qualities of the conventional flashback are subordinated in the service of the diegesis, furthering the present-tense action by providing crucial information, the modernist flashback rejects end-directed sensory-motor psychologisms in favour of an on-screen time-space in which the protagonist's psyche is allegorized; rather than a backwards shift towards a pre-modern paradigm, however, this shift is post-modern, or even posthumanist, in its rejection of the prescribed clichés of modern subjectivity.[16]

Symptomatic of the modernist thematization of death in its allegories of subjectivity, *8 ½* famously opens with a dream sequence, echoing *Wild Strawberries'* second scene,[17] and establishing it as a "mental movie" (Vanelli 2020, 212), or "mental journey film" (Kovács 2007, 321), a Deleuzian time-image film built around a journey through mnemic chronotopes. The second dream scene in *8 ½* exemplifies Marco Vanelli's

(2020, 211) point that the close-up is not a major trait in Fellini's films before 1963. The scene opens in medium shot, after a significant ellipsis, with post-coital Guido in bed with Carla (Sandra Milo), who is reading a comic book. A higher angle shot reveals Guido's mother (Giuditta Rissone) on the left, dressed in black, wiping an invisible window. A cut to his mother from behind shows her facing an actual windowpane inside a different room in which Guido's father (Annibale Ninchi) is reflected, outside the room, in a shot that is only spatially possible in memory (or cinema). The camera pans to follow Guido's mother as she moves into the outdoor space. An abrupt cut to a deep-focus shot, his mother in the distant background, shows Guido in close-up profile. By now it is apparent that this is another dream scene, one that makes explicit the past's role as prick of conscience; here, Guido's evident guilty feelings about betraying his wife elide with deeper feelings of having disappointed his father. Guido's father suddenly appears in the background, and Guido speaks in voice-over ("What is this place? Do you like it here?"[18]) as his father enters what appears to be his own mausoleum, which he criticizes for its design flaws. Guido's producer (Guido Alberti) and his assistant (Mario Conocchia) arrive, and Guido moves back into extreme close-up profile. As the producer departs, Guido's father urges his son not to worry about him in this "lonely" place. It is now apparent that Guido is wearing the adult version of his childhood Catholic school uniform, complete with cap and cape. With Guido's help, his father descends into a grave-like hole, cutting him off mid-sentence. As Guido covers his face with his hands, his mother appears again in foreground close-up. They embrace in a reverse angle shot; she looks up to him, holding his head in her hands, and suddenly pulls his face to hers. The embrace ends with a jump cut and his mother is replaced by his wife Luisa (Anouk Aimée). Clearly there is more at stake here than mere paternal disappointment, as Fellini alludes – ironically, in my view – to Guido's pseudo-Oedipal confusion. In extreme close-up Luisa asks him if he recognizes her; cut to a high angle long shot of Luisa standing alone in the ruins of the cemetery space. Of the film's psycho-*katabases*, this one grants to Guido not special insight but confusion, and to the viewer an ambiguously elegiac affect.

The first proper flashback in *8 ½*[19] is instigated in Proustian style by Guido's recollection of the childhood phrase "Asa Nisi Masa,"[20] which triggers a long scene, set in what appears to be his idyllic early childhood, in a rural house full of other children, with female relatives and servants. To borrow Gaudenzi's (2002, 157) words, just as in Proust's *Recherche*, when the madeleine cake, dipped in tea and tasted by the narrator, calls up a whole train of reminiscences about Combray, so does the childish phrase evoke his boyhood in Guido. Apart from superficial similarities in setting, the contrast with Borg's childhood flashbacks in *Wild Strawberries* could not be greater. The flashback begins abruptly, with a straight cut from the stage magician (Ian Dallas) to Guido's mother, now youthful and vivacious. Various women bathe and dry Guido before putting him to bed in an atmosphere full of love, despite the wide angles and expressive use of depth, with grotesque faces in the foreground and scampering children in the background. The phrase "Asa Nisi Masa" is rather more akin to Proust's madeleine cake and lime tea combination: a random fragment from Guido's past that, rediscovered by chance in the present, allows the past to return in its wholeness – in a manner that exploits film's perpetual present-tenseness to render memory's ongoing reinvention. The sequence ends with a close-up on the fireplace that dissolves into a panning shot in the hotel foyer. Tellingly, in the subsequent "harem" fantasy sequence, the adult Guido, while in the same farmhouse bathtub, repeats the distinctive fluttering hand gestures that accompany the magic phrase, linking the two scenes together graphically and motivically – provided the viewer remembers this detail from the earlier scene.

The "Asa Nisi Masa" scene is therefore related formally to the film's second proper flashback scene, which is the most classically Proustian in its set-up. The dialogue between Guido and a priest that precedes the scene in question tacitly establishes the themes to be explored. The priest remarks to Guido: "I just don't believe cinema lends itself to certain topics. You mix sacred and profane love too casually."[21] The camera tracks in as they approach the seated cardinal (Tito Masini) with whom Guido seeks an audience. As the cardinal discourses about songbirds, Guido is distracted by the bared legs of a middle-aged woman carrying a basket, walking down a nearby slope. The shot of the woman is answered by a close-up on a pensive Guido as he lowers his glasses. A shrill whistle bridges to the next scene, the flashback itself, in which school-age Guido with his classmates visits Saraghina in her beach bunker. Saraghina's appearance, although more exaggerated in every aspect, is obviously what the present Guido recalled at the sight of the woman, which is the madeleine-image or precipitant of the past's unsought return. To be precise, the woman's derriere, in its proleptic echo of Saraghina's considerably larger one, triggers the flashback.[22] This supposition is supported by several moments in other Fellini films – for example, the scene in *Amarcord* (discussed above) in which Titta recounts to the viewer what he cannot confess to Father Balosa: that the boys only go to church on St. Anthony's Day to watch the women hitch up their dresses to mount their bicycles. It would not be an overstatement to say that this "culità," what Frank Burke calls Fellini's "derriere mentality" (2020, 190), is an important motif across Fellini's oeuvre.[23] "Watch out! Recollection," indeed.

As in the previous flashback, episodes in Guido's childhood unfold on-screen with minimal prompting, suggesting an ease of recall that has no equivalent in Proust's narrator's experience. The Saraghina flashback concludes, and a dissolve returns us to the present-tense narrative, the action now shifted to a different time and place. In the spa restaurant, the critic (Jean Rougeul) offers his critique of Guido's proposed exploration of "Catholic consciousness," which we have just watched unfold on-screen, even though the crew has not even begun production on the film-within-the-film: "So what does it mean? It's a character based on your childhood memories. It has no connection with a true critical conscience ... Your little nostalgia-bathed memories, your harmless and essentially sentimental evocations ... You set out to denounce, but you end up an accomplice. I'm sure you see the confusion and ambiguity."[24] As it transpires, the special knowledge that Guido acquires as a result of his personal psycho-*katabasis*, as he admits to Luisa, is that "all the confusion of my life ... has been a reflection of myself! Myself as I am, not as I'd like to be ... Life is a celebration. Let's live it together."[25]

Conclusion

From the foregoing, it should be clear that Fellini's innovations in the representation of memory, the techniques and tropes, the Proustian triggers of embodied memory, or the three-dimensional chronotopography of the past's unbidden return, opening out into the landscape of the hero's mental journey through the realm of the dead – all of this invokes and reinforces what are in fact the clichés of the language of memory, which in this context is a function of the counterhegemonic language of a new kind of cinema. This consists, in Deleuze's words, of "floating images, these anonymous clichés, which circulate in the external world, but which also penetrate each one of us and constitute his internal world, so that everyone possesses only psychic clichés by which he thinks and feels, is thought and felt, being himself a cliché among others in the world which surround him" (1989, 208). This allows us to resolve the contradiction between the approach that grounds Fellini's spectacular images in an auteurist theory of self-expression, and the alternative, an approach that foregrounds the always already-constructed or mediated nature of any act of recollection. For, just as no individual owns the language in which they express themselves, so is there no such a thing as a private memory.

NOTES

1 For Maureen Turim (1989, 19), the classic flashback is not necessarily identical to a scene of memory. Fellini's recollection-image, however, is irreducibly subjective in its meanings, even as its formal properties make it an object of public consumption.
2 Regarding the relation of time and space to cinematic subjectivity in postwar Italian film, see Waller (1997). Regarding the significance of time for cinematic narration, see Waller (1990, 129).
3 "A literary work's artistic unity in relationship to an actual reality is defined by its chronotope" (Bakhtin 1981, 243); that is, the work's *realism* (or lack thereof) is dependent upon its represented spatio-temporal relations. See also the work of Robert Stam, who refers to "cinema's variegated chronotopic capacities" (2000, 15).
4 "solo un po', ma me ne sono pentito subito." In an ironic parallel, the very next sequence, the arrival of the fascist federale, features Gradisca in the crowd lining the street shouting hysterically, "Fatemelo toccare! Io lo voglio toccare!" (Let me touch him! I want to touch him!).
5 I use the term "madeleine-object" or "madeleine-image" also partly in homage to Hitchcock's *Vertigo* (1958), made just four years before *8 ½* (see Kilbourn 2010, 60–7).
6 "Al so, al so, al so, / Che un om a zinquent'ann / L'ha sempre al meni puloidi / E me a li lev do, trè volti e dè. / Ma l'è sultent s'a me vaid al meni sporchi / Che me a m'arcord / Ad quand ch'a s'era burdell."
7 Cf. Fellini's words about his hometown: "I cannot see Rimini as an objective fact, that's it. It is a dimension of my memory and nothing more. And in fact, when I am in Rimini, I always find myself assailed by ghosts that have already been filed away, put in their place" (2006, 24).
8 For a comparable omission, see Kilbourn (2010).
9 The modernist metaphorical connotations of "flashback" – suddenness, shock, illumination within darkness, return or recursivity, and so on – underpin the psychological term, crucial for trauma studies, of "flashback" as a "highly persistent memor[y] of traumatic experience … activated automatically by features of the current environment and … accompanied by much reliving" (Berntsen and Rubin 2002, 649). Psychology had to wait for cinema to be invented so that it could appropriate this term.
10 Regarding Fellini's relation to Dante's *Commedia*, see Bondanella and Pacchioni (2019); Waller (1990); Welle (1993). See also Mirko Tavoni's chapter in this volume.
11 See Turim regarding Proust's "interest in the evocative power of common objects or sensations perceived in the present to initiate recall of the past" (1989, 66).

12 As Stam puts it, "*8 ½ is personal but not private; the associative processes of Guido's mind are not without analogies to our own*" (2000, 104).
13 See Paraskeva (2017) for an insightful analysis of this scene in the context of Proustian "embodied memory."
14 "Thanks to this loosening of the sensory-motor linkage, it is time, 'a little time in the pure state,' which rises up to the surface of the screen. Time ceases to be derived from the movement, it appears in itself. Hence the importance of *false continuity* in modern cinema: the images are no longer linked by rational cuts and continuity, but are relinked by means of false continuity and irrational cuts" (Deleuze 1989, 121).
15 Regarding the relation between Resnais's and Fellini's films, see Kovács (2007, 316–21).
16 "Consciousness of clichés" is one of "the five apparent characteristics of the new image," forged, as Deleuze (following Bazin) claims under the influence of Italian neorealism. The other four are the dispersive situation; the deliberately weak links; the voyage form; … the condemnation of the plot" (1989, 208).
17 *Wild Strawberries'* first major set piece is a dream scene in which the protagonist appears to confront his own mortality in a blatant allegory that – like this scene in *8 ½* – satirizes psychoanalytic tropes. The opening of *8 ½* is also parodied in the opening of Woody Allen's *Stardust Memories* (1980).
18 "Ma che cos'è questo posto? Come ti trovi qui?"
19 The scene is even described as a "flashback" on the Wikipedia page devoted to it (https://en.wikipedia.org/wiki/Asa_Nisi_Masa).
20 By all accounts this phrase is a childish corruption (with added nonsense syllables) of *anima*, the feminine Latin/Italian word for "soul."
21 "Il cinematografo, mi pare, non si presta tanto a certi argomenti. Voi mescolate con troppa disinvoltura l'amor sacro e l'amor profano."
22 On Fellini's treatment of female bodies in his films (and the Saraghina in particular), see Dishani Samarasinghe's and Eleonora Lima's chapters in this volume.
23 Burke provides a convincing analysis of "the seeming obsession in [the] later films with women's derrieres. Because women, as the embodiment of male desire, are inevitably inaccessible, men can only approach them (with awe, fear, fascination, and so on) 'from behind.' What in some respects seems a highly sexist and demeaning view of women becomes, in another respect, a revealing representation of masculine desire, especially in a prohibitive Italian Catholic context" (2020, 185).
24 "E che significato ha? È un personaggio dei suoi ricordi d'infanzia. Non ha niente a che vedere con una vera coscienza critica … I suoi piccoli ricordi bagnati di nostalgia, le sue evocazioni inoffensive e in fondo emotive …

No, lei parte con una ambizione di denuncia e arriva al favoreggiamento di un complice. Ma lei vede che confusione, che ambiguità."
25 "ma questa confusione sono io. Io come sono, Non come vorrei essere … È una festa la vita, viviamola insieme"

REFERENCES

Bakhtin, Mikhail. 1981. "Forms of Time and of the Chronotope in the Novel." In *The Dialogic Imagination*, edited by Michael Holquist, 84–258. Translated by Caryl Emerson and Michael Holquist. Austin: University of Texas Press.

Berntsen, Dorthe, and David Rubin. 2002. "Emotionally Charged Autobiographical Memories across the Life Span: The Recall of Happy, Sad, Traumatic, and Involuntary Memories." *Psychology and Aging* 17, no. 4: 636–52. https://doi.org/10.1037//0882-7974.17.4.636.

Bondanella, Peter. 1992. *The Cinema of Federico Fellini*. Princeton, NJ: Princeton University Press.

Bondanella, Peter, and Federico Pacchioni. 2019. *A History of Italian Cinema*. 2nd ed. London: Bloomsbury.

Bordwell, David. 2019. "The Art Cinema as a Mode of Film Practice." In *Film Theory and Criticism: Introductory Readings*, edited by Leo Braudy and Marshall Cohen, 774–82. 6th ed. Oxford: Oxford University Press.

Bordwell, David, and Kristin Thompson. 2004. *Film Art: An Introduction*. 7th ed. Boston: McGraw-Hill.

Brecht, Bertolt. 1977. *Brecht on Theatre: The Development of an Aesthetic*. Translated by John Willet. New York: Hill and Wang.

Burke, Frank. 1996. *Fellini's Films: From Postwar to Postmodern*. Woodbridge, CT: Twayne Publishers.

– 2020. *Fellini's Films and Commercials: From Postwar to Postmodern*. Bristol, UK: Intellect.

Deleuze, Gilles. 1989. *Cinema 2: The Time Image*. Translated by Hugh Tomlinson and Robert Galeta. Minneapolis: University of Minnesota Press.

Erll, Astrid. 2011. *Memory in Culture*. Translated by Sara B. Young. New York: Palgrave Macmillan.

Fellini, Federico. 2006. *My Rimini*. Translated by Isabel Quigly. Booklet included in *Amarcord*, DVD collection. Irvington, NY: Criterion Collection.

Fellini, Federico, and Tonino Guerra, eds. 1974. *Amarcord, Portrait of a Town*. London: Abelard-Schuman.

Gaudenzi, Cosetta. 2002. "Memory, Dialect, and Politics: Linguistic Strategies in Fellini's *Amarcord*." In *Federico Fellini: Contemporary Perspectives*, edited by Frank Burke and Marguerite R. Waller, 155–68. Toronto: University of Toronto Press.

Holtsmark, Erling B. 2001. "The *Katabasis* Theme in Modern Cinema." In *Classical Myth and Culture in the Cinema*, edited by Martin M. Winkler, 23–50 New York: Oxford University Press.

Kilbourn, Russell J.A. 2010. *Cinema, Memory, Modernity: The Representation of Memory from the Art Film to Transnational Cinema*. New York: Routledge.

Kovács, András Bálint. 2007. *Screening Modernism: European Art Cinema, 1950–1980*. Chicago: University of Chicago Press.

Marrone, Gaetana. 1993. "Memory in Fellini's *City of Women*." In *Perspectives on Federico Fellini*, edited by Peter Bondanella and Cristina Degli-Esposti, 240–8. New York: G.K. Hall & Co.

Münsterberg, Hugo. (1916) 2002. "Memory and Imagination." In *The Photoplay: A Psychological Study and Other Writings*. New York: Routledge.

Murfin, Ross, and Supriya M. Ray. 1997. *The Bedford Glossary of Critical and Literary Terms*. Boston: Bedford Books.

Paraskeva, Anthony. 2017. *Samuel Beckett and Cinema*. London: Bloomsbury Academic.

Plate, Liedeke, and Anneke Smelik. 2013. "Performing Memory in Art and Popular Culture: An Introduction." In *Performing Memory in Art and Popular Culture*, edited by Liedeke Plate and Anneke Smelik, 1–23. New York: Routledge.

Pramaggiore, Maria, and Tom Wallis. 2011. *Film: A Critical Introduction*. 3rd ed. Boston: Pearson.

Proust, Marcel. (1923) 1996. *In Search of Lost Time I: Swann's Way*. Translated by Scott Moncrief and Terence Kilmartin. London: Vintage.

Rothberg, Michael. 2009. *Multidirectional Memory: Remembering the Holocaust in the Age of Decolonization*. Stanford, CA: Stanford University Press.

Stam, Robert. 2000. "Beyond Fidelity: The Dialogics of Adaptation." In *Film Adaptation*, edited by James Naremore, 54–76. New Brunswick, NJ: Rutgers University Press.

Turim, Maureen. 1989. *Flashbacks in Film: Memory and History*. New York: Routledge.

van Dijck, José. 2007. *Mediated Memories in the Digital Age*. Stanford, CA: Stanford University Press.

Vanelli, Marco. 2020. "'Io non me ne intendo': Fellini's Relationship to Film Language." In *A Companion to Federico Fellini*, edited by Frank Burke, Marguerite Waller, and Marita Gubareva, 207–22. Hoboken, NJ: Wiley Blackwell.

Waller, Marguerite R. 1990. "Whose Dolce Vita Is This, Anyhow? The Language of Fellini's Cinema." *Quaderni d'italianistica* 11, no. 1: 127–35.

– 1997. "Decolonizing the Screen: From *Ladri di bidclette* to *Ladri di saponette*." In *Revisioning Italy: National Identity and Global Culture*, edited by Beverly Allen and Mary Russo, 253–74. Minneapolis: University of Minnesota Press.

- 2002. "Introduction." In *Federico Fellini: Contemporary Perspectives*, edited by Frank Burke and Marguerite R. Waller, 3–25. Toronto: University of Toronto Press.
Welle, John. 1993. "Fellini's Use of Dante in *La Dolce Vita*." In *Perspectives on Federico Fellini*, edited by Peter Bondanella and Cristina Degli-Esposti, 110–18. New York: G.K. Hall & Co.

Fellini's Notes on Camp to John Waters

ELEONORA LIMA

When Federico Fellini's *8 ½* (1963) premiered at the Charles Theatre in Baltimore, a seventeen-year-old John Waters – later known, thanks to William Burroughs, as the Pope of Trash – was in attendance. To this day, in the American director's private collection of memorabilia, there is an 8 ½ inch-long wooden ruler that he bought as a souvenir after the screening, a testament to how significant that night at the theatre must have been for him (Sherman 2019, 101–2). Indeed, as Waters declared years later, *8 ½* and Fellini's cinema more generally, had a deep impact on him and his fellow "Dreamlanders," Waters's group of friends who were regularly featured in his early films and with whom he often liked to indulge in LSD-fuelled screenings of *Giulietta degli spiriti* (1965) (Jeffries 2015).

The similarity between Fellini and Waters's aesthetics and penchant for the grotesque was clear to film critic Pauline Kael as early as 1970, when she wrote a review for *The New Yorker* comparing *Fellini Satyricon* (1969) to Waters's first feature-length film *Mondo Trasho* (1969) as a way to insult the work of the Italian director. Indeed, equating the last endeavour of an internationally acclaimed artist like Fellini to *Mondo Trasho* – an independent low-budget film that begins with the beheading of a chicken, continues with the apparition of the Virgin Mary in a laundromat, and concludes with Divine, the drag queen and beloved star of many of Waters's films, rolling over a pig-shed – was to hyperbolically dismiss *Fellini Satyricon*. Kael described it using outdated and problematic language as "one long orgy of eating, drinking, cruelty, and copulation" of "freaks with painted faces and protruding tongues," in which Fellini "goes all the way with his infatuation with transvestism [sic], nymphomania, homosexuality, monsters" (1973, 162).

To be sure, this was precisely what Waters also tried to accomplish with his muse, drag queen Divine, and his cohort of Baltimore outcasts. It was, however, a case of him learning from Fellini, rather than the Maestro borrowing from the young director. The idea that Waters's films have an undeniable Felliniesque quality has been recently claimed by Vito Zagarrio (2020, 279), who points out a striking resemblance between the exuberant corporeality of some of Fellini's most iconic female characters, like Saraghina and the tobacconist, and Waters's regular interpreters, such as Divine and Edith Massey (images 32, 33, 34, and 35).

Certainly, Fellini was not the only Italian director influencing Waters: in some of his early films shot in his own Baltimore apartment, it is easy to spot the posters of Pier Paolo Pasolini's *Il vangelo secondo Matteo* (1964) and *Teorema* (1968) hanging on the walls. Moreover, as a testament of his life-long admiration, on 22 April 2021, the day of his seventy-fifth birthday, Waters released *Prayers to Pasolini*, a number of audio recordings he made in Rome, celebrating the Italian director (see Legaspi 2021).[1] Beyond art cinema, other sources of inspiration, declared by the director himself, are the cult documentary *Mondo cane* (1962) by Paolo Cavara, Franco Prosperi, and Gualtiero Jacopetti (Egan 2011, 78, 216) and the eccentric thriller *La morte ha fatto l'uovo* (1968) by Giulio Questi, that Waters first watched while filming *Pink Flamingos* (1972) (Waters 1985, 16). Such heterogeneous interests in Italian cinema should not elicit any surprise, as Waters's eclectic genius is no stranger to contaminations. However, while these other sources might have influenced him only to a certain extent – with the exception of Pasolini – the impact of Fellini's aesthetics holds quite a different role, especially in his early production, as this chapter aims to demonstrate.

The reason Waters must have found Fellini's work so congenial resides in the Italian director's Camp aesthetics, or rather his aesthetics of bad taste, also a defining trait of Waters's cinematic production.[2] Undoubtedly, there are crucial differences in their shared Camp sensibilities which are largely due to their different approach to politics and aesthetics. The language of "bad taste" is spelled differently in Fellini's decadently rich and extravagant cinema, and in Waters's unpolished and rough-edged low-budget films. While such divergent aesthetics might have originated from the great disparity in budget and technical proficiency – Waters was shooting films in his backyard while Fellini had the entire Cinecittà at his disposal – this soon became a conscious choice, Waters's personal approach to Camp. Moreover, as further discussed later, the level of awareness and involvement with the gender politics discourse intrinsic to Camp sensibility varies greatly when considering the two directors. Evidently, this has to do with their personal identities and roles within the queer community, but also with the fact

Image 32. Saraghina (Eddra Gale) in *8 ½* (1963).

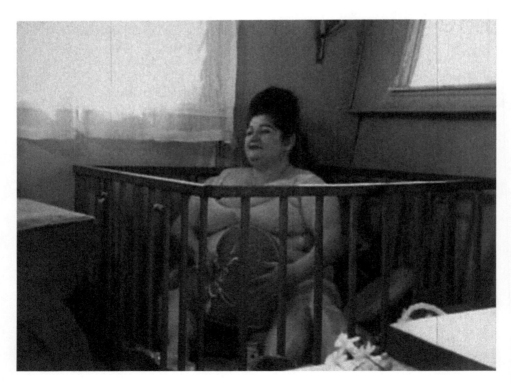

Image 33. Edie (Edith Massey) in *Pink Flamingos* (1972).

Fellini's Notes on Camp to John Waters 325

Image 34. The tobacconist (Maria Antonietta Beluzzi) in *Amarcord* (1973).

Image 35. Aunt Ida (Edith Massey) in *Female Trouble* (1974).

that, while for Waters, Camp is a strategy to challenge heteronormativity, Fellini rather uses it as a more general provocation against bourgeois decency.

According to Susan Sontag's pivotal essay on the matter, "the essence of Camp is its love of the unnatural: of artifice and exaggeration" (1966, 1). Moreover, Camp sensibility allows us to recognize bad taste and to appreciate and celebrate it, and precisely this awareness is what distinguishes "Camp" from "kitsch," as the latter is instead to be understood as the experience of somebody who mistakes tackiness for luxury (Eco 2007). That Fellini was well versed in Camp aesthetics did not escape Sontag, who listed the self-parody of Anita Ekberg in *La dolce vita* (1960) among the highest examples of the genre (1966, 16), together with Tiffany lamps, feathers, and beaded dresses, the fictional characters King Kong and Maciste, and Flash Gordon's comics, all elements dear to Fellini's vision and sensitivity.

Making a catalogue of all the visual elements ascribable to Camp that are present in Fellini and then passed onto Waters would be quite a pointless exercise. What is worth analysing, instead, are the reasons why the Italian director chose to adhere to this aesthetics, and how Waters was influenced by Fellini's vision precisely because he agreed with its premises. There are three main ideological stances implied by Camp aesthetics that this chapter considers: the desire to blur the boundaries between low and high culture; the refusal of any moral posture; and the love for the unnatural. To each of these stances corresponds one of the following recursive and peculiar themes in Fellini's work: the analysis of self-reflexivity in cinema; the disengaged parody of bourgeois values and sense of decency; and the performativity of gender and embodiment. The same convergence between these three ideological claims and corresponding thematic elements is also to be found in Waters, who embraced Fellini's Camp aesthetics on an ideological as well as on a visual level.

The transgression of the boundaries between good and bad taste, as well as between high and low culture is an important and well-known constant in Fellini, who famously contaminated art cinema with popular genres, such as comics, B-movies, and *fotoromanzi* (see Risset 1990; Pacchioni 2013; Bellano 2020). Such ease in playing with different registers was something that the young Waters noticed in him, as well as in other European directors like Bergman (Egan 2011, 10, 74, 219; Sherman 2019, 102), and found extremely enticing and creatively liberating. Indeed, he quickly learned the lesson, to the point of often declaring that all he ever wanted to make are "exploitation films for art theatres" (Waters 1985, 214). Precisely this pleasure in contaminating genres and betraying viewers' expectations is at the root of Fellini's and Waters's peculiarly ironic take on self-reflexivity in cinema.[3] Portraying the world of film production is for them to parody its conventions, to take away its distant allure, and to reveal the more prosaic reality of what happens behind the scenes, while also celebrating its glamour.

One point of convergence is to be found in the way the two directors recur to Camp aesthetics so as to represent the making of their beloved cinematic divas, respectively Anita Ekberg, who in Fellini's *La dolce vita* (1960) offers a "deliciously ironic portrait of the fetishized celluloid woman" (Waller 2002, 114) and Divine, who in many of Waters's films interprets a fame-crazed and egocentric woman, obsessed with her beauty and worshiped by fans and paparazzi. While in Waters the parody of the diva is more explicit and irreverent, as she is an overweight drag queen who interprets a semi-goddess idolized for her looks, the American director does not seem to diverge too much from Fellini's Camp depiction of Anita Ekberg. This is particularly evident when considering, for instance, the scene from *La dolce vita* in which the actress – who plays a version of herself, just like Divine does in many of Waters's works – has freshly landed in Rome and is interviewed by a group of journalists. The comedic effect is reached through the larger-than-life performance of the diva, who does not have any interesting opinion to offer and does not try to hide it, as she knows well that her attractiveness and notoriety is what people – journalists and fans alike – are after. Her performance of ingenuity is matched by one of the reporters, who pretends to be a serious news professional while instead asking her, in the same breath, about her sleeping attire and neorealist cinema, politics, and *maccheroni*. In the spirit of Camp, Fellini takes pleasure in showing the tacky sides of cinema-glamour and the scene constitutes an enjoyable sneak-peek into the backstage, rather than a critical exposé on the vapidity of the film industry.

Similarly, Waters's fascination for stardom in popular culture does not prevent him from taking pleasure in mocking its excesses and idiosyncrasies, as in the case of one of the concluding scenes of *Pink Flamingos*, which closely resembles the scene from *La dolce vita* described above. Divine has just kidnapped her two archnemeses, who tried to steal from her the title of "filthiest person alive." Before executing them, she calls for a press conference to publicize the event and revel in the media spotlight. Whereas Fellini gives us the overblown Camp performance of Ekberg, looking like a distant goddess while being fed pizza as a commercial stunt, Waters chooses to shoot Divine dressed in a bright evening gown and wearing chandelier earrings while standing in front of her trailer, where she is being interviewed by the local paparazzi. Mainly enticed by the promise of witnessing a capital execution, the journalists are also attracted by Divine's fame and diva status, and, as in *La dolce vita*, their questions are vapid and incongruous, as much as the woman's answers are bold and nonsensical. Set aside Waters's peculiar trash aesthetics and shock value, and the scene relies on the same comedic exaggeration and overblown Camp performance of Fellini's portrait of Ekberg, through which he reflects on celebrity culture, mass media's obsession with Hollywood divas, and their influence over society at large.

The desire to blur the boundaries between cinematic glamour and everyday mundane experiences is common to Fellini and Waters, who both refer to the metaphor of the circus to describe life as a theatrical performance and cinema as the art of creating illusions.[4] Indeed, Camp is instrumental in accomplishing their carnivalesque aesthetics, through which they playfully mix genres and registers as in, for instance, when they choose to turn their beloved divas, Ekberg and Divine, into B-movie monsters. The Swedish actress becomes an extremely erotic version of Godzilla, chasing the moralizer and sexphobic protagonist of *Le tentazioni del dottor Antonio* (1962), while Divine, in *Multiple Maniacs* (1970), after being raped by a giant lobster, becomes monstruous and starts ravaging the streets until she is killed by the National Guard – another instance of men trying to police and suppress the unruly hypersexual woman. Ekberg's and Divine's larger-than-life persona and their fame-crazed and egocentric fictional selves turned them into supernatural characters of an action film, in which cheap special effects and plot twists typical of B-movies are interpreted by Hollywood glamourous actresses, or at least by their drag impersonators.

Indeed, Fellini's pleasure in contaminating art cinema with popular genres and low-culture references is deeply shared by the American director, to the point that Wagner's *Ride of the Valkyries*, used for comedic and estrangement effects by Fellini in *8 ½* in the famous scene of Guido at the thermal water fountain, is reprised by Waters with the same intention in *Mondo Trasho*. Wagner is in fact the background music for the concluding scene in which Divine rolls over feces in a pig-shed until the Virgin Mary materializes, a heavenly apparition second only to the one of Claudia Cardinale to Guido in Fellini's classic.

Even when the clash is not as evident as in these instances, both directors take pleasure in hiding very cultured references under their Camp aesthetics. This is the case, for instance, of Fellini's short film *Toby Dammit* (1968), in which the protagonist is cast to perform in a Catholic Western movie about Jesus' second coming as a cowboy. This odd and almost sacrilegious project, while very much in line with Fellini's love for contamination, was not his original idea, but rather the plot of Mark Twain's short story, "The Second Advent" (1881), defined as a "burlesque of the Christ story" (Fulton 2006, 90). Similarly, the infamous closing scene in Waters's *Pink Flamingos* – in which Divine eats dog feces – hides a very cultured reference to Jean Genet's statement about poetry as "the art of using remains. Of using shit and getting you to eat it"[5] (Stephens 2009, 4). The celebration of bad taste, be it a Catholic Western movie or coprophagy, therefore succeeds in blurring the lines between high and low culture.

However, and this is the second reason why Camp sensitivity was so congenial to Fellini and consequently to Waters, the adoption of bad-taste aesthetics has nothing to do with satire nor reflects a moral stance. As Sontag points out, "the whole point of Camp is to dethrone the serious," therefore its aesthetics "neutralizes moral indignation, sponsors playfulness," because it is "above all, a mode of enjoyment, of appreciation … It relishes, rather than judges" (1966, 32–3). Certainly, Fellini and Waters alike do not wish to chastize the subject of their Camp representation – be it the Catholic Church, middle-class decorum, or B-movies. Their fascination is purely aesthetic and free from any desire to belittle or reprimand. This does not mean that their cinematic representations are free from any form of judgment against social conventions, but rather that, in subverting the norms through exuberant mise-en-scène, they aim for theatricality first and foremost, while the critical commentary comes second as a natural consequence.

This is obvious when considering, for instance, the subversion of the rules governing domestic life, as well as women's respectability, in Fellini's *Giulietta degli spiriti* and in Waters's *Polyester* (1981). In both films, the protagonists are women who, after having fully dedicated themselves to creating a perfect conjugal nest, realize that the devotion to their husbands is misplaced, not only because they are unfaithful and careless but also because the role of spouses and housewives is detrimental to their ability to live life fully. The struggle to subvert gender roles and expectations faced by Giulietta in Fellini's film and Francine – again played by Divine – in Waters's film, is the perfect storyline to enable the two directors' aesthetics, and to allow them to queer the bourgeois domestic space by playing with shocking costumes and extravagant characters. In both films, supporting the protagonist's rebellion against gender expectations, is a defiant "unruly woman" (Rowe 1995): the sexually promiscuous and mysterious neighbour Suzy (Sandra Milo) in *Giulietta degli spiriti*, and, in *Polyester*, Cuddles Kovinsky (Edith Massey), Francine's ex-housekeeper who, now a rich heiress, enjoys her nouveau riche life and the sexual favours of her young limousine driver. Undoubtedly, the comedic and Camp elements in these films do not erase their critique against the hypocrisy and oppressiveness of married life in suburbia, but, nonetheless, the love for theatricality seems to exceed the desire to stigmatize society's shortcomings. Suzy sliding into her private pool from a shell-shaped tunnel, or Cuddles, a dishevelled old woman, sporting immaculate tennis attire, attest more to Fellini's and Waters's attraction for aesthetically conscious bad taste than to their commitment to taking down patriarchal values.

Indeed, both directors have always been adamant in declaring their lack of interest in making any moral or political stance with their films. While this may partly be a disingenuous pose, it is nonetheless telling that Fellini, trying to stop the many intellectual overinterpretations of *La dolce vita*, stated: "I believe I never had any specific intention to denounce, criticize, scourge, or satirize" (quoted in Bondanella 2002, 81). An assertion so dear to the director that he lends his words to his alter ego Guido, who, at the end of *8 ½*, candidly and defiantly declares: "I have really nothing to say. But I want to say it anyway" (Fellini 1987, 132). Waters too has repeatedly offered the very same evasive answer when asked about the hidden message of his visually provocative films: "I am really not trying to say anything"[6] (Egan 2011, 84). Evidently, such rejection towards engagement takes on different meanings, as for Fellini it is a mark of distinction between the political art cinema of the 1960s and 1970s, and of his dislike for Leftist *engagé* intellectuals, while for Waters it is part of his nihilist punk aesthetics that opposes a blasé, apathetic performance to the political activism of hippy culture. Leaving the question about the earnestness of this claimed ingenuity aside, it is nonetheless true that Fellini and Waters regularly refused to take any moral stance and instead engaged with their subjects on a purely aesthetic level, for the visual and comedic pleasure that they produce, and this is most evident when considering their treatment of Catholic iconography.

Probably one of the campiest scenes in the history of cinema is the Vatican fashion show in *Roma* (1972). In a crescendo that culminates with the pope framed by feather fans, viewers are presented with priests on roller-skates, nuns with dove-shaped hats, and cardinals dressed in neon lights. However, the scene is "essentially an exercise in theatricality" (Inglis and Thorpe 2019, 10), not at all a sharp condemnation against the lush lifestyle promoted by the Vatican. Fellini invites us to marvel at the exuberant and dramatic quality of Catholic rites and robes rather than provoke our disdain for the Church's immoral love for luxury. If anything, the detraction comes from the choice of applying the same aesthetics to depict Trimalchio's dinner party in *Fellini Satyricon* and the Apostolic Palace: for the director, they are equally enticing subjects, perfect for unleashing his Camp sensitivity.

Similarly, Waters, who shares with Fellini a Catholic upbringing, declares the importance of this experience for his cinematic vision, asserting that "being Catholic always makes you more theatrical" (1985, 65). Expectedly, the Virgin Mary is a recurring presence in his work: from his first full-feature film *Mondo Trasho*, where the Virgin repeatedly appears to Divine in the least holy of places, to the more recent *Pecker* (1998), in which the protagonist's grandmother pretends to be blessed with a talking statue of the Madonna – indeed a ventriloquist dummy – and is finally discovered and reprimanded by the press. It is impossible, again, not to think of Fellini and the episode from *La dolce vita* when the appearance of the Virgin Mary to a little girl leads to a media circus.

Perhaps one of the most telling examples of Waters's attraction for Catholic theatricality is his blasphemous re-enactment of the Passion of the Christ in *Multiple Maniacs*. While the director mentions *Il vangelo secondo Matteo* as his prime source of inspiration – a comparison that makes his rendition even more outrageous – the scene retains nothing of the sober tone of Pasolini's film, nor his "intimate, profound, archaic Catholicism."[7] In the Gospel according to Waters, Jesus turns the loaves of bread and fish into a mountain of canned tuna and packages of pre-sliced bread, like in a cheap TV commercial, and among his followers is Divine wrapped in bedsheets. As in Fellini's Vatican fashion show, theatricality, comedic elements, and a penchant for the grotesque is what interested Waters, not a pointed criticism towards the Church. Offending the Catholics is an inevitable consequence of the two directors' Camp aesthetics, not necessarily their main goal.

Ultimately, their shared fascination for the theatrical and performative aspects of religious rites and iconography points to the third and final reason why Camp sensitivity suited Fellini, and in turn Waters, best. Camp, in Sontag's words, is "not a natural mode of sensibility" but rather "the love of the exaggerated, the 'off,' of things-being-what-they-are-not" (1966, 8), and it therefore allows the two directors to playfully reveal the artificiality of social conventions, gender identities, and reality at large. Indeed, Camp is Ekberg in *La dolce vita* when, by offering a parody of herself, shows how both cinema and femininity are for Fellini nothing but a projection of male desire (Bachman 1980–1). Camp is Giulietta, her absurdly overdressed mother and sisters, her licentious neighbour Suzy, who overperforms stereotypical female roles – the devoted wife, the perfect bourgeois, the libertine – all exaggerated because they are all artificial (De Lauretis 1987). Camp is, of course,

Divine, who offers "a twisted version of Elizabeth Taylor" (as quoted by Waters in 2016)[8] in *Multiple Maniacs*, a hypersexualized and queer interpretation of femininity in *Pink Flamingos*, a failed wife and housewife coming to terms with oppressive gender roles in *Polyester*. All of this, while being in drag, therefore reinforcing the claim that any form of identity is nothing but a staged performance.

However, the intent of the two directors is not to denounce artificiality as shallowness, underneath which lies a deeper meaning longing to be discovered, but rather to celebrate its multiform appearance in the spirit of Camp, which, as Sontag explains, equals "to understand Being-as-Playing-a-Role" (1966, 8). Although Fellini and Waters do succeed in deconstructing, or at least questioning, stereotypes and fixed identities, they do so not with the intent to replace them with something more genuine: they simply recognize them as performances and exploit their staginess for comedic purposes.[9]

This is especially true when it comes to their Camp rendition of what Julia Kristeva defines as "the abject body," which transgresses the boundaries and upsets social norms (1982, 4). Fellini and Waters alike are attracted by non-conventional corporeality – obesity, ungracefully aging bodies, deformities and mutilations – and seek to explore the liminal space between gender roles, as well as between humans and animality.[10] Indeed, the list of visually analogous frames in Fellini's and Waters's films prove beyond any doubt their shared obsession with the unnatural and the abject, if not even a direct line linking the work of the American director to the production of his Italian maestro (images 36, 37, 38, 39, 40, and 41). Belonging to this shared repertoire is, for example, the character of Carla, Guido's mistress in *8 ½*. As part of a playful erotic game, he exaggerates her make-up and draws fake eyebrows so as to make her look "more like a whore"[11] (Fellini 1987, 55), therefore creating a caricatural and unnatural version of her.[12] Those clownish, imperfectly shaped eyebrows, which design an arch almost reaching Carla's hairline, will become – perhaps as a tribute – Divine's signature make-up (images 42 and 43).[13]

A more general lesson that Fellini seems to teach Waters, however, is the ability to celebrate the sexual appeal of the grotesque: the gory equivalent of Carla's make-up mask, is Dawn Davenport – again interpreted by Divine – in *Female Trouble* (1974), who proudly shows off her face disfigured by an acid attack as a mark of beauty. Dawn's uneven, burned skin – on which Waters's camera likes to indulge – is reminiscent of the make-up worn by some of the characters in *Fellini Satyricon* who, because they are painted images from a fresco who magically come to life, have horrid faces made of cracked plaster (images 44 and 45). Again,

Image 36. Suzy (Sandra Milo) in *Giulietta degli spiriti* (1965).

Image 37. Lady Divine (Divine) in *Multiple Maniacs* (1970).

Image 38. The Marquis Du Bois (Daniel Emilfork Berenstein) in *Il Casanova di Federico Fellini* (1976).

Image 39. Aunt Ida (Edith Massey) in *Female Trouble* (1974).

Fellini's Notes on Camp to John Waters   335

Image 40. Partygoer (Franca Pasut) in *La dolce vita* (1960).

Image 41. Raymond and Connie Marble (David Lochary and Mink Stole) in *Pink Flamingos* (1972).

Image 42. Carla (Sandra Milo) in *8 ½* (1963).

Image 43. Divine/Babs Johnson (Divine) in *Pink Flamingos* (1972).

Image 44. Frame from *Fellini Satyricon* (1969).

Image 45. Dawn Davenport (Divine) in *Female Trouble* (1974).

it is not possible, and perhaps beyond the scope of this chapter, to prove that Divine's make-up is directly inspired by one of Fellini's characters. However, what matters is that Waters follows the Italian directors in his celebration of everything that is considered monstrous and perverted, unapologetically against "nature," when nature stands for whatever common sense intends as normal.

Also framed within this Camp celebration of the unnatural – at least according to traditional bigoted standards – is the representation of homosexuality and transgenderism, and this is perhaps the point on which the two directors diverge the most in their approach to Camp sensitivity. In Waters, the accusation made by conservatives to queer people as being against nature and therefore an abomination, is made void by the claim that any identity is in fact an artifice, an act of theatre. Camp is therefore a tool for Waters to denounce bigotry, while also celebrating the carnivalesque and exuberant elements of the queer community of which he is an integral part.[14] Indeed, the level of connection and personal involvement with their subjects is where the difference between Waters and Fellini lies. While the first heavily draws from real-life experiences and is organic to the community he depicts, the second is quite alien to queer culture, which he knows, due to his profession, but only as an external spectator. Like Sontag in her attraction to Camp, Fellini, in his exploration of queerness seems to be guided by "a deep sympathy modified by revulsion" (Sontag 1966, 2), and his work demonstrates a fascination cultivated from a privileged heterosexual stance (Suderburg 2020, 84). As a result, Camp aesthetics for Fellini appear to be a strategy through which he tries to appropriate queer culture via a cultural lens, one of extravagant theatricality that he fully masters. For Waters, the exact opposite is true, as he embraces Camp aesthetics to distance his personal experience from his artistic production.

Closing this comparative analysis by pointing to this fundamental difference is crucial to avoid overstating Fellini's influence on Waters's cinema. Indeed, the aim of this chapter was not to trace back to the Italian director stylistic and thematic elements that can very well have a polygenic origin, but rather to demonstrate how Waters's predilection for Camp aesthetics, often explained through his belonging to queer counterculture, was instead nurtured and inspired, at least in part, by the model of Fellini's cinema, thus validating the claim that what the Baltimore director has always tried to make are indeed "exploitation movies for art theatres."

NOTES

1. Pasolini's long-standing impact is declared by Waters, as he mentions two of the Italian director's works – *Salò* and *Teorema* – among the art films that have deeply influenced him since his early years (Waters 1983, 125–6). Surprisingly, none of Fellini's films make it to the list of art films that Waters, the self-proclaimed champion of exploitation movies, reluctantly – and jokingly – admits to love: "I blab on ad nauseam about how much I love films like *Dr. Butcher, M.D.* or *My Friends Need Killing*, but what really shames me is that I'm also secretly a fan of what is unfortunately known as the 'art film'" (Legaspi 2021, 120).
2. Elaborating on his aesthetics of bad taste, Waters writes: "One must remember that there is such a thing as good bad taste and bad bad taste. It's easy to disgust someone; I could make a ninety-minute film of people getting their limbs hacked off, but this would only be bad bad taste and not very stylish or original. To understand bad taste one must have very good taste. Good bad taste can be creatively nauseating but must, at the same time, appeal to the especially twisted sense of humor, which is anything but universal" (Waters 1985, 2).
3. Kane-Maddock analyses the convergence between Waters's subversive parody and contamination of genre and gender norms "in order to cast a critical eye on that evocative symbol of normalcy and repository of morality, the family" (2012, 106).
4. For more on this, see Fellini (1976, 98); Waters (1985, 33); Ravetto (2005); and Stoddart (2002).
5. "l'art d'utiliser des restes. D'utiliser la merde et de vous la faire bouffer"; English translation in Stephens taken from Genet's *Pompes funèbres* (1948). Divine's stage name, that Waters suggested to his friend, is also a tribute to Genet's scandalous novel *Notre-Dame-des-Fleurs* (1943), in which the character of a drag queen is indeed named Divine.
6. This early position has been partially amended in more recent years by Waters, who declared: "I prided myself on having no social redemption, but they [the films] do. Because outsiders win. Fat girl gets the boy. Things that don't happen in real life happen in my films" (Egan 2011, 143). Furthermore, for an analysis that challenges Waters's early claim about the lack of political engagement in his films, see Breckon (2013).
7. This is a famous line delivered by Orson Welles in Pasolini's *La ricotta* (1962), in which the American director plays Pasolini's alter ego.
8. Quoted from the *Multiple Maniacs* audio commentary recorded by Waters for Criterion in 2016.
9. For a discussion of this deconstruction, please see Picchietti (2002).

10 For a political reading of Waters's early cinema – specifically of *Pink Flamingos* – against Kristeva's concept of "the abject," see Breckon (2013).
11 "più porca"
12 This entire scene is missing in the Italian screenplay. This, however, is not the only discrepancy as a note preceding the text explains that the differences between the script and the actual film are preserved in order to show Fellini's creative interventions. "This screenplay differs in many places from the final film. But we believe it was important to publish it because a comparison with the film allows to evaluate the creative work of the director during the shoot" (Questa sceneggiatura differisce in molte parti dal film girato. Ma s'è ritenuto utile pubblicarla perché un confronto col film permetta di misurare il lavoro creativo del regista durante le riprese) (Fellini 1965, 87).
13 Describing Divine's signature look, Waters writes: "His hairline was shaved back to his crown and his eyebrows were just a memory" (1985, 11), which could also be the perfect description for Donald Sutherland's appearance in *Fellini's Casanova* (1976), another prime example of Fellini's Camp aesthetics (image 42).
14 For an analysis of the social and cultural significance of Camp cinema in shaping and expressing "gay sensibility," see Babuscio (1999).

REFERENCES

Babuscio, Jack. 1999. "The Cinema of Camp (Aka Camp and the Gay Sensibility)." In *Camp: Queer Aesthetics and the Performing Subject*, edited by Fabio Cleto, 117–35. Edinburgh: Edinburgh University Press.

Bachman, Gideon. 1980–1. "Federico Fellini: The Cinema Seen as a Woman." *Film Quarterly* 34, no. 2: 2–9. https://doi.org/10.2307/1211908.

Bellano, Marco. 2020. "Fellini's Graphic Heritage: Drawings, Comics, Animation, and Beyond." In *A Companion to Federico Fellini*, edited by Frank Burke, Marguerite Waller, and Marita Gubareva, 59–78. Hoboken, NJ: Wiley Blackwell.

Bondanella, Peter. 2002. *The Films of Federico Fellini*. Cambridge: Cambridge University Press.

Breckon, Anna. 2013. "The Erotic Politics of Disgust: *Pink Flamingos* as Queer Political Cinema." *Screen* 54, no. 4: 514–33. https://doi.org/10.1093/screen/hjt041.

De Lauretis, Teresa. 1987. "Fellini 9 ½." In *Technologies of Gender: Essays on Theory, Film, and Fiction*, 95–106. Bloomington: Indiana University Press.

Eco, Umberto. 2007. *On Ugliness*. Translated by Alastair McEwen. London: Harvill Secker.

Egan, James, ed. 2011. *John Waters Interviews*. Jackson: University of Mississippi Press.
Fellini, Federico. 1965. *8 1/2*. Edited by Camilla Cederna. Modena: Cappelli Editore.
– 1976. *Fellini on Fellini*. Translated by Isabel Quigley. New York: Delacorte Press.
Fulton, Joe B. 2006. *The Reverend Mark Twain: Theological Burlesque, Form, and Content*. Columbus: Ohio State University Press.
Inglis, David, and Chris Thorpe. 2019. "Catwalk Catholicism: On the Ongoing Significance of Federico Fellini's Ecclesiastical Fashion Show." *Religions* 10, no. 520: 1–19. https://doi.org/10.3390/rel10090520.
Jeffries, Stuart. 2015. "John Waters: I Want to Be Despised." *The Guardian*, 30 June. www.theguardian.com/artanddesign/2015/jun/30/john-waters-art-lassie-justin-bieber-ansel-adams.
Kael, Pauline. 1973. "Fellini's Mondo Trasho." In *Deeper into Movies*, 160–6. Boston: Little, Brown and Company.
Kane-Maddock, Derek. 2012. "Trash Comes Home: Gender/Genre Subversion in the Films of John Waters." In *Gender Meets Genre in Postwar Cinemas*, edited by Christine Gladhill, 205–18. Urbana: University of Illinois Press.
Kristeva, Julia. 1982. *Powers of Horror: An Essay on Abjection*. Translated by Leon S. Roudinez: New York: Columbia University Press.
Legaspi, Althea. 2021. "John Waters Marks 75th Birthday with 'Prayer to Pasolini.'" *Rolling Stone*, 22 April. www.rollingstone.com/movies/movie-news/john-waters-prayer-to-pasolini-1159583/.
Pacchioni, Federico. 2014. "Bernardino Zapponi." In *Inspiring Fellini: Literary Collaborations Behind the Scenes*, 79–95. Toronto: University of Toronto Press.
Picchietti, Virginia. 2002. "When in Rome Do as the Romans Do? Federico Fellini's Problematization of Femininity (*The White Sheik*)." In *Fellini: Contemporary Perspectives*, edited by Frank Burke, Marguerite R. Waller, 92–106. Toronto: University of Toronto Press.
Ravetto, Kriss. 2005. "The Circus of the Self: Fellini's *8 1/2*." In *Film Analysis: The New Norton Anthology*, edited by Jeffrey Geiger and R.L. Rutsky, 582–601. New York: Norton.
Risset, Jacqueline. 1990. *Fellini, "Le cheik blanc": L'annonce faite à Federico*. Paris: Adam Birro.
Rowe, Kathleen. 1995. *The Unruly Woman: Gender and the Genres of Laughter*. Austin: University of Texas Press.
Sherman, Dale. 2019. *John Waters FAQ: All That's Left to Know about the Provocateur of Bad Taste*. Guildford, CT: Applause.
Sontag, Susan. 1966. *Notes on "Camp."* London: Penguin Books, 2018.
Stephens, Elizabeth. 2009. *Queer Writing: Homoeroticism in Jean Genet's Fiction*. New York: Palgrave.

Stoddart, Helen. 2002. "Subtle Wasted Traces: Fellini and the Circus." In *Federico Fellini: Contemporary Perspectives*, edited by Frank Burke, Marguerite R. Waller, 47–64. Toronto: University of Toronto Press.

Suderburg, Erika. 2020. "In Bed with Fellini: Jung, Ernst Bernhard, Night Work, and *Il libro dei sogni*." In *A Companion to Federico Fellini*, edited by Frank Burke, Marguerite Waller, and Marita Gubareva, 79–92. Hoboken, NJ: Wiley Blackwell.

Waller, Marguerite R. 2002. "Whose *Dolce Vita* Is This, Anyway? The Language of Fellini's Cinema." In *Fellini: Contemporary Perspectives*, edited by Frank Burke and Marguerite R. Waller, 107–20. Toronto: University of Toronto Press.

Waters, John. 1983. *Crackpot: The Obsessions of John Waters*. Scribner: New York, 2003.

– 1985. *Shock Value. A Tasteless Book about Bad Taste*. Philadelphia: Running Press.

Zagarrio, Vito. 2020. "*Egli Danza*: Fellini's Contexts and Influence from Before Rossellini to Sorrentino and Beyond." In *A Companion to Federico Fellini*, edited by Frank Burke, Marguerite Waller, Marita Gubareva, 279–92. Hoboken, NJ: Wiley Blackwell.

The Mastrangelo Collection and Fellini's Distribution in Canada

JESSICA WHITEHEAD AND CHRISTINA STEWART

Introduction: Fellini in North America

Federico Fellini occupies a venerated place in North American cinema. In 2021, director Martin Scorsese published an essay in *Harper's Magazine* entitled "Il Maestro: Federico Fellini and the Lost Magic of Cinema," which outlines Fellini's lasting impact. He wrote:

> In the Sixties, Federico Fellini became more than a filmmaker. Like Chaplin and Picasso and the Beatles, he was much bigger than his own art. At a certain point, it was no longer a matter of this or that film but all the films combined as one grand gesture written across the galaxy. Going to see a Fellini film was like going to hear Callas sing or Olivier act or Nureyev dance. His films even started to incorporate his name – *Fellini Satyricon*, *Fellini's Casanova*. The only comparable example in film was Hitchcock, but that was something else: a brand, a genre in and of itself. Fellini was the cinema's virtuoso. (Scorsese 2021)

This quote perfectly exemplifies Fellini both as a cultural icon and as a brand in North America. He shifted global cinema culture, and his films influenced the development of "New Hollywood," in which, of course, Scorsese played a crucial role.

Fellini also had a significant impact on Canadian film-makers, from Deepa Mehta to Atom Egoyan and Guy Maddin.[1] While this larger cultural stature is undeniable, our interest lies in understanding how Fellini's films permeated through Canadian culture, a culture that in the postwar period was already grappling with an influx of Italian immigrants who brought with them a new understanding of cinema. Our chapter will explore the everyday interactions of the audience in Canada and how the business of Italian film distribution and exhibition negotiated the arrival of Italian art house cinema. In Canada, unlike the United States, Italian film distribution was largely driven by diasporic audiences who were interested in popular titles. Fellini was able to bridge the popular and art house audiences, and he was one of the first international directors to have his films regularly screened in mainstream theatres.

Our chapter examines four of Fellini's films – *La strada* (1954), *I vitelloni* (1953), *La dolce vita* (1960), and *Fellini Satyricon* (1969) – focusing on how these films were distributed and received in Canada. We will also look at the material history of Italian-language film through an exploration of the Rocco Mastrangelo Italian Cinema Collection, which is the largest collection of Italian films in North America. Rather than being an organized industry, international film distribution in Canada was largely done through grass-roots movements. Fellini's films deviated from this typical trajectory, and he had wider releases for his later titles after becoming his own film brand in the 1960s. We can see through the distribution of these four films how Fellini evolved from grass roots to mainstream.

Italian-Language Film Distribution in North America

After the Second World War, with the rise of neorealist cinema, Italian film became popular in American urban centres. The Italian films *Sciuscià* (1946) and *Ladri di biciclette* (1948) were of course the first international films to be recognized at the Academy Awards. Films from Italian directors such as Vittorio De Sica and Roberto Rossellini drew in large audiences in cities like New York, Chicago, and Los Angeles. As Nathaniel Brennan (2011) pointed out, Italian cinema appealed to "sophisticated" urban audiences with distributors marketing these films in two seemingly contradictory ways (88). One technique relied on by distributors was to emphasize the critical merit and aesthetic qualities of Italian cinema, and the other technique suggested that the films contained sexualized and exotic content that could not be found in American films.

Italian neorealism pushed American film culture towards "a more sustained engagement with cinematic realism" (Brennan 2011, 87). As Robert Sklar (2011) noted, Italian films appealed to American intellectuals and helped to change film cultures and practices in the country. Sklar documents the role writer James Agee played in promoting neorealism through his critical writings for publications like *The Nation* and *Time* magazine. Sklar also examined how Agee was a link between aesthetic theory and production through his role as a screenwriter for the documentary films *The Quiet One* (1948) and *In the Street* (1948). Both films depict childhood poverty and were clearly influenced by De Sica.

Selling Italian film in urban America became a profitable business, as evidenced through several articles in the American trade papers. In 1952, the *Motion Picture Herald* published a report on the "Salute to Italian Film week," which was held at the little Carnegie theatre in New York City and included many well-connected guests, including the president of the Motion Picture Association, Eric Johnson, the director of the Metropolitan Opera, Rudolph Bing, US Senator Irving Ives, and then president of the Screen Actors Guild Ronald Reagan alongside the top executives from theatres circuits across the United States. This report indicated that films from Italy were the most popular international productions, and these films helped break down traditional barriers to foreign exports (*Motion Picture Herald* 1952, 34). Italian Films Export (IFE) was created to aid in the distribution of Italian films in the United States, and the president of Lux Film, Renato Gualino, was its managing director. IFE had an office in New York where it facilitated contracts and stored, edited, and subtitled films for the American market (*Motion Picture Herald* 1952, 35).

Of course, a large reason for the popularity of Italian cinema, alongside its critical merits, was the perceived sexual content and attractive female actresses who would later become stars in the United States. A notable early film that received a sexualized marketing campaign was Giuseppe De Santis's *Riso amaro* (1949), starring Silvana Mangano and produced by Lux Film. The film, about the plight of rice workers in Northern Italy, was marketed heavily around the sexuality of Mangano, whose scantily clad figure was prominently featured in promotional material. Another marketing campaign devised by IFE to help promote Italian film in the United States was a brochure outlining popular Italian actresses and their film credits, body measurements, and how to pronounce their names – and "when in doubt," the brochure advised, "pronounce it Bella Bella" (*Film Bulletin* 1954, 19).

In Canada, film distribution has always been tied to the United States and was treated as part of the domestic market by the American industry. However, in terms of international film distribution, it was difficult and expensive for Canadian exhibitors to get access to Italian films through distributors in New York, and instead diasporic exhibitors created new channels of distribution. While there were urban audiences in places like Toronto interested in viewing films from the great Italian neorealist directors, a larger audience for Italian films was the diasporic audience. Although this audience also existed in the United States, American film distributors seemed to be more interested in appealing to urban audiences. In Canada, on the other hand, Italian-language film distributors focused more on the newly arrived post–Second World War Italian immigrants who were eager to view films directly from Italy and were able to do so without English subtitles. This could be because distributors in Canada in many cases were part of the diasporic community themselves.

Canada's Unique Italian Cinema Cultures

The unique Italian-language cinema culture of Canada compared to the United States was largely based on different immigration patterns between the two countries. In Canada, Italians tended to stay in the country on a temporary basis because both the Canadian and Italian governments discouraged permanent settlement (Harney 1979). It was not until after the Second World War that permanent Italian settlement increased greatly in the country. This was because the Canadian government changed immigration policies after the war due to lobbying from business and industry groups to help contribute to expanding the Canadian economy. A sizable percentage of these new immigrants were Italian, and they played a significant role in the construction industry, particularly in urban centres. There are clear differences between the degree of integration and diasporic ties of earlier and later generations of Italians in Canada. The new wave of immigrants in the 1950s was more assertive in maintaining its ethnic differences and was sometimes at odds with the older generation over cultural heritage and distinctiveness (Di Giacomo 2011). Postwar Italian immigrants created ways to keep their language and cultural practices. Diasporic media such as Italian films at community theatres were important to many of these new immigrants and helped to create profitable businesses as well.

Starting in the 1950s, Italian-language theatres began to appear in Canadian cities. One of the first of these theatres was the Studio, which opened in 1951 as an art house theatre specializing in internationally produced films. The Studio was located in Toronto's historic Little Italy and close to the University of Toronto. The *Toronto Star* reported that the theatre opened with an Italian film, which the newspaper called *This Woman Is Mine*, starring Elli Parvo (Whittaker 1951, 8).[2] When the Studio first opened, it attempted to attract University of Toronto students interested in European art house cinema. The school's student newspaper, the *Varsity*, regularly promoted the theatre through its "Critic in the Dark" column. Despite this promotion, by the late 1950s the paper reported that the Studio now only ran second- and third-rate Italian films that no longer had English subtitles, and rarely screened films that were of interest to the film society at the university (Green 1957; Wilson 1958).

Most of the other theatres in the city screening Italian films were also generally catering to a popular Italian-Canadian audience rather than patrons interested in art house cinema, which was not profitable in Toronto. The University of Toronto's *Varsity* newspaper reported that this was partly due to the failure of the Towne theatre, one of Toronto's first art house cinemas, which had a colossal flop when it screened *Ladri di biciclette*. After that failure, the *Varsity* reported that European films needed to run twice as long as Hollywood films to be considered a financial success (Green 1957, 5). The newspaper also reported that European art house cinema was not often screened because it was expensive and difficult to get from distributors in New York. The film critics at the *Varsity* pointed out that the only European films to be regularly screened in the city were on the Italian circuit, but only occasionally were subtitled films screened. For example, when the Pylon theatre screened Fellini's *I vitelloni*, it was reported with excitement in the *Varsity* that the film had English subtitles. However, this excitement did not necessarily translate into more art house cinema at the Pylon. In fact, the owner of the Pylon theatre that same year was quoted in the *Toronto Star* as saying that 99 per cent of their audience were members of the Italian diaspora with only 1 per cent being University of Toronto students (*Toronto Star* 1959, 3).

Rocco Mastrangelo (1933–2021) was the first of the newly arrived Italian immigrants to get involved with the importing and screening of Italian films. Mastrangelo arrived in Toronto in 1957 and quickly became a successful presence in College Street's Little Italy with a variety of profitable businesses. In the 1960s, he purchased the Pylon, operated the Radio City, and started the Radio City Film Exchange. He also ran the Vogue in suburban Port Credit and operated a distribution office in Montreal. Until the 1980s, Radio City Film Exchange supplied films to Italian communities in numerous cities across Canada and even in the United States. Mastrangelo's film exchange provided older movie titles to local multicultural television broadcasters and eventually transferred these films to video for home viewing, importing new tapes and discs to rent and sell even after his theatres closed. The focus of his distribution circuit was largely popular and un-subtitled films that were likely not intended for North American distribution. In an interview in 2011, Mastrangelo said he tried to screen films from Pasolini, Fellini, and Antonioni but received criticism from his working-class Italian-Canadian audience. Some did not understand these films, while others did not want to watch "serious" films because of the struggles of daily life and instead preferred comedies and lighter fare (Ricci 2011), not unlike working-class audiences in Italy (Treveri Gennari et al. 2020).

The Rocco Mastrangelo Italian Cinema Collection

Over a span of three years, from 2015 to 2018, Media Commons Archives at the University of Toronto Libraries acquired a large collection of audiovisual material from Rocco Mastrangelo. Now referred to as the Rocco Mastrangelo Italian Cinema Collection, it consisted of two separate donations. An initial donation of 3,700 video masters, high-resolution copies on professional video formats that were used to create copies for home viewing, and over 5,000 reels of 35mm film from his Toronto, Ontario, office was made in 2015. A later accrual in 2018 contained an additional 3,000 video masters and over 4,000 reels of 35mm film from a separate office in Montreal, Quebec. The film reels are all from distribution prints that had been shown publicly in Canada, and the video masters are transfers from distribution prints. The prints from the Toronto office date primarily from the late 1960s through to the early 1980s, while those from Montreal are from roughly the mid-1950s to the early 1970s. Altogether, the films from both donations make up an estimated 1,500 titles with approximately 4,000 titles on multi-tape video masters. Almost all are Italian-language features, but the collection also includes a number of trailers, short subjects, and newsreels. There is potential overlap between the film and video master titles that remains to be explored.

The Rocco Mastrangelo Italian Cinema Collection is still being processed by archivists. As an archival acquisition, it raises some conservation challenges. Prior to being donated, both sets of video masters had been stored in offices, however, due to their size and quantity, the films were stored in the basements of buildings owned by Mastrangelo. Sadly, the films in Toronto were subjected to water leaks and minor flooding, concrete dust, temperature fluctuations, and high humidity. These conditions have led to problems with dirt and contributed to the colour fading and warping and brittleness that accompanies the loss of moisture in the film base. Mould is present on a considerable number of reels. Often this is very mild, but on occasion the mould can be severe and as a consequence the film must be destroyed. Fortunately, there are many titles in good condition, and there has been no evidence of water damage on the films from Montreal.

Both as individual films and as a collection these materials hold a tremendous amount of archival value and can provide insights into the cinema-going habits of Italian diasporic communities in Canada during these decades. The collection is heavy on popular entertainment. Comedies starring Totò (*Il coraggio*, 1955; *Totò contro Maciste*, 1962) and Franco Franchi (*Due mafiosi contro Al Capone*, 1966; *Paolo il freddo*, 1974; *Il sogno di Zorro*, 1975) feature prominently, as do Westerns with Franco Nero (*Django*, 1966; *L'uomo, l'orgoglio, la vendetta*, 1967) and sex comedies with Edwige Fenech (*La soldatessa alle grandi manovre*, 1978; *La poliziotta a New York*, 1981). None of the films processed to date contain English subtitles. The absence of subtitles implies a viewership with a functional knowledge of Italian, and the selection of films from popular genres suggest a committed interest in Italian popular culture. Together these details indicate that the films were not intended for a broader audience.

To date, no Fellini titles have been found among the film prints. However, there are several in the video masters, including *Lo sceicco bianco* (1952), *I vitelloni* (1953), *La strada* (1954), *La dolce vita* (1960), *Boccaccio '70* (1962), *8½* (1963), *Amarcord* (1973), and *La città delle donne* (1980). The presence of these titles suggests that Mastrangelo had access to prints of these films at some point. Their absence in the film prints show that "art films" and popular cinema were treated differently by Mastrangelo's businesses and underline the positioning of the Italian diasporic communities as his primary customer base.

In addition to the collection of titles, the physical objects themselves provide clues to the films' histories and their screenings. Many reels have their original provincial censorship board band, which notes the original title, language, total reel count, country of origin, distributor exchange, production on code rating, and provincial certificate number. On occasion, the censor bands contain further information, such as theatres where the film played, dates of the film's censorship approval, and handwritten projectionist notes. Earlier films contain an embossed provincial censor stamp within the image near the head and tail of each reel. Some of these have multiple stamps from different provincial censorship boards. Later films, typically those from the early 1980s, have a sticker with the board name and censor number on the leader before or after the image. The shipping cases containing the prints offer potentially valuable information in labels that indicate the delivery companies used, dates, theatre names and addresses, theatre manager or projectionist names, and sometimes any fees associated with shipment or screening.

The films carry on them the traces of this activity. Scratches and other forms of damage are relatively common. In some cases these are a minor detraction, in others the damage may require serious intervention. Some films have had their head and tail leaders replaced with those from a different film.³ Many films have multiple sets of platter splices at the head and tail of each reel indicating they were assembled and disassembled onto large platters for projection several times. These splices are often messy and poorly executed.⁴ While platter projection systems are fairly modern, the films in this collection frequently also have more than one set of cue marks for older multi-projector systems.⁵ Like the platter splices, many of these are crudely and carelessly done. This sheds light on both the projection set-up of the theatres showing Mastrangelo films and their projectionists. The presence of both additional cue marks and platter splices on the same print provides a glimpse into the storied history many of these prints went through in their active lives.

As these films have transitioned from being distribution prints to archival materials, this information takes on new significance. It allows scholars to situate a particular print at a specific place and time. This changes the role of film prints in historical research, and it is no longer just a distribution print. Film archivists frequently draw a distinction between the content of a film, as an abstract creative or intellectual entity, the various ways it can be embodied, and the particular form that it takes in an individual object. Seen in this light, a film print becomes a unique physical object that links scholars in the present to the equally unique circumstances of identifiable screenings in the past, opening the door to a more technically and materially informed historical scholarship.⁶ In turn this emphasizes the importance of maintaining archival film materials, as they provide something extra and special that gets lost when research is done with digital versions alone, while providing an impetus for closer collaboration between archivists and scholars.

Distribution of Fellini's Films in Canada

In addition to addressing the material history of Fellini's films through assessing the Rocco Mastrangelo Italian Cinema Collection, we also want to explore how these films circulated in Canada. As Richard Maltby (2011) argued, to understand the totality of cinema history we need to include exhibition data. Following Jessica's previous newspaper research protocols (Whitehead 2020), we consulted newspaper databases – Newspapers.com, ProQuest Historical Newspapers, and the University of Toronto's *Varsity* student newspaper – that published information on international films that were not often found in mainstream newspapers. We tracked premier dates, locations, and the trajectory of each film. Films in Canada generally (but not always) premiered in Toronto, with Montreal, Ottawa, Vancouver, and sometimes even the border city of Windsor premiering films first (Whitehead 2020). Our research examined film advertisements and reviews to determine how these films travelled across Canada and how they were received in each location.

In Canada, unlike the more organized industry of international film distribution in the United States, it was film societies along with diasporic distributors like Rocco Mastrangelo that drove the grass-roots movement of Italian film distribution in the country. Film societies were an integral part of international film distribution in Canada, and these groups would pool resources together to rent prints and distribute them. Pat Thomson of the Toronto Film Society discussed in an interview for the Picture Pioneer Archive how difficult it was to run the national network of film societies. Because she was based in Toronto, it was often her role to obtain expensive prints from New York and organize the schedule for these film prints to fly across the country. Volunteer members of film societies would wait at airports, sometimes overnight during snowstorms, to obtain and pass off prints to the next city (Whitehead, Moore, and Copeland 2017). The president of the Vancouver Film Society, John Hunter, also noted that the impetus behind film societies was to screen international films that had not been released commercially in Canada (*The Province* 1958, 32). It was through these networks that many of Fellini's early films were screened. Because of the nature of these societies, their screenings were not always advertised in newspapers, but their yearly schedule was usually advertised in newspapers in Vancouver and Ottawa and could also sometimes be found in the *Varsity* student newspaper. It is also notable that it was out of the film society movement that many popular film festivals emerged.

La strada (1954) was the first of Fellini's films to receive widespread distribution in North America. It opened in Toronto first in August 1956 before screening in both Montreal and Vancouver in the fall of that same year. The film was not screened in Windsor until a full year later. Most of the coverage focused on its award-winning status. Many film critics praised the film and reported that it was an unforgettable cinematic experience, although some reviews noted that the film was unusual and highlighted that Giulietta Masina was not a typical "sexy" Italian actress. Despite the good reviews the film proved to be another failure for the Towne theatre, and theatre manager Barney Simons said in an interview published in the *Toronto Star* that patrons did not want to see films like *La strada* (Johnson 1959, 15). The film did screen across Canada in both the 1950s and 1960s, however, and it was screened again in the late 1950s at Mastrangelo's Radio City theatre, indicating that this film was able to appeal to both audiences.

I vitelloni (1953), despite being released in Europe before *La strada*, did not reach Canada until 1958. It was the film society network that first brought the film to Canada with the Vancouver Film Society, screening *I vitelloni* as part of their 1958–9 season, although the film was misidentified as being directed by Visconti in Vancouver's *The Province* newspaper. It also was screened in Regina, Saskatchewan, for the Regina Film Society in November 1958, indicating that the print may have been part of the film society network. It was also screened as part of the Ottawa Film Society's 1959–60 program in October 1959. It finally officially opened in Toronto at the Kent theatre in December 1959, with famous Canadian film critic and historian Gerald Pratley (1959) lamenting that it took six years to screen in Toronto after showing at the Venice Film Festival. It had only previously played in the city in a special screening for the University of Toronto's Film Society in February 1959 at the theatre located at the Royal Ontario Museum as well as at the Pylon theatre in January 1959, both screenings being reported in the *Varsity* but not in other mainstream newspapers. It does not seem to have been screened in Montreal until the 1960s. In Windsor, there was an advertisement for a screening in the nearby town of Sarnia at a local resident's house in 1960 as part of a film society series. It did finally screen in Windsor theatres in 1964 for an Italian programming night at the Park theatre.

La dolce vita (1960) received the most press and widest release of any other Fellini film to date. With *La dolce vita*, Fellini became part of mainstream film coverage with gossip reported in newspapers accompanied by larger film ads. The film had its Canadian premiere at the Capitol theatre in Windsor, Ontario, in July 1961. As mentioned above, because of Windsor's border town status, the smaller city sometimes premiered films in Canada. It then opened in Vancouver and then Montreal as part of the film festival circuit, and finally came to Toronto in August 1961. In Toronto, it opened at the more mainstream Tivoli theatre and proved extremely popular, running until September. It also played for one night at Ottawa's Nelson theatre in October 1961. Much of the newspaper coverage focused on the celebrities in the film, how controversial the film was with both the Catholic Church and the Italian aristocracy, and how much it made at the box office in Europe and South America. One of the repeated gossip items published in several Canadian newspapers was that an Italian aristocrat had challenged Fellini to a duel when the film premiered in Milan. Despite the film's popularity, the *Varsity* newspaper published a scathing review critiquing Fellini for catering to mainstream audiences (Thomas 1961).

It is clear from the Canadian media coverage that by the 1960s Fellini had become a brand unto himself with many editorials, interviews, and articles focused on his unique film style and eccentric persona. Fellini was a fascinating figure to Canadian reporters, and his celebrity status in the United States also garnered interest. In 1969, the *Toronto Star* published a report from Shari Steiner, who had been sent to Rome to interview Fellini on the set of *Fellini Satyricon*. In the piece, Fellini is depicted as an almost bipolar figure whose emotions change at the drop of a hat. His strange behaviour and his obsession with his work is noted throughout the article. He disagreed vehemently with Steiner's characterization that he had moved away from realism, with Steiner reporting that he "gestured compactly with a hand cutting down like a guillotine" after she asked her question. He is quoted as saying the following:

> For an artist everything he does is reality. It ... it doesn't exist this kind of division. We are put into a big mess of a world, and we have the wrong idea to call something real, another unreal. It's because we're sick. We have divided things in a very silly way. What is more real than dreams for example? They are much more real because they are the expression of something deeper ... An artist is obliged to live in the imagination. For him reality is imagination. So I don't find any difference between *Vitelloni* and *Dolce Vita* [sic]. (Steiner 1969, 43)

Steiner's piece exemplifies Fellini's unique status as an artistic director who was able to get media attention through his ability to capture reporters' interest. Steiner ends the interview by asking him, "You love faces, don't you?" and ever the playful interview subject, Fellini responded, "Your face ... Sure I love faces," before grinning and walking back to his set (Steiner 1969, 43).

Fellini Satyricon (1969) continued to receive mainstream press coverage with many articles published about Fellini and the strangeness of the film in the lead up to its Canadian release. It opened in Montreal in May 1970, then shortly after in Toronto in June, and July in Vancouver as part of the Don Barnes Varsity Theatre Film Festival. It did not play in Ottawa until February 1971 and then was released in Windsor in April of that year. In Toronto, it opened at the mainstream York theatre and received wide coverage and advertising. The reviews in the Toronto and Vancouver papers were generally positive with critics focusing on the bizarre and perverse nature of the film. Martin Knelman in the *Globe and Mail* wrote that the film was fantastic and described the experience of watching it as akin to having "someone else's dreams piped into your head" (1970, 25). This positive reception was not the case everywhere, however, and in Montreal the film critic for *The Gazette*, Herbert Aronoff (1970), wrote that the film was an utter failure with tired images and a dull story. Despite this negative review, the film still made headlines and contributed to the mystique surrounding Fellini's persona and films in North America that helped to make him mainstream.

Conclusions

Italian film distribution was distinctive in Canada because it was driven by grass-roots movements. This was because many art house Italian films, such as *Ladri di biciclette* and even *La strada*, were not profitable at the box office and were also expensive to rent from distributors in New York. Fellini had a unique place in North American film culture, and unlike many other Italian directors in the Canadian market his later films received wider releases. His films were also occasionally screened for the diasporic community alongside the Canadian audience. By catering to a more mainstream audience in *La dolce vita*, Fellini was able to become a new type of international film-maker in Canada – one that was popular. Because of his celebrity status, his films went from being relegated to the art house film society network to more mainstream distribution.

In Canada, Italian film was treated differently than in the United States, and the great Italian directors did not have the same cultural cachet. While Italian film was a profitable business in the urban United States, and Italian Films Export had offices in New York City to facilitate Italian film distribution for the American market, this did not always extend to Canada. Instead, it was un-subtitled Italian films that were likely not originally intended for North American distribution that made up a substantial portion of the Italian films screened in Canada. This was because of the very engaged postwar Italian audience who was interested in maintaining cultural ties through consuming popular Italian-language media and not as interested in art house cinema.

The Rocco Mastrangelo Italian Cinema Collection also demonstrates that Italian art house cinema was treated differently in Canada in terms of availability and distribution practices. None of Fellini's films have been found among the film reels, but some of his films are in the video master collection indicating that Mastrangelo did have access to them at some point. Most of the films in the collection are comedies, melodramas, and Italian Westerns that appealed to the working-class diasporic audience, although Fellini was able to appeal to a more mainstream audience, which is a large part of his legacy in North America. His unique cultural status allowed him to be accepted by diverse audiences. Like Martin Scorsese wrote, he became his own film genre, and he was able to transcend the problems associated with traditional Italian art house distribution. He came a long way from the days of being misidentified as Visconti when *I vitelloni* was first screened in Vancouver.

NOTES

1 For more on Fellini's influence on Canadian film-makers, see the chapters collected in the first section of this volume.
2 Both the *Toronto Star* and the *Globe and Mail* identified the opening film as *This Woman Is Mine*. Neither paper reported on the director of the film, but the *Toronto Star* reported that the film featured "a new Italian Glamour Girl Elli Parvo" and that the film had English subtitles. It appears this film was *Desiderio*, released in 1946 and directed by Marcello Pagliero and Roberto Rossellini (uncredited). In the United States, the film was released as *Woman*, so it is likely the same film.
3 Leaders are the sections of the film before and after the image that allow the film to be handled without undue risk to the content. Leaders typically include identifying information and a countdown at the head.
4 In modern projection systems, all the reels of a film are assembled together on a large horizontal disc from which the film is fed to the projector. To use this equipment, head and tail leaders need to be removed and the reels spliced together and assembled.
5 Prior to the use of platter projection systems, each film reel would be projected individually. This required two separate projectors, with the projectionist alternating between them at the end of each reel for continuous and uninterrupted presentation. Cue marks are the indicators in the upper-right corner of the image shortly before the end of the reel. These tell the projectionist when to start and switch over (i.e., change over) between projectors during the screening.
6 This distinction comes from the Functional Requirements for Bibliographic Records, a conceptual model of the information universe developed by the library science community (IFLA Study Group on the Functional Requirements for Bibliographic Records 1998). Distinguishing entities at different levels of abstraction allows connections to be drawn between different objects and for individual items to be understood within the context of all of the items related to a title.

REFERENCES

Aronoff, Herbert. 1970. "Tired Images, Dull Story; *Fellini Satyricon* Fails." *The Gazette* (Montreal), 16 May, 42.

Brennan, Nathaniel. 2011. "Marketing Meaning, Branding Neorealism: Advertising and Promoting Italian Cinema in Postwar America." In *Global Neorealism: The Transnational History of a Film Style*, edited by Saverio Giovacchini and Robert Sklar, 87–102. Jackson: University Press of Mississippi.

Di Giacomo, Michael. 2011. "Identity and Change: The Story of the Italian-Canadian Pentecostal Community." *Canadian Journal of Pentecostal-Charismatic Christianity* 2, no. 1: 83–130. http://journal.twu.ca/index.php/CJPC/article/view/40.

Film Bulletin. 1954. "Roman Beauties Stunt." 31 May 1954, 19.

Green, Guy. 1957. "Toronto Closed City." *Varsity*, 14 March, 5.

Harney, Robert F. 1979. *Italians in Canada*. Toronto: Multicultural History Society of Ontario.

IFLA Study Group on the Functional Requirements for Bibliographic Records. 1998. *Functional Requirements for Bibliographic Records: Final Report*. Munich: Saur.

Johnson, Ron. 1959. "Show Time: Nothing like Mediocrity." *Toronto Star*, 29 May, 15.

Knelman, Martin. 1970. "The *Satyricon*: Fellini's Pagan Circus." *Globe and Mail*, 6 June, 25.

Maltby, Richard. 2011. "New Cinema Histories." In *Explorations in New Cinema History: Approaches and Case Studies*, edited by Richard Maltby, Daniel Biltereyst, and Philippe Meers, 3–40. Hoboken, NJ: Wiley-Blackwell.

Motion Picture Herald. 1952. "Italian Salute." 4 October 1952, 24–35.

Pratley, Gerald. 1959. "The Wastrels' Finally Come to Town." *Toronto Star*, 22 December, 21.

The Province. 1958. "French Film Launches Stellar Society Year." 13 September 1958, 32.

Ricci, Dalma. 2011. "Scenes, Nostalgia and the Integration of Italians in Toronto's Little Italy." *Local Film Cultures: Toronto* (blog). https://localfilmculturestoronto.wordpress.com/sites-and-scenes-2/scenes-out-of-site/scenes-nostalgia-and-the-integration-of-italians-in-torontos-little-italy.

Scorsese, Martin. 2021. "Il Maestro: Federico Fellini and the Lost Magic of Cinema." *Harper's Magazine*, March, 25–32. https://harpers.org/archive/2021/03/il-maestro-federico-fellini-martin-scorsese.

Sklar, Robert. 2011. "'The Exalted Spirit of the Actual': James Agee, Critic and Filmmaker, and the US Response to Neorealism." In *Global Neorealism: The Transnational History of a Film Style*, edited by Saverio Giovacchini and Robert Sklar, 71–86. Jackson: University Press of Mississippi.

Steiner, Shari. 1969. "Face to Face with the Formidable Frederico Fellini." *Toronto Star*, 22 March, 43.

Thomas, Ralph. "*La Dolce Vita* Not a Sample of the Best of Fellini." *Varsity*, 29 September, 48.
Toronto Star. 1959. "Newcomers Invest in Foreign Films." 4 July 1959, 3.
Treveri Gennari, Daniela, Catherine O'Rawe, Danielle Hipkins, Silvia Dibeltulo, and Sarah Culhane. 2020. *Italian Cinema Audiences: Histories and Memories of Cinema-Going in Post-War Italy*. London: Bloomsbury.
Whitehead, Jessica L. 2020. "Comparison of Canadian Urban and Small-Town Exhibition Practices 1914–1929." *TMG Journal for Media History* 23, no. 1–2: 1–32. https://doi.org/10.18146/tmg.648.
Whitehead, Jessica L., Paul Moore, and Stacy Copeland. 2017. *Pioneer Archive*. Film.
Whittaker, Herbert. 1951. "Show Business." *Toronto Star*, 5 October, 8.
Wilson, Warren. 1958. "Worth Watching." *Varsity*, 4 March, 5.

"Women with Big Breasts and Wide Hips": Fellini's Cinema in Chinese Media Essays

GAOHENG ZHANG

The year 2020 marked the fiftieth anniversary of the establishment of diplomatic relations between Italy and the People's Republic of China. Among the many celebratory events scheduled on this occasion, most of which moved online owing to the COVID-19 pandemic, a centennial retrospective of Federico Fellini's films was staged in a select group of Chinese cities in late 2020, after restrictions on public gatherings had been lifted. Presented with a Chinese-English-Italian title, "费德里科•费里尼百年诞辰纪念放映/Ciao! Federico Fellini: A Retrospective/Ciao, Federico! Rassegna retrospettiva per il centenario di Federico Fellini," the retrospective included nineteen feature films and three short films in Beijing in October and November of 2020. In November and December, eight representative works were screened in Suzhou, Changsha, Xiamen, Chengdu, and Guangzhou. In addition, the 2020 editions of the Hong Kong International Film Festival (HKIFF) and the Shanghai International Film Festival (SIFF) dedicated special programming to review well-known films from Fellini's oeuvre, and the Italian Cultural Institute (ICI) in Shanghai staged an "Italian Film Retrospective" in both Shanghai and Hangzhou, where several classic Fellini films were included in the program (妖灵妖 2020). Although other public retrospectives of Fellini's films had taken place in China before, the centenary retrospective was the first-ever large-scale tour of his films, and Italian cinema in general, in the country.

News releases from the sponsors in the nine Chinese cities praised Fellini's achievements in several ways. China Film Archive (CFA), the main Chinese organizer, published an English-language communiqué announcing the "luxurious programming list [that] includes 19 most important films of Fellini representing different periods of his whole creation and 3 shorts related to his art to review the magnificent cinema life of this genius in the world film history" (CFA 2020). The ICI in Beijing highlighted Fellini's capacity to create wonder (*stupore*) and to strike (*folgorare*) the viewer, unsettling their narrative expectations. According to 保利文化集团 (Poly Culture Group), the Chinese company that hosted the centennial in its own movie theatres in the five-city tour, "China and Italy are working together to promote cultural exchanges between the East and the West through the medium of film" (Poly 2020). In anticipation of its special programming, the HKIFF restated Fellini's aesthetics and legacy: "His phantasmagorical works, which were at once humorous, imaginative and bewildering, leave behind a legacy that continues to awe and inspire generations of filmmakers" (HKIFF 2020).[1] Chinese and Italian official organizers, as well as their commercial partners, exalted Fellini's cinema and the Italian lifestyle or creativity that it represented. These announcements refer to the impressive range of films screened (CFA), the Italian-Chinese friendship (Poly), and Fellini's style and influence (ICI and HKIFF), thereby offering us an overview of the emphases in public communications by officialdom of various stripes.[2]

What these news releases fail to capture is how culture actually works on the ground: What themes and critical dimensions of Fellini's films did Chinese viewers most care about? How did they discuss Fellini's cinema? In this chapter, I examine extended Fellini-focused media essays that were prompted by the centenary, in order to paint a portrait of the popular reception and appreciation of an Italian filmmaker in contemporary China. Gleaned from online sources, this body of primary resources targets the educated but non-expert Chinese public in the country's vibrant digital culture.[3] My analysis reveals aspects of Fellini-related transculturation in China at the level of media narratives, which register concrete deliberations about approaching Fellini, and which significantly mould public opinion of the director.

A quick word on transculturation, or transculturality. In the introduction to a large-scale edited volume titled *Engaging Transculturality*, the editors deploy Giorgio Agamben's concept of "urphenomenon" to argue that transculturation, insofar as it focuses on analyzing connectivity and the lack thereof, is a critical tool that is less marked by the historical concreteness of its content than by its paradigmatic and ontological significance (Abu-Er-Rub et al. 2019). According to them, transculturality is also a fundamental social process which, by reference to Gilles Deleuze and Félix Guattari's theorizing of rhizome, privileges an understanding of interactions among cultural entities in multilayered, non-linear, and transgressive ways. In so doing, the authors have expanded the intellectual horizons of the initially anthropological concept of transculturation as understood by the forerunners Fernando

Ortiz and Mary Louise Pratt (Abu-Er-Rub et al. 2019, xxiv–xxvii).[4] In plain terms, *Engaging Transculturality* reiterates a somewhat prosaic point: while mundane human practices and narratives always have some transcultural dimension when engaged in cultural interactions, much previous scholarship works within the framework of a specific single nation-state, ethnic group, or cultural entity. To me, the critical matter which this volume's introduction does not explicitly articulate, but which is an essential component of the research agenda it proposes, concerns the role that a transcultural lens can play in shedding light on how culture truly functions. My chapter analyzes several interfaces where such cross-cultural transactions occur to pinpoint transcultural moments of Fellini in China.

Domestication and Remix of Western Criticism

Inspired by the centenary, two Chinese media essays (电影杂志 MOVIE 2020; 导管 directube 2020) introduce Fellini's cinema by way of excerpting from the film-maker's own interpretations of his artistic vision – *Fare un film* (1980), which enjoys a Chinese translation, and *Il libro dei sogni/The Book of Dreams* (2007/2019), which the Chinese cineastes know through an English translation (although a Chinese edition exists). The title of the first Chinese edition of the former work is taken from a French documentary film about Fellini, *Fellini, je suis un grand menteur/Fellini: I'm a Born Liar* (2002), thereby accentuating the drama of reality and make-believe in his cinematic world.[5] *Il libro dei sogni* then increases the value of viewing Fellini's films in relation to his dreams and desires. The essays are exemplary Chinese reinterpretations of Fellini through an established analytical arsenal encouraged by Fellini himself and perfected by critics in the West.

Indeed, Chinese essayists extensively draw from Western criticism on Fellini, partially thanks to Chinese translations of relevant critical literature and possibly to seminars on Fellini held by academics in China. Thus, traces of the auteur theory, neorealism, (Carl Jung's) psychoanalysis, and Marxian cultural materialism intermix in this body of texts. The author of an extended essay begins by following a well-established convention in the West in viewing Fellini's career in three stages from the perspective of his film narratives and artistry. According to this account, while narratives were still traceable in his 1950s films, beginning in the 1960s, the plots veered towards a "mosaics" style, showing a tendency of "anti-story." This experimentation progressed during the 1970s so that his films became dreams and his cinema was transformed into "pure cinema. To better contextualize the upcoming centenary screenings for the audience, the author then refers to Italy's socio-historical conditions, the country's film industry, Pier Paolo Pasolini's assessment of *La dolce vita* (1960), Fellini's friendship with Marcello Mastroianni, and anecdotes from Fellini's private life – in particular, his parents' troubled relationship and his own relationship with wife and actor Giulietta Masina. At the end of the article, the Chinese translation of *I, Fellini* by Charlotte Chandler (1995) is proposed for further reading. Notably, the author frames the discussion of Italy's film industry and trends through the rise and fall of neorealism. When examining Italian cinema, many Chinese cineastes mention this subject; for example, one article cites André Bazin's theorization of neorealism to argue, somewhat imprecisely, that the use of non-professional actors and an improvised script characterize Fellini's oeuvre. A video report of the Changsha retrospective provides a similar account of Fellini's career, stressing, however, the roles that the circus and clowns have played in his work. Another commentary uses the terms "Fellinian" and "Felliniesque" in English (上海国际电影节 2020) in describing Fellini's style, which crucially means the use of the "metacinema" in such films as *8 ½* (1963), a topic which was discussed during a symposium held by the Shanghai Film Museum in 2013. The "Fellinian" style was also explored from multiple angles in a seminar held in Hangzhou in 2020 during the Italian film week organized there. Among the diverse topics discussed, the seminar leader explained the figures of the clown, the nomad, and the mentally ill by way of Jungian archetypes, an interpretation said to be preferred by Fellini himself, as well as Michel Foucault's studies on madness.[6] While not manifestly original in their presentations of Fellini from a (Western) critical standpoint, these essays render a composite and contemporary picture of his art for the appreciating Chinese readers.

Even specific topics which are often not considered fundamental to his work, but which were previously examined by Western critics, surface in the essays. One author (李啸洋 2020) argues that full of "luxury, hedonism, passion, romanticism, and imagination," the Fellinian style is quintessentially baroque. According to this author, the obscurity of *8 ½* owes not only to the director's intentional ambiguity but also to his baroque style that requires a "rediscovery through senses." An essay (Anonymous 2020b) notes the male bonding and collaboration between Fellini and Mastroianni, who is reputed to be the filmmaker's "muse." This concern with Italian masculinity is associated with fashion in another essay (黑择明 2020b), which praises Fellini's sartorial choices throughout his career and the fashionable men and women seen in *La dolce vita*, a time when the Milan-based ready-to-wear model was emerging.[7] While it is difficult to ascertain whether these observations made by Chinese authors were directly influenced by previous Western reception of Fellini, it is clear that the interpretive repertoire is broadly Western in origin.

Appreciation and Scepticism with Chinese Characteristics

Apart from the reading and retelling of Western interpretations of Fellini in Chinese media essays, another way of transculturating Fellini's films is to make connections with the authors' Chinese milieus. There are several trends in the media essays in this regard. Sharpened by highly subjective and idiosyncratic interpretations of Fellini's films, some cineastes transpose his cinematic world to their own lives and surroundings. After viewing *La strada* (1954) during Beijing's centennial retrospective, an author captured the film's impact on his or her interiority by describing the journey home. The street or path in the film's title parallels the walk "on the streets of the capital city for half an hour in the early-winter coldness, reluctantly and slowly, towards home" (得得 2020). On another night, the same author first saw *Le notti di Cabiria* (1957) and then went to see a Beijing opera on Su Shi, a famed Song dynasty poet, whose life was underscored by government office held in various cities outside of his hometown and by a prolonged period of political exile. "In a state of trance, the two things unexpectedly created a queer adhesion," the author claims, referring to the positive attitudes that both the prostitute in Fellini's film and the exiled poet held firm in challenging times of their lives. Presumably, this understanding mirrors the author's own life circumstances (as a migrant or an exile?) at the time of writing and life as a journey, as the essay ends with an emphasis on the "healing" and "consolatory" power of great art.

This article (得得 2020) also exhibits another trend, which is to put Fellini's cinema into dialogue with some aspect of ancient Chinese or "Eastern" cultural and philosophical traditions. Such cultural operations are often applied to specific fundamental but cognitively difficult dimensions in Fellini appreciation. In this instance, the author 得得 compares *Amarcord* (1973) to 清明上河圖/*Along the River During the Qingming Festival*, a well-known Northern Song dynasty (960–1127) scroll painting by Zhang Zeduan, which, in a long sequence of scenes, depicts the landscape and the daily life of residents in the capital city, Bianjing (today's Kaifeng). This comparison abandons the afore-mentioned Western description of the Fellinian style as mosaics, which is indeed a Western art, in favour of a Chinese scroll painting, which is typically viewed by gradually unfolding from the right-hand end of the scroll, thereby resembling the viewing of a film as it progresses in time. This example shows the Chinese author's attempt to give shape to the episodic structure of the film and to highlight its anthropological quality.

Focusing on Fellini's dreams, another thorny issue for popular comprehension, the author of an essay (黑择明 2020b) argues that, for the director, reality and dream are not dichotomous, "just like the implied meaning of the Chinese proverb 庄周梦蝶 (zhuang zhou meng die)." The popular proverb, known as "Zhuangzi's Butterfly Dream," originates from "齊物論/The Adjustment of Controversies," a chapter in the book 莊子/Zhuangzi, with the title bearing the philosopher's name (350–250 BCE). In the story, Zhuangzi slept and dreamed that he was a butterfly flying about and enjoying himself. When waking up, he mused: "I did not know whether it had formerly been Zhou [i.e., Zhuangzi] dreaming that he was a butterfly, or it was now a butterfly dreaming that it was Zhou" (Legge 2006). The conclusion of this paragraph asks us to consider "the Transformation of Things." In referencing this proverb when explaining Fellini's view of dreams, the essayist implies that the empirical reality and the dream state become fused into a succession of transformations between the two elements. Instead of using the Western concept of "stream of consciousness," which is a more mainstream way of describing Fellini's method, this author points to a rich ancient Chinese tradition of dream interpretation.

China's deep repertoire for dream and divination interpretation also functions in a surprising way as the end paragraph of this essay makes a bold claim. Because Fellini was an avid Jung follower and because Jungian analysis had an intimate relationship with Eastern philosophy and Tibetan Buddhism, by practising mediumship, which is depicted in *Giulietta degli spiriti* (1965), Fellini resorted to the book 易经/*I Ching* (or *Book of Changes*), an ancient Chinese divination manual (1000–750 BCE), to help "him determine the births of many of the greatest films in the history of cinema" (黑择明 2020b.). The author does not support this interpretation of his film-making practice with concrete examples, thereby lacking persuasion. But the author is referring to Fellini's various mentions of *I Ching* in *Il libro dei sogni*. For example, Fellini draws Hexagram 6 訟 (*song*, arguing) in describing his feeling of "depression, distrust, sense of guilt, inertia, humiliation, and disdain for myself" (2019, 267). Perhaps the clearest example of Fellini attempting to relate *I Ching* to his film-making experience is a diagram dated 13 August 1974, which depicts a transformation from Hexagram 23 剝 (*bo*, stripping) to Hexagram 27 頤 (*yi*, swallowing). Interpreting this "oracle" on a previous dream as a change from "crumbling" to "nourishment," Fellini seems to try to calm his doubts about finishing *Il Casanova di Federico*

Fellini (1976) (Fellini 2019, 269).[8] Generally, Fellini uses *I Ching* to interpret his dreams and states of mind, occasionally in relation to specific film projects. Such use is utilitarian in that he does not probe any deeper meaning of the Chinese signs, and it is also not related to any Chinese tradition, for his interpretation is purely based on the non-historical abstraction of the hexagrams. Moreover, *I Ching* should not be confused with the various ancient Chinese classics in dream interpretation.[9] Nevertheless, the essay remains a key example of how Chinese reviewers occasionally go to great lengths to make Fellini comprehensible and endearing to their Chinese readers.

Finally, some media essays refute a scepticism about the potential irrelevance of Fellini's cinema to contemporary Chinese audiences because it may be seen as dated and untimely. In essays published in 北京青年报/*Beijing Youth Daily*, an influential newspaper in the capital city, and in 澎湃新闻/*The Paper*, a popular Shanghai-based digital newspaper, the author Mei 梅生 provides three reasons for the unease that some of today's viewers may feel when encountering Fellini's films. First, Mei points out that Fellini's cinematic vision, which paints "the picture of a secular and even vulgar carnival in the human world," is in stark contrast to the "otherworldliness" of the works by "masters enjoying the same status as Fellini" (梅生 2020), including Robert Bresson, Ingmar Bergman, and Andrej Tarkovskij. Mei seems to imply that the Chinese viewers may be offended by the Fellinian "clowns of every stripe, women with big breasts and wide hips, noises, and chimerical scenes" (梅生 2020). Mei attributes the second reason of commonly-experienced disquiet to Fellini's later films with no apparent storytelling; instead, they "use fantasies and dreams to decorate carnivalesque spectacles, resulting in seemingly chaotic mazes" (梅生 2021). Here, Mei refers to the impenetrable and inscrutable quality of Fellini's films that turned away impatient Chinese audiences, because too much interpretive energy seems to be required of them to overcome obstacles ranging from the geographical, temporal, and cultural distances to the director's artistic innovations and auteurist idiosyncrasies. The final point that Mei makes is relevant to viewing behaviours: in the 1970s and 1980s, television replaced cinema in the West as a dominant audio-visual media; and in the 2010s, compared to European films, the "microcinema" – essentially short video clips or films – as well as Hollywood, Japanese, and Korean movies, became increasingly popular for Chinese audiences. Similar to how the previous circumstance sealed the demise of a popular fan base of Fellini's films in the West, the current conditions in China do not favour a growth of followers of his cinema.

In order to recover a sense of wonder and appreciation for Fellini, Mei resorts to the aforementioned established approaches and themes imported from the West and domesticated at home, in particular the biographical approach and the interpretation of dreams. Similarly, an essay on 文艺报, a well-respected Beijing-based literature and art newspaper, provides counterarguments to the discourse on untimeliness by suggesting ways to appreciate the wall painting-like quality of Fellini's films, his love for "women with big breasts and wide hips" (黑择明 2020a) and the act of whispering in his work which resonates with our inner voices.[10] While the detailed arguments should not deter us here, we can observe this author's return to an established Western canon in asserting the positive aspects of Fellini's oeuvre. The sway that the cultural transfer from Western criticism to Chinese appreciation of Fellini's art exerts over these media essays is long-lasting. The authors evidently take delight in being the ambassadors of transculturation in the enterprise of translating Fellini in China.

"Women with Big Breasts and Wide Hips"

In this chapter, I have offered two main vantage points from which to probe the modus operandi of Fellini's transculturation in Chinese digital reading culture. The diffusion of Western criticism of Fellini in China is pervasive. Although the use of this critical tradition in its specifics may not always be accurate, in the main it has helped promote an up-to-date and variegated understanding of Fellini's art. Frequent references are also made to concepts, stories, and phenomena that are dear to, or disliked by, the popular Chinese sensibility. While the quality of these media essays varies, they help us understand the thematic and methodological milieu in which the non-expert, but educated moviegoers, interpret and care about Fellini's cinema.

Adopting a framework that examines transcultural details and operations at the level of media essays, I contend that it is difficult to determine whether this case study shows the West's epistemological domination over Chinese reviewers in interpreting Fellini. When *La strada* leads the viewers to contemplate their own personal paths, and when the commentators believe that *I Ching* manifests itself in Fellini's artistic deliberations, agency overwhelms any foreordained Western interpretive frame of Fellini. Meanwhile, many Chinese essayists keep returning to, for example, Jungian analysis and film theories, which make them feel empowered as users of an interpretive repertoire that not any single country, but humanity, has achieved.

What we can be certain of in this regard is transculturality enacted from a China versus West standpoint, as opposed to, say, a "trans-Asia" method of comparing China with other Asian countries vis-à-vis Fellini.[11] The media essays analyzed do not refer to other Asian understandings of Fellini; very rarely do they compare Fellini to Asian film-makers, except for, occasionally, the Japanese director Akira Kurosawa. The China versus West perspective may also help explain why such films as *Satyricon* (1969), *Roma* (1972), and *Il Casanova di Federico Fellini* (1976) were not included in any centenary screenings in China. Among other things, these films' dosage of Western libertinism, decadence, and "alternative" sexualities may have been too heavy for the eyes of the Chinese organizers. Curiously, the centenary retrospectives in Tokyo and in Seoul also omitted these films. In East Asia, Hong Kong showed *Roma*, and Taiwan alone staged a retrospective of the complete twenty-four Fellini films within the Taipei Golden Horse Film Festival and Awards.[12]

Perhaps the Chinese expression used to describe Fellini's women, which appears twice in the above-mentioned essays, best encapsulates some of the critical cultural issues that I explored in this chapter.[13] Possibly mirroring the Italian term *maggiorata* (a well-endowed woman), "women with big breasts and wide hips" is the conventional translation of 丰乳肥臀 (*fengru feitun*), famously coined by the writer and awardee of the Nobel Prize in Literature, Mo Yan (born in 1955), and used as the title of his 1995 novel. While the reader of this and other novels of Mo, which often feature women, can make up their own minds about the meaning of this expression for each specific female character, unconventionality is arguably a quality of these women that most would agree upon. While not all of Mo's female characters, and for that matter Fellini's women, fit the bodily type that this expression conveys, they are "lush" (*feng*) and "fertile" (*fei*) in personalities and experiences, quite unlike the typical women either exalted or criticized by Chinese patriarchy. For the Chinese reviewers and essayists surveyed here, Fellini's cinema is like these women and exhibits a much-valued and coveted quality of abundance and opulence, which enriches the cinematic art, grows our interpretive ability with the help of Western film criticism, and prods us to dream for ourselves.

NOTES

1 Anonymous, "Ciao! Federico Fellini"; Anonymous, "Ciao! Federico Fellini: A Retrospective," Istituto Italiano di Cultura in Pechino, 29 November 2020, https://iicpechino.esteri.it/iic_pechino/it/gli_eventi/calendario

/ciao-federico-fellini-a-retrospective.html; Anonymous, "Fellini Film Festival Hosted by Poly Film Opened in Guangzhou," Poly.com.cn, 24 December 2020, www.poly.com.cn/polyen/s/1883-6536-25081.html; and Anonymous, "HKIFF Celebrates FELLINI 100 with a Full Retrospective, Exhibition and Concert," Hong Kong International Film Festival, 18 June 2020, www.hkiff.org.hk/news/detail?id=461.

2 Film criticism on Fellini's cinema has also been on the rise. Thanks to the integrated database of 中国知网/China National Knowledge Infrastructure (CNKI), the largest of its kind for Chinese-language academic resources, we can be precise about the trajectory of film criticism of Fellini in China in academic journals, by inputting the Chinese transliteration of Fellini – "费里尼" – in the subject line of the search engine. In total, there are fourteen academic essays that were published in the 1980s and 1990s, several of which are translations of Western criticism, and there are twenty-three Chinese-authored papers that were published in the 2000s and 2010s. There are also numerous Chinese translations of Western-language books on Fellini that were published, some of which are mentioned in subsequent notes.

3 This chapter contains certain internet resources that have no author information, or their author names are obviously pseudonyms. Such phenomena are not unusual in the Chinese mediascape. The articles I have selected for the chapter reflect public opinion in this milieu.

4 For Italian migrant communities in some parts of the world and their transculturality, see Burdett et al. (2020).

5 For Chinese translations of *Fare un film*, see Fellini, *Wo shi shuohuang zhe* (2000) and Fellini, *Pai dianying* (2017). For the Chinese translation of *Il libro dei sogni*, see Fellini, *Meng shu* (2014).

6 For a full discussion of these topics, see Anonymous (2020a), "'百年费里尼'"; 肥内 (2020), "笔记费里尼"; 上海国际电影节 (2020), "向大师致敬 | 共同迎接他的百年诞辰华丽狂欢节"; federicofellini.info (2013), "FELLINI IN CINA—费里尼在中国"; and 大屋顶 (2021), "现场 | 费里尼是一个孤独的游历者." For an article that is focused on Fellini's personal life and his art, see 夏姑娘 (2021), "成为费里尼." For the Chinese edition of Chandler's book, see Chandler, *Wo, Fei li ni* (2006).

7 For Western criticisms on the topics and approaches analyzed in this section, see Burke et al. (2020).

8 For other examples of *I Ching* hexagrams, see Fellini, *The Book of Dreams* (2019, 276, 346, 349, 370, 394, 416). Fellini also conceives the number combination 69 in the form of what he calls the "sign of Destiny," 太极 (*taiji*, roughly, "Supreme Ultimate"), which *I Ching* also explains, when contemplating a scene of death by hanging and choking (148–9).

9 On the ancient Chinese tradition of dream interpretation, see Liu 刘文英 and Cao 曹田玉 (2023).
10 Hei Zeming 黑择明 (2020a), "纪念费德里科•费里尼诞辰百年: 打开费里尼," 文艺报, 10 February 2020, www.chinawriter.com.cn/n1/2020/0210/c404005-31578968.html.
11 On such a method, see Iwabuchi, "Trans-Asia as Method."
12 For Tokyo, see @fellinifilmfes, 28 July 2020, Twitter, accessed 13 July 2021, https://twitter.com/fellinifilmfes/status/1287975397884223488; for Seoul, see Istituto Italiano di Cultura in Seoul, "Retrospettiva Fellini," 29 July 2020, https://iicseoul.esteri.it/iic_seoul/it/gli_eventi/calendario/2020/07/coming-soon-retrospettiva-fellini.html; for Hong Kong, see Anonymous, "HKIFF Celebrates FELLINI 100 with a Full Retrospective, Exhibition and Concert"; and for Taiwan, see Anonymous, "金馬經典影展: 費里尼 100," 13 May 2020, www.goldenhorse.org.tw/news/detail/1375. For a Weibo post speculating why *Satyricon* was not selected for the Beijing retrospective, see Weibo.com, accessed 13 July 2021, https://weibo.com/1404675262/JykgoligY.
13 For examples of the expression used in Sina Weibo on the occasion of the centennial screenings, see Weibo.com, accessed 11 July 2021, https://weibo.com/2655058447/IB8FH5WmZ?refer_flag=1001030103, and Weibo.com, accessed 11 July 2021, https://weibo.com/1684737447/JpFaW2iA6.

REFERENCES

Abu-Er-Rub, Laila, Christiane Brosius, Sebastian Meurer, Diamiantis Panagiotopoulos, and Susan Richter. 2019. "Introduction." In *Engaging Transculturality. Concepts, Key Terms, Case Studies*, edited by Laila Abu-Er-Rub, Christiane Brosius, Sebastian Meurer, Diamiantis Panagiotopoulos, and Susan Richter, 1–17. London: Routledge.

Anonymous. 2020a. "'百年费里尼' 电影导航：一本正经地拍摄不正经." 星期五文艺, 23 July. https://zhuanlan.zhihu.com/p/163329360.

— 2020b. "费德里科•费里尼: 许多耳熟能详的经典作品, 都在他的影子里." 上海文艺, 31 July. www.shwenyi.com.cn/renda/2012shwl/n/zt/u1ai6263145.html.

Burdett, Charles, Loredana Polezzi, and Barbara Spadaro. 2020. *Transcultural Italies: Mobilities, Memory and Translation*. Liverpool: Liverpool University Press.

Burke, Frank, Marguerite Waller, and Marita Gubareva, eds. 2020. *A Companion to Federico Fellini*. Hoboken, NJ and Chichester, West Sussex, UK: Wiley Blackwell.

Chandler, Charlotte. 1995. *I, Fellini*. New York: Random House.

– 2006. *Wo, Fei li ni* 我, 费里尼 (I, Fellini). Translated by Huang Cuihua 黄翠华. Guilin: Guangxi shifan daxue chubanshe 广西师范大学出版社.

China Film Archive. 2020. "Ciao! Federico Fellini: A Retrospective." Last modified 1 May 2020. www.cfa.org.cn/cfaen/highlights/index.html?articleKey=4acdd5993b4d4aba9269aed2c3c2d8a3.

大屋顶. 2021. "现场 | 费里尼是一个孤独的游历者." NetEase, Last accessed 11 July 2021. www.163.com/dy/article/FRJGTO6B0514BVS4.html.

导管directube. 2020. "绘画巨匠费里尼." 20 January. https://mp.weixin.qq.com/s/MC6HpWyg4EM2cqkD5fRbXg.

电影杂志 MOVIE. 2020. "康妮, "费里尼的4部电影笔记." 18 October. https://mp.weixin.qq.com/s/tV5ka1p5Vk9rZhGQTu4-bg.

得得. 2020. "守护天使的秘密通道布满了全宇宙." 北京青年报, 4 December. http://epaper.ynet.com/images/2020-12/04/B02/bjbqb20201204B02.pdf.

Federicofellini.info. 2013. "FELLINI IN CINA – 费里尼在中国." 16 December. www.federicofellini.info/federico-fellini-in-cina-费里尼在中国/.

肥内. 2020. "笔记费里尼." 掘火档案. 19 January. www.digforfire.net/?p=17661.

Fellini, Federico. 1980. *Fare un film*. Turin: Einaudi.

– 2007. *Il libro dei sogni*. Edited by Tullio Kezich and Vittorio Boarini with a contribution by Vincenzo Mollica. Milan: Rizzoli.

– 2019. *The Book of Dreams*. Edited by Sergio Toffetti. Translated by Aaron Maines and David Stanton. New York: Rizzoli.

– 2014. *Meng shu* 梦书 (Il libro dei sogni). Translated by He Yan 何演 and Zhang Xiaoling 张晓玲. Beijing: Zhongyang bianyi chubanshe 中央编译出版社.

– 2017. *Pai dianying* 拍电影 (Fare un film). Translated by Ni Anyu 倪安宇. Haikou: Nanhai chuban gongsi 南海出版公司.

– 2000. *Wo shi shuohuang zhe* 我是说谎者 (Fare un film). Translated by Ni Anyu 倪安宇. Beijing: Sanlian shudian 三联书店.

黑择明 2020a. "纪念费德里科•费里尼诞辰百年: 打开费里尼." 文艺报, 10 February. www.chinawriter.com.cn/n1/2020/0210/c404005-31578968.html.

– 2020b. "费里尼的梦与梦书." 北京青年报, 23 October. http://epaper.ynet.com/html/2020-10/23/content_364607.htm?div=0.

Hong Kong International Film Festival. 2020. "HKIFF celebrates FELLINI 100 with a full retrospective, exhibition and concert." Last modified 18 June 2020. www.hkiff.org.hk/news/detail?id=461.

Iwabuchi, Koichi. 2019. "Trans-Asia as Method: A Collaborative and Dialogic Project in a Globalized World." In *Trans-Asia as Method: Theory and Practices*, edited by Jeroen de Floet, Yiu Fai Chow, and Gladys Pak Lei Chong, 25–41. London: Rowman & Littlefield International.

Legge, James. 2006. *Chinese Text Project*. https://ctext.org/zhuangzi/adjustment-of-controversies?filter=430901.

Liu, Wenying 刘文英, and Cao Tianyu 曹田玉. 2003. *Meng yu zhongguo wenhua* 梦与中国文化 [Dream and Chinese Culture]. Beijing: Renmin chubanshe 人民出版社.

梅生. 2020. "被嫌弃的费里尼: 大师已经不合时宜?" 北京青年报, 14 August. http://epaper.ynet.com/html/2020-08/14/content_359256.htm?div=-1.

— 2021. "费里尼的梦境, 是否已然褪去动人的色彩?," 澎湃新闻, 20 January. https://m.thepaper.cn/rss_newsDetail_10866984?from.

Poly. 2020. "Fellini Film Festival Hosted by Poly Film Opened in Guangzhou." Last modified 24 December 2020. www.poly.com.cn/polyen/s/1883-6536-25081.html.

上海国际电影节. 2020. "向大师致敬 | 共同迎接他的百年诞辰华丽狂欢节." Weixin, 20 January. https://mp.weixin.qq.com/s?__biz=MjM5MTY3NTkyMQ==&mid=2653764116&idx=1&sn=d5d169b7481583ea47ed8a31a5f295c2&chksm=bd68796a8a1ff07cc57841f2a54c0a5b4776fab82a4fb79dbb2e7b27cf11a3db68c47c792965&token=689340843&lang=zh_CN#rd.

Shanghai International Film Festival. 2020. "向大师致敬 | 费德里科•费里尼." Last modified 20 July. www.siff.com/content?aid=import-cms-4203.

夏姑娘. 2021. "成为费里尼." 澎湃新闻, 6 April. www.thepaper.cn/newsDetail_forward_12058218.

妖灵妖. 2020. "孙瑜的《大路》放了, 那费里尼的《大路》......" 电影山海经, Weixin, 18 September. https://mp.weixin.qq.com/s?__biz=MzA3Mzc4MzI3MA==&mid=2650210504&idx=1&sn=f81e655a849c45385ca7d44844bf9a75&chksm=870a6241b07deb57dc8569fd66193a48fc905e341dec496f869f6c186ddd1b0694eee2149e40#rd.

Contributors

Frank Burke has published five books on Fellini, most recently *A Companion to Federico Fellini* with Marguerite Waller and Marita Gubareva (2020) and *Fellini's Films and Commercials: From Postwar to Postmodern* (2020). He has provided the audio commentary for the Criterion releases of *Il bidone, Roma,* and *Amarcord*. He has co-edited with Amy Hough-Dugdale and Marita Gubareva a collection of essays on Tonino Guerra in the *Journal of Italian Cinema and Media* (2023). In addition to his work on Fellini, Burke has published on numerous Italian directors, various American directors, horror cinema, experimental cinema, peplum film, and Canadian cinema.

Atom Egoyan is one of the most celebrated contemporary film-makers on the international scene. His body of work – which includes theatre, music, and art installations – delves into issues of memory, displacement, and the impact of technology and media on modern life. Egoyan has won numerous prizes at international film festivals, including the Grand Prix and International Critics Awards from the Cannes Film Festival, two Academy Award® nominations, and numerous other honours. His most acclaimed works include *Ararat* (2002) and *The Sweet Hereafter* (1997).

Manuela Gieri is Associate Professor of Film, Television and Photography Studies at the University of Basilicata. Gieri has published extensively in learned journals; she has edited volumes on Italian cinema and on theatre, as well as on Italian cinema and ecology. Her main research interests are Italian and world film history, Federico Fellini, Luigi Pirandello, contemporary Italian women's writing, and new historiography; in recent years much of her research efforts have been focused on film and ecology. Among her works, the following deserve special mention:

La Strada: Federico Fellini, Director (1990), *Contemporary Italian Filmmaking: Strategies of Subversion* (1995), *Cinema. Dalle origini allo studio system (1895–1945)* (2009), *Twentieth-Century Italian Filmmakers* (2020), and *Basilicata and Southern Italy between Film and Ecology* (2023).

Shelleen Greene is Associate Professor of Cinema and Media Studies in the Department of Film, Television and Digital Media at the University of California, Los Angeles. She was the 2020–1 Fulbright Distinguished Chair at the University of Leeds. Her book, *Equivocal Subjects: Between Italy and Africa* (2012), examines discourses of race and nation in the Italian cinema. Her recent work appears in *Italian Culture*, *Feminist Media Histories*, *California Italian Studies*, the *African American Review*, and the *Journal of Italian Cinema and Media Studies*.

Russell J.A. Kilbourn is Professor of English and Film Studies at Wilfrid Laurier University. Dr. Kilbourn publishes on memory, critical posthumanism, Italian film, and postsecular cinema. His books include *Feminist Posthumanism in Contemporary Science Fiction Film and Media: From* Annihilation *to* High Life *and Beyond* (2023); *The Cinema of Paolo Sorrentino: Commitment to Style* (2020); *W.G. Sebald's Postsecular Redemption: Catastrophe with Spectator* (2018); *The Memory Effect: The Remediation of Memory in Literature and Film* (2013); and *Cinema, Memory, Modernity: The Representation of Memory from the Art Film to Transnational Cinema* (2010).

Eleonora Lima is a Research Fellow in Digital Humanities at Trinity College Dublin, where she works on the EU-funded project Knowledge Technologies for Democracy (KT4D). She has published on the interconnection between literature, science, and technology, as well as on Italian cinema, and visual arts, often with an eye to gender issues. She is currently working on the first comprehensive history of computing in Italian literature, provisionally titled *Narrating Computing: Italian Authors Write Computer Culture*. Her monograph dedicated to the impact of information technology on the work of Italo Calvino and Paolo Volponi was published in 2020.

Giovanna Caterina Lisena is a PhD candidate in the Department of Italian Studies at the University of Toronto. Lisena's doctoral thesis focuses on Giulietta Masina's career through the media ("Masina beyond Fellini: Theatre, Radio, Cinema and Television," under the supervision of Professor Alberto Zambenedetti). In addition to Italian cinema, her interests include Italian pedagogy, Italian-Canadian studies, the history of the Italian language, Italian linguistics, dialectology, the Middle Ages, the contemporary (1800–present), Italian literature and culture, and Italian religious texts.

Guy Maddin has directed twelve feature-length movies, including *The Forbidden Room* (2015), *My Winnipeg* (2007), and *The Saddest Music in the World* (2003), and innumerable short films. He has mounted over seventy performances of his films around the world, featuring the live elements of orchestra, sound effects, singing, and narration. Maddin won the National Society of Film Critics Award for Best Experimental Film for both *Archangel* (1991) and *The Heart of the World* (2001). He has received many other awards, including the Telluride Silver Medal in 1995, the San Francisco International Film Festival's Persistence of Vision Award in 2006, and an Emmy for his ballet film *Dracula – Pages from a Virgin's Diary* (2002). *The Green Fog,* co-directed with Galen Johnson and Evan Johnson, won the Los Angeles Film Critics Association Best Experimental Film Award for 2018. Maddin is the author of three books, and his writing has appeared in *Lapham's Quarterly*, *The Believer*, *Cinema Scope*, *Sight and Sound*, and *Film Comment*. He is a member of the Order of Canada and the Order of Manitoba.

Gaia Malnati is a PhD candidate in the Centre for Comparative Literature and the Jewish Studies Collaborative Program at the University of Toronto. She received her MA in Comparative Literature from the University of Bologna. Malnati's research spans the fields of voice studies, oral literature, oral history, and public theory. She is currently writing a doctoral thesis on Holocaust poetry and testimony, as well as migrant songs and life stories. In 2020 she published her article "Variantistica e semantica nella poesia giovanile di Leonard Cohen," in which she analysed unedited variants of Leonard Cohen's early poetry through seminal works on oral literature. In her day-to-day life, Malnati wonders at the myriad ways people tell their stories, modulating meaning through their voices. She is actively engaged in the Toronto community, volunteering at a Community Art Centre, where she can chat with participants and hear about the stories that are hidden behind their artworks.

Marco Malvestio is Assistant Professor of Comparative Literature at the University of Padua. He was a Postdoctoral Fellow at the University of Toronto and an EU Marie Skłodowska-Curie Postdoctoral Fellow at the University of Padua and at the University of North Carolina at Chapel Hill. His publications include *The Conflict Revisited: The Second World War in Post-Postmodern Fiction* (2021) and *Raccontare la fine* *del mondo: Fantascienza e Antropocene* (2021). He co-edited *Vecchi maestri e nuovi mostri: Tendenze e prospettive della narrativa horror all'inizio del nuovo millennio* with Valentina Sturli (2019), *Italian Gothic: An Edinburgh Companion* with Stefano Serafini (2023), and *Italian Science Fiction and the Environmental Humanities* with Emiliano Guaraldo and Daniel A. Finch-Race (2023).

Deepa Mehta is an Oscar-nominated (*Water*) transnational film-maker whose work is celebrated on an international scale. Her emotionally resonating, award-winning films have played every major film festival, and many remain audience favourites. She is best known for her Elemental Trilogy: *Earth* (1996), *Fire* (1998), and *Water* (2005). Other films include *Bollywood/Hollywood* (2002), *Heaven on Earth* (2008), and the epic adaptation of *Midnight's Children* (2012) – Salman Rushdie's three-time Booker Prize winning novel.

Giuliana Minghelli is an independent scholar and photographer. She works on questions of history, ethics, and memory at the intersection of literature, cinema, and photography. She is the author of *In the Shadow of the Mammoth: Italo Svevo and the Emergence of Modernism* (2003) and *Landscape and Memory in Post-Fascist Italian Film: Cinema Year Zero* (2013). She edited *The Modern Image* (2009), and co-edited *Stillness in Motion: Italy, Photography and the Meanings of Modernity* with Sally Hill (2015). She is currently working on a book on postwar shame and on an essay film about the memory of Fascism, *Family Remains*.

Andrea Minuz is Full Professor of Film and Media Studies in the Department of Art History and Performing Arts, University of Rome "La Sapienza." He is the author of *La Shoah e la cultura visuale. Cinema, memoria, spazio pubblico* (The Holocaust and visual culture: Film, memory, the public sphere) (2010); *Viaggio al termine dell'Italia. Fellini politico* (2012), which was published in English translation as *Political Fellini: Journey to the End of Italy* (2015); and *Fellini, Roma* (2019).

Andrew A. Monti is Assistant Professor of Strategic Communications at Trent University Durham, where he leads an Insight Development Grant funded research project on digital propaganda and directs undergraduate courses and professional placements in the Communications Program. Before academia, Monti worked as an assistant at the Legislative Assembly of Ontario, as a TV news reporter at Omni Television, and as an analyst at the Italian Trade Agency's Toronto Office. He holds a BSc in International Economics and Management from Bocconi

University, an MA in Communication from York University, and a PhD in Communication and Culture from Toronto Metropolitan University.

Emiliano Morreale is Full Professor at Sapienza University of Rome. His principal research interest lies in Italian cinema from 1945 on, with reference to relationships between film and society, in a cultural and gender perspective. Among his books are *L'invenzione della nostalgia. Il vintage nel cinema italiano e oltre* (2009), *Così piangevano. Il cinema melò nell'Italia degli anni '50* (2011), *Cinema d'autore degli anni sessanta* (2011), and *La mafia immaginaria. 70 anni di Cosa Nostra al cinema* (2020). He co-edited the anthology *Racconti di cinema* with M. Pierini (2014). He has been the Italian correspondent for *Cahiers du cinéma*, a member of the selection board of the Turin Film Festival and the Venice Film Festival, and a curator for the Cineteca Nazionale.

Federico Pacchioni is Full Professor of Italian Studies at Chapman University, where he holds the Musco Endowed Chair and serves as the founding director of the Ferrucci Institute for Italian Experience and Research. He has authored numerous publications and has lectured nationally and internationally about the subjects of his books, which include *Inspiring Fellini: Literary Collaborations behind the Scenes* (2014), *A History of Italian Cinema* co-authored with Peter Bondanella (2017), *The Image of the Puppet in Italian Theater, Literature and Film* (2020 and 2022), and *Southwest of Italy: Stanzas for a Travel Memoir* (2022).

Veronica Pravadelli is Professor of Film Studies at Roma Tre University. She has been Visiting Professor at Brown University and New York University. Her research blends historical and theoretical frameworks and has focused on Italian post-neorealist cinema, Hollywood cinema, women's cinema, and gender studies. Her publications include *Dal classico al postmoderno al global* (2019), *Contemporary Women's Cinema, Global Scenarios and Transnational Contexts* (2017), *Classic Hollywood: Lifestyles and Film Styles of American Cinema, 1930–1960* (2015), *Le donne del cinema. Dive, registe, spettatrici* (2014), *Performance, Rewriting, Identity: Chantal Akerman's Postmodern Cinema* (2000), *Visconti a Volterra. La genesi di Vaghe stelle dell'Orsa...* (2000), and *Il cinema di Luchino Visconti* (2000).

Dishani Samarasinghe is a PhD student in communications at the Université du Québec à Montréal under the supervision of Professor Viva Paci. Her research focuses on the diversity of female bodies in mainstream American cinema of the 2020s. She has worked as an assistant in film-making workshops, film methodology courses, and in set design for theatres. She currently works as a teaching and research assistant on seminars and projects on history of cinema and documentary. She is a member of labdoc (Le laboratoire de recherche sur les pratiques audiovisuelles documentaires), RéQEF (Réseau Québécois en études féministes), and IREF (Institut de recherches et d'études féministes).

Eleonora Sartoni is Assistant Teaching Professor of Italian at Penn State. She received her PhD in Italian from Rutgers University (2020). Her research interests focus on urban studies, biopolitics, ecocriticism, cinema, and literature exploring the relationship between body, society, and space. She published the articles "*The Hawks and the Sparrows* and *Sacro GRA* as Peripatetic Analyses of Capitalist Society" in the *Journal of Italian Cinema & Media Studies* (2019) and "(*Mamma*) *Roma* between Archaic and Modern Italy" in *Senses of Cinema* (2015). She is also a contributor to the project Postcolonial Italy: Mapping Colonial Heritage.

Christina Stewart is a film and media archivist at Media Commons Archives, University of Toronto Libraries. A graduate of the L. Jeffrey Selznick School of Film Preservation at George Eastman Museum, she has worked with collections at George Eastman Museum, Northeast Historic Film, Canadian Filmmakers Distribution Centre, and Canadian National Exhibition Archives. She has taught film preservation workshops through provincial archival associations across Canada and in graduate programs at the University of Toronto and Toronto Metropolitan University. In 2016, Christina discovered *Secrets of the Night* (1924), a previously lost film directed by Herbert Blaché and released by Universal Studios.

Giacomo Tagliani is Associate Professor of Film and Media at the University of Modena and Reggio Emilia, Italy. He has taught and conducted research at the University of Palermo, the Filmuniversität "Konrad Wolf" Babelsberg, Dickinson College, and the California Institute of the Arts, among others. His research interests include Italian biopics and political cinema, the representation of materials, substances, and fuels in modern visual culture, and the theory and practice of sustainable media. His publications include *Estetiche della verità. Pasolini, Foucault, Petri* (2020), *Biografie della nazione. Vita, storia, politica nel biopic italiano* (2019), *Homeland. Paura e sicurezza nella Guerra al terrore* (2016), and *Lo spazio del reale nel cinema italiano* co-edited with R. Guerrini and F. Zucconi (2009).

Mirko Tavoni is Emeritus Professor of Italian Linguistics at the University of Pisa. He is the author of studies on Dante: *De vulgari eloquentia*, translator and commentator (2011 and 2017); *Qualche idea su Dante* (2015);

and *Dante e la dimensione visionaria fra medioevo e prima età moderna* with Bernhard Huss (2019). He has published on the history of linguistic ideas: *Latino, grammatica, volgare* (1984); *Italy and Europe in Renaissance Linguistics* (1996); and *Essays in Renaissance Linguistics* (in press); and has published for Dante Search, digital resources for literary studies (https://dantesearch.dantenetwork.it/). He is a full member of the Accademia della Crusca.

Marina Vargau, PhD in Comparative Literature and Cinema at the University of Montreal, is a Lecturer in Italian Studies and Film Studies at the same university. Her research interests include Italian cinema, the relationship between arts and media, the representations of cities in cinema and literature. Her first book, *Romarcord. Flânerie, spectacle et mémoire dans la Rome de Federico Fellini* (2021), focuses on the cinematic poetics of Rome in Federico Fellini's films and its effect in cinema and literature. On Fellini, she has also authored book chapters in *Federico Fellini: Riprese, riletture, (re) visioni* (2016) and *The Cinema of Ettore Scola* (2020), and articles in the *Journal of Italian Cinema & Media Studies, Mnemosyne o la costruzione del senso, Images secondes, PRISMI*, and *Art Research Journal*. She is currently working on a book about the *8 ½* effect.

Jessica Leonora Whitehead is Assistant Professor in the Communication and Languages Department at Cape Breton University. Her scholarly work includes exploring local and diasporic filmgoing and Federico Fellini's impact on global cinema. Additionally, she co-leads the CHiMERA project, an initiative digitizing Canadian film and media periodicals to create an online archive dedicated to the exhibition and business history of cinema in Canada. Her writing has appeared in the *Canadian Journal of Film Studies, Transformative Works and Cultures, TMG Journal for Media History*, and *Italian Canadiana*, and she has published chapters in the books *Rural Cinema Exhibition and Audiences in a Global Context* (2018), *Handbook of Ethnic Media in Canada* (2023), and *Mapping Movie Magazines* (2020). She was awarded the University of Toronto's Superior Teaching Award and Excellence through Innovation Award, and was appointed a Teaching Chair at CBU for her work with digital pedagogies.

Alberto Zambenedetti is Associate Professor in the Department of Italian Studies and the Cinema Studies Institute at the University of Toronto. He is the author of *Acting across Borders: Mobility and Identity in Italian Cinema* (2021), and the editor of *World Film Locations: Florence* (2014) and *World Film Locations: Cleveland* (2016). He also co-edited *Federico Fellini. Riprese, riletture, (re)visioni* (2016). His scholarship has appeared in journals such as *Annali d'Italianistica, Studies in European Cinema, Journal of Adaptation in Film and Performance, Short Film Studies*,

The Italianist, Quaderni d'Italianistica, The University of Toronto Quarterly, ACME, and *Space and Culture*. He has contributed essays to the home video releases of *Fire at Sea* (Gianfranco Rosi), *Dawson City: Frozen Time* (Bill Morrison), and *Fellini's Casanova* (Federico Fellini). His criticism is posted on *Gli Spietati* (www.spietati.it).

Ottavio Cirio Zanetti (1983–2020) was a film director, film critic, and photographer. He directed several documentaries for RAI and two prize-winning short films: *The Honey of Luxembourg* and *Sipario*. In 2015, he was invited to work with the photography team at the Hermitage Museum in St. Petersburg, and for seven years he wrote a weekly column of film criticism for the online magazine *InPiù*. He worked as a subject matter expert at the University of Roma Tre and authored two books: *Tre passi nel genio. Fellini tra fumetto, circo e varietà* (2020) and *300 dichiarazioni di amore al cinema. Racconti di film, registi, attori, sceneggiatori* (2021), which is a collection of his film reviews.

Gaoheng Zhang is Associate Professor of Italian Studies at the University of British Columbia. His first book, *Migration and the Media: Debating Chinese Migration to Italy, 1992–2012* (2019), is the first media and cultural study of the Chinese migration from both Italian and Chinese migrant perspectives. He is the co-editor of *Cultural Mobilities between China and Italy* (2023), which offers a critical analysis of global mobilities across China and Italy in modern history. His current book projects examine cultural representations and dynamics about Italy-China food and fashion mobilities that migration and tourism help deepen.

Index

Abbagnano, Nicola, 182
Adolphe, Hylette, 115
Adorno, Theodor, 101, 105
Agamben, Giorgio, 359
Age (Incrocci, Agenore), 40
Agee, James, 344
Agel, Jerome, 126n6
Agnew, John, 217
Aimée, Anouk, 234, 314
Alba, Tyto, 10, 168–71, 175n20; *Fellini en Roma*, 10, 168–9
Albert the Great, 155; *Liber de natura et origine animae*, 155
Alberti, Guido, 314
Aldouby, Hava, 236; *Federico Fellini: Painting in Film, Painting on Film*, 236
Alighieri, Dante, 8–10, 46, 144–8, 150, 154–5, 157nn3–4, 157nn7–9, 157n11, 158n16, 163, 174n8, 244, 310, 376; *Convivio*, 155; *Divina Commedia* (*Divine Comedy*), 144, 146, 155, 157n7, 174n8 (*Inferno*, 144, 148, 244, 310; *Paradiso*, 145; *Purgatorio*, 144, 174); *Vita nuova*, 145, 154–5, 157n4
Allen, Woody, 318n17; *Stardust Memories*, 318n17
Aloisi, Alessandra, 206

Alsop, Elizabeth, 289
Altman, Rick, 291
Alvaro, Corrado, 220, 227n16
Angelucci, Gianfranco, 59, 61
Anger, Kenneth, 127n11
Antonioni, Michelangelo, 101, 126n2, 127n11, 168, 347; *Blow-Up*, 126n2; *L'amore in città*, 33, 158n17
Araya, Zeudi, 121
Arbasino, Alberto, 181, 188n8
Argento, Dario, 202; *Profondo rosso*, 202, 203
Ariosto, Ludovico, 209
Aronoff, Herbert, 353
Astaire, Fred, 240
Asti, Adriana, 29
Attalo, 8, 33, 35n5, 38, 40, 42n3, 42n7
Aumont, Jacques, 236
Avedon, Richard, 116–17, 126nn4–5, 223; *Nothing Personal*, 116
Averty, Jean-Christophe, 126n2; *Soft Self-Portrait of Salvador Dali*,126n2
Avicenna (Ibn Sina), 155; *Liber de anima*, 155

Bach, Johann Sebastian, 182–4, 188n11; *Toccata and Fugue in D minor*, 183
Bachelard, Gaston, 47

Bachmann, Gideon, 126n2, 252n9; *Fellinikon* (*Ciao, Fellini!*), 126n2
Bachtin, Michail, 283n12, 302
Bacon, Francis, 5, 236
Bagdassarian, Serge,170
Bailey, David, 116
Baldan Bembo, Alberto,185
Baldwin, James, 116; *Nothing Personal*, 116
Bangerotti, Angelo, 93
Bardo Thodol (*Tibetan Book of the Dead, The*), 174n8
Barrymore Jr., John, 174n11
Barthes, Roland, 74, 86, 88, 102, 279, 288, 294; *Mythologies*, 102
Baudelaire, Charles, 34
Baudrillard, Jean, 12, 244, 282
Baudry, Jean-Louis, 107
Bava, Mario, 203–4; *Operazione paura*, 203
Bazin, André, 80, 92, 97n11, 108, 305, 312, 318n16
Beatles, the, 125, 223, 343
Beau Geste (Wellman, William A.), 303
Bene, Carmelo, 122–3, 127n11, 224; *Salomè*, 122–3, 125, 127n11, 224
Benedetti, Francesca, 29
Benigni, Roberto, 266, 282, 284n18
Benjamin, Walter, 222
Benzi, Titta (Luigi), 191
Bergman, Ingmar, 310, 326, 364; *Wild Strawberries*, 310–11, 313, 315, 318n17
Berlusconi, Silvio, 5, 35, 252n13, 252n15
Bernhard, Ernst, 56, 60, 145, 152, 154–5, 157n3, 231
Bertolucci, Bernardo, 192, 198, 199n15; *Il conformista*, 192, 199n15; *Novecento*, 198
Bertozzi, Marco, 6; *L'Italia di Fellini. Immagini, paesaggi, forme di vita*, 6

Betti, Liliana, 170
Biagi, Enzo, 148
Bing, Rudolph, 345
Bispuri, Ennio, 251n6, 253n18
Böcklin, Arnold, 206
Bolognini, Mauro, 168
Bond, Julian, 117
Bondanella, Peter, 166, 193, 271, 289–90
Bonzi, Leonardo, 220
Boorstin, Daniel J., 102, 110; *The Image: A Guide to Pseudo-Events in America*, 102, 110
Bordwell, David, 303, 312
Bosch, Hieronymus, 225, 263–4, 268n22
Boym, Svetlana, 242–3
Brennan, Nathaniel, 344
Bresson, Robert, 364
Brignone, Guido, 148; *Maciste all'inferno*, 148
Brooks, Peter, 228
Brown, Elspeth, 117
Brunetta, Gian Piero, 145, 165–6
Buñuel, Luis, 23
Burchiellaro, Giantito, 32
Burke, Frank, 6, 7, 120–1, 256, 289–90, 294, 296–7, 316, 318n23; *A Companion to Federico Fellini*, 6, 22; *Federico Fellini's Film and Commercials: From Postwar to Postmodern*, 7
Burroughs, William, 322
Burton, Tim, 168
Buzzati, Dino, 148, 151, 163, 167, 174n8, 203; *I misteri d'Italia*, 151; *I sette messaggeri*, 151; *Poema a fumetti*, 151, 167

Cabiria (Pastrone, Giovanni), 21
Calamai, Clara, 220
Callas, Maria, 343

Calvino, Italo, 146, 148, 163, 196–7, 207, 272
Camilletti, Fabio, 206
Campany, David, 74
Campbell, Naomi, 116
Caponetto, Rosetta Giuliani, 121
Caporale, Aristide, 304
Cappuccio, Eugenio, 175n22; *Fellini fine mai*, 175n22
Capucine (Lefebvre, Germaine Hélène Irène), 119
Carcano, Gianfilippo, 303
Cardinale, Claudia, 30, 235, 328
Cardone, Lucia, 106
Carrera, Alessandro, 6, 57, 174n12; *Fellini's Eternal Rome: Paganism and Christianity in the Films of Federico Fellini*, 6
Cartier-Bresson, Henri, 73–4, 91; *Image à la sauvette (Decisive Moment, The)*, 73
Casanova, Giacomo, 201, 204–8, 212
Casby, William, 117
Cassirer, Ernst, 47
Castañeda, Carlos, 40
Cataluccio, Francesco, 193
Cavara, Paolo, 221, 323; *Mondo cane*, 220–1, 323
Cavazzoni, Ermanno, 148, 150
Cavell, Stanley, 211
Cazzaniga, Dream, 116
Cazzaniga, Luigi, 124, 126n4
Ceruti, Giacomo, 206
Chandler, Charlotte, 61, 65nn16–17, 281, 361; *I, Fellini*, 65n16, 361; *The Ultimate Seduction*, 61
Chaplin, Charlie, 108, 275, 278, 283n9, 343
Cheddle, Janice, 116
Chiamenti, Massimiliano, 147
Chiesi, Roberto, 6, *8 ½ di Federico Fellini*, 6

Chion, Michel, 289, 291
Cinema Paradiso (Tornatore, Giuseppe), 17
Cixous, Hélène, 52; *The Laugh of the Medusa*, 52
Clouzot, Henri-George, 127n11
Conocchia, Mario, 314
Contini, Gianfranco, 151, 207; *Italie magique*, 151
Cooper, Gary, 303
Copioli, Rosita, 6, 210–1; *Il Casanova di Fellini: ieri e oggi 1976–2016*, 6
Corbucci, Sergio, 34; *Totò, Peppino e… la dolce vita*, 34
Corman, Roger, 203; *House of Usher*, 203
Cortese, Valentina, 29
Corvi, Lorenzo, 10, 167–8; *Il viaggio di G. Mastorna, esperimento di ricostruzione*, 10, 167–8
Costa, Antonio, 166
Croce, Benedetto, 9, 101; *Estetica*, 101
Cunningham, Beryl, 121
Cuny, Alain, 177, 184
Curti, Roberto, 204

Dalí, Salvador, 116, 223, 227n23
Dalla, Lucio, 244
Dallas, Ian, 315
Dalle Vacche, Angela, 21; *Diva: Defiance and Passion in Early Italian Cinema*, 21
D'Annunzio, Gabriele, 148, 157n11, 220, 227n16
Daumier, Honoré, 263, 268n22
Davis, Miles, 117
Davis Jr., Sammy, 117
d'Azeglio, Massimo, 206
de Carlo, Andrea, 173n1; *Yucatan*, 173n1
de Chirico, Giorgio, 148, 206, 236
de Chomón, Segundo, 148

De Filippo, Peppino, 34, 191, 277–8, 280, 284n13
De Laurentiis, Dino, 163–4, 174n11, 175n20, 218, 267n2
De Maistre, Xavier, 219; *Voyage autour de ma chambre*, 219
De Matteis, Stefano, 103–4
de Robespierre, Maximilien, 205, 213n3
De Santi, Pier Marco, 146; *Federico Fellini dai disegni ai film*, 146; *I disegni di Fellini*, 146
De Santis, Giuseppe, 345; *Riso amaro*, 345
De Sica, Vittorio, 21, 168, 173, 219, 276, 344–5; *Boccaccio '70*, 9, 34, 191, 276, 349; *Ladri di biciclette*, 344, 347, 354; *Sciuscià*, 344
de Toro, Alfonso, 173n4
de Toulouse-Lautrec, Henri, 236
de Vaucanson, Jacques, 210
Debord, Guy, 102, 110, 112n2, 130, 133–5, 245, 252n10, 268n4; *The Society of the Spectacle*, 102, 245
Decker, Jennifer, 170
Del Buono, Oreste, 196, 225
Deledda, Grazia, 220, 227n16
Deleuze, Gilles, 8, 47–9, 51, 57, 64, 305–6, 308, 311, 312, 318n16, 359; *Cinema 2*, 308, 312
Diderot, Denis, 205, 213n3
Dijon, Alain, 139
Disney, Walt, 39
Divine (Milstead, Harris Glenn), 322–3, 327–9, 331–2, 338, 339n5, 340n13
Django (Corbucci, Sergio), 349
Doane, Mary Ann, 288–9, 294, 296
Dockstader, Tod, 184
Dolar, Mladen, 288
Donati, Danilo, 32–3, 114
Dorigo, Francesco, 295

Dr. Butcher, M.D., (Girolami, Marino), 339n1
Due mafiosi contro Al Capone (Simonelli, Giorgio), 349
Dulac, Germaine, 106; *La souriante Mme Beudet*, 106–7
Dyer, Richard, 6, 103; *La Dolce Vita*, 6

Ebner, Michael, 140n5
Eco, Umberto, 29, 102, 105, 263–4, 271; *Apocalittici e integrati*, 102
Eger, Raymond, 203
Ekberg, Anita, 34, 39, 52, 110, 119, 130, 132–40, 191, 263, 277, 280, 282, 294, 326–8, 331
Enciclopédie de la Divination (Le Scouëzec, Gwenc'hlan, Larcher, Hubert, Alleau, René), 210
Engaging Transculturality (Abu-Er-Rub, Laila et al.), 359
Engels, Friedrich, 109
Ensor, James, 41

Fabbri, Paolo, 273–4
Falana, Lola, 121
Falk, Lee, 8, 34, 38–9
Fatty (Arbuckle, Roscoe), 275, 283n9
Feist, Felix, 21; *Deluge*, 21
Fellini, Federico, 3–13, 17, 19, 21–6, 30–5, 37–41, 42n3, 42n5, 42n11, 45–64, 64nn1–2, 64n7, 65nn12–13, 65nn17, 71–8, 80–2, 84–5, 87–8, 91–4, 96, 97n1, 100–11, 114–15, 118–24, 127n11, 130–9, 141n8, 144–8, 150–2, 154–155, 157nn4–5, 157n9, 158n17, 159n22, 162–72, 173n1, 173n3, 174nn8–9, 174n11–13, 175nn16–17, 175n20, 177, 179–81, 183, 185–6, 186nn1–2, 187n7, 188n9, 190–8, 198n4, 201–12, 213n9, 213n11, 214nn13–14, 216–22, 224–5, 226n1, 226n5, 226n8, 226nn10–11,

Index

227nn18–19, 227n22, 228n25, 228n27, 231–8, 238nn1–2, 240–50, 251n2, 251n5, 251n8, 252n9, 252n12, 252n15, 255–67, 267n2, 268nn7–8, 268n19, 268n22, 271–82, 283n6, 283n11, 284n12, 284nn17–18, 287–99, 300n21, 302–16, 317n1, 317n7, 322–3, 326–32, 338, 339n1, 340nn12–13, 343–4, 347, 349–54, 358–66, 367n2, 367n8; *8 ½*, 7,11, 17, 19–20, 46, 53, 144–5, 148, 154–5, 157n2, 157n4, 165–6, 173n1, 174n10, 190–1, 193, 198, 202, 216, 231–7, 238n2, 273, 276, 278, 302, 310–14, 317n5, 318n12, 318n17, 322, 328, 330, 332, 349, 361; *Agenzia matrimoniale*, 33, 158n17; *Amarcord*, 10, 26, 32–3, 38, 46, 56, 62, 148, 167, 190–8, 213n9, 216–17, 222, 258, 282, 303, 305–6, 308, 313, 315, 349, 362; *Boccaccio '70*, 9, 34, 191, 276, 349; *E la nave va (Ship Sails On, The)*, 166–7, 217, 255, 262–3, 307; *Fare un film (Making a Film)*, 61, 65n17, 272, 360; *Fellini: A Director's Notebook*, 12, 54, 163–4, 167–8, 170, 202, 217–8, 240, 264, 280–1, 288, 291–2, 294–5, 297; *Fellini Satyricon*, 9, 33–4, 114–15, 118–25, 126n2, 166–7, 184, 191, 193, 198n4, 202, 216, 218, 221, 224, 227, 231, 236–7, 280, 282, 322, 330, 332, 343–4, 353, 366; *Ginger e Fred*, 11–12, 34, 167, 240–1, 244–6, 252n9, 263–5; *Giulietta degli spiriti*, 46, 51–3, 63, 146, 151, 191, 193, 198n4, 203, 231, 236, 308, 322, 329, 363; *I clowns*, 12, 39, 54, 190, 192, 202, 216, 218, 240, 257, 264, 281, 288–9, 292–6, 308; *I vitelloni*, 12, 22, 33, 46, 72, 109, 166, 191, 201, 216, 273, 275, 282, 287–8, 290–2, 344, 347, 349, 352–3, 355; *Il bidone*, 46, 75–6, 101, 109; *Il Casanova di Federico Fellini*, 10, 32, 46, 166–7, 191, 201–2, 204–5, 212, 213, 236–7, 258, 282, 340, 343, 363, 366; *Il libro dei sogni (Book of Dreams)*, 8, 11, 17, 41, 45, 56–7, 61, 64, 65nn11–12, 146, 152, 154, 167, 168, 231–3, 235, 360, 363; *Il viaggio di G. Mastorna detto Fernet (Journey of G. Mastorna nicknamed Fernet, The)*, 10, 40, 42, 54, 56–7, 63–4, 120, 148, 150, 162–8, 170, 172, 173n1, 174n10, 190, 207, 218, 274, 291; *Intervista*, 12, 34, 38–9, 41, 46, 60, 158n17, 234, 263, 288, 290, 297, 300n21, 308; *L'amore in città*, 33, 158n17; *La città delle donne (City of Women)*, 11, 46, 52–3, 56, 64, 166, 201, 223, 231–5, 237–8, 238n2, 258–9, 262, 267, 310, 349; *La dolce vita*, 25–6, 34, 39, 49, 50, 52, 61, 71–3, 75, 80, 97n1, 100, 109–11, 118–19, 126, 136, 139, 144–6, 154, 157n4, 164, 166, 174n10, 177–8, 180, 182, 184–6, 196, 199n12, 216, 218–22, 224, 231, 260, 263, 276–8, 280, 282, 306, 326–8, 330–1, 344, 349, 352–4, 361; *La mia Rimini*, 190; *La strada*, 7, 24, 39, 46, 101, 109, 146, 179, 216, 273, 275, 344, 349, 351–2, 354, 362, 365; *La voce della luna*, 41, 46, 100, 146, 166–7, 175n14, 217, 252n15, 256, 258, 264–5, 273, 282, 284n17; *Le notti di Cabiria*, 7–8, 25, 37, 71–2, 75–8, 80, 88, 94, 107–9, 256, 273, 277, 362; *Le tentazioni del dottor Antonio*, 9, 34, 46, 52, 130–1, 136, 139, 166, 191, 231, 273, 276–7, 279–80, 328; *Lo sceicco bianco*, 62, 75, 104–8, 250, 256, 349; *Luci del varietà (Variety Lights)*, 100–2, 104, 242–3, 251n8, 273; *Prova d'orchestra (Orchestra Rehearsal)*, 166, 260–1,

Fellini, Federico (*continued*)
264, 281, 300n21; *Quattro film. I vitelloni, La dolce vita, Otto e mezzo, Giulietta degli spiriti*, 272; *Roma*, 11–12, 32–4, 35n5, 38–40, 42n3, 46, 54–6, 100, 109, 111, 122, 167, 170, 190, 192, 195–6, 202, 213n9, 216–19, 221–5, 226n2, 226n5, 257–8, 268n11, 280, 288–9, 295–9, 300n15, 308, 330, 366; *Toby Dammit*, 46, 54, 57, 120, 202, 203–4, 206, 218, 226n8, 236, 256, 260, 328; *Tre passi nel delirio* 203–4, 226n8; *Viaggio a Tulum: Da un soggetto di Federico Fellini per un film da fare*, 40, 163, 167, 173n1, 175n22
Fellini, je suis un grand menteur/*Fellini: I'm a Born Liar* (Pettigrew, Damian), 360
Fellini, Riccardo, 62
Feltrinelli, Giangiacomo, 72
Fenech, Edwige, 349
Ferretti, Dante, 30
Ferroni, Giorgio, 211; *Il mulino delle donne di pietra*, 211
Fink, Guido, 145
Fisher, Terence, 208; *Dracula*, 208
Flaiano, Ennio, 177, 276–7, 299n2; *Un marziano a Roma*, 276; *Diario notturno*, 276
Flaubert, Gustave, 106, 276
Fofi, Goffredo, 151
Foreman, Walter C., 54
Forgacs, David, 222
Foucault, Michel, 130, 132, 134, 260, 361
Franchi, Franco (Benenato, Francesco), 173, 349
Franco, Francisco, 138
Freda, Riccardo, 205; *Il cavaliere misterioso*, 205
Freeman, Nathaniel, 126n3

Freeman, Peggy, 126n3
Freud, Sigmund, 145, 157n3, 211, 307; *The Uncanny*, 211
Fried, Robert, 132
Frigeri, Francesco, 168
Fulci, Lucio, 209; *Il cav. Costante Nicosia demoniaco, ovvero: Dracula in Brianza*, 209
Fuller, Mia, 131

Gaillard, Christian, 154; *L'inconscio creatore*, 154
Gale, Eddra, 312
Gallippi, Franco, 244, 249
Gassiorowsky, Yoann, 170
Gassman, Vittorio, 276
Gastaldi, Ernesto, 202
Gaudenzi, Cosetta, 305, 314
Geleng, Antonello, 32
Geleng, Rinaldo, 32, 223
Genet, Jean, 329, 339n5; *Notre-Dame-des-Fleurs*, 339n5; *Pompes funèbres*, 339n5
Ghatak, Ritwik, 25; *Subarnarekha*, 25
Ghirotti, Gigi, 123–4
Giacomini, Lea, 61
Giannesi, Giovanni, 32
Gilroy, Paul, 121
Ginzburg, Natalia, 196
Giolitti, Giovanni, 137
Giovannini, Giorgio, 32
Goldin, Nan, 125, 127n11
Gramazio, Ernesto Ugo, 210
Grasso, Aldo, 251n3, 252n13
Greene, Shelleen, 136, 227n21
Greimas, Algirdas Julien, 273
Grifi, Alberto, 126n2; *Il Festival del proletariato giovanile al Parco Lambro*, 126n2
Grosz, George, 263, 268n22
Gualino, Renato, 345
Guattari, Félix, 306, 359

Gubareva, Marita, 6; *A Companion to Federico Fellini*, 6, 22
Guerra, Tonino, 195, 222, 305
Gündo du, Cihan, 62

Hall, Stuart, 102–3, 121; *The Popular Arts*, 102
Hallström, Lasse, 205; *Casanova*, 205
Hamard-Padis, Aurélien, 170; *Le voyage de G. Mastorna*, 10, 168, 170
Hegel, Georg Wilhelm Friedrich, 109
Heidegger, Martin, 173n5, 184, 189n16
Herriman, George, 275, 283n9
Hillman, James, 47–8
Hitchcock, Alfred, 30, 317n5, 343; *Vertigo*, 317n5
Hitler, Adolf, 278
Hoffmann, Ernst Theodor Amadeus, 211; *The Sandman*, 211
Hogarth, William, 5, 206
Holzer, Jane, 119
Homer, 310; *Odyssey*, 310
Horkheimer, Max, 101, 105
Horowitz, Daniel, 102
Hunter, John, 351
Huyssen, Andreas, 106

I Ching (Book of Changes), 363–5, 367n8
Iarussi, Oscar, 6; *Amarcord Fellini. L'alfabeto di Federico*, 6
Il coraggio (Paolella, Domenico), 349
Il segno del comando (D'Anza, Daniele), 203
Il sogno di Zorro (Soldati, Mario), 349
Iman (Mohamed Abdulmajid, Iman), 116
Ingrassia, Ciccio (Francesco), 173; *Paolo il freddo*, 349
Irigaray, Luce, 52
Ives, Irving, 345

Izzo, Pietro, 10, 167–8; *Il viaggio di G. Mastorna, esperimento di ricostruzione*, 10, 167–8

Jacopetti, Gualtiero, 221, 323
Jentsch, Ernst, 211
Johnson, Beverly, 116
Johnson, Eric, 345
Johnson, Evan, 22
Jones, Archie, 115
Jones, Gloria, 115
Jones, Grace, 116
Jung, Carl Gustav, 8, 47–8, 145, 151–2, 155, 157n3, 158n20, 231, 360, 363; *Ricordi, sogni, riflessioni*, 152

Kael, Pauline, 227n19, 322
Kafka, Franz, 34, 38, 150–2, 158n17, 158n20, 174n8, 224; *America*, 34, 38, 174n8; *The Trial (Il processo)*, 150–1, 158n19, 174n8, 224
Kandinsky, Wassily, 76
Kane-Maddock, Dave, 339n3
Keaton, Buster, 275, 283n9
Keller, Hiram, 114
Kezich, Tullio, 133, 147, 154, 164, 174n9, 177, 193–4, 222, 242, 251nn1–2; *Federico Fellini: His Life and Work*, 147
Kitzmiller, John, 115
Klein, William, 8–9, 71–5, 77–82, 84, 87–8, 91–4, 97n3, 97n8, 98n12, 125; *Broadway by Light*, 97n8; *Life Is Good and Good for You in New York: Trance Witness Revels*, 8, 71–2, 74, 87; *Rome*, 72, 94, 97n5, 98n12; *Who Are You, Polly Maggoo?*, 125, 126n2
Knelman, Martin, 353
Kovács, András Bálint, 310–12
Kristeva, Julia, 332

Index 385

Kubrick, Stanley, 32, 260; *A Clockwork Orange*, 17, 260; *Barry Lyndon*, 32
Kurosawa, Akira, 366

La poliziotta a New York (Tarantini, Michele Massimo), 349
La soldatessa alle grandi manovre (Cicero, Nando), 349
Lacan, Jacques, 47
Langton, Harry, 275, 283n9
Langer, Susanne, 47
Lattuada, Alberto, 102, 104, 242, 273; *L'amore in città*, 33, 158n17; *Luci del varietà*, 100–2, 104, 242–3, 273
Lawrence, David Herbert, 48
Leavis, Frank Raymond, 103
Leavis, Queenie Dorothy, 103
Léger, Ferdinand, 93
Lenglet, Alain, 170
Levi, Mica, 125
Lewalski, Barbara, 144
Linder, Max, 275, 283n9
Lindsay-Hogg, Michael, 126n2; *The Rolling Stones Rock and Roll Circus*, 126n2
Lo Vetro, Gianluca, 119
Longhi, Pietro, 206
Longhi, Roberto, 10, 177, 185
Lopez, Jérémy, 170
Lorde, Audre, 53
Lormeau, Nicolas, 170
Lucas, George, 190; *American Graffiti*, 190
Lukács, György, 101
Luna, Donyale (Freeman, Peggy Ann), 9, 114–25, 126n2, 126nn4–6, 126nn8–9, 127n11, 222–4, 227n21, 227n23
L'uomo, l'orgoglio, la vendetta (Bazzoni, Luigi), 349
Luzzati, Emanuele, 29
Lyotard, Jean-François, 111

Maccari, Mino, 40
Maccario, Angelo, 223, 227n22
Macdonald, Dwight, 102, 105; *Masscult and Midcult*, 102
Machado, China (Machado, Noelie Dasouza), 117
Maddin, Guy, 343; *Dracula, Pages from a Virgin's Diary*, 7; *My Winnipeg*, 7, 22; *The Rabbit Hunters*, 7, 22; *The Saddest Music in the World*, 7
Magi, Luca, 173n1; *Anita*, 173n1
Magia verde (*Green Magic*, Gian Gaspare Napolitano), 219–20
Magnani, Anna, 33, 55, 64n7, 223, 296
Malcolm X (Little, Malcolm), 117
Malle, Louis, 203, 226n8; *Tre passi nel delirio* (*Spirits of the Dead*), 203–4, 226n8; *William Wilson*, 203
Maltby, Richard, 350
Manara, Milo, 5, 10, 30, 40–1, 42n11, 150, 163, 165, 167–9, 173n1, 175n17, 274; *Due viaggi con Federico Fellini*, 150; *Viaggio a Tulum: Da un soggetto di Federico Fellini per un film da fare*, 40, 163, 167, 173n1, 175n22
Mangano, Silvana, 345
Manni, Ettore, 258
Manzoni, Alessandro, 206
Mao Zedong, 218–19, 226nn10–11
Marchesi, Marcello, 40
Marcus, Millicent, 131, 133, 139, 209, 212, 240, 245, 252n13, 253n17, 284n17; *Filmmaking by the Book: Italian Cinema and Literary Adaptation*, 284n17
Margheriti, Antonio, 203; *Danza Macabra*, 203
Mariniello, Silvestra, 173n5, 174n7
Marker, Chris, 72

Marquis de Sade (de Sade, Donatien-Alphonse-François), 205, 213n3
Marrone, Gaetana, 306
Marx, Karl, 109–10
Masina, Giulietta, 5, 23, 63, 72, 146, 167, 170, 180, 203, 234, 240, 251n8, 351, 361
Masini, Tito, 315
Massey, Edith, 323, 329
Mastrangelo, Rocco, 347–51, 354
Mastroianni, Marcello, 20, 34, 38–9, 41, 54, 137, 163–5, 169, 170, 173, 174nn1–2, 177, 234, 240, 243, 251n8, 252n9, 258, 263, 282, 292, 294, 310–11, 361
Matisse, Henri, 76
Mattei, Enrico, 138
McCabe, David, 116–17
McLuhan, Marshall, 102, 248; *The Medium Is the Message*, 248; *Understanding Media*, 102
McMullan, Chelsea, 10, 167–8, 175n17; *Deragliamenti/Derailments*, 10, 167–8
McQueen, Steve, 174n11
Mehta, Deepa, 343; *Anatomy of Violence*, 26; *Earth*, 7; *Fire*, 7; *Water*, 7
Mei, 364–5
Méliès, Georges, 168
Metz, Vittorio, 40
Mileto, Alma, 289
Miller, Beatrix, 116
Milo, Sandra, 314, 329
Mina (Mazzini, Mina Anna Maria), 173
Minuz, Andrea, 6, 122, 251nn4–5; *Fellini, Roma*, 6; *Political Fellini: Journey to the End of Italy*, 6
Mion, Marco, 10, 167–8; *Il viaggio di G. Mastorna, esperimento di ricostruzione*, 10, 167–8
Mo Yan, 366

Mollica, Vincenzo, 56, 148, 164
Monicelli, Mario, 173n1, 205, 276; *Boccaccio '70*, 9, 34, 191, 276, 349; *Casanova '70*, 205; *Viaggio con Anita*, 173n1
Monroe, Marilyn, 34
Moravia, Alberto, 72, 196, 199n15, 216
Moretti, Franco, 109–10
Morin, Edgar, 102, 108–9; *The Cinema, or The Imaginary Man*, 102, 108; *L'esprit du temps*, 102; *The Stars*, 102
Morin, Gérard, 6, 207–8; *Il Casanova di Fellini: ieri e oggi 1976–2016*, 6
Moser, Walter, 174n6
Mulvey, Laura, 51, 110
Münsterberg, Hugo, 309
Mussolini, Benito, 38, 122, 131–2, 138
My Friends Need Killing (Leder, Paul), 339n1

Nazzari, Amedeo, 97n9, 107
Needham, Gary, 118, 126n7
Nero, Franco, 349
Newman, Paul, 174n11
Nichetti, Maurizio, 252n14; *Ladri di saponette*, 252n14
Nico (Päffgen, Christa), 118–19, 126n7
Nietzsche, Friedrich, 106
Ninchi, Annibale, 314
Noël, Magali, 166, 303
Nureyev, Rudolf, 343

O'Healy, Àine, 121
Olivier, Laurence, 174n11, 343
Ombra, Gennaro, 304
Ophüs, Max, 21; *La signora di tutti*, 21
Orfei, Nando, 38
Ortiz, Fernando, 360
Osiris, Wanda, 173

Pacchioni, Federico, 203, 207
Pagliero, Marcello, 355n2; *Desiderio (This Woman Is Mine* and *Woman*), 346, 355n2
Pallavicini, Renato, 274
Parise, Goffredo, 276
Partridge, Christopher, 202
Parvo, Elli, 346, 355n2
Pascoli, Giovanni, 148, 157n11
Pasolini, Pier Paolo, 5, 55, 64n7, 72–3, 92–3, 168, 170–1, 173n1, 175n20, 185, 194–5, 198, 217, 219, 255, 323, 331, 339n1, 339n7, 347, 361; *Il vangelo secondo Matteo*, 323, 331; *La ricotta*, 339n7; *Salò o le 120 giornate di Sodoma*, 198, 339n1; *Teorema*; 323, 339n1
Pavese, Cesare, 10, 177–8
Pecori, Franco, 297
Perry, Eleanor, 222
Perryman, Marcus, 57
Petrarch, Francis, 8, 209, 211; *Rime in morte di madonna Laura*, 211
Petronius Arbiter, 9, 33, 114, 119, 218, 224; *Satyricon*, 9, 114
Piacentini, Marcello, 131
Picasso, Pablo, 5, 11, 75, 232, 237–8, 343
Pinelli, Carlo, 178
Pinelli, Tullio, 5, 10, 40, 173n1, 177–86, 188n9, 276; *Lotta con l'angelo*, 178–9
Pinto, Raffaele,
Piovani, Nicola, 29–30, 39
Piovene, Guido, 218
Pirandello, Luigi, 284n13; *Il fu Mattia Pascal*, 284n13
Plate, Liedeke, 307
Plazzi, Giuseppe, 154
Plotinus, 47
Poe, Edgar Allan, 57, 174n11, 203–4, 206, 213n7; *Berenice*, 206; *Metzengerstein*, 204; *The Black Cat*, 206; *The Cask of Amontillado*, 206; *The Fall of the House of Usher*, 206; *The Premature Burial*, 206; *The Oval Portrait*, 204; *William Wilson*, 204
Polidori, John, 208; *The Vampyre*, 208
Pollock, Jackson, 75
Ponti, Gio (Giovanni), 93
Ponti, Marco, 29
Ponzanezi, Sandra, 122
Potter, Martin, 114
Powell, Richard, 123–4
Pratley, Gerald, 352
Pratt, Mary Louise, 360
Pravo, Patty, 125
Preminger, Otto, 126n2; *Skiddo*, 126n2
Presley, Elvis, 24
Prosperi, Francesco, 221, 323
Proust, Marcel, 305, 307, 312–16, 317n11; *À la recherche du temps perdu*, 305, 307, 314 (*Swann's Way*, 306)
Prucnal, Anna, 234
Punter, David, 201; *The Literature of Terror*, 201

Questi, Giulio, 323; *La morte ha fatto l'uovo*, 323
Quillardet, Thomas, 170; *Le voyage de G. Mastorna*, 10, 168, 170

Rabelais, François, 284n12
Rancière, Jacques, 91
Ravasi Bellocchio, Lella, 154; *L'inconscio creatore*, 154
Ravetto-Biagioli, Kriss, 266
Ray, Satyajit, 8, 24–5; *Devi*, 8, 25
Reagan, Ronald, 345
Rembrandt (van Rijn, Rembrandt Harmenszoon), 236

Rémond, Marie, 10, 168, 170–1; *Le voyage de G. Mastorna*, 10, 168, 170
Rémy, Tristan, 294
Renzi, Renzo, 190
Rèpaci, Leonida, 185
Resnais, Alain, 311; *Hiroshima, My Love*, 311; *Last Year at Marienbad*, 311
Rhodie, Sam, 245, 251n8, 253n16
Richard, Cliff, 24
Riesman, David, 105
Risset, Jacqueline, 145–7; *L'incantatore*, 146
Rissone, Giuditta, 314
Rogers, Ginger, 240
Rol, Gustavo Adolfo, 42n11, 164–5, 170, 174n9
Rolling Stones, the, 223
Roman Holiday (William Wyler), 219
Romanini, Alessandro, 168
Ronconi, Luca, 29
Rondi, Brunello, 10, 148, 163, 177, 180–6, 188n9, 276; *I prosseneti*, 184; *Velluto nero*, 184–5
Rootstein, Adel, 116, 124, 223
Rossellini, Isabella, 7, 21–3
Rossellini, Roberto, 101, 168, 170, 218–19, 344, 355n2; *Desiderio (This Woman Is Mine* or *Woman)*, 346, 355n2
Rossi, Luigi, 304
Rossini, Gioachino, 235; *Il barbiere di Siviglia*, 235
Rota, Nino, 5, 39, 165, 183, 292
Rothberg, Michael, 307
Rothko, Mark, 75
Rougeul, Jean, 316
Rubini, Sergio, 298

Salerno, Enrico Maria, 174n11
Salvatore, Anna, 185
Sanguineti, Tatti, 290
Scaccianoce, Luigi, 34

Scala, Delia, 58, 60, 65n13
Scalliet, Georgia, 170
Scarpelli, Furio, 40
Scattini, Luigi, 121
Schaeffer, Pierre, 184
Schoenberg, Arnold, 182
Schoonover, Karl, 98n13
Scola, Ettore, 40, 168; *Che strano chiamarsi Federico*, 40
Scorsese, Martin, 343, 354; *Taxi Driver*, 17
Secchiaroli, Tazio, 168
Sedgwick, Edie, 119
Sella, Quintino, 140n4
Servadio, Emilio, 145, 157n3
Seven Year Itch, The (Wilder, Billy), 34
Shakespeare, William, 8
Shelley, Mary, 52, 212; *Frankenstein*, 212
Simons, Barney, 351
Sims, Naomi, 116
Sjöström, Victor, 311
Sklar, Robert, 344
Smargiassi, Michele, 97n5
Smelik, Annette, 307
Smithson, Robert, 94
Soavi, Michele, 29
Sontag, Susan, 326, 329, 331–2, 338
Sordi, Alberto, 3, 33
Sorrentino, Paolo, 26; *È stata la mano di Dio*, 26
Spaini, Alberto, 150
Spielberg, Steven, 168
Spinazzola, Vittorio, 220
Spivak, Gayatri, 121
Stamp, Terence, 203
Steele, Barbara, 202
Steiner, Shari, 353
Steno (Vanzina, Stefano), 40, 208–9; *Tempi duri per i vampiri*, 208
Stoddart, Helen, 102
Stoker, Bram, 209; *Dracula*, 209
Stravinsky, Igor, 182

Strehler, Giorgio, 93
Sunset Boulevard (Wilder, Billy), 17
Sutherland, Donald, 208, 340n13
Swift, Jonathan, 278; *Gulliver's Travels*, 278

Tarantino, Quentin, 168; *Inglourious Basterds*, 168
Tarkovsky, Andrei, 364
Tasso, Torquato, 209
Tassone, Aldo, 6, 174n9; *Fellini 23½*, 6
Taylor, Elizabeth, 332
Terdiman, Richard, 307
Thompson, Kristen, 303
Thomson, Pat, 351
Tobey, Mark, 75
Toffler, Alvin, 257, 268n9; *Future Shock*, 268n9
Tognazzi, Ugo, 174n11
Tonti, Aldo, 78
Toppi, Giove, 39
Tornabuoni, Lietta, 147; *Federico Fellini*, 147
Totò (De Curtis, Antonio), 173, 349
Totò contro Maciste (Cerchio, Fernando), 349
Trombadori, Antonello, 226n2
Turim, Maureen, 303–4, 307–9, 313, 317n1; *Flashbacks in Film: Memory and History*, 308
Turpin, Ben, 275, 283n9
Twain, Mark, 329; *The Second Advent*, 329

Vadim, Roger, 203–4, 226n8; *Metzengerstein*, 203; *Tre passi nel delirio (Spirits of the Dead)*, 203–4, 226n8
Vanelli, Marco, 307, 313
Vargau, Marina, 6, 238n3; *Romarcord: Flânerie, spectacle et mémoire dans la Rome de Federico Fellini*, 6

Velazquez, Diego, 5
Vidal, Gore, 257
Villaggio, Paolo, 30, 41, 165, 167, 169, 173, 174n11
Virgil, 310; *Aeneid*, 310
Visconti, Luchino, 37, 78, 101, 276, 352, 355; *Ossessione*, 78; *Senso*, 101; *Boccaccio '70*, 9, 34, 191, 276, 349
Vivarelli, Piero, 123; *Black Decameron*, 123
Volpi, Gianni, 151
von Kempelen, Wolfgang, 210

Wagner, Richard, 328
Wallace, Michelle, 124
Waller, Marguerite, 6, 45, 47, 49–53, 56, 63, 211, 306; *A Companion to Federico Fellini*, 6, 22
Walpole, Horace, 204, 209; *The Castle of Otranto*, 204, 209
Warhol, Andy, 117–20, 126n2, 126nn5–7, 223; *Camp*, 117, 126n2, 223; *Exploding Plastic Inevitable*, 120; *Four Stars*, 117; *Screen Tests*, 117–18, 120, 125, 126n5, 223
Waters, John, 13, 227n19, 322–3, 326–32, 338, 339nn1–3, 339nn5–6, 340n13; *Female Trouble*, 332; *Mondo Trasho*, 322, 328, 331; *Multiple Maniacs*, 328, 331–2; *Pecker*, 331; *Pink Flamingos*, 323, 327, 329, 332; *Polyester*, 329, 332
Watson, Van, 47
Weingart, Brigitte, 118
Welles, Orson, 224, 339n7
Wertmüller, Lina, 29–30
West, Cornell, 121
Whannel, Paddy, 102–3; *The Popular Arts*, 102
White, Nancy, 117
Whitehead, Alfred North, 47

Whitehead, Peter, 126n2; *Tonite Let's All Make Love in London*, 126n2
Who, the, 223
Wilde, Oscar, 122, 126n2; *Salomè*, 126n2
Wollstonecraft, Mary, 52; *A Vindication of the Rights of Woman*, 52

Yaru, Marina, 203

Zagarrio, Vito, 323
Zambenedetti, Alberto, 131, 133, 141n8
Zanelli, Dario, 150; *L'Inferno immaginario di Federico Fellini*, 150
Zanetti, Ottavio Cirio, 6, 29–31, 166; *300 dichiarazioni d'amore al Cinema*, 30; *Honey of Luxembourg, The*, 29; *Tre passi nel genio: Fellini tra fumetto circo e varietà*, 6, 8, 30; *Sipario*, 29
Zanin, Bruno, 303
Zanoli, Anna, 131
Zanzotto, Andrea, 5, 147
Zapponi, Bernardino, 5, 11, 40, 167, 175n16, 195, 202–5, 207–8, 211, 213n9, 224–5, 228n25; *Gobal*, 202; *Nostra signora dello spasimo*, 202, 213n9
Zavattini, Cesare, 33, 40, 221; *I misteri di Roma*, 221; *L'amore in città*, 33, 158n17
Zhang Zeduan, 362
Zhuangzi, 363; *Zhuangzi*, 363